FOG CITY FORUM

Fundamentals
of the
Construction
Process

Fundamentals of the Construction Process

Kweku K. Bentil, AIC

Illustrated by Carl W. Linde

R.S. Means Company, Inc.

R. S. MEANS COMPANY, INC.
CONSTRUCTION CONSULTANTS & PUBLISHERS
100 Construction Plaza
P.O. Box 800
Kingston, MA 02364-0800
(617) 585-7880

DEC 17 1990   90-919

© 1989

In keeping with the general policy of R.S. Means Company, Inc., its authors, editors, and engineers apply diligence and judgment in locating and using reliable sources for the information published. However, no guarantee or warranty can be given, and all responsibility and liability for loss or damage are hereby disclaimed by the authors, editors, engineers and publisher of this publication with respect to the accuracy, correctness, value and sufficiency of the data, methods and other information contained herein as applied for any particular purpose or use.

This book was edited by Dwayne Lehigh and Julia Willard. Typesetting was supervised by Joan Marshman. The book and Jacket were designed by Norman Forgit. Illustrations by Carl Linde.

Printed in the United States of America

10   9   8   7   6   5   4   3   2

Library of Congress Catalog Card Number 89-189292

ISBN 0-87629-138-8

Dedication

To my mother, Ms. Mary K. Edu-Sam; Dr. Dave and Ellen Godfrey; Paul and Diane Williams; and their respective families, for making my education and career possible.

Table of Contents

PART II: THE BUILDING PROCESS

APPENDIXES

Foreword

Every year, the construction industry employs over a million general contractors, over 1-1/2 million subcontractors and suppliers, over 40,000 registered architects, and over 150,000 registered engineers. In addition, many auxiliary professions and industries profit from involvement in construction—accountants, attorneys, data processing and administrative personnel, and the trucking, materials, oil, computers, financial, banking, insurance, chemical, and manufacturing industries. Because of its magnitude, the structure, method, and sequence of events in construction are not always clear.

Answering this need, this book is an introduction to the principles of the construction process. It is designed for anyone overseeing, budgeting, or otherwise involved in the construction of a building or facility. *Fundamentals of Construction* provides simplified information on the fundamentals of the construction process, construction technology, contract documents, the bidding process, computer applications, and effective contract administration. Although this handbook was written with nontechnical personnel in mind, it is a handy reference and may serve as a refresher course for seasoned construction professionals.

Part I reviews the roles of the key players and the major activities that take place before the physical construction process begins. The preconstruction processes, from estimating and bidding to signing the contract documents, are described in this part. Basic materials, methods, and installation techniques of each phase of the building process, from getting started to installing the finishes, are described in Part II. Even the well-planned project will fail without proper management. The final part of the book addresses project management. A chapter on computer applications in the construction process is included in this section. The appendices contain terminology, abbreviations, symbols tables, and formulae commonly used in the construction industry.

Acknowledgments

The author wishes to express his deepest appreciation to the United States Air Force Office of Scientific Research, the Air Force Systems Command, and the Contracting Directorate at the Air Force Logistics Management Center for the opportunity to participate in its summer Faculty Research program and for the permission to use some of the ideas developed by the author, while in the program, in this handbook; to the R.S. Means editorial staff for their encouragement and support; and to Dr. Brisbane Brown of the School of Building Construction, University of Florida, for his motivation and guidance.

Finally, the author would like to thank his wife Phyllis and children Daniel, Sandra, and Leslie for their loving support, trust, and understanding; for tolerating those long days and nights spent working on this book; and for being there when he needed them most.

Part One

An Overview of the Construction Industry

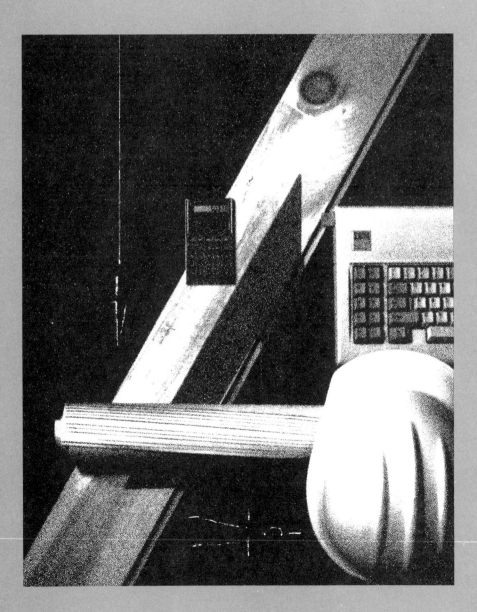

Chapter One

Introduction to the Construction Process

"The road to success is constantly under construction."

The construction process has become increasingly more complex in recent times as the industry attempts to meet the demands of a constantly growing and changing world. As a result, facilities, institutions, manufacturing companies, and other businesses are perpetually engaged in construction – creating new structures, adding to existing ones, or renovating, restoring, and preserving old buildings. For the professional who is not initiated into the field of construction, this many-faceted process may seem difficult to sort through and fully understand. To begin, the novice must be familiar with the key people involved in the construction process, the different phases of construction, the various types of construction, and ways to procure projects. These fundamental distinctions are described in this chapter.

The Key Players in Construction

There are myriad individuals, professionals, and other entities involved in the construction of a building, but the key players in the industry are:

- the owner(s),
- the architect/engineer,
- general contractor,
- subcontractors,
- suppliers, and
- other consultants.

The relationships among these key parties are illustrated in Figure 1.1. Each party plays a distinct role in the construction process, described in the following paragraphs.

The Owner

Every construction project, no matter how large, small, complex, or simple, has an owner who recognizes the need for that project. The owner is the person, firm, organization, or agency that needs the construction work accomplished.

3

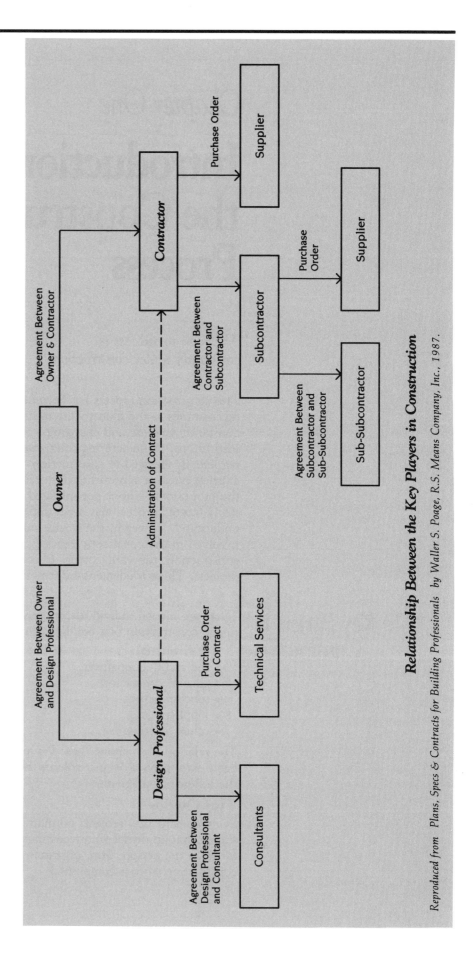

Relationship Between the Key Players in Construction

Reproduced from Plans, Specs & Contracts for Building Professionals by Waller S. Poage, R.S. Means Company, Inc., 1987.

Figure 1.1

The owner may be:
- an individual;
- a group of people;
- a firm (corporation, partnership, etc.);
- an organization (such as a church, civic club, etc.); or
- the government (such as federal agencies, states, counties or cities, and the military – the army, navy, air force, and marines).

Generally, the owner provides the financial resources to fund the project and the property on which the structure is to be built. The owner also makes binding decisions and approvals throughout the duration of a project. These decisions and approvals are, in some projects, delegated to a professional or consultant hired by the owner.

Traditionally, the owner initiates the construction process by his desire to invest in a structure or to meet his need for a structure. The owner then selects a construction professional (an architect, construction manager, or other) to assist him through the complex process, unless he has the required expertise himself, or within his own company. This professional, in serving his client, may secure the services of other professionals such as architects, engineers, real estate agencies, and mortgage and financing specialists.

Architect/Engineer

The architect/engineer transforms the dreams and ideas of the owner into plans and specifications. If hired by the owner in the early stages of the project, this professional may assist with some of the preliminary conceptual work, such as selecting a site and providing conceptual estimates.

During the design phase, the architect/engineer performs the design in several stages, each stage undergoing extensive review and approval by the owner and/or his representative. First, a **conceptual design** is prepared based on information provided by the owner. Then, a **preliminary design** is prepared. Once that is approved by the owner or his representative, a **semi-detailed design** is prepared. The next stage is the final detailed or **working drawings**, to be used for bidding or negotiating a construction contract. (These drawings are defined in more detail in Chapter 2.)

The architect/engineer's responsibilities do not end here. He is responsible for the interpretation of the plans and specifications until the completion of the project and, depending on his contract with the owner, may be responsible for bid administration, inspections, and approval of progress payments.

General Contractor

The general (or prime) contractor transforms the plans and specifications prepared by the architect/engineer and owner into a physical structure. The contractor coordinates the work of the craftsmen (laborers, carpenters, plumbers, electricians), subcontractors, and material suppliers.

The prime contractor accepts the responsibility of completing the project for the agreed terms. Normally, the contractor signs an agreement with the owner to provide the labor, materials, equipment, and subcontracts required to complete the project in accordance with the plans and specifications, within a specified time period, for an agreed-upon price. (The common types of agreements between an owner and contractor are discussed in Chapter 2.)

Subcontractors

Subcontractors play a major role in the construction phase of a project. The general contractor depends on subcontractors to perform portions of the work at appropriate intervals in order to maintain the project schedule. The subcontractor signs an agreement with the general contractor to provide all labor, equipment, and materials necessary to perform a specific portion of a given project for a designated price. These are portions of work the general contractor cannot or does not choose to perform with his own work force, such as masonry, finish carpentry, plumbing, and electrical work.

Suppliers

Another form of subcontractor is the supplier. Both contractors and subcontractors deal with suppliers. Suppliers are responsible for furnishing the materials and equipment to be incorporated into the project being constructed.

Other Consultants

On most construction projects, there is a need for consultants. These consultants may be hired by the contractor to provide expertise not available within the contractor's organization. Consultants on a construction project might include the following.

- **Specialists** (such as testing laboratories) perform the testing of soil, and concrete, steel, asphalt, plumbing, and air conditioning work.
- **Schedulers** plan the progress of the project.
- **Claims Specialists** help prepare, negotiate, settle, or litigate claims that a contractor may have against an owner.
- **Certified Public Accountants** prepare independent and audited financial statements and offer tax planning advice.
- **Attorneys** offer legal advice.
- **Surveyors** locate the building properly on the site.

Phases of the Construction Process

While every construction project is unique, most follow a consistent pattern. The projects go through the following *five* major phases.

- Pre-bid phase
- Contract procurement phase
- Contract award phase
- Construction phase
- Operating and maintenance phase

These five phases are illustrated in Figure 1.2.

Pre-bid Phase

The pre-bid phase has two sub-phases: **the conceptual phase** and the **design phase.** The sub-phases are described in the following paragraphs.

Conceptual Phase

The conceptual phase usually begins with an owner (or owners) recognizing the need for a structure, or having the desire to invest in a building. In this phase, all factors are considered and carefully examined to determine if the project is feasible. Factors such as the type of structure, size, possible locations, cost, availability of funds, source of the funding, market analysis, availability of utilities at the proposed site, and selection of the designer are weighed and parameters set. This early phase of a project is generally handled by the owner. However, an owner may consult other professionals during this phase to analyze the above factors.

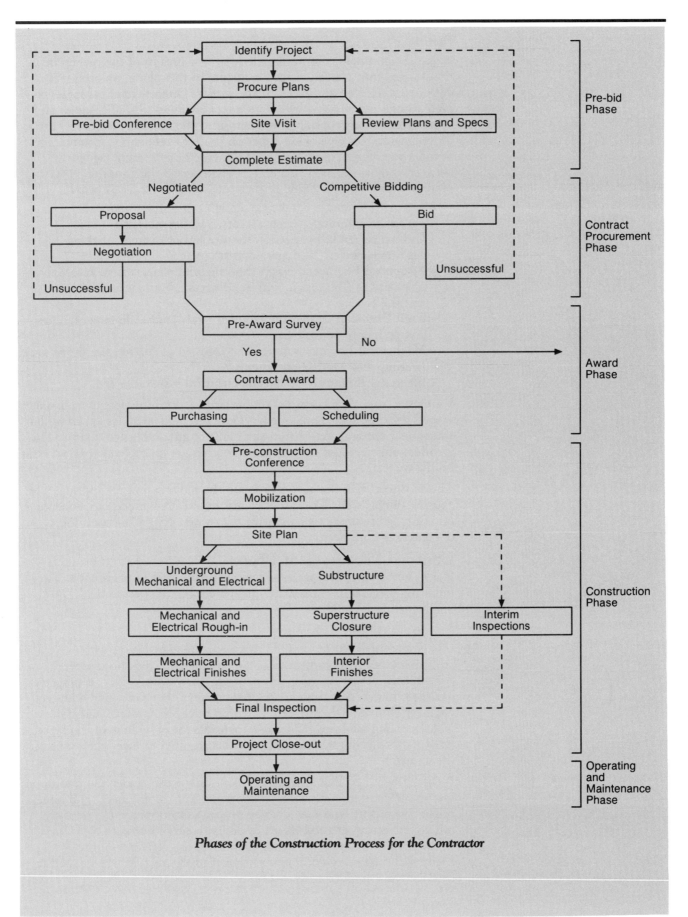

Phases of the Construction Process for the Contractor

Figure 1.2

Design Phase

In the design phase, the needs, ideas, and/or dreams of the owner are transformed into plans and specifications. In this phase, an architect/engineer is selected and hired by the owner. Often several other design professionals are engaged by the architect/engineer. Specific design and other professionals consulted in addition to the architect/engineer vary depending on the type of construction project – residential, commercial, or industrial. Size, complexity, and the type of agreement signed between the owner and the architect/engineer also dictate the professionals involved. Some of these consultants are listed below.

- **Interior Designers** handle the design of the floor and wall coverings, painting scheme, colors, and furnishings.
- **Landscape Architects** design the site layout of trees, parking lots, roadways, flowers, and grassed areas.
- **Structural Engineers** design the structural elements, such as slabs, columns, and beams, to withstand stresses from all loads during its useful life.
- **Civil Engineers** design the required roads, curbs, drainage systems, and underground utilities.
- **Mechanical Engineers** design the required plumbing, fire protection, heating, and ventilation systems.
- **Electrical Engineers** design the electrical system needed.

For most commercial construction projects, an architect/engineer assumes overall responsibility for the design function. This includes ensuring that the project is completed within the limits of an established budget. The architect/engineer also coordinates the other design professionals working on the project.

The architect/engineer may coordinate the bidding process and supervise construction as well. The duties of the architect/engineer vary depending on the type of contract signed with the owner. (See Chapter 2 for a discussion of contracts.)

Contract Procurement Phase

Construction contracts are either **competitively bid** or **negotiated**. The following paragraphs explain the differences between these two arrangements.

Competitive Bid Contracts

In a competitive bid process, contract procurement begins with advertisement of the project to obtain competitive bids from several general contractors. In government work, the lowest bidder, if properly qualified, always gets the job. In private work, the owner and architect/engineer choose one contractor based on price, reputation, and skill. The successful qualified bidder is responsible for providing all the labor, equipment, subcontractors, and materials required to meet the terms of the contract.

It should be noted that this arrangement only exists under the traditional method of contracting (owner hires an architect or engineer, and one prime contractor, who may oversee several subcontractors). There are other contracting methods, such as design/build, construction management or turn-key, but for simplicity, the elements of the traditional method of contracting (shown in Figure 1.3) will be used to describe the phases of construction.

Negotiated Contracts

While most government, state, and city projects must be publicly advertised and competitively bid, owners of private projects can negotiate with a contractor of their choice. In a negotiated contract, owners request bids from one or more selected contractors, based on factors such as past performance, reputation, experience, and previous contractual relationship. In some instances, the "finalists" are requested to make more elaborate presentations regarding their qualifications and the proposed schedules. A contractor is then selected from the finalists for negotiation and contract award.

Award Phase

During this phase, the owner finalizes the necessary administrative matters such as final verification of the contractor's references, surety bonds, insurance, and proposed schedules. The contractor, if a contract award appears to be imminent, often begins to prepare the schedule of values, progress schedule, and assignment of the prospective site personnel such as the superintendent and the project manager.

Once the owner and the contractor sign a formal contract, most contractors immediately begin negotiating with prospective subcontractors and material suppliers. One must devote priority to subcontract work and materials needed at the beginning of the project, such as site preparation work, site utilities, reinforcing steel, door frames, and items to be embedded in the foundation and slab. Long lead items (items not manufactured or fabricated until an order is placed), or items that must be modified to meet project specifications and require several months advance notice in order to meet production and delivery schedules (such as mechanical and electrical equipment and elevators), should be ordered immediately.

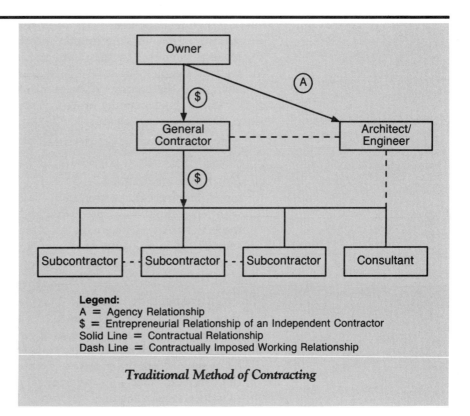

Legend:
A = Agency Relationship
$ = Entrepreneurial Relationship of an Independent Contractor
Solid Line = Contractual Relationship
Dash Line = Contractually Imposed Working Relationship

Traditional Method of Contracting

Figure 1.3

9

Pre-Construction Conference

A pre-construction conference between the architect/engineer, the owner's representation, and the contractor takes place after the contract is awarded, before construction begins. This meeting is a forum to ask questions on technical and administrative aspects of the project.

Contractor's representatives attending this meeting include the following personnel.

- **Authorized Officer** – such as the president, vice-president, or construction manager.
- **Designated Project Manager** – usually based at the home office of the contractor who handles more than one contract at any given time.
- **Field Supervision Personnel** – any number of field supervision personnel, depending on the size, type, and complexity of a project; usually includes at least a superintendent, an office engineer, and an administrative employee.

In addition to the contractor's representatives, major subcontractors (mechanical, electrical, and sitework), the architect/engineer, and owner's site representative should attend the pre-construction meeting. At this meeting, all parties agree on responsibilities for portions of the project. Soon after the pre-construction conference – often within ten to fifteen days – the project moves into the construction phase.

Construction Phase

The construction phase transforms the needs, ideas, and dreams of the owner – plans and specifications – into a physical structure. The key players in this phase are the general contractor's project management team (project manager, superintendent, and office engineer), field work force (laborers, carpenters, etc.), subcontractors, suppliers of materials and equipment, and other consultants such as material testing laboratories, schedulers, and surveyors.

The architect/engineer plays an important supporting role in contract administration, making interim inspections, approving progress payment requests submitted by the contractor, reviewing shop drawings, approving material samples, interpreting the plans and specifications, and reviewing changes to the contract. The exact scope of the architect/engineer's duties varies, depending on the contractual requirements of the owner.

Procedures for change orders, which occur frequently during the construction process, are described in Chapter 15, "Project Management."

Pre-Final Inspection

Once the physical construction is complete, the architect/engineer, often with representatives of the owner and contractor, conducts a pre-final inspection. Any deficiencies uncovered during this inspection are summarized in a document known as a **punch list**, shown in Figure 1.4. The owner gives the contractor a copy of this list, and the contractor must complete the listed items before receiving the final payment.

Final Inspection

When the contractor has remedied all the deficiencies on the punch list, he requests a final inspection by the architect/engineer. If the contractor corrects all punch list items to the satisfaction of the architect/engineer, he or she accepts the project as complete on behalf of the owner. When the contractor meets all the necessary administrative requirements, he submits a request for final payment.

PUNCH LIST

PROJECT:__Admin. Bldg. & F.S.__   DATE OF WALKTHROUGH__10/1/89__

TIME START_____9:15 AM_____   TIME COMPLETE_12:00 Noon_

REPRESENTING SPONSOR:

Chris Bell, Architect

Chuck Bloomfield, Engineer

N. Neilson, Inspector

REPRESENTING CONTRACTOR:

Buck Buttress, Superintendent

U.N. Level, Foreman

S.O. Beit, Manager

Doug Piper, Piper Piping Co.

E.C. Hull, Sparks Electric

ITEMS REQUIRING CORRECTION	CORRECTIVE ACTION
1. M.H. cover too high at station 14+10	1. Piper Piping Co. will lower to proper elevation
2. Entrance door closer needs adjusting	2. Foreman will adjust
3. Sprinkler piping not painted	3. Painter was notified
4. Sheet metal flashing not straight	4. Sub was notified
5. Landscaping not completed	5. Sub promises completion by Friday
6. Parking light doesn't turn on	6. Elec. sub is checking it
7. Rollup door needs adjusting	7. Sub was notified
8. Robe hook missing in men's room	8. Foreman will supply

Reproduced from Superintending for the General Contractor by Paul J. Cook, R.S. Means Company, Inc., 1987.

Figure 1.4

The administrative tasks necessary to finalize, or "close," a job are listed below.

- **Submit an affidavit of release of liens:** This document states that all the labor, materials, equipment, subcontractors, and consultants used on the project have been paid in full and that all applicable taxes (sales tax, payroll taxes, etc.) have been paid.
- **As-built drawings:** This is a set of the final drawings for the project, showing all changes made during construction. The changes are usually highlighted with red pen or pencil, or surrounded by an irregular line or "cloud."
- **Submit operating and maintenance manuals:** These are instructions for operating and maintaining all equipment and specialty items installed on the project. Manufacturers' warranties are included in this package.

Operating and Maintenance Phase

The operating and maintenance phase begins as soon as the owner accepts the completed structure. It involves periodic maintenance of the structure and the equipment installed within it. This phase may be simple or complicated, depending on the type of structure, its size, and the type of equipment housed within the structure.

Types of Construction Projects

In the U.S., construction projects may be classified into **five major categories**. These categories are shown in Figure 1.5 and described in the following paragraphs.

Residential Construction

This category consists of single family housing such as individual houses, or multi-family housing such as apartments and condominiums.

Heavy Construction

This category includes earth-moving projects such as roads, bridges, dams, tunnels, railroads, mass transit, underground utility work, and land reclamation.

Commercial Construction

Projects are considered commercial construction if they are office buildings, shopping centers, malls, hotels, gas stations, sports complexes (stadiums, skating rinks, and other recreational facilities), convention centers, movie theaters, and restaurants. Commercial construction is further classified as **small**, **medium**, or **large**, depending on such criteria as building size and type of owner. Building size is expressed in total square footage and number of stories. Commercial projects are owned by private individuals, firms, cities, counties, states, or the federal government.

Institutional Construction

Projects that are normally built for institutions (schools, colleges, etc.) include dormitories, classrooms, hospitals, and correctional facilities. These projects may be further divided into two categories – **civilian** and **military**. While there are similarities in the functions served by civilian and military institutional structures, their standards of design and construction are completely different. Military structures are designed with rigid requirements and standards, depending on factors such as location and role in the National Defense system. For example, housing and classroom structures for military personnel are designed with much more reinforcing than required in similar structures on a college campus.

Industrial Construction

This category includes projects such as manufacturing plants (for clothing, and automobiles), processing plants (for chemicals and petroleum), sewage treatment plants, power generating plants (coal and oil), and factories (such as steel, glass, electrical, and mechanical equipment). Industrial projects often require complex installations of piping and specialized equipment.

Sources of Construction Project Information

To stay in business, construction professionals are always seeking new projects. There are numerous ways by which construction professionals find out about future or upcoming projects. The following are the most common sources.

- **Published listings:** These include publications such as *Engineering News Record*, newspapers, *Commerce Business Daily* and the *Dodge Reports*. The *Dodge Reports* list detailed information on prospective projects. This information includes: the name of the owner; the location of the project; the approximate size (dollar value, square footage, etc.); the architect/engineer; the status of the project; the anticipated bid date; and any other requirements or deadlines. This particular publication provides such information as a service to subscribers, catering to either nationwide projects or to local or regional projects.

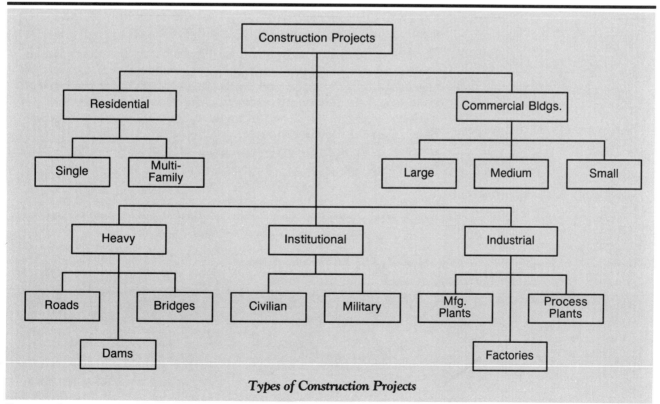

Types of Construction Projects

Figure 1.5

- **Owners and/or former clients:** Sometimes contractors, architects, and engineers are invited by an owner to negotiate or bid on a contract. This may occur if the owner had a previously positive team relationship with the contractor.
- **Word of mouth:** Word of upcoming projects is frequently passed along by contractors, subcontractors, and material suppliers. This source is most effective when contractors or suppliers associate with each other regularly. This association may or may not be a formal one.
- **Architects and engineers:** Sometimes contractors hear about prospective projects from designers with whom they have previously worked. Maintaining close contact with designers has been found by many to be a source of prospective new projects. Designers for private projects sometimes even have the option of inviting selected contractors to submit bids or cost proposals for negotiation, chosen on the basis of their prior experience, reputation, and performance.
- **The Builder's Exchange:** In some cities, contractors may obtain membership in a Builder's Exchange, which makes available to its members – at a designated location – information, plans, specifications, and all the necessary documents needed to negotiate or bid a job. These exchanges usually procure several sets of documents for each project and contain adequate furnishings and work areas to enable members to review the documents and perform a quantity takeoff.

Summary

Understanding the construction process begins with defining the basic roles of the parties involved in a construction project: the owner, the architect/engineer, the general contractor, subcontractors, and suppliers. Also critical are how their roles change during the phases of construction – the pre-bid phase, the contract procurement phase, the award phase, the construction phase, and the operating and maintenance phase.

Construction projects fall into one of five major categories: residential, heavy, commercial, institutional, and industrial construction. Various regulations, qualifications, and standards govern each of these types of projects and the novice to construction should be aware of these distinctions. Finally, it is helpful for advertising and bidding purposes to be aware of the sources contractors use to locate jobs. From this elementary foundation, an integrated understanding of the construction process begins.

Chapter Two

Construction Contract Documents

"A problem well stated
is a problem half solved."
Charles Kettering

The construction process is a concerted undertaking requiring the efforts of numerous professionals; the commitment of large sums of money; and considerable increments of construction professionals' time. In the past, this process was simple and there were relatively few people involved. Parties relied on trust, spoken agreements, and handshakes to uphold commitments. These handshake agreements have evolved into written, legally binding contracts, because of the complexity, magnitude, and the number of participants involved. Knowledge of the contents of construction documents simplifies the potentially overwhelming collection of agreements, plans, drawings, specifications, and other documents of the construction contract. This chapter describes the basic elements of construction contract documents.

Definition of a Contract

A contract is an agreement made in good faith between two or more capable parties to perform an act or acts. A contract may be invalid if signed under duress, under influence of another person, or if the objective is fraudulent. Contracts may be spoken or written, but are usually written because oral contracts are generally not recognized in court.

Elements of a Valid Contract
Every contract is unique, but certain elements are common to all valid contracts. These are listed below.

- The agreement must be mutual. (Both parties must agree to enter into the contract. In other words, there must be mutual consent between all parties to the contract.)
- There must be an offer and an acceptance.
- There must be some sort of consideration. (This is usually the promised value of the contract.)
- The purpose or objective of the contract must be clearly stated and must be lawful.

- There must be good faith or genuine intention on the part of the parties involved to fulfill the contents.
- The parties to the agreement must be capable of performing the designated tasks.

Types of Construction Contracts

There are many types of construction contracts. However, the following contracts are most commonly used in construction.

- Unit price contract
- Lump sum contract (also called the single fixed-price contract)
- Cost plus fixed fee contract
- Guaranteed maximum price contract

Unit Price Contract

Under the unit price contract, a contractor agrees to perform specific portions of work for predetermined unit prices. These unit prices usually include the contractor's direct and indirect costs, as well as the mark-up for job overhead, home office overhead, and profit. Since this type of contract is best used in situations where the quantities involved may vary or the scope may change, the total contract price is not firm, but depends on the actual quantities of units of work measured when the job is complete.

Unit price contracts may be used for heavy construction projects such as roads and highways. Contractors in these trades may be paid for the total number of cubic yards of base or tons of asphalt actually placed.

In this contractual arrangement, the contractor bids or negotiates unit prices on the project based on approximate quantities furnished by the owner.

Lump Sum Contract

Fixed lump sum contracts are used on most traditional, competitively bid projects. This contractual arrangement binds the contractor to perform all the work in accordance with the plans, specifications, terms, and general conditions of a contract for a **fixed lump sum price**, based on the materials and equipment described in the contract documents.

With this type of contract, most general contractors perform some portions of construction (such as masonry and concrete) with their own work forces. The remainder of the work is subcontracted to specialty contractors – painters, electricians, plumbers, air-conditioning mechanics, steel erectors, or roofers. The general contractor assumes the responsibility for all work done by his own forces and the subcontractors.

Cost Plus Fixed Fee Contract

This agreement is used primarily for negotiated contracts. With this type of contract, a contractor agrees to perform the work and the owner agrees to pay the contractor for the **direct** field costs, **plus a fee** to cover the contractor's home office costs and profit. The fee is usually based on the size and/or complexity of the work and may be expressed as a flat dollar amount or as a percentage of the total estimated cost of the project. One disadvantage with this type of contract, to an owner, is that the total cost of the project is unknown until the project is completed. Another problem is that the contractor does not have the incentive to minimize field costs. The advantages are that the owner can change design or materials during construction without complicated change orders or can start the project before the design is complete.

Guaranteed Maximum Price Contract

With this type of contract, the contractor agrees to perform all the work necessary to complete a construction project for a price that will not exceed a **pre-established maximum price**. Any costs above the guaranteed price are absorbed by the contractor. However, if the contractor completes the work for a price under the guaranteed maximum price, the savings is passed on to the owner unless there is an agreement (in the contract) to share any savings with the contractor. Contracts of this type may have a specific **cost savings clause** to motivate the contractor to perform the contract in the most economical manner, without sacrificing quality. Guaranteed maximum price contracts are used primarily for negotiated contracts.

Common Methods of Contracting

In the construction industry, it is not unusual to find many variations and/or combinations of the four main types of contracts being used. However, there are several established methods in which these four types are used. The most common methods are described in the following paragraphs.

The Traditional Method

Under this method, the owner selects an architect/engineer to design a project that can be built within a predetermined budget. When the design is completed and approved by the owner, one general contractor is selected to build the project. The contractor is selected through a competitive bid or negotiated process and reports directly to the owner or his representative.

The general contractor performs part of the work (usually between 15 and 40 percent) with his own work force and subcontracts the remainder to specialty contractors. The percentage performed by the general contractor could be more or less than the percentages quoted above. On most public contracts, a general contractor is required to perform at least 25 percent of the work with his own forces. For private or other contracts where no percentage is specified, general contractors perform only those portions of the work that do not require a specialist. The rest of the work is then subcontracted, since most subcontractors are specialists in their field and can buy materials and perform the work at a more productive and economical rate.

This method is used with any of the four types of contracts described in the previous section.

One of the main advantages of the traditional method is that the owner deals with only one contractor (the general contractor who coordinates and schedules all the work of his subcontractors). One of the main disadvantages of this method is that an adversarial situation could develop, with the general contractor on one side, the architect/engineer on the other, and the owner in the middle.

The Construction Management Method

This method, in its purest form, is run by a three-party team consisting of the owner, architect/engineer, and a construction manager. The owner contracts directly with several prime contractors (subcontractors who normally contract with the general contractor) instead of one general contractor. Unlike methods involving a general contractor, the owner assumes responsibility for work done by the subcontractors. The organization of the construction management method of contracting is illustrated in Figure 2.1. The major differences between the construction management method and the traditional method are presented in Figure 2.2.

The Turn-key Method

As the name turn-key implies, the owner accepts a project and pays for it when he can insert the key into the lock of the main entrance and take possession of the completed building.

In its purest form, the owner contracts with one organization, to whom he presents his building needs, an architectural program, a time frame for completion, and a budget. The turn-key organization then accepts overall responsibility for locating a site, completing the design, financing, and constructing a project. Often, this is accomplished by assembling a team of specialists that may include architects, engineers, bankers, contractors, and subcontractors to complete the project within a pre-established budget.

Design/Build

The design/build contract is similar to the turn-key contract in that the owner has only one contract for the design and construction of a project. The owner may provide the site, a schedule, and a budget. The sum and dates of progress payments are agreed upon by the contractor and the owner in advance.

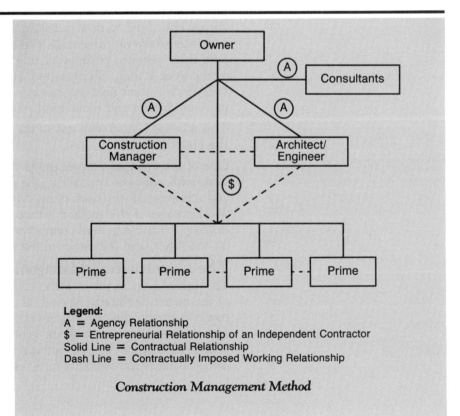

Legend:
A = Agency Relationship
$ = Entrepreneurial Relationship of an Independent Contractor
Solid Line = Contractual Relationship
Dash Line = Contractually Imposed Working Relationship

Construction Management Method

Figure 2.1

The Contract Package

The contract package for most construction projects consists of the following three elements.

- **The Contract** – owner-contractor agreement
- **The Specifications** – including the general conditions as well as addenda and any special provisions of the contract, where applicable
- **The Contract Drawings** – plans, with any revisions issued prior to the bid or negotiation date

An overview of these components is shown in Figure 2.3.

The Construction Contract

Every construction project involves a high cash flow and a high degree of risk. It is, therefore, important that written, legally binding, agreements are executed between all parties involved in the design and construction process. The main objectives of a construction contract are: to define the practical and legal responsibilities and commitment of the parties involved; and to ensure that common-law risks, liabilities, and leverage are ascribed to the responsible party.

Differences Between the Construction Management Method and the Traditional Method	
Construction Management Method	**Traditional Method**
1. Several prime contractors contract directly with owner.	1. One general contractor contracts with owner.
2. Design and construction are handled as one single effort and has continuity.	2. Design and construction are two seperate efforts— no continuity.
3. Cohesive team effort between architect/engineer and construction manager.	3. Adversarial relationship between architect/engineer and general contractor.
4. Reduces layering of bonding.	4. Layering of bonding occurs with the general contractor furnishing bonds to the owner and subcontractors furnishing bonds to the general contractor.
5. Value analysis and cost control during design.	
6. No guaranteed costs at the onset of the project (unless it is a guaranteed maximum price contract).	5. Usually less value analysis during the design phase.
7. Integrated system but permits phased construction.	6. Usually a guaranteed lump sum bid at the beginning of the project.
8. Construction manager has incentive to reduce costs to owner through value engineering.	7. Phased construction coordinated by general contractor.
9. Owner retains more control of the schedule and can plan cash flow to his or her advantage.	8. General contractor has lump sum contract with owner.
10. Involvement of the construction manager during the planning and design phases provides the owner with source of independent information about probable costs and schedules.	9. General contractor controls schedule.
	10. Owner depends on the architect and general contractor for design, costs, and schedules.

Figure 2.2

Construction contracts, like other contracts, are written in cumbersome legal language that reflects years of previous lawsuits and case law (judicial precedent). As such, the contents of a contract are often unclear to nonlegal people. An experienced construction attorney should be consulted during the development, review, and/or interpretation of a legal agreement.

A construction contract, should, at least, include the following information.

- The date of the agreement
- The parties involved and their addresses
- A description or name of the project and its location
- The name of the architect/engineer, including an address
- A list of contract documents to be attached (drawings, specifications, addenda, etc.)

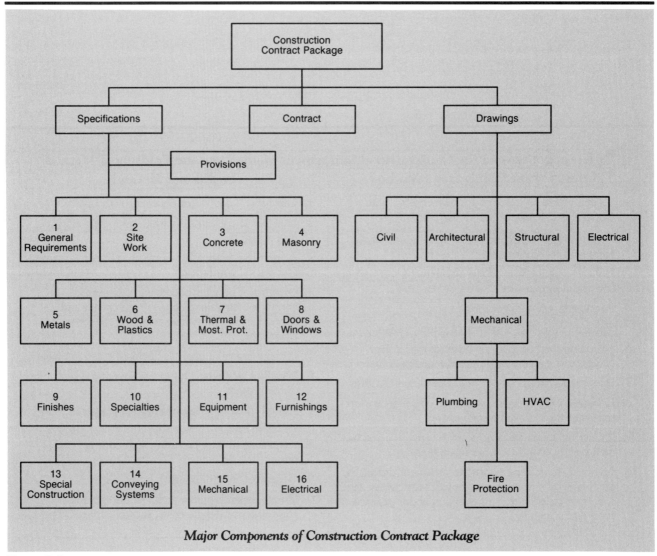

Major Components of Construction Contract Package

Figure 2.3

- A description of the scope of work to be performed
- The required starting date and completion date (including the number of calendar days)
- The amount of the contract
- Method and frequency of payment
- The rights and duties of all parties
- How changes in the work will be handled
- Provisions for termination by either party
- Other provisions as needed

While some firms often develop their own agreements, there are several standard forms available, developed by the American Institute of Architects (AIA) and the Associated General Contractors of America, Inc. (AGC).

Contract Specifications

In order to build a structure from a set of drawings, the architect/engineer must describe the materials and equipment used to build that structure (and the correct method of installation) in the form of specifications. Specifications, or "specs," enable a contractor to clearly understand the concept of the architect/engineer. These documents define the quality of the materials, products, and workmanship required in the construction contract.

The specifications are one of the most critical documents in any construction contract; whenever there is a difference or conflict between the drawings and specifications of a project, the specifications always take precedence. Examples of a section from a set of specifications are shown in Figures 2.4a and 2.4b.

Specifications are printed or typed on 8-1/2 x 11 inch paper and have a stiff cover listing information about the project, its owner, and the project architect/engineer. The size and contents of a set of specifications vary depending on the type, size, or complexity of the construction project.

There are several formats for specifications, but the format used by most architects and engineers is the one developed by the Construction Specifications Institute (CSI). The CSI format breaks the specifications down into the five major sections shown below.

- **Bidding Requirements**
- **Legal Requirements:** such as contract forms.
- **General Conditions:** These articles of the contract define the separate parties and their specific roles and responsibilities in the contract. The General Conditions addresses such issues as remedying conflicts, time constraints, methods of payment, insurance, and changes to the work. These conditions are standard ("boiler plate") sections of a contract and, rather than recreating them for each project, are available as preprinted forms from the American Institute of Architects (AIA) or, for federal (government) projects, from the General Services Administration (GSA). These documents should never be modified, and any differences from standard General Conditions should appear in separate articles of the contract known as Supplemental General Conditions. The reader is referred to *Plans, Specs and Contracts for Building Professionals*, by Waller S. Poage, R. S. Means Company, Inc., for sample AIA forms.

SECTION 03300
CAST-IN-PLACE CONCRETE

PART 1 - GENERAL

1.01 REQUIREMENTS INCLUDED

Poured-in place concrete, foundations and other concrete items specified in other Sections.

1.02 RELATED REQUIREMENTS

A. Section 02800 - Site Improvements.

B. Section 03100 - Concrete Formwork.

C. Section 03200 - Concrete Reinforcement.

D. Section 03320 - Concrete Topping: Concrete topping and curbs over existing construction.

E. Section 03346 - Finishing Concrete Surfaces.

1.03 QUALITY ASSURANCE

A. Reference Standards: Comply with all applicable Federal, State and local codes, safety regulations, Portland Cement Assoc. Standards, Ready Mixed Concrete Assoc. Standards, Texas Aggregates Assoc. Standards and others referred to herein.

B. Tests and Submittals in accordance with Section 01410.

1. Mix Design and Tests: The mix design for all concrete be established by a testing laboratory under provisions of Section 01410. All tests shall be performed in accordance with standard procedures as follows:

a. ASTM C 172 Standard Method of Sampling fresh concrete

b. ASTM C 31 Standard Method of Making and Curing Concrete compressive and Flexural Strength. Test Specimens in the field.

c. ASTM C 143 Standard Method of test for Slump of Portland Cement Concrete.

d. ASTM C 39 Standard Method of test for Compressive Strength of Molded Concrete Cylinders.

2. Access: The Architect shall have access to all places where materials are stored, proportioned or mixed.

3. Proportions: The testing laboratory shall submit, prior to the start of concrete work, contemplated proportions and the results of preliminary 7 day compression test. Submit a separate set of proportions and test results for pumpcrete if used.

4. Slump test shall be made by the testing laboratory of concrete delivered to the site for each set of test cylinders.

5. Standard test cylinders of all concrete placed in the work shall be made by the testing laboratory. One (1) set of four (4) cylinders shall be taken for each 100 cubic yards or fraction there of poured on each day.

6. Two (2) cylinders of each set shall be tested at 7 days and two (2) cylinders to be tested at 28 days

7. Reports of above tests and field quality control tests: Provide copies of test reports:

   1 copy to Engineer

   2 copies to Architect

   2 copies to Contractor

8. Mill reports: The Contractor shall furnish mill reports of test of cement showing compliance with specifications.

9. All expenses for concrete design and testing shall be paid by the General Contractor

Section 03300 Page 1

Sample Specifications

Reproduced from Plans, Specs & Contracts for Building Professionals by Waller S. Poage, R.S. Means Company, Inc., 1987.

Figure 2.4a

C.   Inspection: Inspection of Reinforcing Steel and Concrete Placement: Before any concrete is poured on any particular portion of project, reinforcing steel will be checked and approved by Architect or Engineer. Correct any errors or discrepancies before concrete is placed. Such checking and approval shall not relieve Contractor from his responsibility to comply with the Contract requirements.

1.04   REFERENCE STANDARDS

A.   ASTM C33 - Concrete Aggregates.

B.   ASTM C150 - Portland Cement

C.   ACI 318 - Building Code Requirements for Reinforced Concrete

D.   ASTM C494 - Chemical Admixtures for Concrete.

E.   ASTM C94 - Ready-Mixed Concrete.

F.   ACI 304 - Recommended Practice for Measuring, Mixing, Transporting and Placing Concrete.

G.   ACI 305 - Recommended Practice for Hot Weather Concreting.

H.   ACI 306 - Recommended Practice for Cold weather Concreting

I.   ACI 301 - Specifications for Structural Concrete for Buildings

J.   ACI 311 - Recommended Practice for Concrete Inspection.

1.05   SUBMITTALS

A.   Submit product data in accordance with Section 01300.

B.   Provide product data for specified products.

C.   Submit manufactures' instructions in accordance with Section 01400.

D.   Provide shop Drawings showing construction joints.

E.   Provide schedule of pouring operations for approval before concreting operations begin.

F.   Conform to Mix Design in accordance with 1.03-B.

1.06   PRODUCT DELIVERY, STORAGE AND HANDLING

Store materials delivered to the job and protect from foreign matter and exposure to any element which would reduce the properties of the material.

1.07   COORDINATION

A.   Obtain information and instructions from other trades and suppliers in ample time to schedule and coordinate the installation of items furnished by them to be embedded in concrete so provisions for their work can be made without delaying the project.

B.   Do any cutting and patching made necessary by failure or delay in complying with these requirements at no cost to Owner.

PART 2 - PRODUCTS

2.01   MATERIALS - STANDARD STRUCTURAL CONCRETE

A.   Portland Cement: Type I and III shall conform to "Standard Specifications for Portland Cement" (ASTM C - 150) and shall be of domestic manufacture. Use only one brand of cement unless otherwise authorized by Architect.

B.   Fine Aggregate: ASTM C33, natural bank sand or river sand, washed and screened so as to produce a minimum percentage of voids.

C.   Normal Weight Coarse Aggregate: ASTM C33, gravel or crushed stone suitably processed, washed and screened, and shall consist of hard, durable particles without adherent coatings. Aggregate shall range from 1/4" to 1-1/4", well graded between the size limits.

Section 03300   Page 2

Sample Specifications (continued)

Reproduced from Plans, Specs & Contracts for Building Professionals by Waller S. Poage, R.S. Means Company, Inc., 1987.

Figure 2.4b

- **Special Conditions:** These articles are unique conditions for the individual project and contain sections on shift work (premium time), site security, noise or dust control, and hazardous material handling.
- **Technical Specifications:** In this section, the architect/engineer provides the contractor with a comprehensive description of the required materials and equipment and their fabrication, quality, workmanship, and/or installation details. However, the architect/engineer assumes no responsibility for the adequacy of any procedure specified. The contractor is responsible for installing the final product by using his own skill, resources, experience, and ingenuity. This section is further divided into the sixteen divisions shown in Figure 2.3.

Contract Drawings

It is impossible for an architect/engineer to communicate every thought, concept, and intention in the specifications. To supplement the specifications, architect/engineers prepare contract drawings, or **working drawings**. The number of sheets in a set of drawings depends on such factors as building size, complexity, and level of detail. Most working drawings include: site, architectural, structural, plumbing, mechanical, and electrical drawings, details, and schedules. These drawings are explained in the following paragraphs.

Site Drawings

These drawings provide information such as the geographic location of the project, a plot plan showing the general orientation of the project, contours (existing and proposed elevations), roads, parking lots, and the location of both existing and new site utilities. An example of a civil drawing is shown in Figure 2.5.

Architectural Drawings

All architectural information about a project is recorded here. Architectural drawings usually begin with floor plans starting from the lowest floor and progressing to the highest floor, followed by elevations, sections, schedules, and details. Examples of architectural drawings are provided in Figures 2.6a and 2.6b.

Structural Drawings

These are drawings of all structural supporting systems such as foundations, columns, floor systems, roof supporting systems, beams, and joists, showing their sizes, connection details, and location. Information on the type and strength of concrete and reinforcing may also be found here.

Plumbing Drawings

Plumbing drawings show water distribution piping and types of fixtures (sinks, toilet bowls, urinals, water fountains, etc.). They also show waste and vent systems, internal storm drainage, special piping, and fire protection standpipes.

Mechanical Drawings

These drawings provide information about the heating, ventilating, and air-conditioning system such as ductwork, heating, and cooling equipment, including size, capacity, and arrangement.

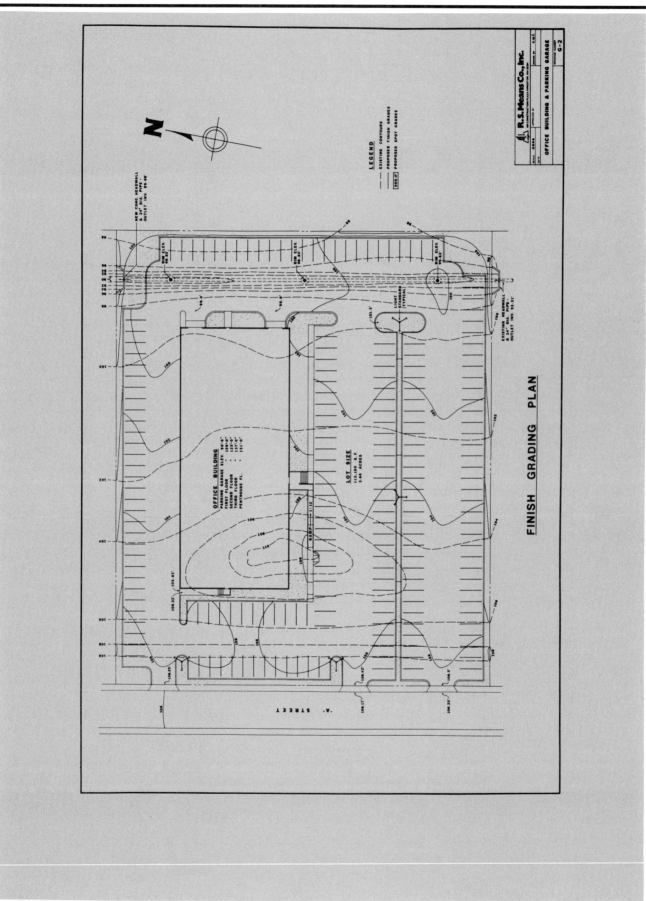

FINISH GRADING PLAN

Figure 2.5

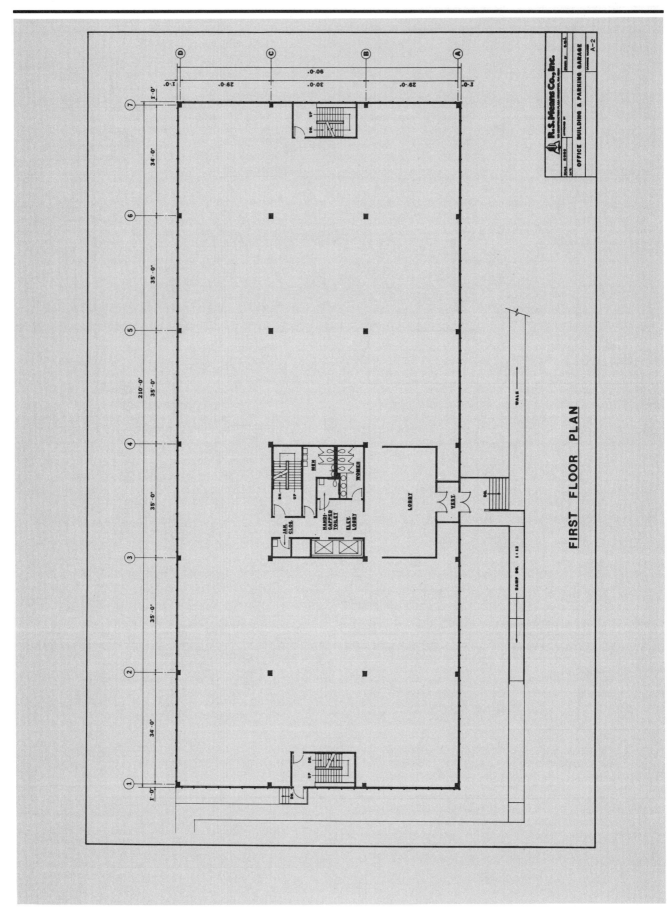

FIRST FLOOR PLAN

Figure 2.6a

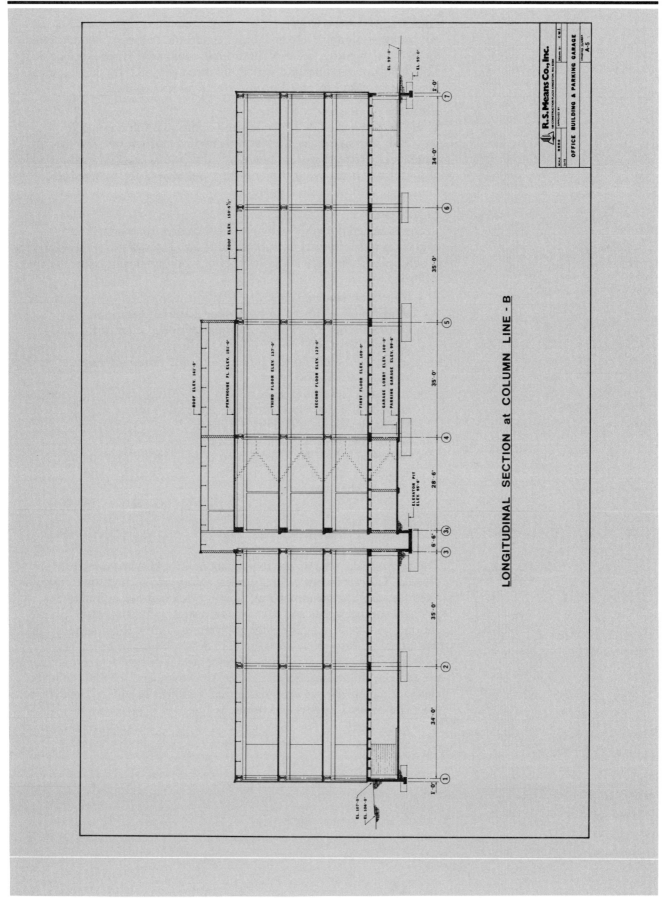

LONGITUDINAL SECTION at COLUMN LINE - B

Figure 2.6b

Electrical Drawings

All information about electrical and electronic requirements of a building for fixtures, lighting, security, and other equipment is recorded here. The details of conduits and wiring are often prepared by the electrical subcontractor and recorded on the electrical shop drawings.

Details

These drawings provide expanded and additional information on items previously shown on the site, architectural, or structural drawings. In some cases, items that were previously drawn too small to read for lack of space, and/or to avoid overcrowding one sheet, are enlarged and illustrated with more detail here.

Schedules

Tables or schedules are usually provided to save time and avoid duplication of information throughout a set of drawings. Some examples of schedules commonly found in a set of working drawings include the following.

- **Door and window schedule:** This is a listing of all the doors and windows on a project by type, size, material, location, etc.
- **Finishes schedule:** This is a listing of all the interior finishes (floors, carpet, and tile; painting, wallpaper, and gypsum wallboard; ceiling tile, etc.) on the project with additional information such as location, color, and type.
- **Structural schedule:** This is a list of footings, columns, beams, and joists by size, location, material, and some form of identification.
- **Mechanical schedule:** This is a list of ducts (by size), fans, and pumps (by type, size, and capacity).
- **Electrical schedule:** This is a list of lighting fixtures, motors, generators, and transformers by size, type, capacity, and other relevant characteristics.

Examples of two types of schedules (room finish and door schedules) are illustrated in Figures 2.7a and 2.7b.

Summary

The contract documents are the backbone of a building construction project. The various types of contracts – unit price, lump sum, cost plus fixed fee, and the guaranteed maximum price – all demand different payment arrangements and divisions of responsibilities. These types of contracts are used judiciously for the various contracting methods – the traditional, construction management, design/build, and turn-key methods. The contents of these documents are critical to the outcome of the project. The plans, specifications, drawings, and schedule must be clear and comprehensive to ensure that a project is built successfully to meet the owner's intents and needs.

Means Forms

**DOOR
AND FRAME SCHEDULE**

PROJECT

LOCATION

ARCHITECT

OWNER

PAGE _____ OF _____

DATE

BY

DOOR NO.	DOOR							FRAME						FIRE RATING		HARDWARE		REMARKS
	SIZE			MAT.	TYPE	GLASS	LOUVER	MAT.	TYPE	DETAILS			LAB	CON	SET NO.	KEYSIDE ROOM NO.	
	W	H	T							JAMB	HEAD	SILL					

Figure 2.7a

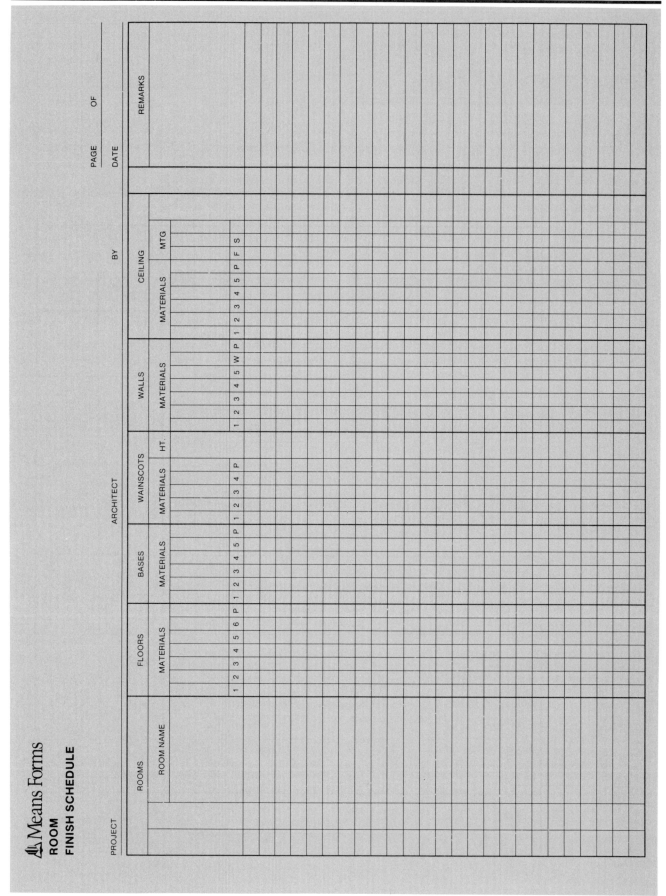

Figure 2.7b

Chapter Three

Construction Cost Estimating

"When we mean to build,
We first survey the plot, then draw the model;
And when we see the figure of the house,
Then we must rate the cost of erection;
Which if we find outweighs ability,
What do we then but draw anew the model,
In fewer offices; or at least,
Desist to build at all."
Henry IV

Construction cost estimating is perhaps the most critical and important function in the construction process for the contractor. The success of a construction contract largely depends on the accuracy of the cost estimate. If a construction cost estimate is too low – lower than the project could actually be built for – there is little or no chance of making any profit. If a construction cost estimate is too high and therefore not competitive, there is also no chance of getting a project. A competitive bid must be low enough to beat competitors and get a job, but high enough to make a "reasonable" profit. A contractor cannot submit a good competitive bid unless he has an accurate cost estimate.

Cost estimates are regularly used by owners; the decision to build a project is often based on an estimate prepared by an in-house staff person or consultant. Cost estimates are also used by architects/engineers, contractors, subcontractors, construction managers, schedulers, attorneys, insurance companies, lending institutions, and all others involved in the construction process for their own special purposes. This chapter discusses the crucial task of estimating.

Definition of a Cost Estimate

A construction cost estimate is a "best judgment" of the future cost of a project. This judgment of a project's probable cost is normally based on the following factors.

- Information from a specific set of drawings
- Information in the related specifications
- Observations and information about the proposed site
- The estimator's knowledge and experience

The main objective of estimating is to prepare an approximate, realistic cost of a project in an orderly, efficient, and comprehensive manner. Although there is always the possibility that a project may actually cost more or less than the estimate, the objective of an estimator is to be as accurate, thorough, and realistic as possible. The estimator is, therefore, a very important member of the construction team, regardless of whether or not he is employed by an owner, architect/engineer, general contractor, subcontractor, or private consultant.

In order to successfully perform the important task of determining costs that could involve millions of dollars, an estimator must not only possess reliable skills and attributes, but also must have a sound knowledge of the elements of the construction process listed and described below.

Plan Reading

The ability to read and understand construction drawings and specifications is indispensable, because the process of estimating requires that the estimator build the project in his mind in order to arrive at a realistic cost. Thus, he must have the ability to interpret the meaning of graphic, written, and oral data, and possess strong mathematical calculating skills.

Construction Costs

The estimator must be familiar with current labor, materials, equipment, and subcontract work costs; have access to such costs; and/or have reliable sources for cost data. The factors that affect cost must be monitored continuously in order to make adjustments when necessary. In short, an estimator must be familiar with current costs; know where and how to find them; and know how to use them to calculate a cost estimate.

Scheduling

While an estimator does not have to be an expert in scheduling, he should understand the basics of scheduling. The estimator must be able to place construction activities in logical sequence as he mentally "builds the project," to determine a realistic duration for the overall project. This is important for the estimator because to perform productivity calculations for various work crews, the estimator must be able to determine the duration of the many activities in a construction project.

Construction Contracts

The estimator must be familiar with the basic elements of contracts commonly used in the construction industry, to determine the scope of work for each subcontractor and to avoid legal pitfalls and claims. Often, the estimator is an expert witness in court, on claims cases, to define the scope of work in a project. For this reason, the estimator must recognize and understand the inferred obligations in a construction contract.

Construction Materials

An estimator should be familiar with basic construction materials and their uses, and keep abreast of material innovations. This may be accomplished by communicating with material suppliers and manufacturers. A working knowledge of construction materials is particularly important on projects where a **value engineering incentive clause** permits the sharing of cost savings with the owner.

Construction Methods

In order to assemble a project in his mind, an estimator must understand the method and sequence by which each component is built. New improved construction methods can be used to the contractor's advantage when a value engineering incentive clause is in the contract.

Types of Estimates

Construction cost estimates are known by several different names within the construction industry. However, most construction professionals agree that they may be classified in three general categories.

- Conceptual
- Semi-detailed
- Detailed

These three types of estimates and their major sub-categories are illustrated in Figure 3.1.

Conceptual Estimates

Sometimes referred to as **order-of-magnitude** or **pre-design estimates**, the accuracy of these estimates is usually within 20%. Conceptual estimates are often "ball-park" figures based on minimal information. These preliminary estimates are calculated by using one of the following

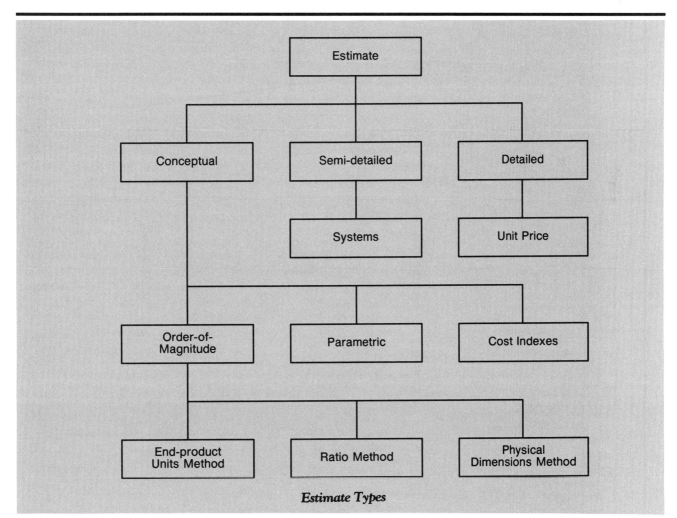

Estimate Types

Figure 3.1

criteria: floor area, number of floors, number of rooms in a hotel, number of beds in a hospital, or the output or capacity of a manufacturing plant. Conceptual estimates are not substitutes for detailed quantity takeoffs and prices needed for bidding or negotiating a contract. Conceptual estimating is used to calculate the **approximate probable cost** or **cost range** of a project before detailed plans and specifications are prepared.

Conceptual estimates are further broken down into three categories: **order-of-magnitude, parametric**, or **cost indexes**.

Order-of-Magnitude

Order-of-magnitude estimates can be prepared in many ways. However, the most commonly used methods are the **end-product units method,** the **ratio method,** and the **physical dimensions method.**

End-product Units Method: This method is used when enough data is available, from historical experience, to establish a relationship between some end-product and construction costs. Examples are the capacity of a power generating plant (in kilowatts) and its construction costs; the capacity of a hospital (number of beds) and the construction cost of that hospital; the number of apartments and the construction cost of an apartment building; and the number of parking spaces and the construction costs of a parking garage.

For example, an owner may be contemplating the construction of a 600-bed hospital in a large city and needs a quick estimate for the preliminary feasibility studies. The owner's estimator may consult publications, such as Means *Building Construction Cost Data* for cost information. A page from this publication (1989 edition) is shown in Figure 3.2, with information on the cost per bed.

According to Figure 3.2, the cost per bed ranges from $28,300 to $65,100. Therefore, the cost of a prospective 600-bed hospital should fall somewhere between $16,980,000 ($28,300 × 600) and $39,060,000 ($65,100 × 600). Adjustments may then be made for the location, required quality, site conditions, etc. Factors for adjustments are listed in the reference section of Means *Building Construction Cost Data.*

For more accuracy, the consultant, through some research, may be able to find the following information on a completed hospital in a similar city:

Capacity (number of beds) = 500
Total cost of construction = $27,500,000

From this information, the cost per bed is calculated:

$$\frac{\$27,500,000}{500} = \$55,000$$

or

$$\frac{\text{Total Cost}}{\text{Number of Beds}} = \text{Cost per Bed}$$

An order-of-magnitude estimate for a 600-bed hospital would be $33,000,000 ($55,000 × 600).

Ratio Method: The ratio method is commonly used in estimating the cost of facilities such as process and chemical plants. For these types of projects, the cost of specialized equipment and machines constitutes a major portion of the total cost. In the ratio method, the cost of all equipment and machinery is multiplied by a ratio determined from historical data. For example, if the total cost of all the major equipment

171 000	S.F. & C.F. Costs	UNIT	UNIT COSTS			% OF TOTAL			
			¼	MEDIAN	¾	¼	MEDIAN	¾	
410	9000	Per car, total cost	Car	5,375	7,325	10,300				410
	9500	Total: Mechanical & Electrical	"	385	580	710				
430	0010	GYMNASIUMS	S.F.	44.10	59.35	76				430
	0020	Total project costs	C.F.	2.20	3.06	3.90				
	1800	Equipment	S.F.	1.14	1.90	3.33	2%	3.20%	6.70%	
	2720	Plumbing		2.72	3.70	4.68	4.80%	7.20%	8.50%	
	2770	Heating, ventilating, air conditioning		2.89	5	8.20	7.40%	9.70%	14%	
	2900	Electrical		3.71	4.53	6.75	6.50%	8.90%	10.70%	
	3100	Total: Mechanical & Electrical	↓	8	12.45	16.35	16.70%	21.80%	27%	
	3500	See also division 114-801 & 114-805								
460	0010	HOSPITALS	S.F.	97.40	118	159				460
	0020	Total project costs	C.F.	7.15	8.60	11.50				
	1120	Roofing	S.F.	.71	1.77	2.88	.50%	1.20%	2.90%	
	1320	Finish hardware		.96	1.04	1.26	.60%	1%	1.20%	
	1540	Floor covering		.67	1.22	3.07	.50%	1.10%	1.60%	
	1800	Equipment		2.40	4.44	6.64	1.60%	3.80%	5.60%	
	2720	Plumbing		8.60	10.95	15	7.50%	9.10%	10.80%	
	2770	Heating, ventilating, air conditioning		9.30	15.50	21.75	8.40%	13%	16.70%	
	2900	Electrical		10.05	13.45	20.45	10%	12.30%	15.10%	
	3100	Total: Mechanical & Electrical	↓	29.45	40.15	59.35	28.20%	36.60%	40.30%	
	9000	Per bed or person, total cost	Bed	26,400	51,400	67,700				
	9900	See also division 117-001								
480	0010	HOUSING For the Elderly	S.F.	47.35	59.40	74.50				480
	0020	Total project costs	C.F.	3.34	4.63	6.05				
	0100	Sitework	S.F.	3.38	5.10	7.35	6%	8.20%	12.10%	
	0500	Masonry		1.42	4.98	7.60	2.10%	6.50%	10.40%	
	0730	Miscellaneous metals		1.39	1.85	4.88	1.40%	2.10%	3.10%	
	1120	Roofing		.92	1.59	2.81	1.20%	2.10%	3%	
	1140	Dampproofing		.27	.37	.85	.20%	.40%	.70%	
	1340	Windows		.64	1.09	2.35	1.10%	1.50%	2.40%	
	1350	Glass & glazing		.17	.49	.91	.20%	.40%	.90%	
	1530	Drywall		2.81	3.69	5.91	3.70%	4.10%	4.60%	
	1540	Floor covering		.76	1.13	1.63	.90%	1.40%	1.90%	
	1570	Tile & marble		.36	.52	.78	.50%	.60%	.80%	
	1580	Painting		1.52	2.14	3.32	2%	2.60%	3.10%	
	1800	Equipment		1.09	1.51	2.39	1.80%	3.20%	4.40%	
	2510	Conveying systems		1.11	1.52	2.02	1.70%	2.30%	2.80%	
	2720	Plumbing		3.58	4.96	7.24	8.30%	9.70%	10.90%	
	2730	Heating, ventilating, air conditioning		1.60	2.48	3.50	3.20%	5.60%	7.10%	
	2900	Electrical		3.48	4.87	6.85	7.50%	9%	10.60%	
	2910	Electrical incl. electric heat		3.98	7.50	8.90	9.60%	11%	13.30%	
	3100	Total: Mechanical & Electrical	↓	8.65	12.20	15.90	18.40%	21.90%	24.70%	
	9000	Per rental unit, total cost	Unit	41,800	49,500	54,400				
	9500	Total: Mechanical & Electrical	"	8,300	10,400	12,300				
500	0010	HOUSING Public (low-rise)	S.F.	36.45	49.90	67.90				500
	0020	Total project costs	C.F.	3.01	3.92	4.95				
	0100	Sitework	S.F.	4.77	6.70	10.35	8.30%	11.70%	16.10%	
	1800	Equipment		1.04	1.69	2.76	2.20%	3.10%	4.60%	
	2720	Plumbing		2.60	3.59	4.61	7.10%	9%	11.50%	
	2730	Heating, ventilating, air conditioning		1.39	2.60	2.95	4.40%	6%	6.40%	
	2900	Electrical		2.29	3.29	4.62	5%	6.50%	8.10%	
	3100	Total: Mechanical & Electrical	↓	6.80	9.70	13.55	15.60%	19.20%	22.20%	
	9000	Per apartment, total cost	Apt.	39,700	45,000	56,200				
	9500	Total: Mechanical & Electrical	"	6,675	9,150	11,500				
510	0010	ICE SKATING RINKS	S.F.	33.90	47.35	77.70				510
	0020	Total project costs	C.F.	1.92	2.41	2.84				
	2720	Plumbing	S.F.	1.02	1.50	2.29	3.10%	3.20%	4.60%	
	2900	Electrical	"	2.67	3.51	4.87	5.70%	7%	10.10%	

362

For expanded coverage of these items see *Means Square Foot Cost Data 1989*

Figure 3.2

and machinery on a chemical manufacturing plant is $5,000,000 and the ratio of plant cost to equipment cost (from historical data) is 5.0, then the projected cost will be approximately $25,000,000 ($5,000,000 × 5). Another method is to multiply the cost of each major item of equipment by its own ratio, and then add the results of each one to obtain the total cost of the project.

Physical Dimension Method: This method is the most common method of conceptual estimating. It is based on a physical dimension such as the square foot, cubic foot, or linear foot. A conceptual estimate for an office building can be calculated by the building's floor space (square feet) or volume (cubic feet). Pipe lines may be estimated by the linear foot or mile. Costs per unit may be based on historical data from a comparable building or obtained from a reliable annual cost publication such as *Means Square Foot Costs*. Sample pages from *Means Square Foot Costs*, 1989, are shown in Figures 3.3a and 3.3b. This book calculates the cost per square foot of a particular type building by adding the cost of the components of a model of a typical building.

Parametric Estimates This type of conceptual estimate is based on parameters that reflect the size and/or scope of a project. These parameters include parking area, total floor area, gross enclosed floor area, net finished area, gross area supported (excluding slab-on-grade), number of floors, area of face brick, area of other exterior wall, interior partitions, area of storefronts, and typical height of floor.

In this method, total parameter costs are obtained from completed projects. From these total costs, unit prices are determined and applied to similar parameters or components of a proposed building. The closer the proposed building is in size, shape, quality, and other features, the more reliable the estimate.

Cost Indexes

A construction cost index number is a percentage ratio of a building component's cost at any stated time and location to the cost of that same component at a base period.

$$\frac{\text{Cost at Stated Time}}{\text{Cost at Base Period}} \times 100 = \text{Index Number}$$

For estimating purposes, index numbers, applied to historical cost data, allow the contractor to evaluate changes in building construction costs from one period to another, and from one location to another.

The four most common types of cost indexes are:
- **General Purpose Construction Cost Indexes** – such as those published by R. S. Means Company, *Engineering News Record* and the *United States Commerce Department*
- **Selling Price Indexes** – including those compiled by *Fru-Con Corp., Lee Saylor, Inc., Turner Construction Company,* and *Smith, Hinchman & Grylls Associates, Inc.*
- **Valuation Indexes** – such as those compiled by the *Boeckh Company,* and *Marshall & Swift Services*
- **Special Purpose Indexes** – including those published by *Nelson-Farrar, New York Port Authority,* the *Environmental Protection Agency,* and the *Bureau of Labor Statistics*

Of the indexes described above, those compiled by the R. S. Means Company and *Engineering News Record* (ENR) are the most widely used in the construction industry and are reviewed in this text.

COMMERCIAL/INDUSTRIAL INSTITUTIONAL | 2.480 | Office, 11-20 Story

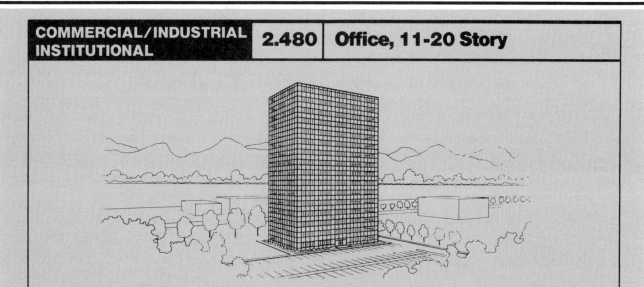

COSTS PER SQUARE FOOT OF FLOOR AREA

EXTERIOR WALL	S.F. Area	90000	100000	110000	120000	130000	140000	150000	160000	170000
	L.F. Perimeter	320	342	364	360	376	393	400	413	426
Double Glazed Heat Absorbing Tinted Plate Glass Panels	Steel Frame	87.10	85.80	84.65	82.35	81.40	**80.60**	79.50	78.75	78.10
	R/Conc. Frame	88.55	86.85	85.45	82.85	81.65	80.70	79.40	78.55	77.75
Face Brick with Concrete Block Back-Up	Steel Frame	81.60	80.20	79.00	77.30	76.40	75.60	74.70	74.05	73.50
	R/Conc. Frame	95.70	94.15	92.75	90.65	89.55	88.65	87.55	86.75	86.10
Precast Concrete Panel With Exposed Aggregate	Steel Frame	81.45	80.10	78.95	77.20	76.30	75.55	74.60	74.00	73.40
	R/Conc. Frame	95.90	94.30	92.90	90.85	89.75	88.85	87.80	87.00	86.35
Perimeter Adj. Add or Deduct	Per 100 L.F.	7.15	6.40	5.85	5.35	4.95	4.60	4.25	4.05	3.80
Story Hgt. Adj. Add or Deduct	Per 1 Ft.	2.20	2.10	2.05	1.90	1.80	1.75	1.65	1.60	1.55
FOR BASEMENT, add $17.70 per square foot of basement area										

The above costs were calculated using the basic specifications shown on the facing page. These costs should be adjusted where necessary for design alternatives and owner's requirements. Reported completed project costs, for this type of structure, range from $34.00 to $125.00 per S.F.

COMMON ADDITIVES

Description	Unit	Cost
CLOCK SYSTEM		
20 Room	Each	$9075
50 Room	Each	22,000
DIRECTORY BOARDS, Plastic, glass covered		
30" x 20"	Each	425
36" x 48"	Each	780
Aluminum, 24" x 18"	Each	385
39" x 27"	Each	510
48" x 32"	Each	575
48" x 60"	Each	1025
ELEVATORS, Electric passenger, 10 stops		
3000# capacity	Each	99,250
4000# capacity	Each	101,350
5000# capacity	Each	103,550
Additional stop, add	Each	6875
EMERGENCY LIGHTING, 25 watt battery operated		
Lead battery	Each	305
Nickel cadmium	Each	460

Description	Unit	Cost
ESCALATORS, Metal		
32" Wide, 10' story height	Each	$88,150
20' Story height	Each	100,080
48" Wide, 10' Story height	Each	98,255
20' Story height	Each	113,090
Glass		
32" Wide, 10' story height	Each	100,730
20' Story height	Each	114,380
48" Wide, 10' story height	Each	110,080
20' Story height	Each	123,625
SMOKE DETECTORS		
Ceiling type	Each	98
Duct type	Each	300
SOUND SYSTEM		
Amplifier, 250 watts	Each	1125
Speaker, ceiling or wall	Each	96
Trumpet	Each	185
TV ANTENNA, Master system, 12 outlet	Outlet	170
30 Outlet	Outlet	110
100 Outlet	Outlet	100

Use LOCATION FACTORS on pages 389 to 393

Figure 3.3a

Model costs calculated for a 15 story building with 10 foot story height and 140,000 square feet of floor area

NO.	SYSTEM/COMPONENT	SPECIFICATIONS		UNIT	UNIT COST	COST PER S.F.
1.0 FOUNDATIONS						
.1	Footings & Foundations	Poured concrete; strip and spread footings and 4' foundation wall		S.F. Ground	17.10	1.14
.4	Piles & Caissons	N/A		—	—	—
.9	Excavation & Backfill	Site preparation for slab and trench for foundation wall and footing		S.F. Ground	.74	.05
2.0 SUBSTRUCTURE						
.1	Slab on Grade	4" reinforced concrete with vapor barrier and granular base		S.F. Slab	2.70	.18
.2	Special Substructures	N/A		—	—	—
3.0 SUPERSTRUCTURE						
.1	Columns & Beams	Steel columns with fireproofing		L.F. Column	88.60	2.41
.4	Structural Walls	N/A		—	—	—
.5	Elevated Floors	Concrete slab, metal deck, beams		S.F. Elev. Floor	10.74	10.03
.7	Roof	Metal deck, open web steel joists, beams, columns		S.F. Roof	3.65	.24
.9	Stairs	Concrete filled metal pan		Flight	4840	1.21
4.0 EXTERIOR CLOSURE						
.1	Walls	N/A		—	—	—
.5	Exterior Wall Finishes	N/A		—	—	—
.6	Doors	Double aluminum & glass doors		Each	3750	.75
.7	Windows & Glazed Walls	Double glazed heat absorbing, tinted plate glass wall panels	100% of wall	S.F. Wall	32.10	13.52
5.0 ROOFING						
.1	Roof Coverings	Built-up tar and gravel with flashing		S.F. Roof	3.30	.22
.7	Insulation	Perlite/urethane composite		S.F. Roof	1.23	.08
.8	Openings & Specialties	N/A		—	—	—
6.0 INTERIOR CONSTRUCTION						
.1	Partitions	Gypsum board on metal studs, toilet partitions	30 S.F. Floor/L.F. Partition	S.F. Partition	2.67	1.15
.4	Interior Doors	Single leaf hollow metal	400 S.F. Floor/Door	Each	480	1.20
.5	Wall Finishes	60% vinyl wall covering, 40% paint		S.F. Surface	.82	.44
.6	Floor Finishes	60% carpet, 30% vinyl composition tile, 10% ceramic tile		S.F. Floor	4.14	4.14
.7	Ceiling Finishes	Mineral fiber tile on concealed zee bars		S.F. Ceiling	3.73	3.73
.9	Interior Surface/Exterior Wall	Painted drywall on metal furring	80% of wall	S.F. Wall	2.97	.79
7.0 CONVEYING						
.1	Elevators	Four passenger elevators		Each	178520	6.20
.2	Special Conveyors	N/A		—	—	—
8.0 MECHANICAL						
.1	Plumbing	Toilet and service fixtures, supply and drainage	1 Fixture/1345 S.F. Floor	Each	1455	1.08
.2	Fire Protection	Standpipes and hose systems and sprinklers, light hazard		S.F. Floor	2.00	2.00
.3	Heating	Oil fired hot water		S.F. Floor	2.20	2.20
.4	Cooling	Chilled water, fan coil units		S.F. Floor	6.47	6.47
.5	Special Systems	N/A		—	—	—
9.0 ELECTRICAL						
.1	Service & Distribution	2400 ampere service, panel board and feeders		S.F. Floor	.83	.83
.2	Lighting & Power	Fluorescent fixtures, receptacles, switches and misc. power		S.F. Floor	5.53	5.53
.4	Special Electrical	Alarm systems and emergency lighting		S.F. Floor	.54	.54
11.0 SPECIAL CONSTRUCTION						
.1	Specialties	N/A		—	—	—
12.0 SITEWORK						
.1	Earthwork	N/A		—	—	—
.3	Utilities	N/A		—	—	—
.5	Roads & Parking	N/A		—	—	—
.7	Site Improvements	N/A		—	—	—
			SUB-TOTAL			66.13
GENERAL CONDITIONS (Overhead and Profit)					15%	9.92
ARCHITECT FEES					6%	4.55
			TOTAL BUILDING COST			80.60

Figure 3.3b

The Means Construction Cost Indexes (CCI), published quarterly, provide adjustment factors for 209 major cities in all 50 states and Canada. The Indexes list material and installation costs of all 16 CSI construction divisions for each city. A separate table shows the average Construction Trade Labor Rates.

Each issue also has indexes for an expanded analysis of 50 individual construction cost divisions and major classifications in 30 key cities and 5 major large cities.

The index numbers in Means Indexes represent relative construction costs for material, labor, and equipment, as well as "in-place" costs. All cost indexes are calculated using the 30-city National Average material costs, labor rates, and equipment rental rates related to the base period January 1, 1975.

The components of this index consist of specific quantities of 84 commonly used construction materials, specific man-hours for 24 building trades, and specific days of equipment rental for 9 types of construction equipment normally used to install these 84 material items by the 24 trades.

The exact material, labor, and equipment quantities are based on a detailed analysis of many building types. Then each quantity is weighed in proportion to the expected annual usage. These various material items, labor hours, and equipment rental rates are thus combined to form a composite building, representing as closely as possible the actual usage of materials, labor, and equipment in the building construction industry.

When using CCI for comparing costs from city to city, it must be remembered that an index number is a percentage ratio of a building component's cost at any stated time to the cost of that same component at a base period:

$$\frac{\text{Cost at Stated Time}}{\text{Cost at Base Period}} \times 100 = \text{Index Number}$$

Therefore, when making cost comparisons between cities, **do not subtract** one city's index number from the index number of another city, reading the result as a percentage difference. Instead, the correct way to compare construction costs between two cities is to **divide** one city's index number by that of the other city. The resulting number may then be used as a **multiplier** to calculate cost differences from city to city.

The formula used to determine cost differences between cities for the purpose of comparison reads as follows:

$$\frac{\text{City A Index}}{\text{City B Index}} \times \text{City B Cost (Known)} = \text{City A Cost (Unknown)}$$

City "A" is that city for which there are no estimated cost figures. City "B" is that city for which you already have an estimated, or "known", cost. The city index numbers used when comparing costs between cities must be taken from the same CCI issue, and must be applicable to the same time period as the "known" cost.

The following example illustrates how to use Means Indexes for comparing a specific city's construction costs with the National Average. When studying construction location feasibility, it is advisable to compare a prospective project's cost index with an index of the National Average costs.

For example, according to the October 1988 issue of Means CCI, the weighted average index of construction costs in Sacramento, CA, as calculated using a January 1975 base of 100.0, is 225.9. By referring to the same Means CCI issue, it can be seen that the weighted average index of construction costs for 30 major cities in the United States (calculated using the same base period) is 206.8. By dividing Sacramento's index by that of the 30-city average,

$$\frac{225.9}{206.8} = 1.092$$

it's clear that construction costs in Sacramento are 9.2% more than the National Average. This gives an indication of Sacramento's feasibility as a construction location in relation to the average throughout the nation. (Note that this comparison was made through a division process—not subtraction. Subtraction would result in a difference of 19.1%, which does not take into account the original difference in 1975 between Sacramento's index and the 30-city average index.)

The final example illustrates the use of CCI for updating and adjusting construction cost data based on a National Average. To update construction cost data from calendar quarter to quarter using *Means Construction Cost Indexes*, a basic formula is used:

$$\frac{\text{Present Cost Index}}{\text{Last Quarter's Cost Index}} \times \text{Last Quarter's Cost} = \text{Current Cost}$$

For example, assume that in October 1987 your "bottom line" estimate for a building in Atlanta, GA totaled $250,000.

In October 1988, it is necessary to update that estimate. Refer to the October 1987 and October 1988 Means Indexes, locate the applicable index numbers for that city, and use them in the stated formula.

$$\frac{\text{October 1988 Atlanta Index (185.5)}}{\text{October 1987 Atlanta Index (180.1)}} \times \begin{array}{c} \text{October 1987 Cost} \\ (\$250,000) \end{array} = \begin{array}{c} \text{October 1988 Cost} \\ (\text{Unknown}) \end{array}$$

$$1.030 \times \$250,000 = \$257,500$$

The updated "bottom line" estimate is $257,500.

Engineering News Record compiles and publishes five kinds of cost indexes. They are:

- Construction Cost Index
- Building Cost Index
- Common Labor Index
- Skilled Labor Index
- Materials Index

These indexes are compiled and published monthly using average costs from twenty cities in the United States and two cities in Canada. They are based on *Weighted Skilled Labor, Structural Steel, Lumber and Cement*, and use a base of 1913 = 100.

While most conceptual estimates may have a low level of accuracy, they have some important applications in the construction industry, including those listed below.

- Establishment of probable costs of the construction portion of an overall development budget
- Quick determination of the general feasibility of a project
- Modification of a previously prepared conceptual estimate
- Control of a construction budget during the design phase
- The screening of several types of alternative designs to determine the most cost-effective design
- The screening of a number of projects to determine the probable cost range to decide which projects to bid

Semi-detailed Estimates

These estimates are sometimes called **design development, budget estimates,** or **systems estimates.** Even though the accuracy level of these estimates is low, they are more definitive and accurate than conceptual estimates. Because semi-detailed estimates are based on partially completed drawings and specifications, their accuracy and usefulness depends on the amount and quality of information available. Semi-detailed estimates may be used for:

- determining project feasibility,
- refining conceptual estimates, and
- establishing and/or controlling budgets.

This method of estimating uses a logical, sequential approach that reflects the order in which a building is constructed. Twelve UNIFORMAT divisions organize building construction into major components that can be used in budget, or systems, estimates. The UNIFORMAT divisions are listed below.

Systems Estimating Divisions:

Division   1 – Foundations
Division   2 – Substructure
Division   3 – Superstructure
Division   4 – Exterior Closure
Division   5 – Roofing
Division   6 – Interior Construction
Division   7 – Conveying
Division   8 – Mechanical
Division   9 – Electrical
Division 10 – General Conditions
Division 11 – Special
Division 12 – Site Work

Each system is further broken down into systems, incorporating several different components into an assemblage that is commonly used in construction.

A great advantage of the systems, or budget estimate, is that the designer or estimator can readily substitute one system for another during design development and can quickly determine the cost differential. In this way, the owner can anticipate budget requirements and make design/costing decisions before establishing the final details and dimensions.

Detailed Estimates

Also known as **bid estimates** or **unit price estimates,** detailed estimates are comprehensive and are based on "100% completed" contract documents (plans and specifications). This is the most accurate type of estimate. Detailed estimates are used for the following purposes.

- Bidding
- Negotiating of projects
- Obtaining financing for a project
- Establishing project budget and cost control systems
- Refining and defining semi-detailed and/or conceptual estimates previously prepared for the same project
- Justifying construction claims
- Preparing schedule of values for payment purposes
- Preparing monthly progress payment requests
- Change order preparation and negotiation
- Guidance in the preparation of future estimates

For detailed unit price estimates, most construction specification manuals and cost reference books compile and present unit price information using the 16 divisions of the MASTERFORMAT developed by the Construction Specifications Institute, Inc. (CSI).

CSI MASTERFORMAT Divisions

Division 1 – General Requirements
Division 2 – Site Work
Division 3 – Concrete
Division 4 – Masonry
Division 5 – Metals
Division 6 – Wood and Plastics
Division 7 – Moisture-Thermal Control
Division 8 – Doors, Windows, and Glass
Division 9 – Finishes
Division 10 – Specialties
Division 11 – Equipment
Division 12 – Furnishings
Division 13 – Special Construction
Division 14 – Conveying Systems
Division 15 – Mechanical
Division 16 – Electrical

Each division is further broken down into subdivisions. Unit prices are obtained for each item in each category. Costs can be obtained from published sources such as Means *Building Construction Cost Data* or from a contractor's, owner's, or estimator's historical cost data file.

Phases of the Estimating Process

The estimating process requires a comprehensive and systematic approach. After a contractor has decided to submit a bid or has been invited to submit a cost proposal for negotiation, he normally goes through the following phases.

- Contract documents procurement
- Contract documents review
- Bid preparation

Contract Documents Procurement

A contractor usually obtains contract documents by one of three methods. The first method is to obtain the documents by paying a specified deposit to the architect/engineer. This deposit may be refundable upon return of the documents if the contractor is not the lowest qualified bidder, or it may be non-refundable.

In the second method, the architect/engineer furnishes the documents to a contractor without a deposit.

In the third method, a contractor goes to a local *Builder's Exchange* or *Plan Room*. Here, documents are available and there is ample space to perform a quantity takeoff. The number of sets of contract documents available depends on the size of the project; and the anticipated number of subcontractors and major suppliers from whom prices will be sought.

Contract Documents Review

In this phase, the contractor thoroughly reviews all contract documents to obtain a clear understanding of the project. Since these documents dictate how the project will be built, as well as how the estimate will be prepared, emphasis during the review must be placed on ensuring that the documents are complete (no missing pages or sheets, for example). The contractor should look for any unusual or unfamiliar items of work. It is also important to clearly define those portions of work to be performed with the contractor's own forces and those portions to be subcontracted.

Bid Preparation

Now the contractor is ready to prepare a cost estimate for bidding the job. A logical sequence should be followed to keep the process or schedule and still make the cost estimate as accurate as possible. (The owner or project manager may also prepare a budget estimate based on the techniques presented in the following paragraphs.)

Summary Sheet

After reviewing the contract documents, the estimator lists each cost element of the project on a summary sheet, grouped into headings of similar items. The summary sheet serves as an estimating checklist, helps the estimator become familiar with the project, and helps determine the items to be performed with the firm's own forces and those to be subcontracted. A preprinted summary sheet is shown in Figures 3.4a and 3.4b. Items can be added or deleted from each division of this summary sheet.

During this phase, a schedule for preparing the estimate is developed to ensure that the estimate will be completed on time. Where more than one estimator is involved, the project coordinator establishes specific responsibilities for various sections of the project. Estimators should always solicit bids from potential subcontractors and suppliers for all contracted items or services, to obtain competitive prices for these services.

Bid File Preparation

Immediately upon obtaining the contract documents, a bid file is set up to store information related to the project in an organized format, and to keep all project documents in one place. The bid file typically contains the following.

- The contract documents
- Quantity takeoff and pricing sheets
- Telephone and written quotations from subcontractors, suppliers, etc. (preferably arranged in order and in accordance with the CSI format)
- The estimate summary sheet and cut/add sheets
- Spread sheet
- Surety bonds
- The bid envelope
- A correspondence file

The correspondence file contains a record of every communication between the contractor and the architect/engineer, subcontractors, suppliers, and the owner.

Site Visit

Prior to beginning the takeoff, the estimating team inspects the site and prepares investigation sheets (shown in Figures 3.5a and 3.5b). If possible, inspectors should use a camera or a video camera to photograph the site. Such recordings are helpful when discussing the project with others who may not have seen the site. Photographs or videos also provide a good record of the existing site conditions for legal purposes or change orders.

4 Means Forms

**ESTIMATE
SUMMARY**

SHEET NO.

PROJECT				ESTIMATE NO.
LOCATION		TOTAL AREA/VOLUME		DATE
ARCHITECT		COST PER S.F./C.F.		NO. OF STORIES
PRICES BY:		EXTENSIONS BY:		CHECKED BY:

DIV.	DESCRIPTION	MATERIAL	LABOR
1.0	**General Requirements**		
	Insurance, Taxes, Bonds		
	Equipment & Tools		
	Design, Engineering, Supervision		
2.0	**Site Work**		
	Site Preparation, Demolition		
	Earthwork		
	Caissons & Piling		
	Drainage & Utilities		
	Paving & Surfacing		
	Site Improvements, Landscaping		
3.0	**Concrete**		
	Formwork		
	Reinforcing Steel & Mesh		
	Foundations		
	Superstructure		
	Precast Concrete		
4.0	**Masonry**		
	Mortar & Reinforcing		
	Brick, Block, Stonework		
5.0	**Metal**		
	Structural Steel		
	Open-Web Joists		
	Steel Deck		
	Misc. & Ornamental Metals		
	Fasteners, Rough Hardware		
6.0	**Carpentry**		
	Rough		
	Finish		
	Architectural Woodwork		
7.0	**Moisture & Thermal Protection**		
	Water & Dampproofing		
	Insulation & Fireproofing		
	Roofing & Sheet Metal		
	Siding		
	Roof Accessories		
8.0	**Doors, Windows, Glass**		
	Doors & Frames		
	Windows		
	Finish Hardware		
	Glass & Glazing		
	Curtain Wall & Entrances		
	PAGE TOTALS		

Page 1 of 2

Figure 3.4a

DIV.	DESCRIPTION	MATERIAL	LABOR	EQUIPMENT	SUBCONTRACT	TOTAL
	Totals Brought Forward					
9.0	**Finishes**					
	Studs & Furring					
	Lath, Plaster & Stucco					
	Drywall					
	Tile, Terrazzo, Etc.					
	Acoustical Treatment					
	Floor Covering					
	Painting & Wall Coverings					
10.0	**Specialties**					
	Bathroom Accessories					
	Lockers					
	Partitions					
	Signs & Bulletin Boards					
11.0	**Equipment**					
	Appliances					
	Dock					
	Kitchen					
12.0	**Furnishings**					
	Blinds					
	Seating					
13.0	**Special Construction**					
	Integrated Ceilings					
	Pedestal Floors					
	Pre Fab Rooms & Bldgs.					
14.0	**Conveying Systems**					
	Elevators, Escalators					
	Pneumatic Tube Systems					
15.0	**Mechanical**					
	Pipe & Fittings					
	Plumbing Fixtures & Appliances					
	Fire Protection					
	Heating					
	Air Conditioning & Ventilation					
16.0	**Electrical**					
	Raceways					
	Conductors & Grounding					
	Boxes & Wiring Devices					
	Starters, Boards & Switches					
	Transformers & Bus Duct					
	Lighting					
	Special Systems					
	Subtotals					
	Sales Tax %					
	Overhead %					
	Subtotal					
	Profit %					
	Adjustments/Contingency					
	TOTAL BID					

Figure 3.4b

Means Forms

JOB SITE ANALYSIS

PROJECT		BID DATE
LOCATION		NEAREST TOWN
ARCHITECT	ENGINEER	OWNER

Access, Highway	Surface	Capacity
Railroad Siding	Freight Station	Bus Station
Airport	Motels/Hotels	Hospital
Post Office	Communications	Police
Distance & Travel Time to Site		Dock Facilities

Water Source	Amount Available	Quality
Distance from Site	Pipe/Pump Required?	Tanks Required?
Owner	Price (MG)	Treatment Necessary?
Natural Water Availability		Amount

Power Availability	Location	Transformer
Distance	Amount Available	
Voltage	Phase	Cycle	KWH or HP Rate

Temporary Roads	Lengths & Widths
Bridges/Culverts	Number & Size
Drainage Problems	
Clearing Problems	
Grading Problems	
Fill Availability	Distance
Mobilization Time	Cost
Camps or Housing	Size of Work Force
Sewage Treatment	
Material Storage Area	Office & Shed Area

Labor Source	Union Affiliation
Common Labor Supply	Skilled Labor Supply
Local Wage Rates	Fringe Benefits
Travel Time	Per Diem

Taxes, Sales	Facilities	Equipment
Hauling	Transportation	Property
Other		

Material Availability: Aggregates	Cement
Ready Mix Concrete	
Reinforcing Steel	Structural Steel
Brick & Block	Lumber & Plywood
Building Supplies	Equipment Repair & Parts

Demolition: Type	Number
Size	Equip. Required
Dump Site	Distance	Dump fees
Permits	

Figure 3.5a

⚓ Means Forms

Clearing: Area | Timber | Diameter | Species

Brush Area | Burn on Site | Disposal Area

Saleable Timber | Useable Timber | Haul

Equipment Required

Weather: Mean Temperatures

Highs | Lows

Working Season Duration | Bad Weather Allowance

Winter Construction

Average Rainfall | Wet Season | Dry Season

Stream or Tide Conditions

Haul Road Problems

Long Range Weather

Soils: Job Borings Adequate? | Test Pits

Additional Borings Needed | Location | Extent

Visible Rock

U.S. Soil & Agriculture Maps

Bureau of Mines Geological Data

County/State Agriculture Agent

Tests Required

Ground Water

Construction Plant Required

Alternate Method

Equipment Available

Rental Equipment | Location

Miscellaneous: Contractor Interest

Sub Contractor Interest

Material Fabricator Availability

Possible Job Delays

Political Situation

Construction Money Availability

Unusual Conditions

Summary

Figure 3.5b

Quantity Takeoff Phase

The takeoff, or quantity survey, involves measuring quantities from a set of plans using the specifications as a guide. The quantity takeoff should be organized in the sequence in which the project will be built. This helps to eliminate gross errors or omissions. A formal takeoff also facilitates coordination when several estimators are working on the same estimate. It is recommended that a pre-printed form, as shown in Figure 3.6, be used for clarity and uniformity. (For more information on this subject, refer to *Quantity Takeoff for the General Contractor* by Paul J. Cook, published by R. S. Means Company, Inc., 1989.)

After the takeoff is complete and the dimensions extended, an estimator should carefully check all quantities and numbers (preferably an estimator who did not perform the takeoff).

Costing

In this phase, "bare costs" – the estimated material and labor unit costs to the contractor – are multiplied by the quantities of each item taken off the plans. Items are organized in groups of similar materials, using predetermined categories such as the sixteen CSI Divisions. Standard pre-printed forms (as shown in Figure 3.7) are helpful in producing a uniform cost estimate.

During costing, the estimator solicits bids from subcontractors, suppliers, and manufacturers of specialty items. It is customary to solicit at least two or three prices for each item of work. Subcontractors furnish these prices in writing or by telephone. One should always record prices received over the telephone on telephone quotation forms, as shown in Figure 3.8.

Components of a Cost Estimate

A construction cost estimate has two main parts – direct and indirect costs. Direct costs include labor, subcontractors, material, and equipment. Indirect costs include escalation, profit, all overhead, and labor burden. The breakdown of a cost estimate is shown in Figure 3.9.

Direct Costs

Costs that can be identified or charged to a specific work item on a construction project are direct costs. Direct costs include the cost of labor, materials, and equipment for all work items that will be physically incorporated into a project by a contractor, subcontractor, or vendor.

Labor costs are the wages, including fringes, paid to the field personnel who work on a construction site. This includes carpenters, laborers, masons, painters, and cement finishers.

Material costs are the cost of materials, building parts, and installed equipment incorporated into a project.

Equipment costs are the costs of the equipment a contractor uses to perform a contract (such as cranes, bulldozers, and backhoes). This does not include equipment that is permanently installed as part of a project.

Subcontract costs are those prices furnished by subcontractors for a specific portion of a given project that the general contractor does not perform with his own workmen. The general contractor usually includes the subcontract price (including indirect costs) as part of his cost estimate with an additional mark-up for overhead and profit.

Indirect Costs

Indirect costs are all costs – other than the direct labor, material, equipment, and subcontract costs – incurred by a contractor in the

Means Forms

QUANTITY SHEET

SHEET NO. _____

PROJECT _____

ESTIMATE NO. _____

LOCATION _____ ARCHITECT _____ DATE _____

TAKE OFF BY _____ EXTENSIONS BY: _____ CHECKED BY: _____

DESCRIPTION	NO.	DIMENSIONS					UNIT			UNIT			UNIT			UNIT

Figure 3.6

49

Figure 3.7

Means Forms

TELEPHONE QUOTATION

DATE _____

PROJECT _____

TIME _____

FIRM QUOTING _____

PHONE (_____)

ADDRESS _____

BY _____

ITEM QUOTED _____

RECEIVED BY _____

WORK INCLUDED	AMOUNT OF QUOTATION

DELIVERY TIME	**TOTAL BID**	
DOES QUOTATION INCLUDE THE FOLLOWING:	If ☐ NO is checked, determine the following:	
STATE & LOCAL SALES TAXES ☐ YES ☐ NO	MATERIAL VALUE	
DELIVERY TO THE JOB SITE ☐ YES ☐ NO	WEIGHT	
COMPLETE INSTALLATION ☐ YES ☐ NO	QUANTITY	
COMPLETE SECTION AS PER PLANS & SPECIFICATIONS ☐ YES ☐ NO	DESCRIBE BELOW	

EXCLUSIONS AND QUALIFICATIONS	

ADDENDA ACKNOWLEDGEMENT	**TOTAL ADJUSTMENTS**	
	ADJUSTED TOTAL BID	

ALTERNATES	
ALTERNATE NO.	
ALTERNATE NO.	
ALTERNATE NO.	
ALTERNATE NO.	
ALTERNATE NO.	
ALTERNATE NO.	
ALTERNATE NO.	

Figure 3.8

performance of projects, that cannot be charged to any specific work element. This category includes other costs found in the general conditions of the specifications, such as general overhead (field office and home office overhead), escalation, and profit. Indirect costs include Workers' Compensation, payroll taxes, insurance, home office overhead allocated to job, and profit.

Labor burden is the sum of various indirect costs applied to the labor costs from the general contractor's own forces, such as taxes, insurance, and overhead costs.

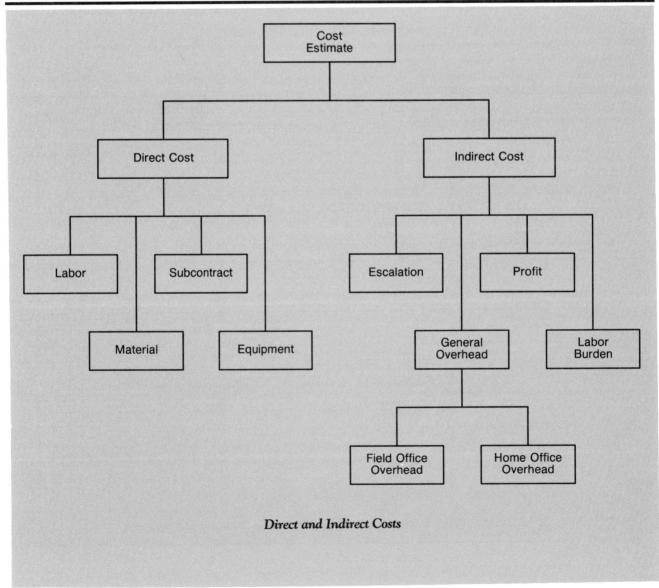

Direct and Indirect Costs

Figure 3.9

Indirect costs are included in the General Conditions of the contract. A sample General Conditions summary sheet is shown in Figures 3.10a and 3.10b.

Home office expense is the fixed cost of "doing business" incurred by a contractor. These costs are calculated yearly. A percentage of the home office expense, based on the annual volume of a contractor, is prorated to every project. A sample listing of a contractor's home office expenses is shown in Figure 3.11.

Profit is the contractor's compensation for his risk, effort, and endeavor to undertake a project. Although the contractor always includes a profit in the initial estimate, the actual profit is the money left after the contractor has met all the costs (both direct and indirect) on a project. By nature, the amount of profit included in an estimate is very subjective, and may be influenced by factors such as competition, the job market, the economy, and the political climate.

Sometimes, the contractor includes an **escalation fee** or percentage to cover any unforeseen but highly probable anticipated price increases he may face in the future on a given project. For example, there is usually a lapse of time from the date when a contractor prepares an estimate to the time when the work begins and the materials and supplies are purchased. During this time, prices may increase due to inflation, shortages, or other factors.

Contractors may also include a percentage of the total cost for **contingencies.** In general, the less complete and specific the plans and specifications, then the higher the contingency.

Sources of Prices

The main sources of prices for construction cost estimates are historical data, productivity calculations, or external sources.

- **Historical Data.** This method uses unit prices compiled from completed work of similar construction updated to the present. These prices are regarded as the most reliable source of cost data for each company.
- **Productivity Calculations.** This method uses man-hour calculations based on the size of a crew and the time to accomplish certain specific tasks. In the absence of, or in conjunction with, prior experience, there are several publications that list productivity data, such as Means *Man-Hour Standards.* Material prices can be obtained from the contractor's data file, suppliers catalogs, and quotes, or cost data manuals.
- **Other (External) Sources.** Other sources are unit prices from published cost data sources such as R. S. Means Company, Inc., McGraw Hill, Richardson Engineering, or Frank R. Walker Co.

Checking a Cost Estimate

Most estimators prepare construction cost estimates under tremendous pressure, time constraints, and deadlines. For this reason, it is not uncommon to find basic arithmetical errors in estimates, that can be costly if not discovered. All costs should be double checked, preferably by an estimator who did not work on the project.

Often Overlooked Items

There are a number of items often overlooked in the estimating process. If these are not addressed early in the process, they can lead to disputes, conflicts, or losses. For example, the cost, scheduling, storage, and

⚖ Means Forms

PROJECT
OVERHEAD SUMMARY

PROJECT

SHEET NO.

ESTIMATE NO.

LOCATION   ARCHITECT   DATE

QUANTITIES BY: PRICES BY: EXTENSIONS BY: CHECKED BY:

DESCRIPTION	QUANTITY	UNIT	MATERIAL/EQUIPMENT		LABOR		TOTAL COST	
			UNIT	TOTAL	UNIT	TOTAL	UNIT	TOTAL
Job Organization: Superintendent								
Project Manager								
Timekeeper & Material Clerk								
Clerical								
Safety, Watchman & First Aid								
Travel Expense: Superintendent								
Project Manager								
Engineering: Layout								
Inspection/Quantities								
Drawings								
CPM Schedule								
Testing: Soil								
Materials								
Structural								
Equipment: Cranes								
Concrete Pump, Conveyor, Etc.								
Elevators, Hoists								
Freight & Hauling								
Loading, Unloading, Erecting, Etc.								
Maintenance								
Pumping								
Scaffolding								
Small Power Equipment/Tools								
Field Offices: Job Office								
Architect/Owner's Office								
Temporary Telephones								
Utilities								
Temporary Toilets								
Storage Areas & Sheds								
Temporary Utilities: Heat								
Light & Power								
Water								
PAGE TOTALS								

Page 1 of 2

Figure 3.10a

54

Means Forms

DESCRIPTION	QUANTITY	UNIT	MATERIAL/EQUIPMENT UNIT	MATERIAL/EQUIPMENT TOTAL	LABOR UNIT	LABOR TOTAL	TOTAL COST UNIT	TOTAL COST TOTAL
Totals Brought Forward								
Winter Protection: Temp. Heat/Protection								
Snow Plowing								
Thawing Materials								
Temporary Roads								
Signs & Barricades: Site Sign								
Temporary Fences								
Temporary Stairs, Ladders & Floors								
Photographs								
Clean Up								
Dumpster								
Final Clean Up								
Punch List								
Permits: Building								
Misc.								
Insurance: Builders Risk								
Owner's Protective Liability								
Umbrella								
Unemployment Ins. & Social Security								
Taxes								
City Sales Tax								
State Sales Tax								
Bonds								
Performance								
Material & Equipment								
Main Office Expense								
Special Items								
TOTALS:								

Page 2 of 2

Figure 3.10b

Annual Main Office Expenses

Salaries

Owner	$ 70,000
Engineer/Estimator	45,000
Assistant Estimator	30,000
Project Manager	60,000
General Superintendent	50,000
Bookkeeper/Officer Manager	24,000
Secretary/Receptionist	18,000

Office Worker Benefits

Workers Compensation FICA & Unemployment Medical Insurance Miscellaneous Benefits	} 37% of salaries	109,890

Physical Plant

Office & Warehouse	30,000
Utilities	2,400
Telephone	3,000
Office Equipment	2,500
Office Supplies	1,000
Auto & Truck (4 vehciles)	24,000

Professional Services

Accounting	1,500
Legal	1,500
Advertising	4,000

Miscellaneous

Dues	1,000
Seminars & Travel	2,000
Entertainment & Gifts	3,000
Uncollected Receivables (2%)	200,000
Total Annual Expenses	$682,790

Figure 3.11

handling of owner-furnished material or equipment is not always clearly defined and therefore should be determined before the contract is signed.

For example, on some projects, specialized material or equipment is specified as "furnished by the owner," but the responsibility of unloading and storing these items on the site until they are incorporated into the project is, by implication, placed on the contractor. This can be expensive if a crane is required for unloading or if the items need to be protected from weather. The cost of crane rental and/or storage should always be included in the estimate in such cases.

Escalation Costs

With inflation being a big factor in recent years, the cost of labor, material, and equipment may increase during construction. Consideration should be given, in the estimate, to escalation of costs. The period of escalation may be calculated from the time the estimate is prepared to the mid-point of the specified construction period.

Weather Impacted Costs

It is important to determine the impact of weather and estimate the costs affected by weather. For example, one day of heavy rains during the excavation phase of a project may result in several days of delay, since it may be too wet to work for several days after the rain.

Lump Sum Items

This category includes items that are paid for by the general contractor but that do not lend themselves to unit pricing, such as the project sign, caulking, and field office expenses. Other examples of lump sum items are building permits, final cleanup, police protection, and trash removal. Although these items are difficult to quantitatively measure, they should be carefully reviewed for scope and difficulty before submitting a price.

Summary

The cost estimate – from the general conceptual estimate to the detailed unit price estimate – is used by all parties involved in the construction of a project. The owner may hire an estimator to determine the project budget. This budget is then used as a comparison to contractor's bids, and to control project costs. Various methods of cost estimating can be used, depending on the status of the design documents.

Chapter Four

Contract Procurement

"Sometimes it is more important
to discover what one cannot do,
than what one can do."
Lin Yutang

Prior to the twentieth century, buildings were constructed by a **master builder** who assembled a project using his own craftsmen (laborers, carpenters, masons, roofers, ironworkers, plumbers, electricians, cement finishers, mechanics, etc.) and his own materials. In contrast, today's general contractor performs only relatively small portions of the work with his own craftsmen, and is more of a supervisor or manager who oversees a construction team. Several subcontractors who are specialists in their fields perform the rest of the construction work.

As the overall supervisor for a project, the general contractor coordinates the work of all the subcontractors. The general contractor manages all other on-site activities as well, to ensure that the work is performed properly in accordance with the contract documents (plans and specifications) in a timely manner.

In the contract procurement phase of the construction process, the owner selects a general contractor to transform the plans and specifications into a physical structure. The process by which the owner selects a general contractor is discussed in this chapter.

Methods of Contract Procurement

The two common methods by which an owner selects a contractor are: **competitive bidding** and **negotiation**. The contract procurement process varies considerably between public and private projects. By law, all public (federal, state, county, or city) projects must be publicly advertised and competitively bid. On such projects, the contracting agency gives notice of a pending bid by posting notices in public places and placing advertisements for bids in trade journals, newspapers, or magazines. For example, advertisements for bids for most federal projects may be found in the *Commerce Business Daily*.

Public Projects

By law, advertisements for bidding federal and state projects must be placed at least thirty days before the bid date. All bid advertisements usually have the following information:

- A project number
- The name of the proposed project and its location
- The name of the contracting agency with an address, phone number, and the name of a contact person
- The name, address, and phone number of the architect/engineer
- A brief description of the proposed work
- The date, time, and place where the bids will be received and how they will be received and opened
- When the contract documents (plans, specifications, etc.) will be available, where they can be examined, and how to obtain them
- Applicable governing laws and regulations, including wage rates
- Requirements for surety bonds (such as a bid bond)
- Proposal submittal procedures (how it must be submitted, owner's right to reject bids, etc.)

Figure 4.1 shows an example of an advertisement to bid.

The U.S. federal government, for example, uses a standard form known as *Standard Form* 1442, *Solicitation, Offer, and Award* of the General Services Administration. A copy of this form is shown in Figure 4.2.

This form contains information on the advertisement to bidders and is usually mailed to general contractors who express interest in the project.

In some situations, the owner has conducted bidding on selected areas of subcontract work and requires the general contractor to incorporate the bids of the successful subcontractors into their overall bid. The bids of the subcontractors are known as **filed sub-bids.**

Privately Owned Projects

Unlike the government, private owners are free to choose the manner by which a contractor is selected. A private owner, with the help of the architect/engineer, may simply select a contractor of his choice to perform the work without any competition from other contractors. The owner may have had prior dealings with a certain contractor and is confident that he (or she) will perform the work proficiently at the lowest possible cost.

In private work, an owner can choose a method known as **invitational bidding** to select a contractor. In this method, the owner, with the help of the architect/engineer, may invite a few contractors considered to be capable and reputable to submit bids for the project. This method retains the elements of competitive bidding while restricting the bidders to a selected group of contractors.

A third contractor selection method available to private owners involves **public advertising** similar to that used on public projects. The owner may be a firm or corporation that must resort to competitive bidding to guarantee a low bid to satisfy the stockholders and other interested parties.

Competitive Bidding

There are two types of competitive bidding: **open competitive bidding** and **closed competitive bidding**. In open competitive bidding, the project is publicly or conspicuously advertised and is open to any responsible and qualified contractor who may wish to submit a bid. In

Advertisement for Bid

The Port Authority of New York
and New Jersey

Sealed proposals for the following contracts will be
received by the Chief Engineer, Room 77N, One World Trade
Center, New York, N.Y. 11088, until 2:30 P.M. on the date
indicated and will then be opened and read in Room 83W.
Contract documents may be seen in Suite 4121 - 41st Floor
and copies may be obtained upon a non-refundable payment
of $25.00 for each contract set. Only company checks or
money orders payable to the order of the Port Authority of
New York and New Jersey will be accepted. (Please call
(212) 466-7083 first for availability of contracts.)
Questions by prospective bidders concerning any one of the
contracts should be directed only to the person whose name
and phone number is listed for the contract in question.

Contract BP-152 -- Brooklyn-Port Authority Marine
Terminal -- Police/Engineering Office Expansion --
Brooklyn Piers Bldg. 186 -- Bids Due Thursday, February
25, 1990 -- Direct Questions to Mr. Jim DiLouie, (201)
924-1233.

Contract HT-110.046 -- Holland Tunnel -- North and South
Tubes -- Catwalk and Handrail Rehabiliation -- Bids Due
Thursday, February 25, 1990 -- Direct Questions to Mr.
Samuel Cruk, (212) 446-7430 or (201) 623-6301, Extension
7521.

Figure 4.1

SOLICITATION, OFFER, AND AWARD (Construction, Alteration, or Repair)	1. SOLICITATION NO.	2. TYPE OF SOLICITATION	3. DATE ISSUED	PAGE OF PAGES
		☐ SEALED BID *(IFB)* ☐ NEGOTIATED *(RFP)*		

IMPORTANT — The "offer" section on the reverse must be fully completed by offeror.

4. CONTRACT NO.	5. REQUISITION/PURCHASE REQUEST NO.	6. PROJECT NO.

7. ISSUED BY	CODE		8. ADDRESS OFFER TO

9. FOR INFORMATION CALL:	A. NAME	B. TELEPHONE NO. *(Include area code)* *(NO COLLECT CALLS)*

SOLICITATION

NOTE: In sealed bid solicitations "offer" and "offeror" mean "bid" and "bidder".

10. THE GOVERNMENT REQUIRES PERFORMANCE OF THE WORK DESCRIBED IN THESE DOCUMENTS *(Title, identifying no., date)*:

11. The Contractor shall begin performance within _____ calendar days and complete it within _____ calendar days after receiving ☐ award, ☐ notice to proceed This performance period is ☐ mandatory, ☐ negotiable *(See _____ .)*

12A. THE CONTRACTOR MUST FURNISH ANY REQUIRED PERFORMANCE AND PAYMENT BONDS? *(If "YES," indicate within how many calendar days after award in Item 12B.)*	12B. CALENDAR DAYS
☐ YES ☐ NO	

13. ADDITIONAL SOLICITATION REQUIREMENTS:

A. Sealed offers in original and _____ copies to perform the work required are due at the place specified in Item 8 by _____ *(hour)* local time _____ *(date)*. If this is a sealed bid solicitation, offers will be publicly opened at that time. Sealed envelopes containing offers shall be marked to show the offeror's name and address, the solicitation number, and the date and time offers are due.

B. An offer guarantee ☐ is, ☐ is not required.

C. All offers are subject to the (1) work requirements, and (2) other provisions and clauses incorporated in the solicitation in full text or by reference.

D. Offers providing less than _____ calendar days for Government acceptance after the date offers are due will not be considered and will be rejected

NSN 7540-01-155-3212

THIS PUBLICATION IS A COURTESY QUICK COPY FROM THE BALTIMORE ARMY PUBLICATIONS CENTER TO MEET YOUR NEEDS WHILE WE ARE REPLENISHING OUR REGULAR STOCK.

1442 102

STANDARD FORM 1442 (REV. 4-85)
Prescribed by GSA
FAR (48 CFR) 53.236-1(d)

Figure 4.2

closed competitive bidding, the owner (often assisted by the architect/engineer) invites only certain selected contractors to compete for the contract.

Open competitive bidding is the method most commonly used to select contractors in the construction industry in the United States. This method follows the steps below.

1. Sealed bids (also known as offers or proposals) are submitted by each bidder on specified forms, and at a specified time and location.
2. At the specified time and location, all the sealed bids are opened and the amount of each bid is publicly announced by a representative of the owner.
3. Usually the contractor with the lowest bid is selected to perform the work, if he is qualified, if there are no irregularities, and if the bid does not exceed the amount budgeted for the project by the owner.

The main advantages of competitive bidding are listed below.

- It theoretically permits an owner to build a project at the lowest possible cost.
- It provides an owner with a way to determine a fair market price for a proposed project.
- It is generally viewed as a way to minimize favoritism and unfairness in the construction contract procurement process.

Even though it is the method most commonly used to procure a contractor, competitive bidding has several limitations that are often overlooked. First, this method does not provide any assurance that the lowest bidder is competent and will be able to complete the work in accordance with the contract documents and in the specified time. Second, competitive bidding is time-consuming – it can take three to four months longer than other procurement methods. Finally, this method may encourage general contractors, particularly during periods when projects are scarce, to submit unrealistically low bids with the hope of making a profit by cutting corners. In such cases, contractors may use cheaper materials or methods that may remain undetected during construction but can lead to costly repairs, maintenance, or replacement in the future. Another way contractors can make a profit on a low bid project is through unethical claims or change orders, or by "beating" and "squeezing" subcontractors and suppliers to reduce costs.

Finally, it is worth noting that the competitive bid method is based on the existence of two critical conditions – **free bids** and **true competition**. If bidders, in violation of anti-trust laws, decide to take turns in submitting artificially low bids, these conditions will not exist. This unethical tactic is known as "bid rigging" and is punishable by fines and imprisonment.

Negotiated Contracts

In this method of selecting a contractor, the owner, usually of a private project, selects and places his trust and confidence in one contractor (without competition) to perform the work at a mutually agreed price. The major advantages of this method are listed below.

- The negotiated method bypasses the time-consuming and often costly process of competitive bidding.
- It permits the owner to use a contractor of his choice.
- On complex, highly technical, or specialty projects that may require specialized equipment, or expertise, the owner can select a

competent contractor with whom he has had successful and satisfactory prior dealings.

- It eliminates the temptation of a contractor to submit an unrealistically low price just to get the job.
- It provides both the owner and the contractor with an opportunity to freely review, discuss, and agree on the scope of the contract, and a mutually satisfactory price.

One major disadvantage of this method is that the owner takes an inherent risk regarding the capability, integrity, and credibility of the contractor he selects. It is therefore important that the owner and his architect/engineer base the budget for the project on a detailed estimate. The experience, capability, and financial resources of the selected contractor should be thoroughly investigated prior to negotiating a price and contract.

In negotiated contracts, the owner is in a position to choose union or non-union contractors to bid on a project. The benefits of choosing open shop contractors could be a savings in overall cost of the project. However, there are arguments that the level of skill of open shop workers does not equal that of the union contractors.

Bid Preparation

The preparation of a bid may be broken down into **nine major phases**. These are described in the following paragraphs.

The Decision-Making Phase

Most contractors do not bid every project that is advertised or all those for which they are invited to submit bids. Instead, they do a certain amount of picking and choosing after they learn of an upcoming project. The decision on which projects to bid is governed by the following factors.

- The location of the project
- The architect/engineer
- The amount of work in progress at the time
- The type and nature of the project and how it relates to the experience of the firm; its availability; and the capability of management, field personnel, and equipment
- Probable competition
- Availability of working capital and cash flow
- Bonding limits

All the above interrelated factors are carefully considered by the contractor before bidding on a project.

Contract Documents Procurement Phase

After desirable projects have been identified, the contractor arranges to obtain the contract documents. These usually include sets of construction drawings, specifications, and any addenda that may have been issued after the completion of the plans and specifications by the architect/engineer. Most architectural firms require a deposit for each set of contract documents obtained. The deposit may range from $0 (no deposit required) to $300 depending on the size and complexity of the proposed project. The deposit may be refundable (if the documents are returned in good condition to the architect by unsuccessful bidders) or they may be non-refundable. It is important to obtain an adequate number of the documents for use by the estimators, subcontractors, and suppliers. It may be possible for the contractor to obtain a set of sepias rather than prints with his deposit. Sepias, in turn, allow the contractor to print as many sets as required to properly bid the work.

The contract documents should be obtained at least 30 to 45 days prior to the bid date to allow sufficient time for preparation of the bid. A bonding agent should be contacted to ensure that a bid bond, and subsequent performance and payment bonds, will be issued for the project. Usually, bonding companies require some basic information to enable them to determine if a contractor is bondable. The information requested usually includes the type of project, projected cost range, location, an updated schedule of work in progress, and completed projects. It is always advisable to ascertain whether a bid bond will be forthcoming well in advance of the bid date.

Documents Review Phase

After the documents are obtained, the following steps are recommended to ensure proper organization.

Step 1

The estimator or estimating team should review the documents for a few days to obtain a general concept of the project.

Step 2

The documents should be numbered sequentially. For example, it is customary to number one set as "set #1" and clearly label it "office set" and "bid set." This process will identify the original bid documents, in the event that the sepias are later altered. Contractors or owners may number another set "set #2" and clearly label it "plan room copy – do not remove from plan room." This is done to ensure that one set stays in the designated plan room to enable subcontractors and suppliers to review the documents and/or perform quantity takeoffs. Any remaining sets of the contract documents should be numbered in sequence so that they may be accounted for during and after the bid process.

Step 3

The project documents should be recorded on a **plan checkout log**. This log, illustrated in Figure 4.3, is used to keep track of the sets of bid documents obtained for a project. The name of each company that borrows a set of the bid documents is entered on the log, along with the checkout date, sections checked out, and the name of the person receiving the documents. The date when the documents are returned is also entered. This system permits the contractor to track the whereabouts of all sets of bid documents obtained by the firm, facilitates their return by subcontractors and suppliers, and makes it possible for them to be returned to the architect for a refund, if appropriate. If the return is mandatory, a deposit should be required from each subcontractor.

Step 4

The project should be recorded on the **bid bulletin**. This is a large chalkboard located in the plan room that lists, in chronological order, the bid schedule of the contractor. An example of a bid bulletin is shown in Figure 4.4. The purpose of this bulletin is to inform the contractor's employees of the bid schedule and to keep suppliers and subcontractors updated about the general contractor's bidding activity.

Plan Check Out Log

Project				Bid Date		

Set No.				Spec. No.		

Foundation	Company				
	Contact				
	Phone				
	Date				
	Return				
Structure	Company				
	Contact				
	Phone				
	Date				
	Return				
Plumbing	Company				
	Contact				
	Phone				
	Date				
	Return				
Mechanical	Company				
	Contact				
	Phone				
	Date				
	Return				
Electrical	Company				
	Contact				
	Phone				
	Date				
	Return				
Interior Finishes	Company				
	Contact				
	Phone				
	Date				
	Return				
Specialties	Company				
	Contact				
	Phone				
	Date				
	Return				
Civil	Company				
	Contact				
	Phone				
	Date				
	Return				
	Company				
	Contact				
	Phone				
	Date				
	Return				
	Company				
	Contact				
	Phone				
	Date				
	Return				

Figure 4.3

Step 5

A subcontractor/supplier solicitation list (also known as a **bidder call list**) should be prepared and given to the appropriate personnel, preferably a junior estimator or a technically-oriented person, who can answer questions about the project, if necessary. The main purpose of this list is to ensure that at least one sub-bid will be received for every section of the specifications not accomplished by the general contractor. Examples of this list are illustrated in Figures 4.5 and 4.6.

Summary Sheet Preparation Phase

A summary sheet for the estimate should be prepared by the chief estimator as soon as he is assigned to the project. It is useful in three ways.

- A summary sheet helps the estimator become familiar with the project.
- It serves as a checklist of important items to be considered during the estimating process.
- It helps the estimator determine which areas of the project to subcontract out and which ones to perform with the general contractor's forces.

(An example of an estimate summary is shown in Chapter 3, Figures 3.4a and 3.4b.)

Bid Organization Phase

The bidding process is usually very hectic. Proper organization is the key to minimizing the chances of gross mistakes normally associated with "bid day scramble." Most contractors begin the organization of the bid documents by setting up two sets of files: **a bid file**, to assemble all the bid information related to the project in an organized manner, and a **correspondence file**, to maintain a record of all the correspondence pertaining to the project (letters, phone conversations, etc.). This includes any communication with the architect/engineer, owner, subcontractors, suppliers, consultants, insurance agent, or bonding agent.

Bid Board — MB General Contractors			
Project Name	**Bid Date**	**Time**	**Addenda**
Boston Tech Office Complex	Sept. 3	2 p.m.	3
Florida High School	Sept. 17	4 p.m.	2
Bentil Inn Riverside	Oct. 12	2 p.m.	2
R.S. Means Plaza	Oct. 29	3 p.m.	0
Gainesville Farms Warehouse	Nov. 1	3 p.m.	4

Figure 4.4

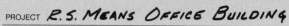

Means Forms

BIDDER
CALL LIST

PROJECT _R.S. MEANS OFFICE BUILDING_   DATE _5-1-89_

ITEM _DIV. 15 MECHANICAL WORK_   BY _R.J.G._

DATE	RESPONSE	PHONE	SUBCONTRACTOR/MATERIAL SUPPLIER	COMMENTS
3-2	YES	617-747-1270	R.S.M. CORP	CALL ON BID DAY
3-2	NO ANSWER	617-747-1274	MECHANICAL INC.	TRY AFTER 5:00
3-2	NOT BIDDING	617-747-1273	MOYLAN PLUMBING & HEATING	
3-2	OUT OF BUSINESS	617-700-0000	COMMERCIAL MECHANICAL	?
3-3	YES	617-747-1270	MOSSMAN PIPING	CALL MEL ON BID DAY
3-3	YES	617-747-0000	PILGRIM MECHANICAL CORP	WILL CALL W/QUOTE
3-3	WILL CALL BACK	617-747-1275	KINGSTON PLUMBING & HEATING	
3-3	YES	617-747-1271	MEANS MECHANICAL SERVICES	WORK WITH BILL

Figure 4.5

Means Forms

BIDDER
CALL LIST

PROJECT R. S. MEANS OFFICE BUILDING

ITEM DIV. 15 MECHANICAL WORK

DATE 1989

BY R. J. G.

| | | RESPONSE | | | | | |
DATE	BIDDING Y/N	NO ANSWER	CALL BACK	WILL CALL	SUBCONTRACTOR/MATERIAL SUPPLIER	PHONE	COMMENTS
3-2	Y				RSM CORP	617-747-1270	CALL ON BID DAY
3-2		✓			MECHANICAL INC	617-747-1274	TRY AFTER 5:00
3-2	N				MOYLAN PLUMBING & HEATING	617-747-1273	
3-2		✓			COMMERCIAL MECHANICAL	617-700-0000	OUT OF BUSINESS
3-3	Y				MOSSMAN PIPING	617-747-1272	CALL MEL ON BID DAY
3-3				✓	PILGRIM MECHANICAL CORP	617-747-0000	W/ QUOTE
3-3			✓		KINGSTON PLUMBING & HEATING	617-747-1275	
3-3	Y				MEANS MECHANICAL SERVICES	617-747-1271	WORK WITH BILL

Figure 4.6

69

Site Visit

The bid documents almost always require that the contractor visit the site. This ensures that the contractor surveys the existing site conditions and becomes familiar with the site before submitting a bid.

Estimating Phase

After reviewing the contract documents, organizing the project, and visiting the site, the estimating of the project begins. For small projects, a contractor may assign one estimator to perform the estimate. For large and/or complex projects, a team of estimators, led by a chief estimator, or project estimator, performs the estimating function. Each estimator in the team is assigned a distinct phase of the project, such as Division 3 – Concrete. This individual then has full responsibility for estimating a price for that division. The chief estimator assembles the various parts of the estimate.

Pre-bid Conference

A meeting, known as the pre-bid conference, is usually held just after the bid documents are issued to contractors. This meeting is a forum for all prospective bidders to clarify any new or outstanding questions they may have concerning the project. Answers to all pertinent questions are usually recorded, issued in the form of addenda, and sent to all planholders. The architect/engineer, other representatives of the owner, and all planholders attend this conference. On some projects, attendance at this conference is mandatory, while it is voluntary on others. In any case, it is highly recommended that prospective bidders attend this meeting.

Bid Finalization Phase

As bid day approaches, the chief estimator should begin to finalize his bid on a **bid spread sheet**. The bid spread sheet is used by the contractor for comparing various costs to arrive at a bid amount. Included in this amount are the contractor's estimated costs, bids from subcontractors and suppliers, as well as the mark-up on these costs. Therefore, there should be a category for each subcontractor or supplier quote. This should be compared with the summary sheet mentioned earlier. This sheet allows the bidding "officer" to review all subcontractors' quotes against one another and the corresponding internal estimate to select the optimum cost. Subcontractor and supplier quotations should also be confirmed by the estimators responsible for each division. All arithmetic should be carefully checked.

Bids submitted by suppliers and subcontractors as listed on telephone bid forms should be carefully evaluated to ensure that the scope of work estimated is in accordance with the bid documents. Next, the low bid is determined for each group of bids submitted. Where subcontractors submit combination bids (for example, one contractor submits a bid that includes plumbing, HVAC, and electrical; another submits one that includes plumbing and electrical; another submits one for electrical and HVAC; another submits one for plumbing only; another submits one for electrical only; and another submits one for HVAC only), a matrix, or bid spread sheet, may be used to determine the best practical combination of bids. A sample bid spread sheet is shown in Figure 4.7.

Note that the blocked out space on the upper left corner of the spread sheet (Figure 4.7) is used to record the contractor's prices as produced by his own estimators. The remainder of the page is composed of smaller blocked out spaces for recording bids for subcontracted items. Within these smaller blocks, there are spaces for entering the item being bid,

Means Forms

BID SPREAD SHEET

PROJECT: R. S. MEANS WAREHOUSE
LOCATION: KINGSTON, MA
BID DATE: OCTOBER 22, 1989
COMPLETION TIME: 365 DAYS
COLOR CODE: BASE BID ——— ; ALT. 1 - - - -

GEN. CONT. WORK — 276,100 (Alt. 1: 320)

		ALT 1	BASE BID
01100	GENERAL CONDITIONS		129,074
03300	C.I.P. CONCRETE	320	99,055
06000	CARPENTRY		17,497
07950	CAULKING & SEALANTS		3,360
06300	INSTALL MISC. METAL		2,004
	SURVEYING		8,000
	WINDOW CLEANING		2,200
	PROGRESS SCHEDULE		6,750
	SHORE PICACHO ST.		8,160
		320	276,100

02200 CLEANING & EARTHWORK — 475,596 (Alt. 1: 48,510)

		EROSION CONTROL	DUMP FEES	ALT 1	BASE BID
BUDGET	441,256	1,350	33,000	48,510	475,596
LEVELERS	595,000	YES	YES	60,510	595,000

02444 CHAIN LINK FENCE — 10,500

	BASE BID
OBSTACLES INC.	10,500
STOP-ALL	11,260
PROP-DIVIDER	10,900

02640 A.C. PAVING — 209,200 (Alt. 1: 82,000)

		PARKING STRIPING	ALT. 1	BASE BID
BUDGET	215,694	1200	88,682	216,694
BLAZERS	208000	NO	82,000	209,200
HARDPAK	218900	YES	90,000	218,900
HILINE	223,000	YES	91,500	223,000

02800 LANDSCAPING — 12,222 (Alt. 1: 2,000)

		SPRINKLERS	ALT. 1	BASE BID
BEANSTIK	15,500	YES	2,990	15,500
PLANTON	14,000	YES	2,850	14,000
GREENER	12,222	YES	2,000	12,222

03320 REINFORCING STEEL — 14,850

		HOISTING	MASONRY REINF	BASE BID
BUDGET		600	2,800	
BETBAR	14,250	NO	NO	14,850
STRAPTIE	18,000	YES	YES	18,000
BENDER	21,300	YES	YES	21,300

04000 MASONRY — 42,000

		REINF STEEL	P.C. WDW SILLS	SHORE OPENINGS	BASE BID
BUDGET	37,864	2,800	1,080	2,880	39,024
HISTACK	36,320	NO	YES	NO	42,000
WALLHEN	48,500	YES	YES	YES	48,500
BLOKSON	47,000	YES	YES	YES	47,000

05120 STRUCTURAL STEEL — 156,600

	STRUC. STEEL	MISC. METAL	BASE BID
L.T. PIZZA	142,200	NO	142,600
RINGER	156,000	YES	156,600
W.F. BEAM	149,000	NO	149,000

05300 MISCELLANEOUS METAL — ☒

	MISC MAT'L	BASE BID
ALUM	18,188	18,188
CARBON	17,000	17,000
ZINC	18,990	18,990

05320 STEEL DECKING — 21,240

		HOISTING	ROOF DECK	FLOOR DECK	BASE BID
HORIZON	24,400	YES	YES	YES	24,400
DEKKO	21,240	YES	YES	YES	21,240

07600 SHEET METAL — 3,800

		WALL LOUVERS	BASE BID
BUDGET		960	
FLASHER	4,400	YES	
LEADER	2840	NO	3,800
DRYER	3,220	NO	4,180

07950 CAULKING & SEALANTS — ☒ SEE GEN CONTR. WORK

	BASE BID
LINERS	3,550

08100 HOLLOW METAL DOORS & FRAMERS — 3,360

	H.M. DOORS & FRAMES	WOOD DOORS	BASE BID
BUDGET		1,260	
SLAMMER	2,100	NO	3,360
ACCESS	2,800	NO	4,060
OPEN	3,000	NO	4,260

08330 OVERHEAD STEEL DOORS — 8,800

		ELEC OPER		BASE BID
SLAMMER	7,900	NO	INCOMPLETE	
SLIDE UP	8,800	YES		8,800

08400 ALUMINUM WINDOWS — 10,750

		CAULKING	INSTALL		BASE BID
SLIDE IN	10,500	NO	NO	INCOMPLETE	
SEETHRU	10,750	YES	YES		10,750
SHINY	12,800	YES	YES		12,880

08720 GLASS & GLAZING — 4200

		GLASS IN DOORS	MIRRORS	BASE BID
BRITTLE	4,200	YES	YES	4,200
GLASSY	4,890	YES	YES	4,890
SPARKLE	5,500	YES	YES	5,500

09110 PAINTING — 28,000

		BASE BID
SMEARS	28,000	28,000
DAUGERS	28,000	28,000
STREAKS	31,400	31,400

15000 MECHANICAL — 98,500

	SAN SEWER	STORM DRAINS	EXTERIOR WATER	EXTERIOR GAS
UTILITY	33,000	YES	YES	YES
PIPER	13,500	YES	14,500	YES
FIXTURES	31,800	YES	YES	YES

	PLUMBING	HEATING	VENT & A.C.	HOSE REELS
UTILITY	26,900	46,000	YES	2,100
PIPER	78,000	YES	YES	YES
FIXTURES	30,000	42,500	YES	NO

16000 ELECTRICAL — 68,000 (Alt. 1: 3,000)

	DOOR OPER	ALT. 1	BASE BID
SHOCKER	NO	3,490	75,500
STATIC	NO	3,700	71,440
SPARKS	NO	3,000	68,000

07320 ROOFING — 30,000

	BASE BID
TILETOP	30,000

BASE BID	
COST	1,473,718
12% MARK-UP	176,846
SUBTOTAL	1,650564
0.6% BOND COST	9900
DEDUCT - ADJUSTMENT	12464
TOTAL	1,648,000

ALT. 1	
COST	135,830
12% MARK-UP	16,300
SUBTOTAL	152,130
0.6% BOND COST	913
ADJUSTMENT	43
DEDUCTIVE TOTAL	153,000

Figure 4.7

subcontractor names, prices, and scope of work. When the best bid is determined, this figure is recorded in the column at the right. The selected bids are totalled and marked up in the block at the bottom right corner of the page. Space is also available here for totalling and marking up alternate bids.

The bid spread sheet helps the contractor organize his bid in a comprehensive manner for use on bid day. For contractors who use computers, the bid spread sheet can be easily done using one of several software programs available on the market.

The final figures from the spread sheet are transferred to the summary sheet. Once the summary sheet is completed, last minute price changes should be handled with a **cut/add sheet.** An example of this sheet is shown in Figure 4.8.

At some point, the chief estimator or "bidding officer" arrives at a final price for the project. This price is entered on the **bid form** (shown in Figure 4.9) and any changes (plus or minus) are made on the envelope (in which the bid is submitted) just before submitting the bid. Note that before the bid is submitted, it should be checked one final time to ensure that all the numbers are correct, that the bid form is properly completed and signed, and that the bid complies with all the instructions in the bid documents.

Surety Bonds

The construction industry, by its nature, may be subject to many uncertainties. As a result, owners are usually concerned about the inherent risks associated with the industry, such as poorly managed or under-capitalized contractors, nonpayment to a general contractor's suppliers and employees, and failure to complete the project in accordance with the contract documents. To insure himself against non-payment, the owner may require that a contractor furnish surety bonds. In the event of default, the owner can then collect damages from a bonding company instead of trying to extract funds from a financially insolvent or bankrupt contractor.

A surety bond is a three-way contract between the bonding company (known as the **surety**), the contractor (known as the **principal**) and the owner (known as the **obligee**), who is the beneficiary. Under this contract, the surety is bound to complete the project in the event that the contractor defaults, up to the face value of the bond. For example, if the owner pays a contractor 75% of the contract sum and the contractor completes only 25% of the contract and then defaults, then the owner only has 25% of the contract sum left with which to finish the project. The surety, by obligation of the bond, must complete the project with the balance (in this case, 25% of the contract sum), and absorb any additional costs itself. The bonding company, in turn, may sue the contractor to recover the additional costs of completing the project.

There are four main types of surety bonds used in the construction process. They are the **bid bond,** the **payment bond,** the **performance bond**, and the **supply bond**. While payment and performance bonds describe separate obligations, they are usually combined in one transaction so that one premium covers both. The premium paid by the contractor ranges from 0.5% to 4% of the total contract amount. Bond premiums may vary considerably depending on the size of the product, the track record of the contractor, and the financial position and bonding history of the contractor. The amount of the bond usually equals 100% of the contract price.

Cut/Add Sheet

Project				Bid Date	
Reference	Work Item	Add	Cut	New Supplier/Sub
				Subtotals
				Net Subtotal
				Plaster Matrix
				Mechanical Matrix
	Add			Cut (to envelope)

Alternate Changes: _____

_____

_____

_____

_____

Figure 4.8

PROPOSAL FORM - GENERAL CONSTRUCTION

PROPOSAL OF:_____
                          (Name of Bidder)

TO: _____

FOR: _____

Gentlemen:

The Undersigned has received the Bidding Documents (Project Manual and
Drawings) for the referenced project including Addenda numbered_____.
The provisions of these Addenda have been included in this Proposal. The
undersigned has examined both the site and the documents, and is fully
informed on the scope and conditions of the work.

The Undersigned hereby proposes to furnish all labor and materials and
perform all work related to the Prime Contract for General Construction
for the new (Name of Project as it appears on all contract documents)
located at (Address of site), in strict accordance with the Contract
Documents included or listed in the Project Manual, for the consideration
of the following:

BASE BID: For all labor and materials and all work related to the General
Construction of the proposed project, including the Plumbing, Mechanical
and Electrical work, in full consideration of all that is required by the
Contract Documents for the sum of:

_____DOLLARS

              ($_____)

If written notice of the acceptance of Bid is mailed, telegraphed, or
delivered to the Undersigned within ninety (90) days after the date of
opening bids, or at any time thereafter before this bid is withdrawn by
writing, the undersigned agrees that he will execute and deliver a
contract, in accordance with the bid as accepted, all within ten (10) days
(unless a longer period of time is allowed) after the prescribed forms are
presented to him for signature.

Notice of acceptance should be mailed, telegraphed or delivered to the
Undersigned at the following address:

              Signed _____

              For   _____
                            (Legal Name of Bidder)

              Address _____

                      _____

Seal
(If Bid is by a Corporation)

Figure 4.9

The Bid Bond

This document is submitted with a bid on a proposed contract, whenever an owner is advertising to bid "at large." A bid bond assures an owner that if the bid submitted by the contractor is accepted by the owner, the contractor will furnish performance and payment bonds and enter into a contract with the owner within a specified time period to perform the contract in accordance with the owner's bid documents. If the contractor fails to do so, the amount of the bid bond becomes payable to the owner as compensation for the damages sustained resulting from the contractor's refusal to proceed with the work, including having to contract with a bidder for a much larger contract sum. The penal sum of the bid bond is usually a percentage (normally 5% to 20%) of the total gross bid price submitted by the contractor. The cost of a bid bond to a contractor ranges from nothing to about $50.

The Payment Bond

This bond is submitted after a contractor's bid is accepted by the owner. It assures the owner that the contractor will pay for all labor, material, equipment, suppliers, and subcontractors used on the project. This bond is sometimes called a **labor and materials payment bond.** Regardless of its name, this bond protects the owner from claims and liens after the project is completed and the final payment is released to the contractor. Bonding benefits subcontractors, material suppliers, and construction workers, because it insures payment.

The Performance Bond

A performance bond is submitted after the acceptance of a contractor's bid. This bond assures the owner that the contractor will perform and complete the contract in accordance with the contract documents. It is intended to protect the owner in the event that the contractor fails to complete the work.

The Supply Bond

This bond is usually provided by a material supplier (when requested) to protect a general contractor. The supply bond ensures that the supplier will furnish the quantity and the quality of a given material or equipment in accordance with the contract documents, delivered to a given location, for an agreed price, within a specified time period.

Bid Submission

Preparing a bid requires a big investment of a contractor's time, money, and resources. Therefore, care must be taken to ensure that the bid is submitted in strict accordance with the owner's requirements, which are summarized in a document known as the **Instructions to Bidders**. (Preprinted forms are available from organizations such as the American Institute of Architects.) It is equally important that the contractor submit the bid on time. A contractor's bid is commonly rejected for reasons such as failure to comply fully with instructions in the bid documents, late submission, failure to include the specified bond, or unnecessary exclusions or qualifications. The following are suggested guidelines for submitting bids.

- The bid amount is normally written in words and figures. In case of a discrepancy between the written amount and the figures, the written amount traditionally takes precedence over the figures.
- The bid envelope must be prepared in advance. Its contents should be carefully checked to ensure that the required number of copies of the bid form are enclosed, along with the bond or any other items specified in the bid documents.

- The bid envelope should include, as a minimum, complete information about the contractor (name, address, telephone number, etc.) on the top left hand corner; the name or identification number of the project being bid in the center; and the dollar amount of the final cut or add, where applicable and permitted.

Courier

All efforts must be made to deliver the bid on time. An employee, preferably an estimator, should be designated as the courier who will deliver the bid. The courier should visit the site in advance and locate a public telephone close to the venue where the bids are designated to be opened. The courier must also know the exact building, floor, and room number where the bids will be received. The designated courier should make a dry run from the telephone to the bid room to determine the amount of time needed to make this trip. Time must also be allowed for unexpected delays, such as slow elevators. The courier should situate himself or herself at the telephone an hour or so before the time of bid opening. It is recommended that the designated person have a couple of good ink pens handy. This advance planning will permit the contractor to communicate any last minute changes (cuts or adds) and ensure that they are correctly written on the envelope before final submission of the bid.

Recording Bids

It is good practice for the contractor to record the results of each bid opening in which he participates. A collection of both "won" and "lost" bids provides a historical record of other competitor's bids in relation to the contractor's own bid for each project. With this data, it is possible to determine the bidding patterns of competitors and develop a bidding strategy for a specific project based on these patterns.

The results of the competitors' bids should be recorded (as they are being read) on a **bid results form**, shown in Figure 4.10.

Means Forms
BID
RESULTS REPORT

PROJECT: _R.S. MEANS OFFICE BUILDING_
LOCATION: _KINGSTON, MA_

A/E ESTIMATE

RANK	BIDDER	BID BOND	BASE BID	1	ALTERNATES 2	3	NOTES
	A/E Estimate	10%	$4,600,000	210,000	64,000	11,000	BUDGET = $4,800,000
4	General Construction	Y	$4,755,000	200,000	72,000	9,900	
2	Contracting Corp	Y	$4,224,000	189,500	67,400	11,200	
1	Office Builders	Y	$4,170,000	226,200	66,400	9,540	CASHIERS CHECK FOR BOND
3	Professional Contracting	Y	$4,676,000	211,400	63,200	12,350	
-	Construction Services	N	$3,954,000	176,400	62,000	9,450	DISQ. - No BOND

Figure 4.10

Part Two

The Building Process

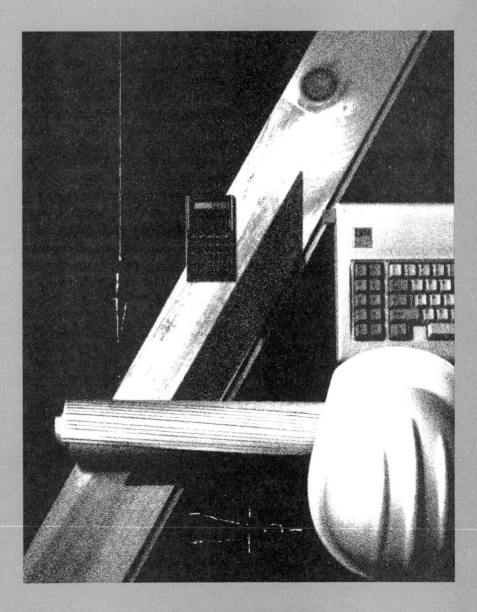

Chapter Five
Getting Started

*"The world is not interested
in the storms you encountered,
but did you bring in the ship?"*
William McFee

Getting the project started properly and on time are essential ingredients in the success of a project. There are so many unknowns in every construction project that a timely start is necessary in order to be prepared for the pitfalls that occur during construction.

Important Preliminary Considerations

The project management team, the contract, the schedule, the bid, budget, subcontractors, and vendors are important elements to be considered at the start of a project. Each of these elements should be addressed before construction begins.

The Project Management Team
A project management team should be selected soon after the contractor receives notice of contract award. This team consists of a project manager (or project managers, depending on the size, complexity, and other parameters of a project), superintendent, and an office engineer. On some government work (such as the U.S. Army Corps of Engineers), and larger private sector projects, a safety or quality control person may also be a member of the team. It is not unusual on large (100M+) projects, especially the construction management type, to have a project manager, a general superintendent with a couple of assistants, a project engineer, other engineer/superintendents (civil, mechanical, electrical), project accountant, purchasing agent, scheduler, expediter, and surveyor.

Pre-construction Conference
The project team and other staff members who may have roles in the execution of the project (such as an officer of the firm, the person who would handle payroll for the project, etc.) should attend the pre-construction meeting.

Contract
The team should study the contract documents (plans, specifications, etc.) before the pre-construction meeting is held.

The contract should be carefully reviewed before it is signed. Most often, the contract is reviewed with an attorney. The attorney may be either an in-house employee or an outside attorney who handles the legal matters of the firm.

Schedule

A detailed progress schedule should be prepared. This schedule should preferably be a CPM schedule, but should at least be a bar chart.

Bid and Budget

The bid should be revised, if alternates were selected by the owner that changed the original bid, and a schedule of values should be prepared for payment purposes. A project budget should be prepared based on the bid revisions, and the revised contract sum written into the contract. A schedule of documents should also be prepared and attached to the contract, listing each drawing and the corresponding revision date. In addition, all applicable addenda should be identified. Any verbal agreements should be committed to writing.

Subcontractors and Vendors

Immediately after the signing of the contract, subcontracts should be chosen for the major specialty trades (such as the plumbing, electrical, HVAC, structural steel, and roofing) and those needed at the beginning of the project (such as sitework, masonry, and exterior underground utilities).

Long lead items are items that take longer than usual to be delivered, either because they are manufactured only after an order is received in the factory, or because the manufacturing process is time-consuming. These items should be ordered as soon as possible after the contract is signed.

Bid Revision

During the bidding process most subcontractors and suppliers, in an effort to protect their prices, quote prices at the last minute, or quote only an approximate number in advance and then adjust it at the last minute. In addition, certain components in the bid may have several alternates, some, all, or none of which may be selected by the owner after the bids are opened. As a result, the figures on the general contractor's **summary sheet** may be different from what was used in the final bid price. In such cases, the contractor revises the entire estimate and summary sheet to reflect the last minute changes and any changes affected by the alternates selected or declined by the owner. This process is known as bid revision.

After the estimate and summary sheet have been revised, the schedule of values is prepared for the project, to which cost codes are assigned, and against which all project costs will be identified.

Pre-construction Submittals

Most contract documents require that the selected general contractor submit certain written information prior to the start of the project. Bonds, a certificate of insurance, a list of subcontractors, and the schedule of values are typically required pre-construction submittals.

Bonds

Owners often require that the contractor submit two types of bonds before construction begins. They are **Performance Bonds** and **Payment Bonds.** (These bonds are explained in detail in Chapter 4.) Failure to submit bonds within the specified time period (usually ten calendar days) can be considered a default and may result in termination of the contract. For protection from default, the contractor should request that his bonding agent issue properly executed bonds (for the appropriate amount, with the appropriate signatures and seals) soon after receiving notice of contract award. The surety (the bonding company) will need sufficient time to perform the underwriting work. For the contractor seeking his first surety bond, this can be a time-consuming process; the bonding agent may ask for a significant amount of information. Information frequently requested by the bonding company is listed below.

- A narrative history of the firm
- Personal Financial Statements of the officers and/or owners of the firm
- Letters of recommendation from previous clients, architect/ engineers, or banks.
- Audited financial statements of the firm (as a minimum, include profit and loss statement, schedule of accounts receivable, schedule of accounts payable, schedule of notes payable, schedule of taxes payable, and schedule of fixed assets)
- The cost estimate for the project
- Schedule of contracts in progress (under construction)
- Schedule of contracts completed in the previous two years
- Certificate of insurance
- A copy of the proposed contract
- Articles of incorporation
- Federal Income Tax returns for the previous two or three years

While the amount of information needed by the surety companies may vary, sufficient time should always be allowed, even if a contractor has an established bonding relationship, because the bonding agent may need to update information previously furnished.

The following paragraphs contain suggested tips for facilitating the acquisition of bonds.

Qualified Personnel

Surety companies often look at the experience and qualifications of a firm's personnel before making a decision to write or decline an application for surety bonds. Therefore, an organizational chart should be prepared showing the key employees of the firm and their functions. The qualifications and experience of these individuals should be emphasized. Qualifications may be presented through the resumes of all the key employees, describing their education and experience (types and sizes of projects previously completed, etc.).

Adequate Records

Accurate records should be kept at all times on all projects, particularly in the areas of cost and financial accounting. A simple filing system should be developed. The administrative staff should file data on each project in the appropriate files to ensure accessibility when needed. Individual files should be prepared for monthly requisitions, changes, subcontractors, suppliers, and correspondence.

Financial Audit

Financial statements should be prepared at regular intervals, at least annually. It is also advisable to hire a construction-oriented independent certified public accountant (CPA) to prepare certified audited financial statements at the end of the firm's fiscal year. Surety companies, as well as bankers, place a lot of confidence in audited and certified financial statements.

Good Credit Record
Payments due to suppliers, subcontractors, and lending institutions should be made on time whenever it is possible to do so. There is no substitute for a good credit history when it comes to seeking bonds or loans.

Good Reputation
A good reputation should be established by doing quality work and completing all projects on time.

Public Relations
Get to know the surety agent well by visiting or talking with him often. Do not wait until a bond is needed before contacting an agent.

Certificate of Insurance
Most business activities involve risks in one form or another. The construction process is no exception. Due to the nature of the construction process, with the many uncertainties and unknowns, it is probably more risky than most other businesses. As a result, most construction contracts require the contractor to assume liability for risks such as:

- Physical damage to work in progress
- Theft or loss of the owner's property at the site
- Theft or loss of the contractor's property at the site
- Physical damage, theft, or loss of the property of third parties (such as subcontractors) at the site
- Personal injuries caused by the work or at the site to the contractor's personnel, owner's personnel, the general public, or other third parties

To ensure that the contractor can assume liability for these risks, most contracts require that insurance policies be obtained.

An insurance policy is an agreement under which an insurance carrier (company), for a premium, agrees to pay the insured or a beneficiary designated by the insured, up to a maximum amount stated in the policy in the event that a loss results from the risk or risks specified in the policy while the policy is in force.

Most general conditions or supplemental conditions require the contractor to submit insurance certification from a reputable insurance carrier. Certification indicates that adequate insurance coverage is in force at the time construction begins, will continue to be in force throughout the period of construction, and that the owner will be notified of the expiration of the insurance policy at least 30 days before the termination date (if the interruption in coverage occurs during the tenure of the contract).

Insurance policies commonly required on construction contracts are described in the following paragraphs.

Workers' Compensation Insurance
This is mandatory in all states. It protects the contractor against loss due to personal injury or death of his employees, by providing the employees (or the designated next of kin) with the benefits (amount of compensation) specified by the various state and federal compensation laws.

General Public Liability Insurance

This protects the contractor against losses in the event of bodily injury or death to a member of the general public caused by the contractor's operations, and damage to the property of others. It may be obtained in a schedule form (where the risks and hazards to be insured are specified) or under a comprehensive general liability form (where all the usual hazards of a general liability nature are covered, unless specifically excluded).

Automobile Liability Insurance

This protects the contractor against losses in the event of bodily injury or death caused by vehicles owned by the contractor, vehicles owned by others, or rented (leased) vehicles.

Fire and Theft Insurance

This protects the contractor against losses due to fire to the contractor's facilities (offices, trailers, tool sheds, warehouses, etc.) and their contents as well as theft of tools and stored materials.

Builder's Risk Insurance

This protects the contractor against losses resulting from damage to the construction work while it is still under construction.

Often, contractors obtain what is known in the industry as **Comprehensive General Liability** (CGL) insurance to cover the contractor's general insurance needs. However, the most important features of a contractor's insurance policy are the **coverage and exclusion clauses,** and the **limits of coverage.** Contractors and owners are encouraged to review insurance policies in detail with their insurance agent before purchasing the policy.

Although most contracts require the contractor to furnish the specified insurance, in the final analysis, the owner pays for it, because the contractor incorporates the cost of insurance into his bid or cost proposal.

List of Subcontractors

Some contracts require that a contractor submit a list of the subcontractors he proposes to use on the project. On some projects, a contractor may be asked to list the dollar amount of each proposed subcontractor. This is typically required for negotiated work and public projects with minority contractor participation requirements.

This practice allows the owner and the architect/engineer an opportunity to object to any subcontractor, particularly if they have had a bad experience on a previous project with the subcontractor in question. Often including the name, address, telephone number, contact person, and specialty or trade, this list is an invaluable directory and permanent record for the owner for future maintenance, repair, or alteration purposes (assuming that the general contractor eventually uses the subcontractors on the list).

Schedule of Values

The schedule of values is a breakdown of the total contract amount by category of work. It is the basis by which periodic (progress) payments are made to the contractor during the course of the project. It is also a means of monitoring actual costs vs. budgeted costs to evaluate the performance of the field forces. Figure 5.1 illustrates a sample schedule of values with work categories listed according to the CSI format.

CONTRACT BREAKDOWN	CONTRACT AMOUNT	PREVIOUS ESTIMATE	THIS ESTIMATE	%	BALANCE
Insurance					
Move In & Bond					
Contingency Fund					
Site Sub-Grade Work					
Drilled Piers					
Concrete & Finish					
Form Work					
Structural Steel					
ReBars & Mesh					
Waterproof, Dampproof & Caulk					
Masonry					
Finish Carpentry					
Demolition					
Rough Carpentry					
Millwork					
Hardware					
Lath & Plaster					
Metal Doors & Frames					
Aluminum Glass & Glaze					
Acoustical Ceilings					
Resilient Floor & Base					
Painting & Vinyl					
Toilet Stalls					
Drywall Partitions					
Roofing & Sheet Metal					
Plumbing Pipe					
Air Conditioning Pipe					
Plumbing Equipment					
Air Conditioning Equip					
Duct Work					
Controls					
Insulation					
Test & Balance					
Fire Protection					
Fire Alarm					
Electrical Fixtures					
Panels & Switches					
Conduit & Rough-In					
Wire					
Job Clean Up					
Poured Roof Deck					
Cubical Track					
Building Insulation					
Folding Doors					
Carpet					
Seamless Floors					
Supervision					
Temporary Facilities					
Contract Sum					
List Change Orders:					
Change Order No. 1					
Change Order No. 2					
etc.					
TOTALS					

Work completed to date . . . .
Stored Material (See attached) . . . . .
Subtotal . . . .
Less 10% Retainage . . . .
Subtotal . . . .
Less Previous Estimates. . . . .
TOTAL AMOUNT DUE THIS ESTIMATE

Schedule of Values

Figure 5.1

Most contractors calculate the price for each category of work by adding a portion of the **total indirect cost**, or **distributable**, of the project to the **direct cost** of each work element (labor, material, subcontract, and equipment). The total indirect cost includes the general conditions, home office overhead, taxes, labor burden, and profit.

The exact portion of indirect cost added to the direct cost of each work category is determined by the contractor. Sometimes, in an effort to minimize the financing costs of working capital borrowed for the project, general contractors request a substantial payment at the beginning of a project. This may be done by distributing the majority of the indirect costs to the categories of work accomplished at the beginning of the project. This is known within the construction industry as **front-end loading**. Front-end loading may distort the perception of the percentage of work completed, if this is the basis for payments to the contractor. If payments are made on the basis of percentage of work completed, the owner or lending institution should be careful to adhere to the correct percentages and not overpay the contractor.

Construction Schedule

Most contracts require that the contractor submit a schedule prior to beginning any construction work. This schedule establishes the degree of completion that the owner can expect at specified intervals (monthly or weekly) to attain the contracted end date. The owner or his representative uses the schedule to monitor the progress of the project, and to predict the approximate amount of progress payment to be made every month.

Definition

Construction scheduling can be defined as the arrangement of a series of tasks or activities involved in a construction project into a logical sequence within the total time specified for the project. Usually a schedule depicts the starting time, duration, and completion time for each activity, task, or work operation in the construction project.

There are *three* major methods of scheduling, illustrated in Figure 5.2 and listed below.

- Program Evaluation Review Technology (PERT)
- Bar Chart
- Critical Path Method (CPM)

Pert

Pert is a system of scheduling that is event-oriented. This method allows three different durations for each activity:

a = optimistic time
m = most likely time
b = pessimistic time

The expected time, $te = \dfrac{a + 4m + b}{6}$

An example of a pert chart is shown in Figure 5.3.

Bar Charts

Bar charts, also known as **Gantt charts**, are simple to develop and very easy to interpret. A sample bar chart is illustrated in Figure 5.4.

Activities on a bar chart are shown graphically on a calendar time scale with bars, each bar representing the start and finish date of each activity. A bar chart graphically depicts the progress of a project in general.

Bar charts are easy to prepare and understand, and are sometimes used in the construction industry as a preliminary schedule and occasionally to manage projects. However, the bar chart's limitations should be considered before making a decision to use the scheduling method; it is an inefficient scheduling tool in its simplified form, without modifications, because it does not depict the exact state of progress of a project at any given time. This scheduling method does not allow for anticipation of problems or delays quickly enough to resolve them before they occur. Finally, the bar chart does not show how changes affect the

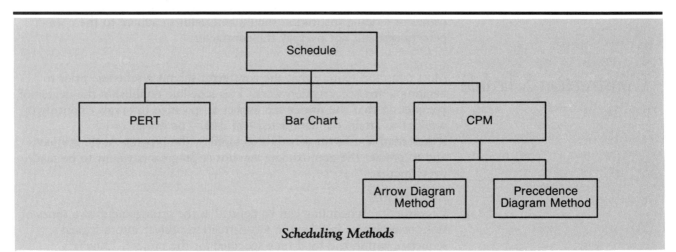

Scheduling Methods

Figure 5.2

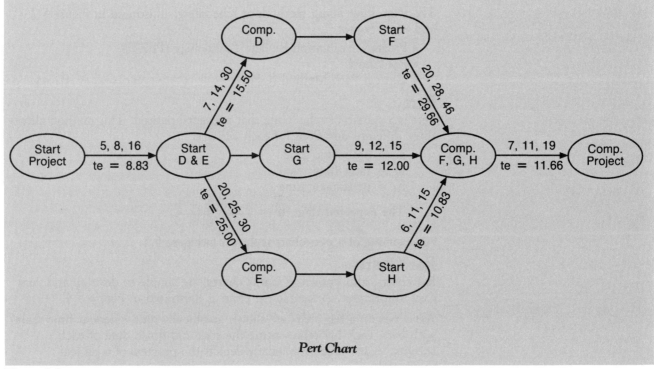

Pert Chart

Figure 5.3

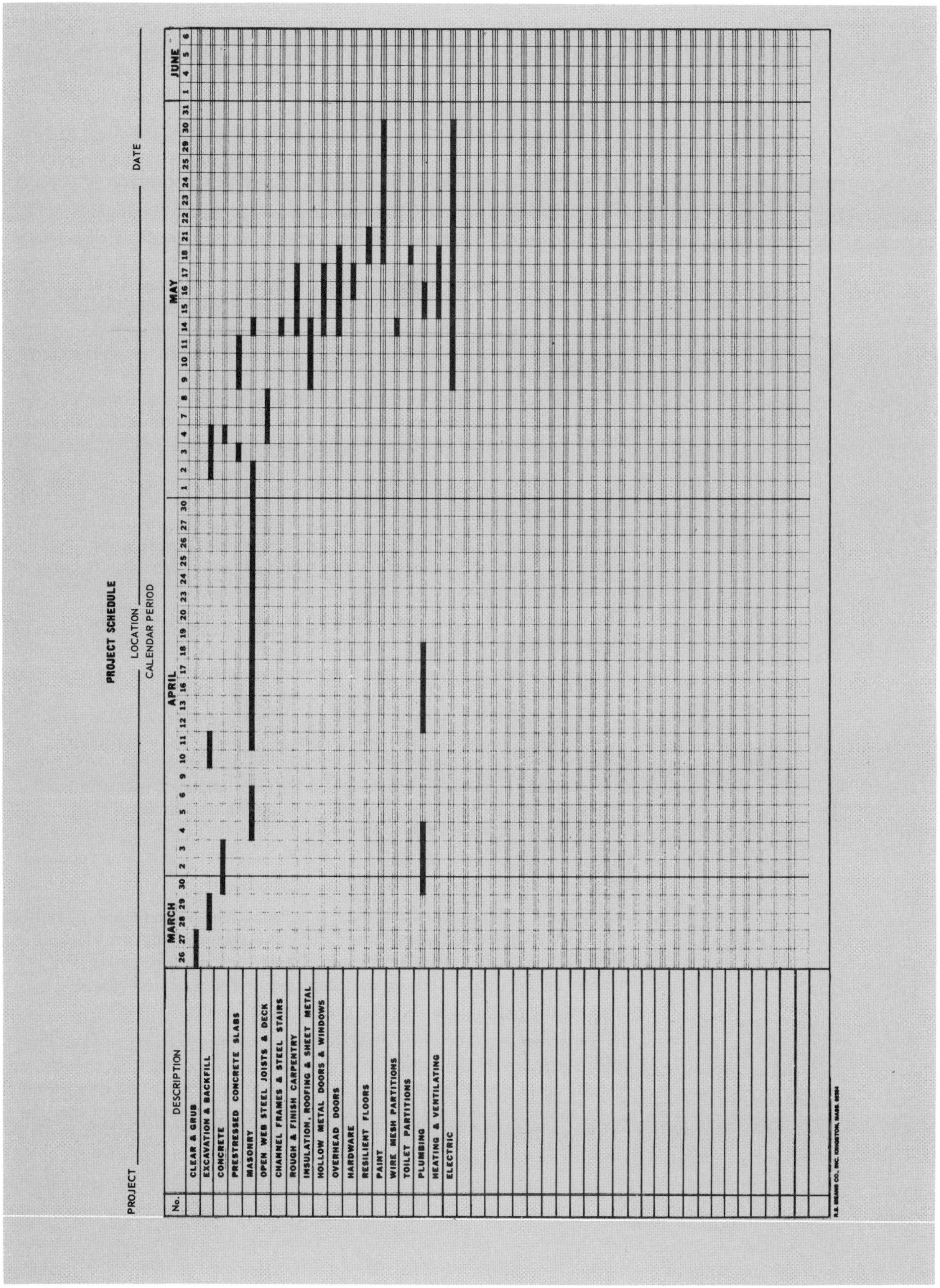

PROJECT SCHEDULE

PROJECT _____
LOCATION _____
CALENDAR PERIOD _____
DATE _____

No.	DESCRIPTION
	CLEAR & GRUB
	EXCAVATION & BACKFILL
	CONCRETE
	PRESTRESSED CONCRETE SLABS
	MASONRY
	OPEN WEB STEEL JOISTS & DECK
	CHANNEL FRAMES & STEEL STAIRS
	ROUGH & FINISH CARPENTRY
	INSULATION, ROOFING & SHEET METAL
	HOLLOW METAL DOORS & WINDOWS
	OVERHEAD DOORS
	HARDWARE
	RESILIENT FLOORS
	PAINT
	WIRE MESH PARTITIONS
	TOILET PARTITIONS
	PLUMBING
	HEATING & VENTILATING
	ELECTRIC

R.S. MEANS CO., INC. KINGSTON, MASS. 02364

Figure 5.4

overall contract duration. For instance, it does not show how a change in one or more activities would affect other dependent and independent activities in the schedule.

Critical Path Method (CPM)

This method of scheduling was developed in the late 1950's and early 1960's. It has been found by many construction professionals to be better and more efficient than a bar chart in managing construction projects.

CPM scheduling has the following major advantages:

- CPM identifies the dependence and interdependence of all activities in a schedule.
- From a CPM schedule, a project manager can immediately determine how a change in one or more activities impacts other activities in a schedule.
- CPM identifies activities that are critical to the timely completion of a project.
- This method enables a project manager to easily determine those activities that are not critical. Non-critical activities are tasks that may be delayed without affecting the overall project completion date.
- The CPM schedule shows the shortest time in which a project can be completed.

CPM is a method of developing a logic network of construction activities. Figure 5.5 shows how to graphically represent logic networks on a CPM schedule.

The components of the logic network (shown in Figure 5.6) are explained below.

- The numbers 1, 2, 3, and 4 designate **Events.**
- The letters A, B, C, D, and E designate **Activities.**
- The dotted line (between events 3 & 4) is known as a **Dummy.**
- The line spanning between events 1 & 4 is called a **Hammock.**
- Event "2" is achieved when activity "B" is completed.
- Activities "C" and "D" cannot start until event "2" is completed; the starts of activities "C" and "D" are **dependent** upon the completion of activity "B".

A CPM network may be prepared in two ways: by the **Arrow Diagram Method** or the **Precedence Diagram Method.**

The Arrow Diagram Method (ADM) is sometimes called the **I-J Method** or the **Activity-on-Arrow Method.** The Precedence Diagram Method (PDM) is also called the **Activity-on-Node Method.** The important aspects of these two methods are discussed in the following paragraphs.

The Arrow Diagram Method (ADM)

In the arrow diagram method, activities are represented by arrows. The arrows are usually not drawn to scale and may go from left to right, right to left, up or down, or at an angle. However, in order to be consistent, avoid confusion, and for ease of use, it is usually recommended that the arrows go from left to right.

Examples of Arrow Diagrams and Interpretations

Diagram	Interpretation
 I — Activity — J	The tail or the arrow ("I") represents the initiation or start of an activity. The arrowhead ("J") represents the completion of an activity.
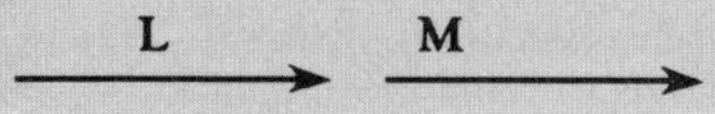 L → M →	Activity "M" cannot start until activity "L" is completed, or the start of activity "M" is dependent upon the completion "L."
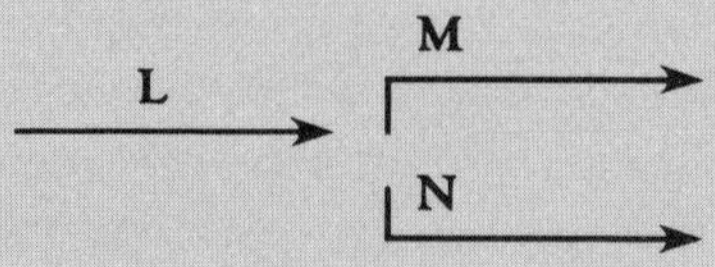 L → M, N	Activity "L" must be completed before activities "M" and "N" can start, i.e., activities "M" and "N" can be done concurrently, but cannot start until "L" is completed.
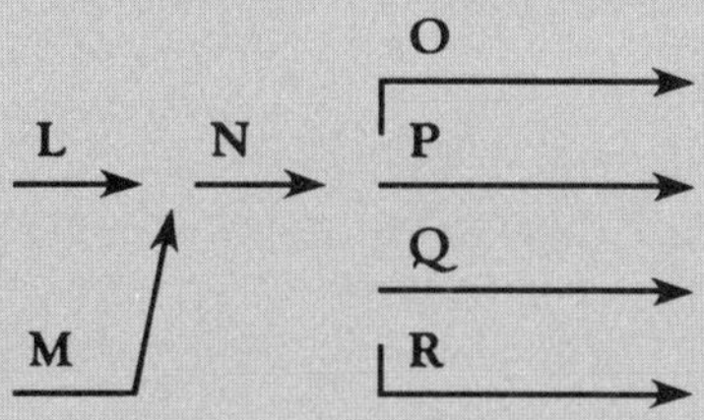 L → N →, M → N; O, P, Q, R	Activities "L" and "M" can be done concurrently. Activity "N" cannot start until "L" and "M" are completed. Activities "O," "P," "Q" and "R" run concurrently, but all four cannot start until "N" is completed.
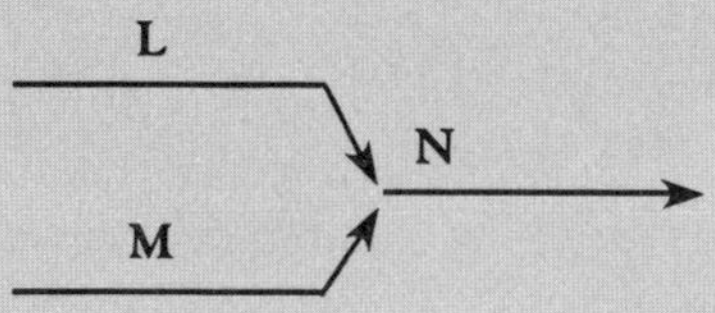 L, M → N →	Activities "L" and "M" run concurrently, and have to be completed before "N" can start.
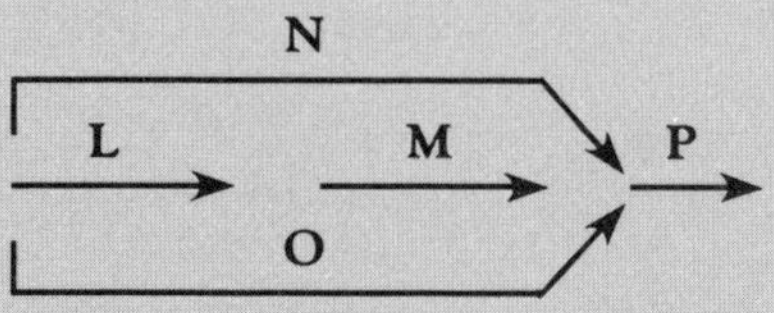 L, M, N, O → P	Activity "L" has to be completed before "M" can start. Activities "N" and "O" run concurrent under "L" and "M." Activity "P" cannot start until "L," "M," "N," and "O" are completed.
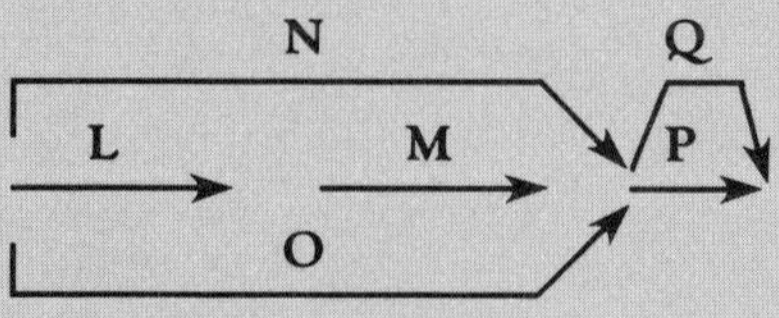 L, M, N, O → P, Q	Activity "M" cannot start until "L" is completed. "N" and "O" run concurrent with "L" and "M." "P" and "Q" are concurrent, but cannot start until "L," "M," "N," and "O" are completed.

Figure 5.5

For each activity (arrow) on the network, the following questions must be answered by the person preparing the schedule:

- When can this activity start and how long will it take to complete it?
- Which activities have to be completed before this activity can start?
- Which activities can be done concurrently with this activity?
- Which activities cannot begin until this activity is completed?

An example of an ADM network is illustrated in Figure 5.7.

The Precedence Diagram Method (PDM)

Four main types of constraints are usually encountered on precedence diagrams. Whereas activities in ADM are represented by arrows, activities in PDM are represented by activity boxes, or nodes. Figure 5.8 is a comparison of ADM and PDM constraints.

In using this method, the node (activity box) may be set up in several different ways. An example of a complete precedence network is illustrated in Figure 5.9.

Basic Scheduling Computation

Certain calculations are required during the preparation of a construction schedule. The following is a simplified guide on how to determine some of the basic values often needed in scheduling, based on the assumption that a project starts on day number one:

- Early Start (ES) plus for the first activity, or
  = EF of the preceding activity for other subsequent activities.
- Early Finish (EF) = ES plus the duration of the activity.

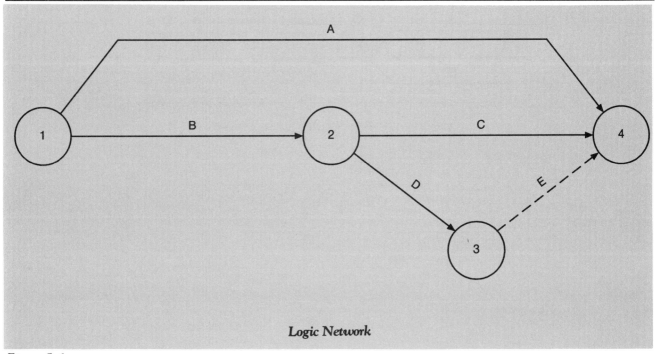

Logic Network

Figure 5.6

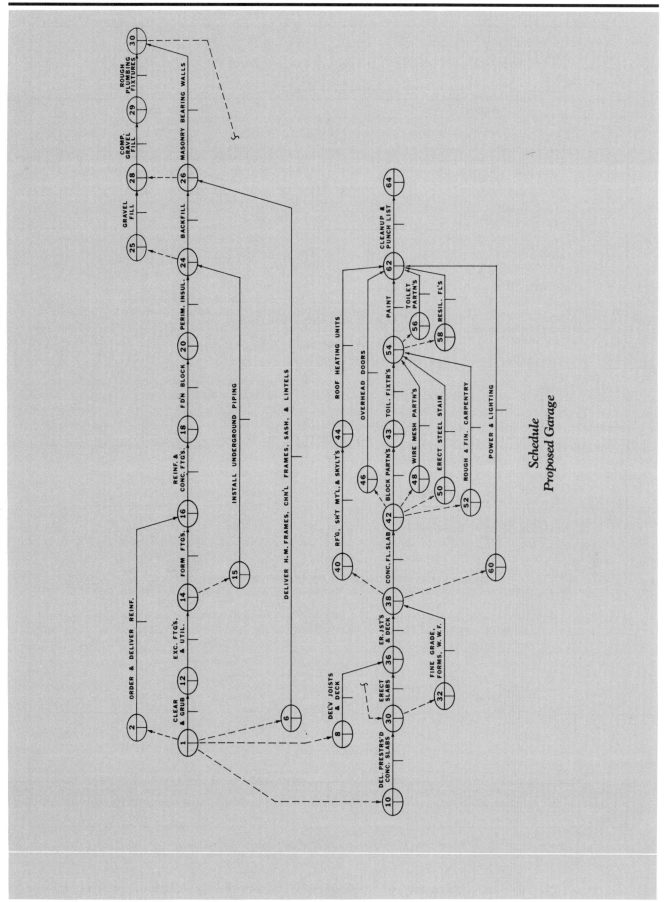

Figure 5.7

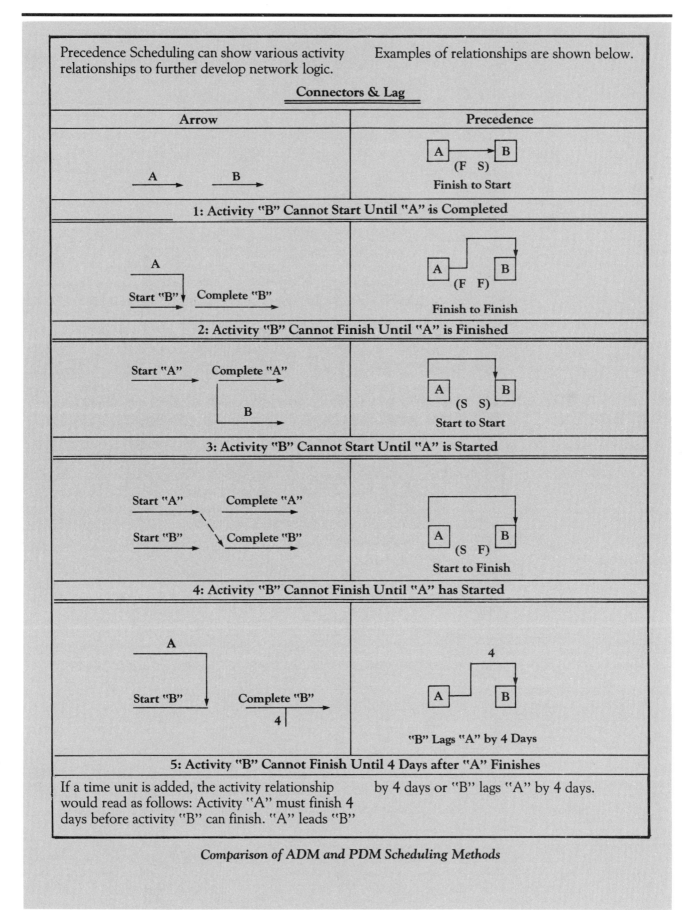

Precedence Scheduling can show various activity relationships to further develop network logic.

Examples of relationships are shown below.

Connectors & Lag

Arrow	Precedence
A → B →	A → B (F S) Finish to Start

1: Activity "B" Cannot Start Until "A" is Completed

A Start "B" Complete "B"	A → B (F F) Finish to Finish

2: Activity "B" Cannot Finish Until "A" is Finished

Start "A" Complete "A" B	A B (S S) Start to Start

3: Activity "B" Cannot Start Until "A" is Started

Start "A" Complete "A" Start "B" Complete "B"	A B (S F) Start to Finish

4: Activity "B" Cannot Finish Until "A" has Started

A Start "B" Complete "B" 4	4 A B "B" Lags "A" by 4 Days

5: Activity "B" Cannot Finish Until 4 Days after "A" Finishes

If a time unit is added, the activity relationship would read as follows: Activity "A" must finish 4 days before activity "B" can finish. "A" leads "B" by 4 days or "B" lags "A" by 4 days.

Comparison of ADM and PDM Scheduling Methods

Figure 5.8

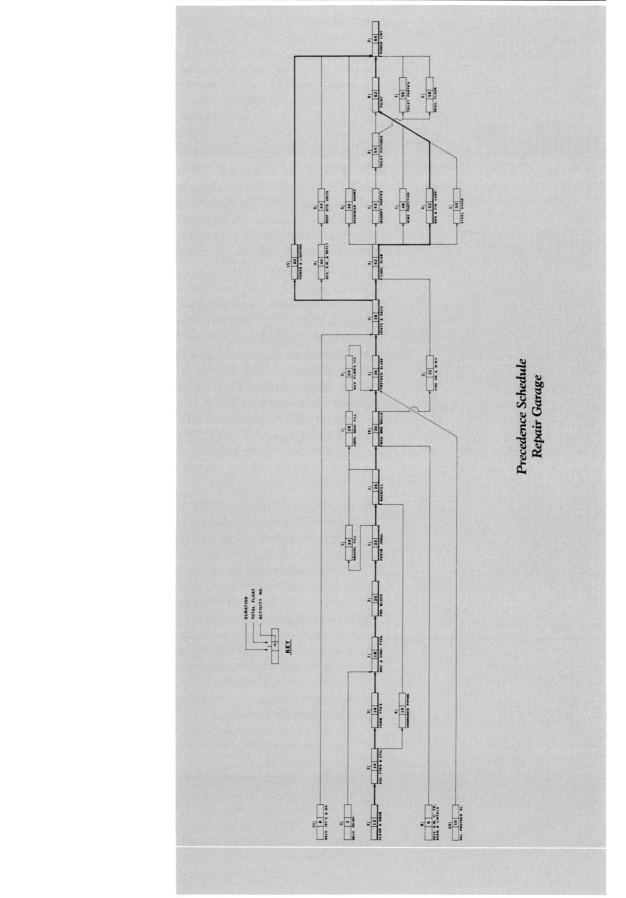

Precedence Schedule
Repair Garage

Figure 5.9

- Late Finish (LF) = LS of the subsequent activities, or
  = EF of the network (for the last activity or activities).
- Late Start (LS) = LF minus duration of the activity.
- Total Float (TF) = LS minus ES
  = LF minus EF
  = LF minus ES minus duration

Pre-construction Conference

As explained in Chapter 2, a pre-construction conference must be held before a Notice to Proceed (NTP) can be issued. The purpose of this meeting is to enable the general contractor and his subcontractors to clarify any remaining questions they have before starting the project. This conference is also an opportunity for the various members of the project team (both the contractor's and the owner's representatives) to meet and clearly establish the roles to all team members.

The meeting is initiated by the owner or his representative, such as the architect/engineer. The pre-construction conference is held at the site of the proposed project, ten to fourteen days before the legal commencement of the project. The following parties attend this meeting.

- A representative of the owner
- The project architect/engineer and his consultants
- An officer of the general contractor's firm (a person who is legally authorized to act on behalf of the firm, such as the corporate secretary, vice-president, etc.)
- The general contractor's project team (project manager, superintendent, office engineer, payroll clerk, etc.)
- Representatives of the general contractor's major subcontractors, consultants, and suppliers

The following is a typical agenda for a pre-construction meeting:

1. Introduction of all parties who will be directly involved in the project and their respective roles and responsibilities
2. Discussion of the working hours permitted for the project
3. Establishment of areas to be used for staging, storage, and location of temporary offices (trailers)
4. Safety and security requirements
5. Project administration requirements, such as reporting procedures, frequency of progress meetings, etc.
6. Submittal and approval system to be used for shop drawings, samples, and other submittals
7. Procedures for the submission and approval of progress payment applications
8. Change order procedures
9. Bonding and insurance requirements
10. Testing requirements and procedures for the inspection of completed work
11. Quality control requirements
12. Distribution of the appropriate documents, such as additional sets of contract documents (plans, specifications, forms for various reports, etc.)
13. Review and discussion of the contractor's proposed progress schedule
14. A question and answer period on the technical aspects of the project

15. Issuance of the Notice to Proceed to the contractor
16. Responsibility for Building Permits

Due to the importance of the subjects discussed at the pre-construction conference, it is imperative that the general contractor's project team, as well as his major subcontractors (plumbing, electrical, HVAC, site work, structural steel, roofing, etc.), attend. It is also a good time for the contractor to submit a schedule of values, a progress schedule, and required shop drawings for approval. Samples for the items that will be accomplished at the beginning of the project – such as reinforcing steel for the foundation and slab-on-grade, hollow metal door frames, anchor bolts, items to be embedded in the concrete foundation and slab, and concrete mix design – should also be submitted. Long lead items that require advanced ordering, such as structural steel, hardware, elevators, and other specialty items should be requisitioned immediately.

On most projects, the contractor has ten calendar days after receiving the Notice to Proceed to begin construction.

Mobilization

Immediately following issuance of the Notice to Proceed, the general contractor begins to mobilize for the commencement of the project. This effort includes obtaining permits for building and utilities. Field offices (trailers) and storage facilities must be set up at the site. If the contractor owns the office trailers, arrangements must be made for their transportation to the site. If trailers will be leased, the lease should be signed immediately and the trailers delivered to the site as soon as possible.

The contractor should submit applications for all utilities needed at the construction site such as telephone, power, water, etc. In some cities, this requires a deposit and may take a few days to begin service, especially if the site is in a remote area. If there is no power source near the site, an alternative power source may be a leased diesel generator.

Vendor accounts should be established within the vicinity of the site for equipment rental, fuel, miscellaneous supplies, lumber, concrete, etc. If the project is in an unfamiliar locale, credit applications or other forms may be required.

Finally, an appropriate project sign must be prepared or acquired.

Purchasing

The procedures for purchasing materials and supplies for a construction project vary from one firm to another. Some firms have a centralized system where all purchases are made by a purchasing agent at the home office. Other firms allow their superintendent to make purchases up to a set limit, after which approval is required from the project manager, while in some firms the major purchases are made directly at the home office and minor purchases are made in the field with some internal control. Regardless of the system used by a firm, it is important that purchase orders or purchase agreements are issued to vendors for all the materials, equipment, and supplies needed for the project as soon as a contract is signed. Failure to do so may result in delays at the beginning of a project that can quickly snowball to delay the entire project.

Chapter Six

Site Work

Most construction projects have a site on which the proposed structure is to be built. The site usually requires some preparatory work before the building process can begin. The contractor must first locate his field office and access roads or ramps into the site for the delivery of materials and lifting equipment to the building. Next, the contractor must establish the rough grade of the site and the building platform. For instance, the site may have trees, stumps, bushes, debris, unsuitable soil, and may be uneven (not level) in several places. Hilly land must be levelled and depressions in the land filled to the level required by the design. Existing old buildings, fences, and any buried utilities (water pipes, sewer pipes, fuel tanks, cables, etc.) may have to be removed or relocated. New utilities must be installed at the appropriate location to suit the new structure. Roads, parking lots, and landscaping may be required. This chapter reviews the major preparatory work that must be done to a piece of land in order to eliminate all existing obstructions, tailor the site to the needs of the proposed structure, and facilitate its construction.

Scope of Work

The scope of site work on construction projects varies tremendously, depending on location, the size of the project, the design of the project, the type and complexity of the project, the natural state of the land, and the time of year when the construction begins. A site and subsurface investigation is first performed by an engineering or testing firm hired by the owner or the project architect/engineer. This often includes a report on the conditions at the site (sometimes with recommendations) and making soil borings.

Soil borings are used to determine the bearing pressure of the soil and its suitability for foundations. Unsuitable soils such as organic matter and clay, the water table, and rock and ledge are also identified by the soil borings. Soil borings are obtained by drilling into the ground at strategic locations over the entire site to obtain soil samples. This procedure is performed in order to determine the condition of the soil below the surface, its bearing capacity, and the level of the water table. The results from these tests are usually included in the specifications for the project. Examples of a subsurface profile and soil boring for a project are illustrated in Figures 6.1a and 6.1b, respectively.

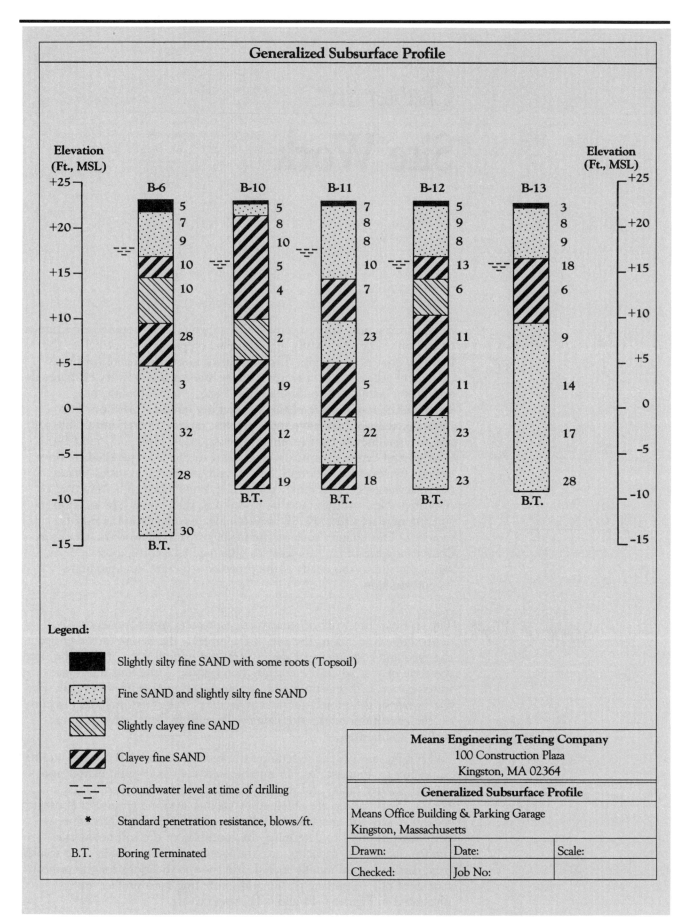

Figure 6.1a

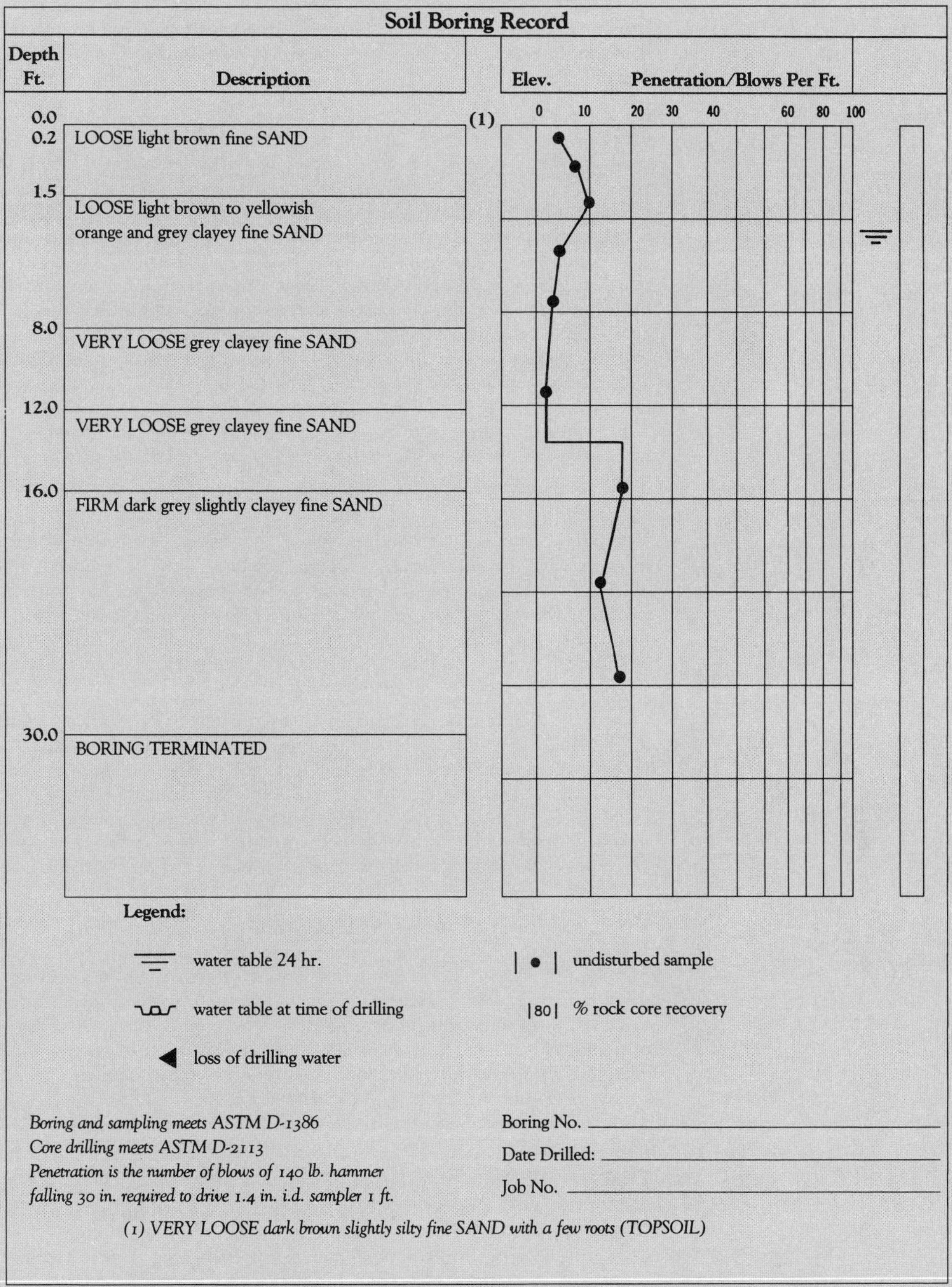

Soil Boring Record

Depth Ft.	Description
0.0	
0.2	LOOSE light brown fine SAND
1.5	LOOSE light brown to yellowish orange and grey clayey fine SAND
8.0	VERY LOOSE grey clayey fine SAND
12.0	VERY LOOSE grey clayey fine SAND
16.0	FIRM dark grey slightly clayey fine SAND
30.0	BORING TERMINATED

Elev. **Penetration/Blows Per Ft.**

(1)

0 10 20 30 40 60 80 100

Legend:

⎯⎯ water table 24 hr.

ᴗᴗ water table at time of drilling

◀ loss of drilling water

| • | undisturbed sample

|80| % rock core recovery

Boring and sampling meets ASTM D-1386
Core drilling meets ASTM D-2113
Penetration is the number of blows of 140 lb. hammer
falling 30 in. required to drive 1.4 in. i.d. sampler 1 ft.

Boring No. _____

Date Drilled: _____

Job No. _____

(1) VERY LOOSE dark brown slightly silty fine SAND with a few roots (TOPSOIL)

Figure 6.1b

From the contractor's perspective, the site work often encountered on construction projects includes the site survey, clearing and grubbing, demolition, and earthwork. These stages are explained in the following sections.

Site Survey

The first task normally undertaken in the site work is a survey of the proposed site. The purpose of this survey is to develop a **rough layout** of the site. A layout should include the location of the proposed structure, roads, and parking lots. Any existing trees are marked in the field. The architect walks through the site and flags any existing trees he wishes to save. Monuments and structures to be retained will be noted on the plans and specifications; all existing objects to be demolished are also clearly identified on the plans. The contractor should note that the conditions in the field are not always clearly identified on the drawings, and this must always be anticipated. Unmarked site conditions should be addressed as construction progresses. The site survey also determines the elevations of the site, which are plotted as contours on the grading plan. The proposed contours will be superimposed on the site plan, from which the site contractor can determine the amount of earthwork involved in grading the site.

Clearing and Grubbing

Vegetation, existing trees, bushes, weeds, and other growth that would interfere with the building of a proposed structure must be removed. This is known as **clearing and grubbing**. This process is accomplished by knocking the trees down with a bulldozer or sawing them down with a chain saw, depending on the type and size of the trees. The removal of tree stumps, bushes, and other undergrowth is referred to as grubbing. Grubbing is normally done with a bulldozer.

Clearing is usually measured and priced by the acre. This is estimated by multiplying the length of the site (in feet) by its width (in feet), to produce the area of the site in square feet (S.F.). The total area of the site (in square feet) is then divided by 43,560 S.F., since 43,560 S.F. is equal to one acre. On large real estate property where the dimensions are in miles, it should be noted that 1 square mile = 640 acres. Clearing can be classified into the caliper (diameter) of trees to be cleared: 0″ to 6″, 6 to 12″, 12″ to 24″.

Protect Vegetation to be Retained

During the clearing and grubbing operations, great care must be exercised to protect and preserve from injury or defacement all existing trees, structures, or monuments designated in the plans and specifications to be retained. Adjacent property must also be protected. Colored flags or markings can be used to designate existing vegetation to be preserved. The flags, coupled with a thorough orientation of the equipment operators or subcontractors, will prevent costly errors. If the site work is well-planned and executed, it sets the tone for a carefully implemented job.

Disposal

One of the major problems to be considered during the site survey phase is the disposal of the trees, stumps, bushes, and other items removed during the clearing and grubbing operations. The two common methods of disposal of stumps are **burning** and **hauling away** to a dump site or designated disposal area. Trees can usually be sold to local wood fuel dealers or mills (paper or lumber).

If on-site burning is permitted, certain permits and approvals may be required by anti-pollution laws and federal, state, and local ordinances.

If on-site burning is not permitted, stumps can be loaded into dump trucks, and hauled off the site to a designated disposal area or buried on site, in accordance with state and local requirements.

Demolition

Demolition often follows or is performed concurrently with clearing and grubbing. Demolition is necessary if the proposed site has existing structures such as old buildings, parts of old buildings (foundations or drainage structures), fences, and other items that must be demolished to make way for the new building or site development.

General contractors sometimes hire subcontractors for specialty work such as removal or relocation; and for capping of underground pipes and cables.

Units of Measure

The units of measure for demolition work vary, depending on the items to be demolished. Fences are usually measured by the square foot, foundations by the cubic yard or the number of foundations (where the size is given), total buildings by the cubic foot, and pipes by the linear foot.

Earthwork

After clearing and demolition work are complete, earthwork operations begin. Earthwork usually includes: stripping of any existing topsoil, general (mass) excavation and fill (also called site grading), and building excavation and backfill.

Stripping of the Site

Unless a construction site is covered by an existing structure or has been previously prepared for construction, the first few inches of the natural ground consist of topsoil, matted root systems, organic material, weeds, leaves, mulch, and loose gravel. This material is not an acceptable base for a building or structure. It is therefore customary to remove the first four to six inches of the proposed building area and stockpile the topsoil for later use.

The building area is defined as the area five feet beyond the limits of the proposed structure (as shown on the site plan) on all sides. (A typical site layout plan is shown in Figure 6.2.) The specifications or drawings also indicate the exact dimensions beyond the proposed structure to which the topsoil is to be removed. Sometimes, the soil removed is worth preserving for later use in landscaping. This soil can be stockpiled on the site and used as topsoil for grassing and other plantings. If the soil removed is unsuitable, then it is loaded and hauled away in trucks to a designated disposal area.

Unsuitable Soil

It is not uncommon for the soil boring to indicate the existence of unsuitable soil over the proposed site or for the contractor to run into unsuitable soil after removing the first six inches. When the soil boring indicates unsuitable material, the engineer recommends that the soil be removed as part of the specifications for the contract. However, if the unsuitable material is not shown on the soil boring and is found by the contractor after he begins construction, then it is considered a "Differing Site Condition," and the contractor is entitled to compensation for removal of the unsuitable soil.

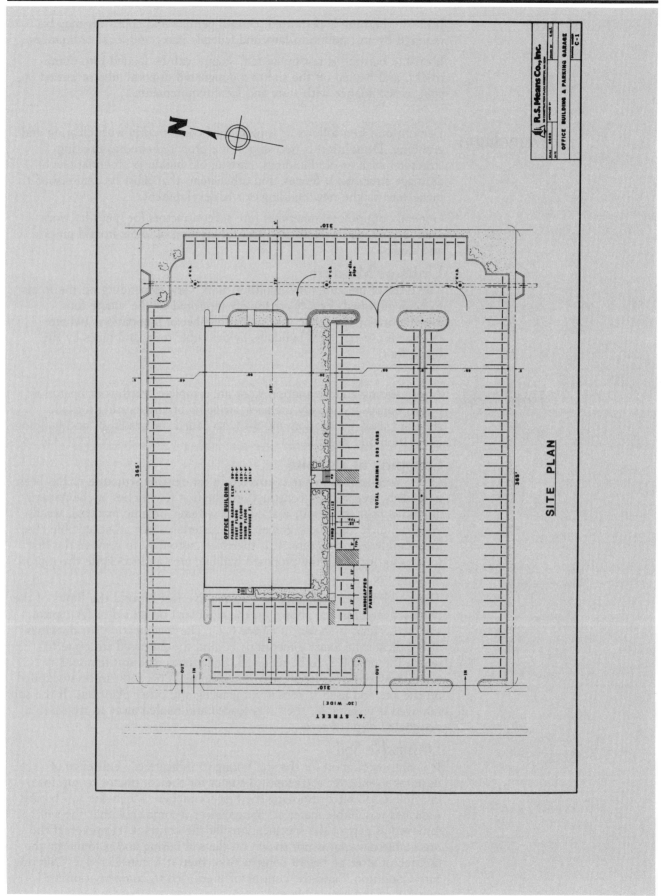

SITE PLAN

Figure 6.2

Units of Measure

Stripping of a site is usually measured by the cubic yard. This is obtained by computing the volume to be removed, called cut, and the corresponding volume to be placed, call fill. Sites often are short of fill and require added material called borrow, or may have excess fill that requires removal from the site. The result is expressed in cubic feet, which is then divided by 27 to convert to cubic yards.

Site Grading

Natural ground is often uneven. Uneven land on a site plan is shown by **contours** established by a surveyor. Contours show the elevation (vertical distance) above sea level. A **topographic survey** of a construction site shows existing contours and proposed finish grades for an office building, as shown in Figure 6.3. This is a simplified example. Usually there are two sets of contours – one solid and the other dotted, one for existing and the other for proposed elevations.

Notice that the elevation shown for a contour is the same all along that contour line.

Filling

When there is a shortage of fill, fill material (also called borrow) must be imported. Fill material may be purchased from a material supplier or excavated and hauled by the contractor from an approved borrow pit. The imported material is then placed in increments of 6 to 12 inches thick at a time, and each layer is compacted. The limits and requirements for compaction are usually indicated in the specifications. When there is an excess of cut material, it must be hauled away to an approved disposal site or sold, if there is an interested buyer.

Swell and Shrinkage

Earth material exists in three principal states: **natural (in-place), loose** and **compacted.** Soil in its natural state is measured in a unit volume known as **bank cubic yard.** Loose soil (after excavation or loading) has a unit volume known as **loose cubic yard.** Soil after compaction has a unit volume referred to as **compacted cubic yard.**

Air (voids) is introduced into soil during excavation, causing it to increase in volume. This increase in volume is called **swell,** and is usually expressed as a percent increase over the original volume. An equation for determining swell is:

$$\text{Swell (\%)} = \frac{\text{Weight of soil/bank cubic yard}}{\text{Weight of soil/loose cubic yard}} - 1 \times 100$$

When soil is excavated from its natural state, it increases in volume. Thus, more soil is needed to fill a hole than is taken out of the same hole. This decrease in volume is known as **shrinkage,** and is usually expressed as a percentage of the original volume. An equation for determining shrinkage is:

$$\text{Shrinkage (\%)} = \frac{\text{Weight of soil/bank cubic yard}}{\text{Weight of soil/compacted cubic yard}} - 1 \times 100$$

Swell and shrinkage factors, which vary depending on the type and characteristics of the earthen materials at a specific site, are applied when earthwork operations involve hauling earth by truck either to or from a project site. Conversion factors for some common materials are provided in Figure 6.4.

It is important to note that all volumes must be converted to a common unit of measure when performing calculations for earthwork. Any of the three units of measure discussed above may be used. However, the bank

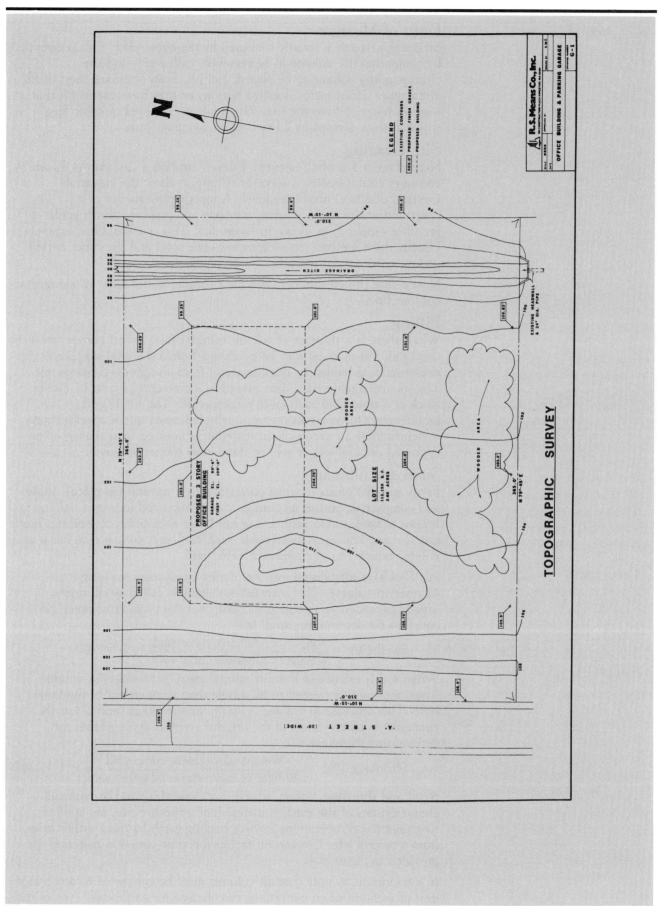

Figure 6.3

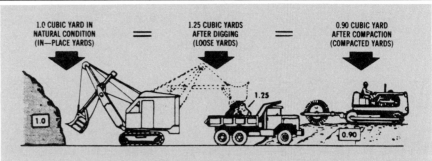

Approximate Material Characteristics*

Material	Loose (lb/c yd)	Bank (lb/cu yd)	Swell (5)	Load Factor
Clay, dry	2,100	2,650	26	0.79
Clay, wet	2,700	3,575	32	0.76
Clay and gravel, dry	2,400	2,800	17	0.85
Clay and gravel, wet	2.600	3,100	17	0.85
Earth, dry	2,215	2,850	29	0.78
Earth, moist	2,410	3,080	28	0.78
Earth, wet	2,750	3,380	23	0.81
Gravel, dry	2,780	3,140	13	0.88
Gravel, wet	3,090	3,620	17	0.85
Sand, dry	2,600	2,920	12	0.89
Sand, wet	3,100	3,520	13	0.88
Sand and gravel, dry	2,900	3,250	12	0.89
Sand and gravel, wet	3,400	3,750	10	0.91

*Exact values will vary with grain size, moisture content, compaction, etc. Test to determine exact values for specific soils.

Typical Soil Volume Conversion Factors

Soil Type	Initial Soil Condition	Bank	Converted to: Loose	Converted to: Compacted
Clay	Bank	1.00	1.27	0.90
	Loose	0.79	1.00	0.71
	Compacted	1.11	1.41	1.00
Common earth	Bank	1.00	1.25	0.90
	Loose	0.80	1.00	0.72
	Compacted	1.11	1.39	1.00
Rock (blasted)	Bank	1.00	1.50	1.30
	Loose	0.67	1.00	0.87
	Compacted	0.77	1.15	1.00
Sand	Bank	1.00	1.12	0.95
	Loose	0.89	1.00	0.85
	Compacted	1.05	1.18	1.00

Figure 6.4

cubic yard is most commonly used for excavation only. Loose cubic yard is used for borrow, and compacted cubic yard for backfill.

Grading

The process of cutting and/or filling a site to achieve the required elevation is known as **grading.** There are two types of grading: **rough grading** (initial grading work) and **finish grading** (final grading work). A finish grading plan for a construction site is shown in Figure 6.5.

Often there is a difference between the existing elevation and the final desired elevation. Some projects can be designed so that the areas to be cut (the high points on a site) and the areas to be filled (the low or depressed points on a site) will balance, as shown in Figure 6.6. However, it is more likely that the cuts and the fills will not balance, as illustrated in Figure 6.7.

The amount of cut and fill is measured by the cubic yard. This portion of a project is often subcontracted out by the general contractor to a subcontractor.

Building Excavation

Digging a hole to make room for construction or engineering improvements is known as excavation. It is sometimes called **bulk excavation** or **structural excavation.** This process is often performed by the general contractor. The excavation may be necessary to build foundations, manholes, vaults, elevators, basements, sub-stories, and ramps. Rock, organic materials, clay, or simply gravel, in any combination, may be encountered during excavation.

Methods of Excavation

There are two common methods of excavation. They are **machine excavation** and **hand excavation.** Machine excavation involves the use of equipment. Today, except on very small jobs, almost all bulk excavation is done using power-operated equipment such as power shovels, scrapers, bulldozers, excavators, and trenching machines.

Hand excavation involves the use of manual labor. On some projects there are types of excavation which, due to size, location, or other factors, cannot be performed by machines. In such cases, manual labor with tools may be necessary to accomplish the task.

There are other situations, such as the excavation of footings, where a combination of hand and machine is most cost-effective. Machines are used for the bulk excavation for footings and manual labor is used to "dress" the bottom, sides, and corners to achieve the precise horizontal and vertical planes required.

When boulders are encountered, they may be dislodged with a piece of equipment such as a backhoe. Other types of rock may be excavated by hydraulic shovels or ripping teeth mounted on a dozer. Small quantities may even be removed by jackhammer. When the size or hardness of the rock is extreme, then explosives provide the extra power to dislodge the material that cannot be removed conventionally.

Safety Considerations

Soils vary in their ability to hold a vertical face at the side of an excavation. This potential to collapse presents a safety hazard for workers, as well as others who may visit the site during construction. Therefore, the edges of an excavation must be stabilized to ensure that they do not cave in. This can be done by cutting the edges of the excavation at a slope known as the **angle of repose.** This is the natural

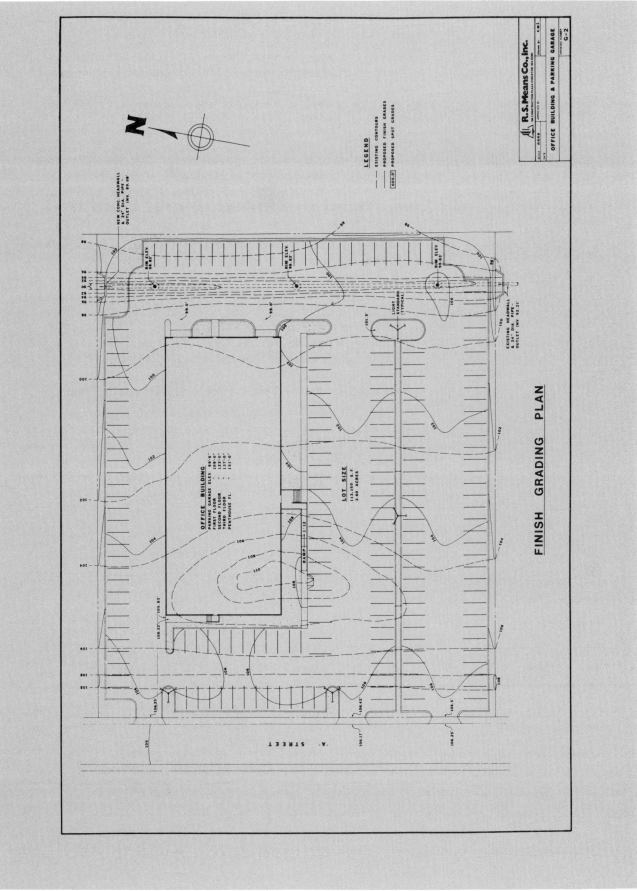

FINISH GRADING PLAN

slope (or maximum angle) which a given material will hold without sliding. An angle of repose is illustrated in Figure 6.8.

When it is impossible to slope the sides of an excavation due to the proximity of adjacent structures or unstable soil, temporary supports of timber or steel sheets known as **shoring** must be used to hold the soil in place. An example of an excavation using shoring is shown in Figure 6.9.

Dewatering

Underground water should be anticipated based on the information collected from the soil borings, unless a water main is broken during excavation. An unanticipated amount of underground water may halt construction, and may increase the cost of the excavation work tremendously.

The unwanted underground water can be removed by a process known as dewatering. Some of the dewatering methods are:

- **Pumping the water out directly** with a submersible pump (see Figure 6.10). Although this method may be the least expensive method of handling underground water, it may not always be feasible or practical.
- **Pumping from one or more sump pits** as illustrated in Figure 6.11.
- **Draining the water to a lower elevation** as illustrated in Figure 6.12.
- **Installation of a well-point system** as illustrated in Figure 6.13.

The well-point system consists of a series of vertical perforated pipes called **well points** driven down into the water table. The well points are connected to horizontal pipes known as **headers** and attached to one or more pumps. Water is pumped from the vertical pipes into the headers where it is discharged above ground. The materials for a well-point system may be partly purchased or partly rented. However, most

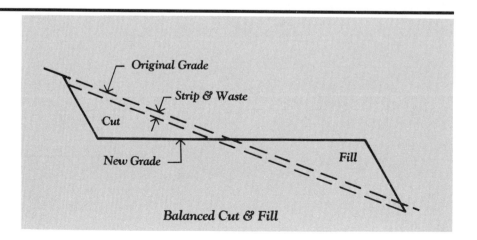

Figure 6.6

contractors sublet the dewatering work to a specialist. The well-point system is usually expensive, but sometimes it is the only practical method of handling sub-surface water.

The cost of dewatering is controlled by variables such as the dewatering method selected, the size of the site, and the hours the pumps will be in operation.

Soil Treatment

Soil treatment, or soil poisoning, is the application of chemicals to the soil to control pests such as termites. The area to be covered by the slab is treated before the concrete is placed. This work is usually subcontracted to a pest control firm licensed to administer the specified chemicals.

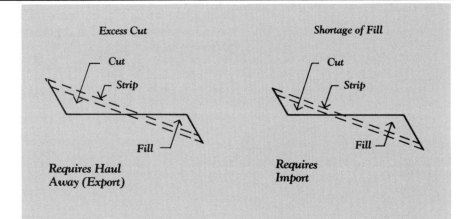

Figure 6.7

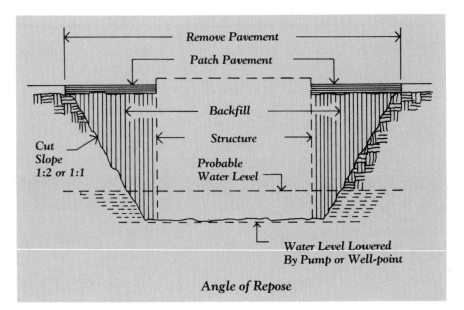

Figure 6.8

Site Utilities

New storm lines, sewer lines, manholes, and catch basins require excavation and backfilling of utility trenches, as well as the connection to, the relocation of, and protection of existing utility lines. Usually this work begins at a point five feet beyond the limits of the proposed structure and goes to the existing storm and sewer mains. This work is normally subcontracted to a site utilities specialist. There are structures for other utilities as well: pump stations, meter pits, desiltation basins, flumes, electrical vaults, and trench drains.

Roads

Two types of roads are encountered in site work: **temporary roads** and **permanent roads.**

Temporary roads are used for access to the construction site during construction and are not a part of the completed project. Under dry conditions, watering of temporary roads may be necessary to control the amount of dust on the job site. Under wet conditions, crushed stone or gravel may be needed to make the roads usable.

Permanent roads are part of the completed project and usually consist of a **base course** (gravel or crushed rock) of a specified thickness, a **primer coat** (asphaltic material applied to the surface of the base course), a **binder course** and a **surface (wearing) course** of asphaltic concrete of a specified thickness. Paving work for roads and parking lots is usually priced by the square yard and performed by a subcontractor who specializes in paving work.

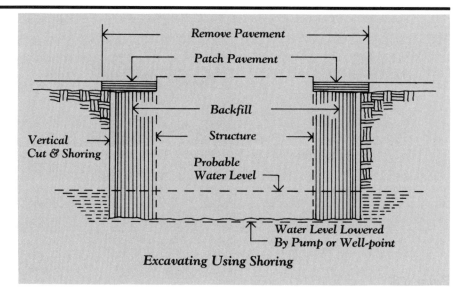

Excavating Using Shoring

Figure 6.9

Landscaping

This phase of site work includes: sodding (placement of layers of soil containing roots of grass), seeding (planting of grass seeds), planting of trees, flowers and shrubs, as well as installation of lawn sprinkler systems. There may be a maintenance period specified, during which the contractor is responsible for watering the grass and replacing dead plants. General contractors usually subcontract the landscaping portion of the work out to a landscaping contractor, who then assumes the responsibility for performing the specified work.

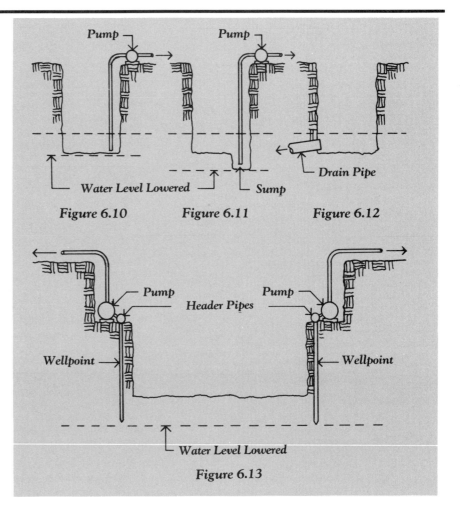

Figure 6.10   Figure 6.11   Figure 6.12

Figure 6.13

Figures 6.10 – 6.13

Summary Most construction jobs require some site work. Clearing and grubbing, demolition, and earthwork are the three categories of site work for removing trees and shrubs, old structures, and preparing the land for the new structure. This work may be performed by subcontractors, or some may be performed by the general contractor, depending on available equipment and staff expertise.

Chapter Seven

Basic Construction Materials

Hundreds of different materials are used on construction projects. However, the major and most commonly used materials are:

- Wood
- Concrete
- Masonry
- Steel

This chapter discusses the fundamental features of the four major materials commonly used in construction. Each material, in the context of its use in construction, will be discussed in subsequent chapters.

Wood

Wood, unlike most processed building materials, is an organic material that can be used in its natural state. Factors that influence its strength are density, natural defects (knots, grain, etc.), and moisture content. Wood can be easily shaped or cut to size on the site, or prefabricated in the shop. Structurally, wood may be used for joists, posts, columns, beams, and trusses. It may also be laminated into columns, beams, rigid frames, arches, vaults, and folded-plate configurations. Various framing systems may be used with fiberboard, particle board, plywood, or wood decking (plain or laminated) to form composite panels. Wood may be exposed and finished for interior or exterior use. It may be pressure-treated to provide resistance to moisture, rot, or exposure. Structural lumber is stress-graded for bending, tension parallel to the grain, horizontal shear, compression perpendicular to the grain, compression parallel to the grain, and modulus of elasticity.

Even though the terms wood, lumber, and timber are often used interchangeably, they have distinct meanings in the construction industry.

Wood

Wood may be classified into two main groups: softwoods such as pine, fir, spruce, and hemlock; or hardwoods such as maple, oak, and mahogany. Hardwoods are most often used for millwork items such as furniture, railings, moldings, carvings, flooring, and other items. Figure 7.1 shows the general classifications of wood.

Lumber

Lumber is sawed from trees that are classified as softwoods. Softwoods are the most widely utilized type of wood for everyday construction. Lumber is classified in terms of size, use, and extent of manufacture according to the American Lumber Standards discussed below and illustrated in Figure 7.2.

Size Classification

Lumber is designated in two ways – **nominal size** or **actual size.** For example, a nominal size of $2'' \times 4''$ is actually $1\text{-}1/2'' \times 3\text{-}1/2''$. The nominal size of lumber is its approximate original size. This original size is normally reduced due to sawing, dressing, and seasoning (the drying out process), resulting in what is described as the actual size. In the construction industry, it is common practice to refer to lumber by its nominal size ($2' \times 4'$, $2' \times 8'$). The difference between the nominal size and the actual size is illustrated in Figure 7.3.

Lumber may be further classified by size into three major groups. They are: **boards,** lumber less than two inches thick and one or more inches wide; **dimension lumber,** lumber two or more inches thick, used in framing, such as studs, joists, and rafters; and **timber,** lumber five or more inches thick, used for beams, columns, posts, girders, and sills.

Use Classification

Lumber may also be classified by use, into **yard lumber, structural lumber**, and **factory and shop lumber**. Yard lumber is lumber of the grade and dimension used in regular construction and general building purposes. Structural lumber is two or more inches thick, used where

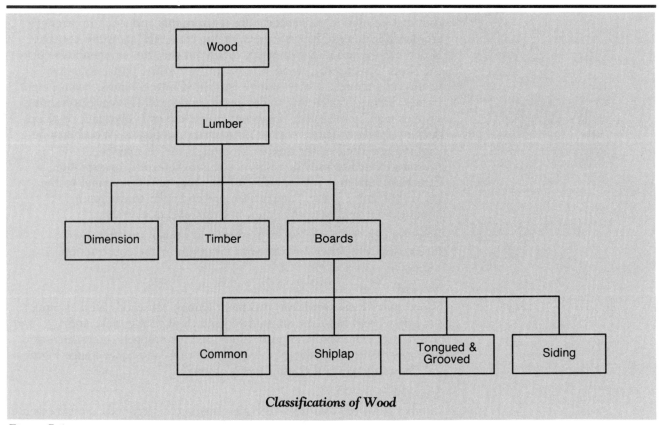

Classifications of Wood

Figure 7.1

working stresses are required. Factory and shop lumber is produced, selected, or intended for re-manufacturing purposes.

Extent of Manufacture Classification

Lumber is sometimes classified into two categories, depending on the extent of manufacture. The two categories are: **rough lumber** and **dressed lumber**. As its name implies, rough lumber is sawed, but not dressed. Dressed lumber is run through a planing machine and may or may not be seasoned. The planing machine provides smoothness and uniformity of size. Dressed lumber may be designated according to the

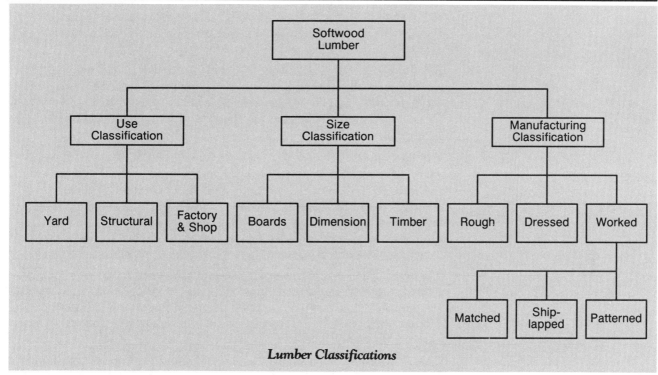

Lumber Classifications

Figure 7.2

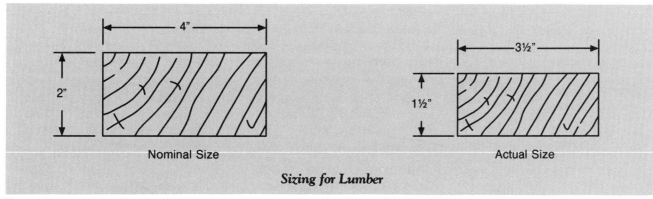

Sizing for Lumber

Figure 7.3

number of dressed sides or edges. For instance, one of the most common designations, S4S, refers to a board that has been surfaced on all four sides.

Rough lumber is used mostly for temporary construction, such as footing formwork, scaffolding, planking, safety railings, and shoring. Dressed lumber is utilized in formwork, framing, blocking, carpentry trim, and the majority of permanent carpentry items in a building.

Worked Lumber

This is lumber that, in addition to being dressed, has been either matched (has a tongue on one edge and a groove on the opposite edge); shiplapped (has been rabbetted on both edges to provide a close-lapped longitudinal joint); or patterned (shaped to some pattern in addition to being dressed, matched, shiplapped, or any combination of these workings). Worked lumber is used in siding, tongue and grooved decking, or shaped moldings, to give a few examples.

Timber

Timber is heavy lumber used for major structural elements in a building such as piles, beams, and columns. The large cross-sectional sizes of these members make them suitable for carrying heavy loads and/or spanning long distances as beams.

Small dimensional lumber (like $2'' \times 4''$s) can be laminated together in the factory with adhesives to form large straight girders and arches that serve the same purpose as timber. These are factory finished and are used for column-free structures such as supermarkets and auditoriums (see Figure 7.4).

Plywood

Plywood is another wood product commonly used in the construction industry. It consists of two or more thin sheets of wood glued together. Plywood is sold in sheets. The most common size is four feet wide and eight feet long. Each sheet usually has grade markings that indicate its quality and the recommended usage. Sample grade marks used by the American Plywood Association are shown in Figure 7.5.

Notice that under the American Plywood Association's grade markings, "group" refers to the species of wood used. The association currently uses five groups – 1, 2, 3, 4 and 5, based on the strength and stiffness of each species, with one being the strongest. A classification of species by group is shown in Figure 7.6.

"A-C" in Figure 7.5 refers to the grade of wood used on the front and back veneer. There are six common grades in use – A, B, C plugged, C, D, and N. A table showing the type of veneer in each grade is provided in Figure 7.7.

Examples of when to use the different grades are as follows; A-A, cabinets and furniture; A-C, soffits and structural diaphragms; B-C, backing for exterior coatings; B-D, utility panel backing; and C-C, flooring underlayment.

In recent years, wood particles (such as sawdust and wood chips) have been processed (by mixing dry wood particles with resins and bonding them together under heat and pressure) to form solid panels known as **particle board**, sometimes used for sheathing and subflooring.

Common Uses of Wood

Dimensional construction grade lumber is commonly used for framing residential structures. A standard member for wall framing was traditionally the 2″ × 4″. In the interest of saving energy, state laws now require 2″ × 6″ members. A typical exterior wall framing system and a typical floor joist framing system are shown in Figure 7.8.

Wall and floor framing members must be aligned to provide a smooth and even surface on which to attach the sheathing, drywall plaster, siding, or other finishes. Occasionally pipes and ductwork protrude beyond the plane of the wall surface. Furring is used to frame around any irregularities to restore the uniformity of the surface.

Plywood sheathing is used to strengthen exterior walls (also shown in Figure 7.8) and as a deck, over floor or roof framing. It varies in thickness depending on the usage, number of layers to be used, and the covering material (wood, carpet, tile, etc.).

Floor systems typically bear (sit) on the walls or girders supporting (underneath) them. In order to increase head room (in basements, for example) floor members can be hung from girders with sheet metal joist hangers, shown in Figure 7.9. Other connections, such as girders to columns, are accomplished with sheet metal connectors.

Wood is also used for trusses for roof systems. Trusses are made up of small dimensional lumber (i.e., 2″ × 4″s) arranged in a geometric pattern based on the triangle which can span long distances, as shown in Figure 7.10. Trusses can be field-fabricated with bolts and gusset plates or factory-fabricated with sheet metal connector plates. They are

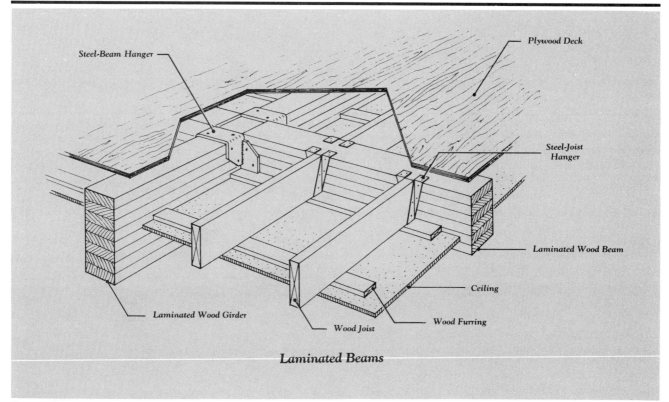

Laminated Beams

Figure 7.4

119

manufactured in many different configurations, for high or low pitched roofs, hipped roofs, mansard roofs, or flat roofs.

Formwork for Concrete

Formwork is largely constructed of wood, although aluminum, fiberglass, and steel may be used or required for architecturally exposed surfaces. Wood planks or plywood, backed by studs and walers and braced by kickers or ties, may be used for forming footings or walls. Plyform held rigidly in steel preformed frames normally 2' or less in width, and varying up to 8' in height, make up the patented forming systems that are often used to form walls and standard foundations. Wood forms are illustrated in Figure 7.11.

Braces or "kickers" are attached to the stakes (pointed pieces of lumber driven into the ground to act as anchors) to stabilize the forms. Pieces of lumber are used as **spreaders** to hold the forms apart and maintain the required shape and dimension until the concrete is cured.

Concrete

Concrete is one of the most universal construction materials in the world because its component raw materials are inorganic, incombustible, highly versatile, and relatively low in cost in comparison to other materials.

Although the terms *concrete* and *cement* are sometimes used interchangeably outside of the construction industry, they have different meanings and are two distinct materials.

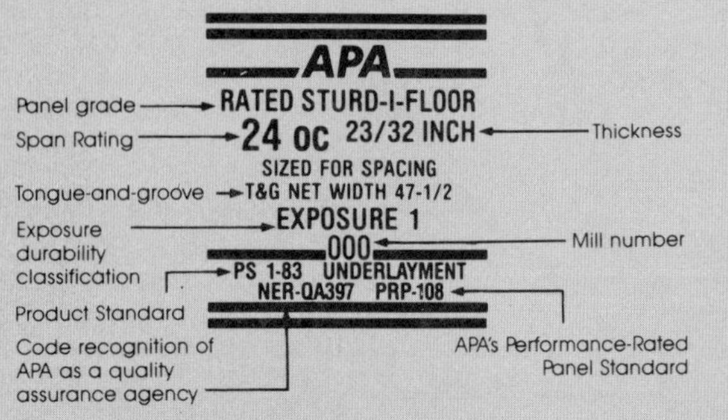

Panel grade ——→ **RATED STURD-I-FLOOR**
Span Rating ——→ **24 oc** 23/32 INCH ←—— Thickness
SIZED FOR SPACING
Tongue-and-groove ——→ T&G NET WIDTH 47-1/2
Exposure durability classification ——→ **EXPOSURE 1**
000 ←—— Mill number
→ PS 1-83 UNDERLAYMENT
NER-QA397 PRP-108 ←
Product Standard
Code recognition of APA as a quality assurance agency
APA's Performance-Rated Panel Standard

TYPICAL TRADEMARK

A-A · G-1 · EXPOSURE1-APA · 000 · PS1-83

Use where appearance of both sides is important for interior applications such as built-ins, cabinets, furniture, partitions; and exterior applications such as fences, signs, boats, shipping containers, tanks, ducts, etc. Smooth surfaces suitable for painting. EXPOSURE DURABILITY CLASSIFICATIONS: Interior, Exposure 1, Exterior. COMMON THICKNESSES: 1/4, 11/32, 3/8, 15/32, 1/2, 19/32, 5/8, 23/32, 3/4.

This information has been reprinted courtesy of American Plywood Association.

Figure 7.5

Cement

Cement, often referred to as Portland cement, is a fine gray powder made from three main ingredients of **silica**, **lime**, and **alumina**. It often includes slag or flue dust from iron furnaces. The appropriate proportions of the above materials are mixed together by crushing, grinding, and blending. The resulting blend is then heated in a rotating kiln to very high temperatures (from 2600 to 3000 degrees Fahrenheit) to produce a vitrified product called **clinker**. The clinker is allowed to cool and then pulverized into powder form, usually with a small amount of gypsum to slow down the curing process. The powder is sold in packaged bags about 1 cubic foot in volume or can be shipped in bulk.

Table 2 Classification of Species

Group 1	Group 2	Group 3	Group 4	Group 5
Apitong	Cedar, Port	Alder, Red	Aspen	Basswood
Beech,	Orford	Birch, Paper	Bigtooth	Poplar,
American	Cypress	Cedar, Alaska	Quaking	Balsam
Birch	Douglas	Fir,	Cativo	
Sweet	Fir 2[a]	Subalpine	Cedar	
Yellow	Fir	Hemlock,	Incense	
Douglas	Balsam	Eastern	Western	
Fir 1[a]	California	Maple,	Red	
Kapur	Red	Bigleaf	Cottonwood	
Keruing	Grand	Pine	Eastern	
Larch,	Noble	Jack	Black	
Western	Pacific	Lodgepole	(Western	
Maple, Sugar	Silver	Ponderosa	Poplar)	
Pine	White	Spruce	Pine	
Caribbean	Hemlock,	Redwood	Eastern	
Ocote	Western	Spruce	White	
Pine, South.	Lauan	Engelmann	Sugar	
Loblolly	Almon	White		
Longleaf	Bagtikan			
Shortleaf	Mayapis			
Slash	Red			
Tanoak	Tangile			
	White			
	Maple, Black			
	Mengkulang			
	Meranti,			
	Red[b]			
	Mersawa			
	Pine			
	Pond			
	Red			
	Virginia			
	Western			
	White			
	Spruce			
	Black			
	Red			
	Sitka			
	Sweetgum			
	Tamarack			
	Yellow-			
	Poplar			

(a) Douglas Fir from trees grown in the states of Washington, Oregon, California, Idaho, Montana, Wyoming, and the Canadian Provinces of Alberta and British Columbia shall be classed as Douglas Fir No. 1. Douglas Fir from trees grown in the states of Nevada, Utah, Colorado, Arizona and New Mexico shall be classed as Douglas Fir No. 2.

(b) Red Meranti shall be limited to species having a specific gravity of 0.41 or more based on green volume and oven dry weight.

This information has been reprinted courtesy of American Plywood Association.

Figure 7.6

Concrete

Concrete is made by mixing a paste of cement and water with sand and crushed stone, gravel, or other inert material. Typical proportions of these components for concrete are shown in Figure 7.12. After mixing, usually accomplished for buildings in a transit mix truck, the plastic mixture is placed in forms and a chemical reaction called hydration takes place and the mass hardens.

Concrete is rated by its compressive strength after a 28-day curing period. The compressive strength most often specified for structures is 3000 pounds per square inch (psi). Concrete that is exposed to freezing temperatures such as curbs and sidewalks is usually 4000 psi. In some cases, concrete with much higher strength is required, from 6000 psi to as high as 19,000 psi. Specified strengths of concrete are produced by varying the proportions of cement, sand, or fine aggregate, coarse aggregate, and water. Test cylinders are taken from each concrete pour

Table 1	Veneer Grades
N	Smooth surface "natural finish" veneer. Select, all heartwood or all sapwood. Free of open defects. Allows not more than 6 repairs, wood only, per 4 x 8 panel, made parallel to grain and well matched for grain and color.
A	Smooth, paintable. Not more than 18 neatly made repairs, boat, sled, or router type, and parallel to grain, permitted. May be used for natural finish in less demanding applications. Synthetic repairs permitted.
B	Solid surface. Shims, circular repair plugs and tight knots to 1 inch across grain permitted. Some minor splits permitted. Synthetic repairs permitted.
C Plugged	Improved C veneer with splits limited to 1/8-inch width and knotholes and borer holes limited to 1/4 x 1/2 inch. Admits some broken grain. Synthetic repairs permitted.
C	Tight knots to 1-1/2 inch. Knotholes to 1 inch across grain and some to 1-1/2 inch if total width of knots and knotholes is within specified limits. Synthetic or wood repairs. Discoloration and sanding defects that do not impair strength permitted. Limited splits allowed. Stitching permitted.
D	Knots and knotholes to 2-1/2 inch width across grain and 1/2 inch larger within specified limits. Limited splits are permitted. Stitching permitted. Limited to Exposure 1 or Interior panels.

This information has been reprinted courtesy of American Plywood Association.

Figure 7.7

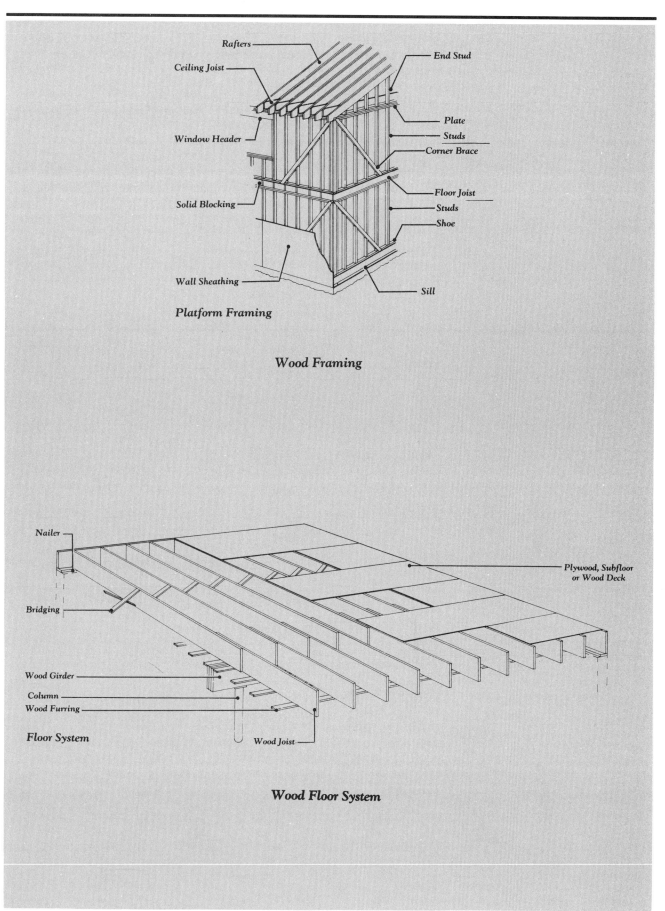

Platform Framing

Rafters
Ceiling Joist
Window Header
Solid Blocking
Wall Sheathing
End Stud
Plate
Studs
Corner Brace
Floor Joist
Studs
Shoe
Sill

Wood Framing

Nailer
Bridging
Wood Girder
Column
Wood Furring
Wood Joist
Plywood, Subfloor or Wood Deck

Floor System

Wood Floor System

Figure 7.8

and broken at the end of the curing period to determine whether the concrete meets the required compressive strength, usually done in a testing lab.

One of the most important factors affecting the strength of concrete is the water-to-cement ratio, expressed in pounds or gallons of water per sack of cement. The use of too much water in the mix may cause segregation of the mid-components, producing non-uniform concrete. Concrete is tested in the field for the water-to-cement ratio by means of a **slump test**, performed by rodding concrete from the transmit mix chute into a conical steel form. When the form is removed, the amount of "drop," or "slump," is measured.

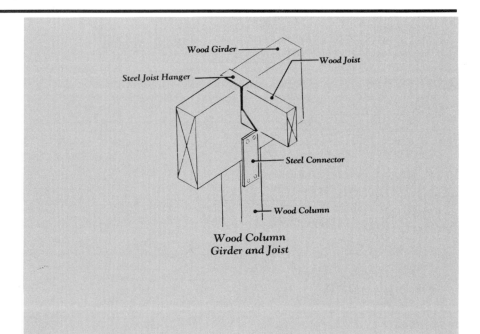

Figure 7.9

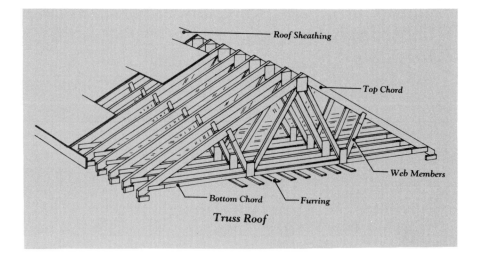

Figure 7.10

Reinforcing

Concrete, although strong in compression, is relatively weak in resisting tension and shear. To resist tension and shear forces, deformed steel bars, called reinforcing, are placed in designated locations. The purpose of the deformations is to develop a bond between the concrete and steel. The bars are held in position during placement of the concrete by tie wires or patented connectors.

Concrete slabs are reinforced by welded wire fabric that consists of longitudinal and horizontal wires fused in position with a designated spacing (see Figure 7.13).

Cast-in-Place

Cast-in-place refers to concrete that is placed in a liquid state in the position and/or location it is to occupy permanently in a finished structure. Figure 7.14 is an illustration of concrete cast-in-place footings.

The majority of general contractors perform all the work related to cast-in-place concrete with their own employees. Most cast-in-place concrete used on construction projects is ready-mixed, delivered to the

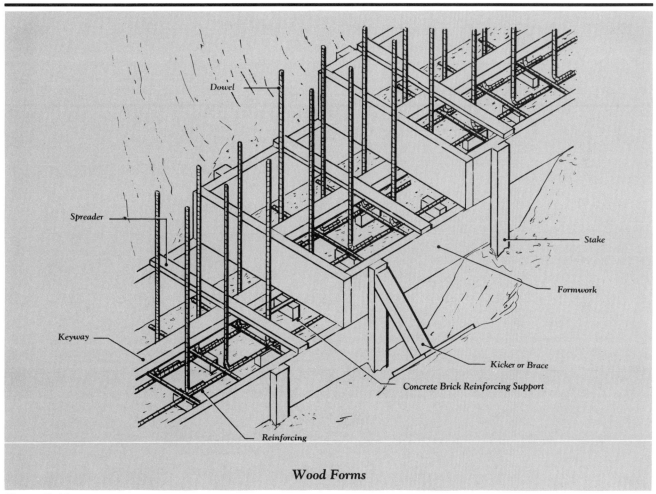

Wood Forms

Figure 7.11

construction site by special trucks, and then placed in the forms by one of several methods: by a chute directly into formwork; into a hopper for distribution by wheelbarrows and mechanical buggies; into buckets to be hoisted by a crane; or into a concrete pump and pushed through a portable pipeline.

Once in the forms, the concrete is vibrated to: eliminate air pockets, surround the reinforcing, and fill any voids in the formwork. Slabs are "struck off" or screeded (leveled) after vibration but require additional finishing (floating and troweling) and curing.

Precast

Precast concrete is cast in the controlled environment of a casting plant where the quality of materials can be controlled to a much greater degree. The finished member is transported by truck to the jobsite and erected by crane.

Three examples of prestressed precast concrete – rectangular, T-shape and L-shape – are illustrated in Figure 7.15.

Prestressed

Concrete may be reinforced, or prestressed, to partially counteract the stresses produced by the loads applied to a structure. The reinforcing can be stressed in the field, but is better controlled in a factory, such as a precast plant.

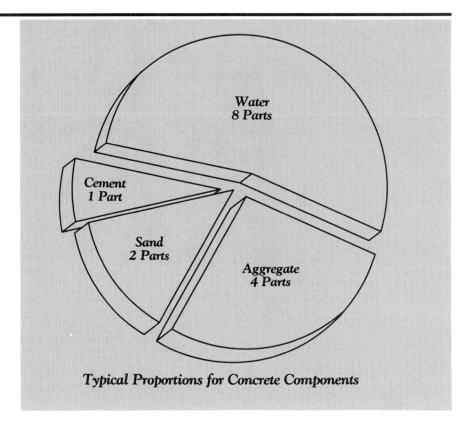

Typical Proportions for Concrete Components

Figure 7.12

Reinforcing Bars

Bar Size Designation	Weight Pounds Per Foot	Nominal Dimensions - Round Sections		
		Diameter Inches	Cross-Sectional Area-Sq. Inches	Perimeter Inches
#3	.376	.375	.11	1.178
#4	.668	.500	.20	1.571
#5	1.043	.625	.31	1.963
#6	1.502	.750	.44	2.356
#7	2.044	.875	.60	2.749
#8	2.670	1.000	.79	3.142
#9	3.400	1.128	1.00	3.544
#10	4.303	1.270	1.27	3.990
#11	5.313	1.410	1.56	4.430
#14	7.650	1.693	2.25	5.320
#18	13.600	2.257	4.00	7.090

Common Stock Styles of Welded Wire Fabric

New Designation	Old Designation	Steel Area Per Foot				Approximate Weight Per 100 Sq. Ft.	
Spacing - Cross Sectional Area (IN.)-(Sq. IN. 100)	Spacing Wire Gauge (IN.)-(AS & W)	Longitudinal		Transverse			
		IN.	CM	IN.	CM	LB	KG
6 x 6-W1.4 x W1.4	6 x 6-10 x 10	0.028	0.071	0.028	0.071	21	9.53
6 x 6-W2.0 x W2.0	6 x 6-8 x 8 (1)	0.040	0.102	0.040	0.102	29	13.15
6 x 6-W2.9 x W2.9	6 x 6-6 x 6	0.058	0.147	0.053	0.147	42	19.05
6 x 6-W4.0 x W4.0	6 x 6-4 x 4	0.080	0.203	0.080	0.203	58	26.31
4 x 4-W1.4 x W1.4	4 x 4-10 x 10	0.042	0.107	0.042	0.107	31	14.06
4 x 4-W2.0 x W2.0	4 x 4-8 x 8 (1)	0.060	0.152	0.060	0.152	43	19.50
4 x 4-W2.9 x W2.9	4 x 4-6 x 6	0.087	0.221	0.087	0.221	62	28.12
4 x 4-W4.0 x W4.0	4 x 4-4 x 4	0.120	0.305	0.120	0.305	85	38.56
6 x 6-W2.9 x W2.9	6 x 6-6 x 6	0.058	0.147	0.058	0.147	42	19.05
6 x 6-W4.0 x W4.0	6 x 6-4 x 4	0.080	0.203	0.080	0.203	58	26.31
6 x 6-W5.5 x W5.5	6 x 6-2 x 2 (2)	0.110	0.279	0.110	0.279	80	36.29
6 x 6-W4.0 x W4.0	4 x 4-4 x 4	0.120	0.305	0.120	0.305	85	38.56

NOTES
1. Exact W-number size for 8 gauge is W2.1
2. Exact W-number size for 2 gauge is W5.4

Figure 7.13

Masonry

Concrete blocks, bricks, and stone are all categorized as masonry units in the construction industry. While the installation of masonry units is said to be the simplest and most ancient of all building techniques, it is also labor intensive and requires the patience and craftsmanship of a skilled mason to achieve the proper final product.

The use of masonry units offers certain advantages over other building materials, which makes their use desirable. Bricks can be obtained in colors that do not fade easily. Concrete blocks and stone are very

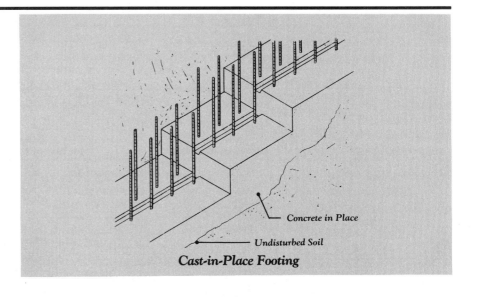

Concrete in Place

Undisturbed Soil

Cast-in-Place Footing

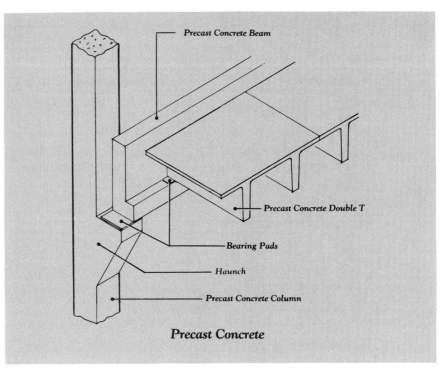

Precast Concrete Beam

Precast Concrete Double T

Bearing Pads

Haunch

Precast Concrete Column

Precast Concrete

durable and can stand up to heavy wear and abuse for long periods of time. In addition, most masonry materials are economical and are not easily affected by the elements of water, air, and fire.

Concrete Block

There are two main weights of concrete masonry units (CMU) or blocks: **standard block** and **lightweight block**. Standard block is made with heavyweight aggregates such as sand and gravel. Lightweight block is made with lightweight aggregates such as coal cinders, clay, or slag.

Concrete block is used for loadbearing exterior walls or nonloadbearing interior partitions. The exposed face dimensions of concrete blocks are usually 8″ high, by 16″ long, whereas the width can vary anywhere from 2″ to 16″ . Concrete blocks are classified in two groups – **solid** and **hollow**. A block is solid if the cross-sectional area, less the voids, is 75 percent or greater of the gross area of the block, and hollow if the solid area is less than 75 percent.

Different shapes are manufactured for incorporation into special conditions in walls. Lintel blocks are used to span over openings; pilaster blocks for thickened walls and additional bearing under beams; bond beam blocks for lateral stiffening of walls at the top and sometimes mid-height; and soap blocks for leveling or starting walls at grade.

A concrete block wall is illustrated in Figure 7.16 showing joint reinforcement, a control joint, and insulation.

Concrete blocks can be installed in different patterns – running bond, offset running bond, or stack bond horizontal, as shown in Figure 7.17.

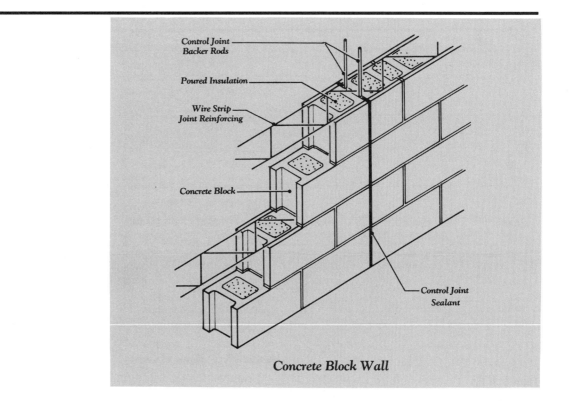

Concrete Block Wall

Figure 7.16

Brick

Brick comes in a variety of colors and shapes, is readily available in most places, and is durable, economical, and easy to maintain. In addition, brick can be installed rapidly with a limited number of specialized tools and equipment.

The most commonly used size of brick measures 2-2/3" × 4" × 8" (2-2/3" high, 4" wide, and 8" long). This is known as the **standard brick**. When the standard brick is 3-1/5" high, it is called **engineer brick**; when it is 4" high it is called **economy brick**; when it is 5-1/3" high it is called **double brick**. The next most commonly used size measures 2" × 4" × 12" (2" high, 4" wide, and 12" long). This is known as **Roman brick**. Brick that is 2-2/3" high is called **Norman brick**; 3-1/5" high is called **Norwegian brick**; 4" high is called **utility brick**; and 5-1/3" high is known as **triple brick**. These shapes are illustrated in Figure 7.18.

Because the two apparent dimensions in any brick wall structure are its length and height, these two measurements are critical in determining the number of units of brick material to be used. Therefore, bricks with larger length and height dimensions are more economically installed because fewer of them have to be laid per square foot of wall area. In addition to the variety of sizes and dimensions, bricks may also be installed in many different positions and patterns within the wall to enhance its structure and appearance. A brick may be laid in one of six basic positions: **stretcher, header, soldier, sailor, rowlock,** and **shiner.** A brick unit is called a stretcher when its length is horizontal and aligned with the plane of the wall. This method of positioning bricks is the most commonly employed format. A brick unit is called a header when its length runs perpendicular to, and its width is aligned with, the

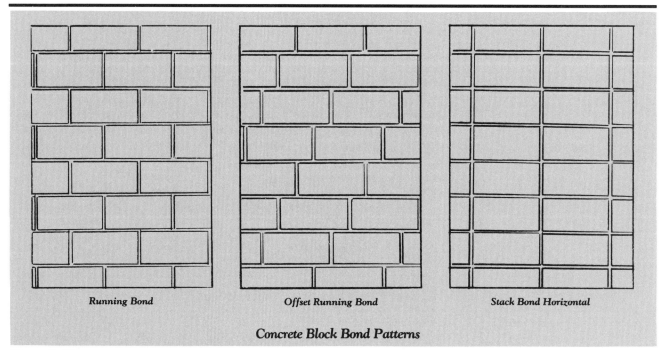

Running Bond   Offset Running Bond   Stack Bond Horizontal

Concrete Block Bond Patterns

Figure 7.17

plane of the wall. Before the development of brick ties, headers were used to attach the brick face to the back-up wall. Soldier brick describes the positioning of the unit with its length placed vertically in the plane of the wall. This method of positioning is often used to accent the fascia above windows or to create a horizontal belt around the building at floor levels.

The various combinations of stretcher and header patterns within brick walls determine its **bond**. Running bond describes courses of stretchers that are laid without any headers and with alternate courses staggered in alignment. If the stretchers line up vertically, the format is called stack bond. Common bond describes the combination of five courses of stretchers and one course of headers. Flemish bond is composed of stretchers and headers laid alternately in the same course. English bond consists of alternating courses of stretchers and headers. Patterns for laying brick are illustrated in Figure 7.19.

Horizontal joint reinforcement can be placed within the brick wall to control shrinkage cracks and to tie the face wythe to the back-up wythe in composite or cavity bearing wall systems. To provide resistance to lateral and flexural loads, bar reinforcement may be grouted vertically into the brick cores or vertically and horizontally into the collar joint between two wythes of bearing wall.

Because brick walls are not waterproof, provisions must be made to limit the amount of water penetration through the exterior face. Flashing should be installed at the junction of walls and floors, as well as over and under openings. In cavity walls, the outside face of the back-up wall or the insulation between the wythes should be waterproofed. Weep holes should be located above the flashing at brick shelves, relieving angles, and lintels to provide a means of escape for moisture that has penetrated the wall.

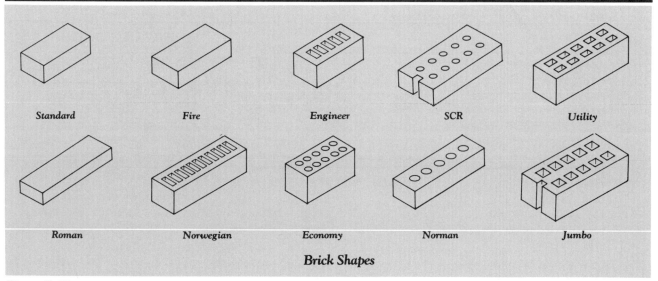

| Standard | Fire | Engineer | SCR | Utility |
| Roman | Norwegian | Economy | Norman | Jumbo |

Brick Shapes

Figure 7.18

Stone

Stone has a wide range of structural and decorative applications as a building material. It can be installed in small units, referred to as "building stone," which can be assembled in many different formats, with or without mortar, to create decorative and structural walls and veneers. Stone can also be employed as a material in larger units, such as stone panels, which are installed with elaborate anchor and framing systems and used as decorative wall facings in high-rise office and other commercial buildings.

Stone used in building construction usually consists of rock excavated or blasted from natural deposits and processed (by cutting, shaping, or sizing) into the required shapes and sizes. Building stone is normally obtained from three main types of rock: igneous rock, sedimentary rock, and metamorphic rock.

Igneous Rock

Rock deposited by volcanic action is igneous rock. Granite is the type of igneous rock most often found in construction. Granite is a non-porous, strong, durable rock whose surface can be polished or textured. It can be obtained in several colors such as black, gray, brown, green and red.

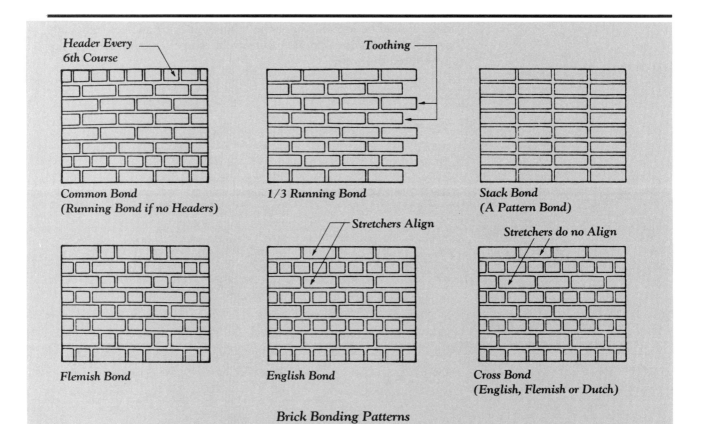

Brick Bonding Patterns

Figure 7.19

Sedimentary Rock

Rock deposited by the action of wind or water is known as sedimentary rock. Limestone and sandstone are the types of sedimentary rock most often used in construction work. Limestone is porous and can be obtained in colors such as white and gray. Richly patterned limestone with marble-like qualities is known as Travertine, and is often used as flooring. The most popular forms of sandstone are brownstone (for exterior walls) and bluestone (for pavings and wall coping).

Metamorphic Rock

The action of intense heat and pressure on either igneous or sedimentary rock converts it into a different, metamorphic rock. Examples of metamorphic rock include quartz (converted sandstone), marble (converted limestone), and slate.

The most popular metamorphic stones used in construction are slate and marble. Slate is utilized in roofs, exterior walls, and for paving. Marble can be carved and is available in black, white, and several other colors. It is often used for flooring, exterior walls, as finish on interior walls, and for decorative items such as counter and cabinet tops.

Uses of Stone

Because of its unique appearance, strength, and durability, stone is widely used as a structural and decorative material in the construction industry. Stone in small random sizes and shapes (called **rubble** or **fieldstone**) can be purchased by the ton and installed dry or with mortar to create small retaining or freestanding walls. Fieldstone may be split to provide pieces suitable for use on exterior walls or fireplaces.

Decorative stone can be purchased in irregular 4″ thick pieces ranging in lengths from 6″ to 14″ and heights from 2″ to 16″. These pieces may be used layered in courses for a face **veneer** over a back-up wall. The method of assembling the stone and mortar in the veneer creates different bond patterns such as random, coursed, uncoursed, squared, and spider web. Examples of stone veneer bond patterns appear in Figure 7.20.

Stones with sawn edges produce rectangular faces. Known as ashlar, these stones can be used as a veneer, arranged in either a regular or random-coursed pattern.

Large stone slabs can be installed as decorative panels on the exterior of commercial buildings. These are available in widths of up to five feet and five inches thick. Examples of stone panels anchored with steel frame with block back-up are shown in Figure 7.21.

These panels are independently hung from the building without the use of mortar. The method for anchoring and supporting stone panels depends on the size of the panel, its weight, and the structural system to which it must be attached.

Stone must be purchased from a reputable quarry that guarantees the stone is uniform in color and texture, and free from defects. Installation is very critical as well; the contractor must create a smooth, aligned surface with consistent joints that will be accepted by the architect or project designer.

Steel Structural steel is well-suited for framing, as it can be erected relatively quickly, particularly on buildings with repetitive framing systems. Steel is strong, flexible, and light in proportion to its strength when compared

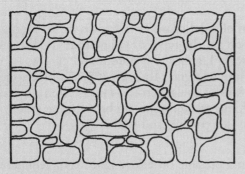

Rubble Stone—Random

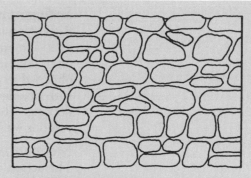

Rubble Stone—Coursed

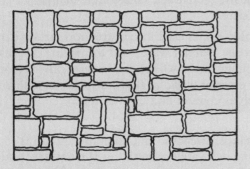

Ashlar Stone—Roughly Squared, Random

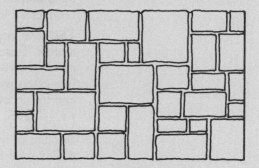

Ashlar Stone—Trimmed, Random

Ashlar Stone—Coursed, Narrow

Ashlar Stone—Coursed

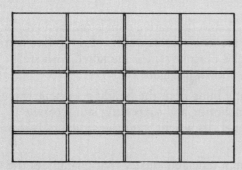

Ashlar Stone—Cut, Stacked Joints

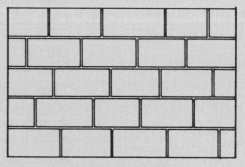

Ashlar Stone—Cut, Broken Joints

Types of Stone Veneers

Figure 7.20

with other materials. Steel does have a tendency to corrode over the years in certain environments and may lose strength when subjected to extreme heat, as is experienced during severe fires. However, steel can be chemically treated to resist corrosion and can be enclosed with fireproofing material to minimize the impact of fire damage.

Steel is produced from three basic materials – iron ore, coal, and limestone. It is produced in several shapes that may be designed and constructed in unlimited combinations of columns, girders, beams, and other shapes. Standard rolled steel shapes are illustrated in Figure 7.22.

Fabrication

Structural steel must be fabricated in the appropriate shapes and lengths before it can be used to form a steel frame on a jobsite. Fabrication starts with detailing all of the beams, girders, and columns on drawings to agree with the structural engineer's design. These shop drawings are reviewed by the architect and then released for fabrication. Detailing involves: listing exact lengths and drawing angles of cuts; coping (cutting out) of flanges; sizing of connection angles; and locating the bolt holes and base plates that enable the steel structure to fit together precisely in

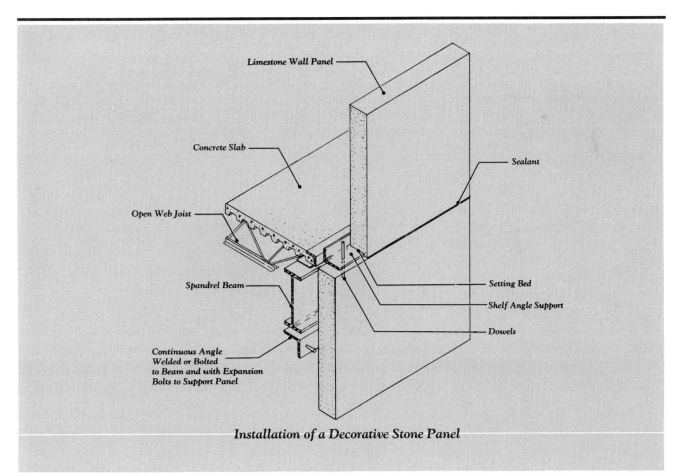

Installation of a Decorative Stone Panel

Figure 7.21

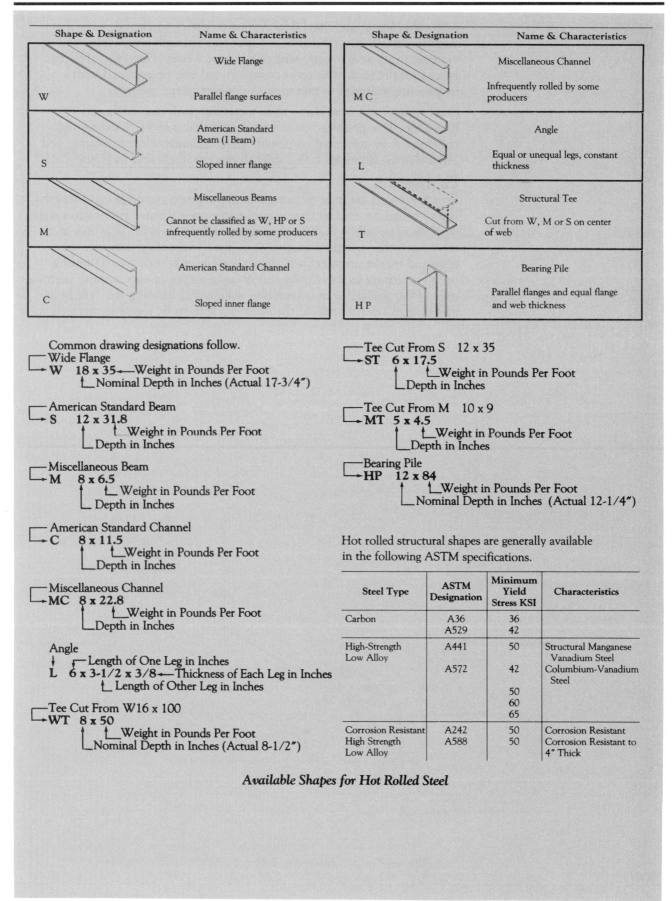

Shape & Designation	Name & Characteristics	Shape & Designation	Name & Characteristics
W	Wide Flange. Parallel flange surfaces	M C	Miscellaneous Channel. Infrequently rolled by some producers
S	American Standard Beam (I Beam). Sloped inner flange	L	Angle. Equal or unequal legs, constant thickness
M	Miscellaneous Beams. Cannot be classified as W, HP or S infrequently rolled by some producers	T	Structural Tee. Cut from W, M or S on center of web
C	American Standard Channel. Sloped inner flange	H P	Bearing Pile. Parallel flanges and equal flange and web thickness

Common drawing designations follow.

Wide Flange
W 18 x 35 ← Weight in Pounds Per Foot
         └ Nominal Depth in Inches (Actual 17-3/4″)

American Standard Beam
S 12 x 31.8
         ↑ Weight in Pounds Per Foot
         └ Depth in Inches

Miscellaneous Beam
M 8 x 6.5
         ↑ Weight in Pounds Per Foot
         └ Depth in Inches

American Standard Channel
C 8 x 11.5
         ↑ Weight in Pounds Per Foot
         └ Depth in Inches

Miscellaneous Channel
MC 8 x 22.8
         ↑ Weight in Pounds Per Foot
         └ Depth in Inches

Angle
   ┌ Length of One Leg in Inches
L 6 x 3-1/2 x 3/8 ← Thickness of Each Leg in Inches
         └ Length of Other Leg in Inches

Tee Cut From W16 x 100
WT 8 x 50
         ↑ Weight in Pounds Per Foot
         └ Nominal Depth in Inches (Actual 8-1/2″)

Tee Cut From S 12 x 35
ST 6 x 17.5
         ↑ Weight in Pounds Per Foot
         └ Depth in Inches

Tee Cut From M 10 x 9
MT 5 x 4.5
         ↑ Weight in Pounds Per Foot
         └ Depth in Inches

Bearing Pile
HP 12 x 84
         ↑ Weight in Pounds Per Foot
         └ Nominal Depth in Inches (Actual 12-1/4″)

Hot rolled structural shapes are generally available in the following ASTM specifications.

Steel Type	ASTM Designation	Minimum Yield Stress KSI	Characteristics
Carbon	A36	36	
	A529	42	
High-Strength Low Alloy	A441	50	Structural Manganese Vanadium Steel
	A572	42	Columbium-Vanadium Steel
		50	
		60	
		65	
Corrosion Resistant High Strength Low Alloy	A242	50	Corrosion Resistant
	A588	50	Corrosion Resistant to 4″ Thick

Available Shapes for Hot Rolled Steel

Figure 7.22

the field. It can take months to produce drawings and manufacture the steel. For this reason, the structural steel system should be ordered as early as possible.

The erection process usually includes: unloading, shake out or spreading, sequencing pieces, hoisting or raising (usually accomplished with a crane), connecting, plumbing and bolting or welding.

Common Uses of Steel

Steel has many uses in the construction industry. The following are some of the most common uses. Steel is used to carry the vertical and horizontal building loads to the foundation. For example, columns, beams, and girders (illustrated in Figure 7.23). Steel floor deck supports the elevated concrete slab. Composite steel floor deck is interlocked into the fill slab to act similar to reinforcing steel and span greater distances. Cellular steel decks are covered with a second sheet of steel which forms longitudinal cells in which utility lines can be run. Steel deck construction is shown in Figure 7.24.

Steel is also used for open-web joists and joist girders which are lightweight, economical, high strength parallel chord members suitable for the support of floors and roof decks. Open-web joists are usually manufactured in three classifications:

- H series – spans of 8 feet to 60 feet and depths of 8 inches to 30 inches

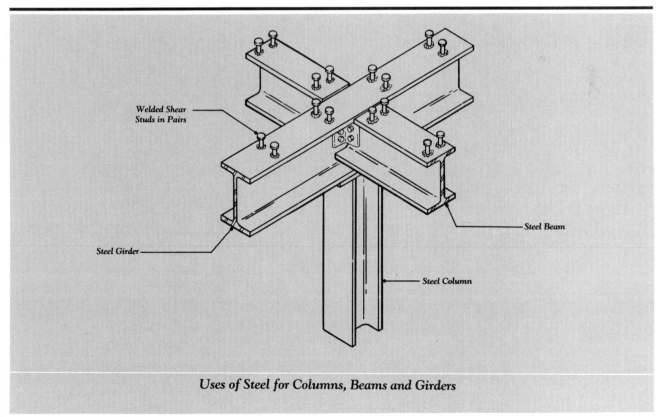

Uses of Steel for Columns, Beams and Girders

Figure 7.23

- LH series – spans of 25' to 96' and depths of 18" to 48"
- DLH series – spans of 89' to 144' and depths of 52" to 72"

H and LH series of joists are suitable for supporting floor and roof decks. When a joist is designated as 18 H 7, it means that it is 18 inches deep, H series, and a chord size of 7. DLH series of joists are suitable for supporting roof decks only. Examples of standard joist details are provided in Figure 7.25.

Structural steel is generally considered as a primary framing system, but often there is a need for secondary framing systems in buildings to carry wind or material loads to the primary members. For example, horizontal girts may be used to carry wind loads to the columns and have intermediate supports called tie rods. Other secondary systems are wind bracing, canopy of signified framing, and ceiling framing.

Steel is also used for roof decking, which has several advantages over other materials. Steel is light, covers a large area, and can be installed very quickly. Steel roof decking is illustrated in Figure 7.24. All steel deck must be spot welded to the structure to fix it permanently in place and is either galvanized or painted to prevent rusting.

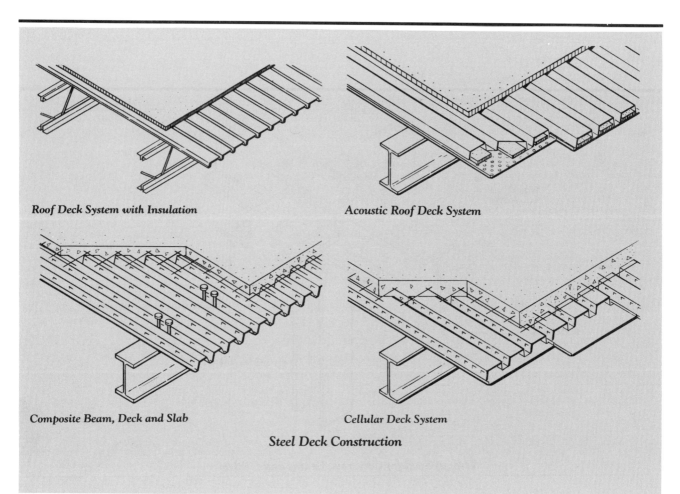

Roof Deck System with Insulation

Acoustic Roof Deck System

Composite Beam, Deck and Slab

Cellular Deck System

Steel Deck Construction

Figure 7.24

Pre-Engineered Buildings

Pre-engineered steel buildings are manufactured by several competitive firms and erected on the chosen site by franchised dealers. The term pre-engineered means that the entire building is designed and fabricated by the same company and includes exterior walls and roof systems, as well as structural framing. These structures are usually single story, relatively low in cost, and are used extensively for industrial, commercial, institutional, and recreational facilities. There are four basic types of steel pre-engineered buildings. They are: **rigid frame**, **truss type**, **post and beam**, and **sloped beam**. An example of a pre-engineered slope beam construction is shown in Figure 7.26.

Roofs and sidewalls of steel pre-engineered buildings are usually covered with steel siding, with several insulation options or factory assembled sandwich panels. A full range of add-on components are available to adapt the steel shell to a customer's needs, including entrance canopies, automatic doors, windows, exterior louvers, and overhead doors.

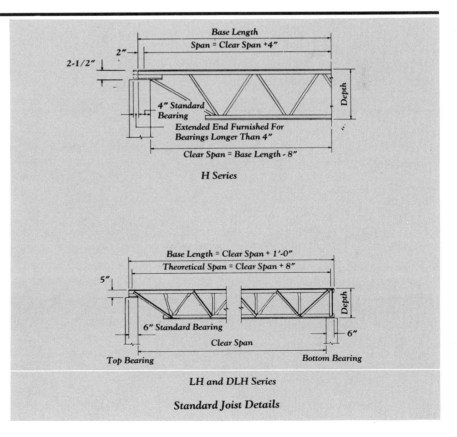

H Series

LH and DLH Series

Standard Joist Details

Figure 7.25

Piping and Tubing

Steel piping and tubing is available in standard, extra strong, and double extra strong weights. In addition, square and rectangular tubing is available in various sizes and wall thicknesses. Examples of steel pipe and tubing are shown in Figure 7.27.

Steel shapes are also used to fabricate miscellaneous items used in buildings such as stairs, platforms, door frames, ladders, and railings.

Summary

Four basic construction materials – wood, concrete, masonry, and steel – were described in this chapter in order to provide an overview of the basic methods of constructing buildings. Working knowledge of each material is not necessary to comprehend the construction process, but a basic understanding of these materials and how they are used in building is essential to comprehending an overall view of the construction process.

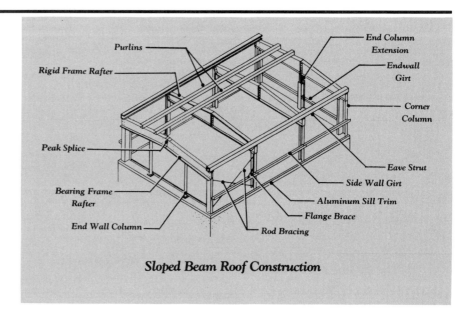

Sloped Beam Roof Construction

Figure 7.26

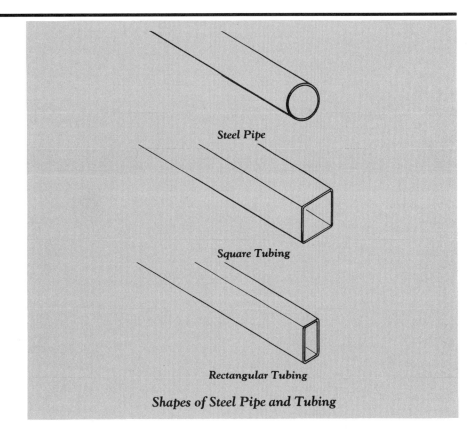

Steel Pipe

Square Tubing

Rectangular Tubing

Shapes of Steel Pipe and Tubing

Figure 7.27

Chapter Eight

Substructure

The substructure is the portion of a building that is at ground level, and below, and transfers structural loads from a building safely into the supporting soil.

The scope of work associated with the substructure portion of a building depends on the ability of the soil at the site to support the building, and the size of the building loads. The substructure, for most buildings, consists of a slab-on-grade, and a foundation.

Slab-On-Grade

A concrete floor placed directly on the ground is known as a slab-on-grade. The slab is placed on compacted granular fill such as gravel or crushed stone. The stone, in turn, is covered with sheets of polyethylene, commonly known in the industry as "visqueen." Polyethylene acts as a vapor barrier to prevent moisture or vapor in the ground from passing into the slab and eventually to the floor above. Slab-on-grade is illustrated in Figure 8.1.

The thickness of the slab depends primarily on the loads acting on the floor, and secondarily on the bearing capacity of the subsoil upon which it is placed.

A concrete slab-on-grade most often is reinforced with welded steel wire fabric – often referred to as "wire mesh." If heavier reinforcement is required, it consists of one or two layers of reinforcing bars, each running both ways (right angles to each other). Any reinforcing, light or heavy, must have adequate concrete coverage to bond it to the concrete and protect it from corrosion. Supports or "chairs" placed at intervals serve as supports until the concrete cures.

Concrete slabs are subject to cracking, as shrinkage occurs during the curing process. Cracking is controlled through the use of joints in the slab and examples of four types of joints are illustrated in Figure 8.2.

Isolation joints occur at the perimeter of the slab and where there are openings to allow for columns. It is a full thickness joint filled with a compressible material that allows the slab to move independently of the wall or column.

Construction joints occur in the slab because of the limits placed on the size of the pour (to control shrinkage). These are also full thickness and are bounded by removable or permanent forms. Where differential (vertical) settlement is anticipated across the joint, dowels can be inserted.

A **control joint**, or **contraction joint**, is a sawed, tooled, or formed groove in the top part of a concrete slab. Its main purpose is to create a weakened plane, thereby predetermining and regulating the location of natural cracking caused by shrinkage as the concrete cures.

An **expansion joint** is generally used to isolate two structurally independent portions of a building, such as a low rise wing adjacent to a high rise tower. The joint is formed with the slab and, once set, filled with an elastomeric material.

The Foundation

Foundations transfer many kinds of loads from a building to the earth below. These include: **dead and live loads, wind loads and earthquake loads.** The dead load is the total weight of the entire building – the structural frame, walls, floors, roof, and foundation. Live load is the combined weight of people, furniture, furnishings, equipment, and any other items expected to occupy the building, as well as the weight of any snow that may accumulate on the roof. Columns carry the dead and live loads down to the foundation.

The structure carries wind and earthquake loads to the foundations by additional strengthening of the columns or by the introduction of stiffening walls into the structure, usually at stairwells or elevator shafts.

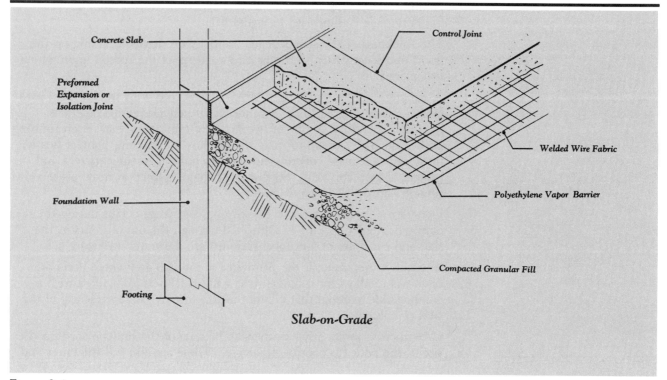

Slab-on-Grade

Figure 8.1

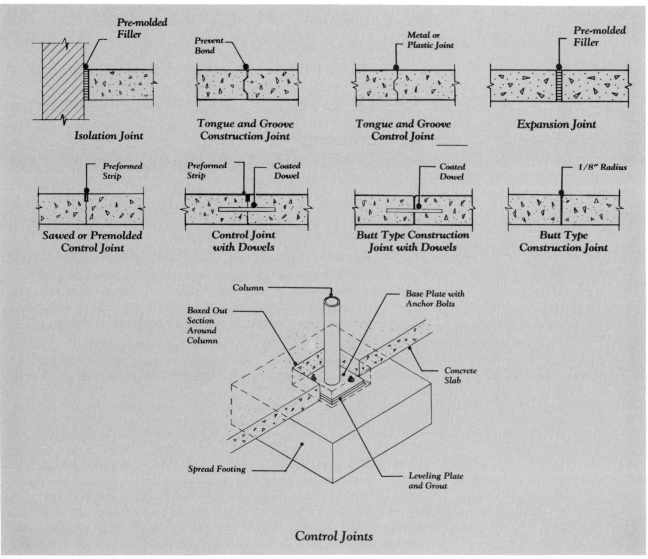

Isolation Joint — Pre-molded Filler

Tongue and Groove Construction Joint — Prevent Bond

Tongue and Groove Control Joint — Metal or Plastic Joint

Expansion Joint — Pre-molded Filler

Sawed or Premolded Control Joint — Preformed Strip

Control Joint with Dowels — Preformed Strip, Coated Dowel

Butt Type Construction Joint with Dowels — Coated Dowel

Butt Type Construction Joint — 1/8" Radius

Column
Boxed Out Section Around Column
Base Plate with Anchor Bolts
Concrete Slab
Spread Footing
Leveling Plate and Grout

Control Joints

Figure 8.2

There are two main types of foundations: **shallow** and **deep**. Shallow foundations for walls or columns are called footings, and transfer loads to the earth below provided they possess sufficient bearing capacity. Deep foundations transfer loads from columns to bedrock when the subgrade lacks sufficient bearing. Bedrock or soils with improved bearing are reached by driving piles or drilling caissons through upper layers of unstable soil.

Shallow Foundations

A footing is a type of foundation that spreads and transmits loads directly to the earth (soil). The weaker the bearing capacity of the soil, the wider the footing must be. Footings are usually cast-in-place concrete. Concrete may be placed by pumping, direct chute, buggies, wheelbarrows, or a crane and bucket. When access permits, the most economical method is the direct chute method.

Under favorable soil conditions, the sides of the excavation can hold a vertical slope, and formwork is not necessary. This is known as **neat excavation** or "excavating to neat lines." However, formwork is required where there is an angle of repose (sloped sides) or the footing is shaped irregularly. In most cases, formwork is required and the excavation is extended to provide working space.

The two most common types of shallow footings are: **spread footings**, and **strip footings**. The important characteristics of each type are discussed below.

Spread Footings

Spread footings are used to distribute column loads to the soil. These are common types of footings because columns are often used to carry building loads. Common configurations of spread footings are rectangular or square. They may be used to support single or multiple column loads. The size of spread footings is governed by the load and the bearing capacity of the soil. Pads, isolated footings, or pier footings are some alternate names for spread footings. Spread footings may be formed with dimension lumber and/or prefabricated plywood. Figure 8.3 illustrates the formwork used to create spread footings with dimension lumber.

Strip Footings

Under walls of concrete, block, brick, or stone, strip footings distribute loads evenly to the supporting soil. Strip footings also act as a levelling pad to facilitate the erection of formwork for the walls. Strip footings are also referred to as **continuous footings** or **wall footings**. An example of strip footing formwork is shown in Figure 8.4.

The bottom of a strip footing is placed on undisturbed soil – usually 12 inches below the deepest frost penetration. The sides may be formed with either dimension lumber or prefabricated panels. Strip footings may have temperature reinforcement running longitudinally. Reinforcing bars may be needed laterally when the width of the footing increases. When reinforced, strip footings should have a minimum of six inches of concrete above the reinforcing. When not reinforced, the footings should be at least eight inches thick.

Structures are commonly built on sloping terrain, or designed with differences in the top of footing elevations. To accommodate such transitions, steps are required in strip footings. Figure 8.5 illustrates a typical stepped footing.

Step footings are generally excavated by hand. Steps should measure at least two feet horizontally, and each vertical step should measure no greater than three-quarters of the horizontal distance between the steps. Vertical risers should be at least six inches thick, and match the footing's width. In comparison to strip and spread footings, stepped footings are time-consuming and costly to construct.

Foundation Walls

Cast-in-place concrete or concrete block are most often used to construct foundation walls. Height and thickness of the walls depends on the height of backfill the wall must retain, the depth of frost penetration, and whether there is a full basement below grade. Plywood forms, steel concrete forming systems, or a combination of the two are typical methods of forming foundation walls. Examples of the two methods are shown in Figure 8.6.

Although there are several methods for erecting foundation wall formwork, the process can be broken down into the following four sequential steps.

1. Build the formwork for one side of the wall.
2. Tie the steel into the wall or place the reinforcing.
3. Form the opposite side wall.
4. Align, adjust, and straighten the entire forming system prior to placing the concrete.

Grade Beams

Grade beams are used to carry loads to the spread footings. Grade beams are economical where there are heavy column loads and light wall loads,

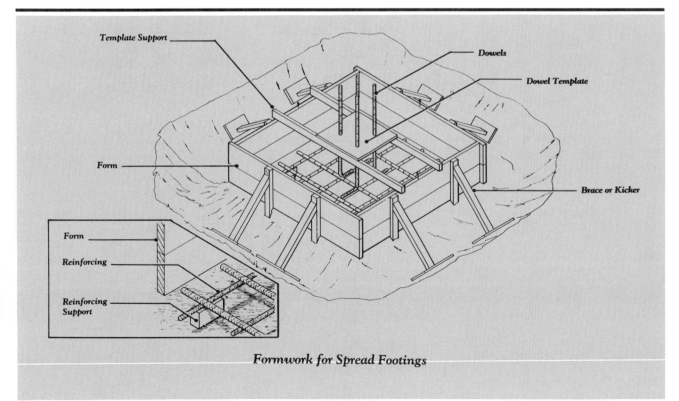

Formwork for Spread Footings

Figure 8.3

in comparison to the cost of other foundation systems. Typical grade beam construction is illustrated in Figure 8.7.

Waterproofing

Ground water must be prevented from seeping through a foundation wall. The foundation wall is waterproofed and, if necessary, underdrains – drain pipes below the slab-on-grade and near the footings – are installed, as shown in Figure 8.8.

The foundation wall is waterproofed by applying a protective coating to the exterior surface, bituminous coating, troweled onto the wall, applied

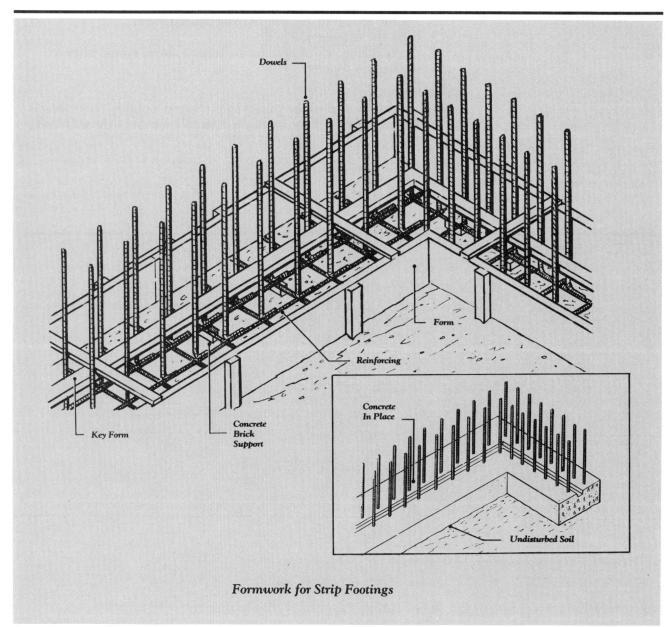

Formwork for Strip Footings

Figure 8.4

by brush, or sprayed on. Other materials used for waterproofing include asphalt protective board, mastic, or a waterproofing membrane.

The underdrain pipes are usually porous and have openings to facilitate the collection of water. Asphalt-coated corrugated metal, porous concrete, vitrified clay, or Polyvinyl Chloride (PVC) pipes are commonly used.

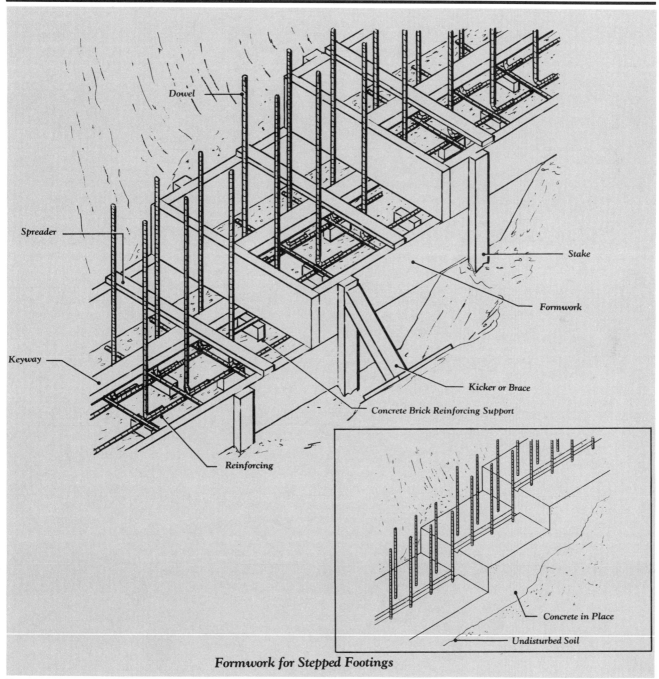

Formwork for Stepped Footings

Figure 8.5

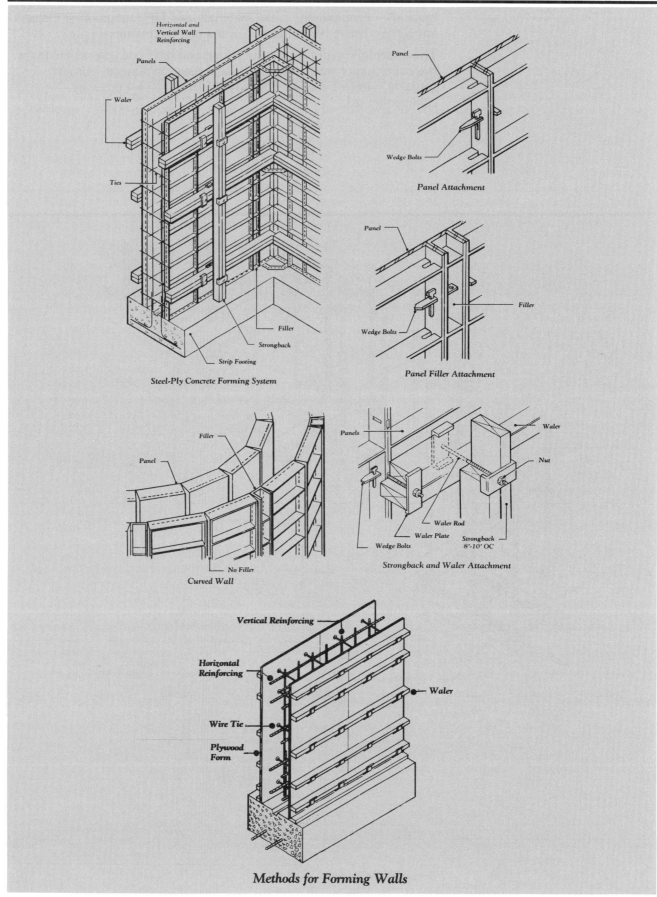

Horizontal and Vertical Wall Reinforcing

Panels

Waler

Ties

Filler

Strongback

Strip Footing

Steel-Ply Concrete Forming System

Panel

Wedge Bolts

Panel Attachment

Panel

Wedge Bolts

Filler

Panel Filler Attachment

Filler

Panel

No Filler

Curved Wall

Panels

Waler

Nut

Waler Rod

Waler Plate

Wedge Bolts

Strongback 8'-10' OC

Strongback and Waler Attachment

Vertical Reinforcing

Horizontal Reinforcing

Waler

Wire Tie

Plywood Form

Methods for Forming Walls

Figure 8.6

Coarse rock or gravel surrounds the pipes to create a channel of least resistance within the fill material. Of course, the pipes should be laid with sufficient slope to give the water adequate velocity to the discharge area.

Deep Foundations

The two most commonly used types of deep foundations are **piles** and **caissons**. A pile is a wood, steel, concrete, or composite shaft driven into place, while a caisson is a large shaft that is drilled into place, and filled with concrete.

Piles

A pile is a column made of timber, concrete, or steel. The pile is driven into the ground to transfer loads from the pile cap through poor soil layers to deeper stable soil (with adequate strength and acceptable settlement) or rock.

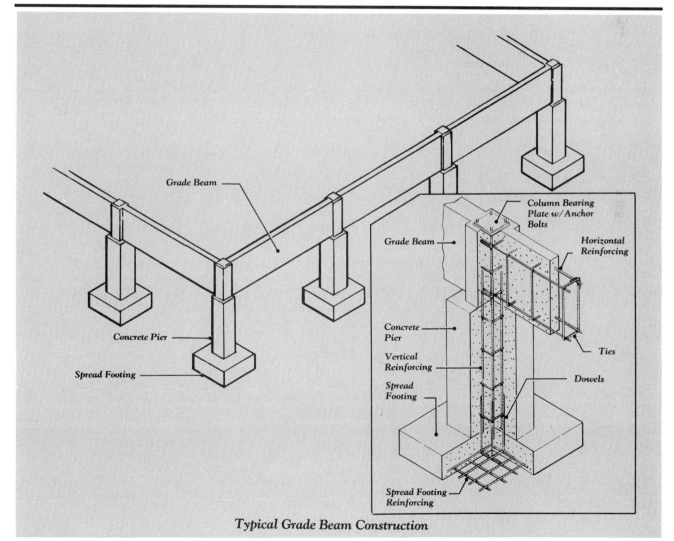

Typical Grade Beam Construction

Figure 8.7

There are two major types of piles: **end-bearing piles** and **friction piles**. End-bearing piles are driven through unstable soil to reach bedrock. Friction piles are driven far enough into cohesive soil to develop load support through "skin friction," between the soil and the outside surface of the pile.

Piles are driven into the ground by a **pile driver**. This is a crane with an attachment known as a **pile hammer**, that consists of weights lifted and then dropped or driven onto the pile head. The load capacity of a single pile is small compared to the loads delivered by the columns to the foundations, so piles are commonly installed in clusters. Pile clusters are capped with a concrete footing known as a **pile cap**, or slab, to evenly distribute loads to the individual piles as illustrated in Figure 8.9.

Piles are usually installed vertically, but occasionally they are installed at a slight angle. Piles installed at an angle are referred to as **battered**.

As previously stated, piles can be made from concrete (cast-in-place or precast), steel (H-pile or pipe pile), or timber. Each type is described below.

Concrete Piles: The first operation for a cast-in-place concrete pile is to drive a cylindrical steel shell with a **mandrel** until it reaches the specified

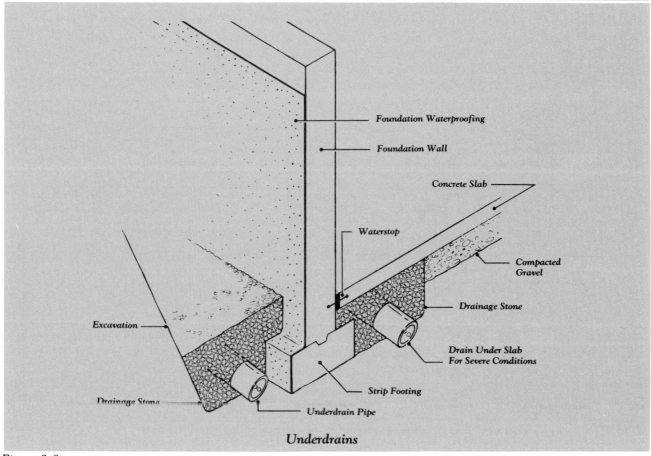

Figure 8.8

152

capacity or location. A mandrel is a heavy metal tube inserted into hollow piles that allows them to be driven. The mandrel absorbs most of the impact and energy of the pile driver. The mandrel is then withdrawn, the shell inspected and, finally, is filled with concrete and reinforcing. Cast-in-place concrete piles may be treated for use in sea water, and can be easily altered in length.

Precast concrete piles are cast at a plant to a specified length and transported by trucks to the job site. They may be reinforced or post-tensioned. Post-tensioning is a method of increasing the strength of concrete by stressing tendons after the concrete has hardened. Like cast-in-place piles, they may be treated for use in sea water, but it is difficult and expensive to alter the lengths of such piles. In addition, precast concrete piles require heavy equipment for handling (unloading from trucks, lifting, etc.) and driving.

Examples of cast-in-place and precast concrete piles are shown in Figure 8.10.

Steel Piles: Steel piles are strong and can withstand rough treatment. However, in some soil conditions, corrosion may be a problem. The two basic types of steel piles are **steel HP piles** and **steel pipe piles.**

Steel HP sections are hot-rolled wide flange members made for use in pile foundations. HP piles are seldom used as friction piles. Most often, they are used as end-bearing piles where long lengths of piles are required to be driven to refusal. HP piles can be brought to the site in convenient lengths and easily spliced as driving progresses, and withstand rough handling and driving conditions.

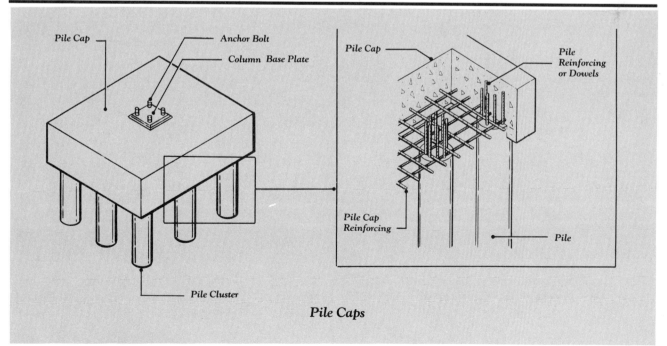

Pile Caps

Figure 8.9

153

Steel pipe piles, also known as **composite piles**, are driven to a specified elevation and then filled with concrete. Steel pipe piles, like HP piles, are flexurally strong and can be easily cut or spliced. They can withstand rough handling and driving conditions and may be driven with a standard hammer without a mandrel.

Examples of steel HP piles and pipe piles, with the necessary accessories, are shown in Figure 8.11.

Timber Piles: Timber piles are known for their relatively low cost and ease of handling. They are best suited under lightly loaded conditions, where driving is through soft strata. These piles can also be pressure-treated with creosote to prevent decay, although generally they are cut-off below the level of the water table to avoid the problem of decay.

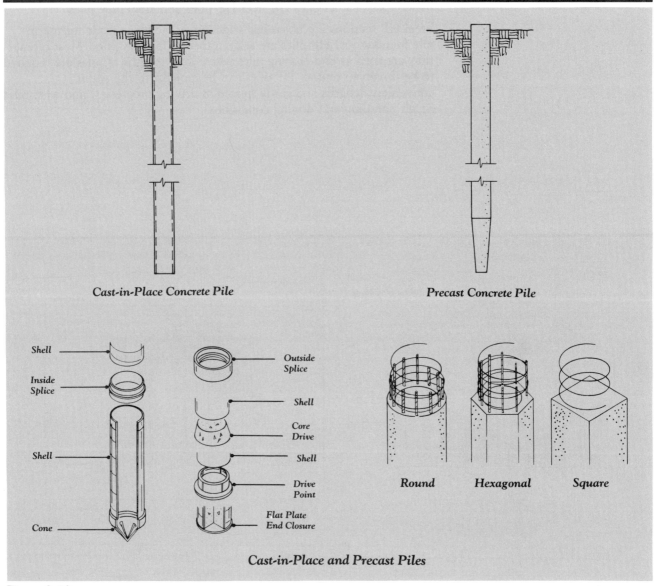

Cast-in-Place Concrete Pile

Precast Concrete Pile

Shell

Inside Splice

Shell

Cone

Outside Splice

Shell

Core Drive

Shell

Drive Point

Flat Plate End Closure

Round   **Hexagonal**   **Square**

Cast-in-Place and Precast Piles

Figure 8.10

154

Soil conditions are critical, however, as timber piles cannot withstand punishing driving through hard strata, rock, or boulders. Other driving limitations are that relatively small hammers must be used and timbers cannot be readily spliced. An illustration of a timber pile is shown in Figure 8.12.

Caissons

Placing concrete into a deep drilled hole at least two feet in diameter creates a columnar foundation known as a caisson. This construction functions as a compression member and transfers building loads through the unstable soil to bedrock or stable hard stratum. The advantage of using a caisson over a pile is that there is no soil heaving, displacement vibration, or noise during installation, and the underlying bedrock can

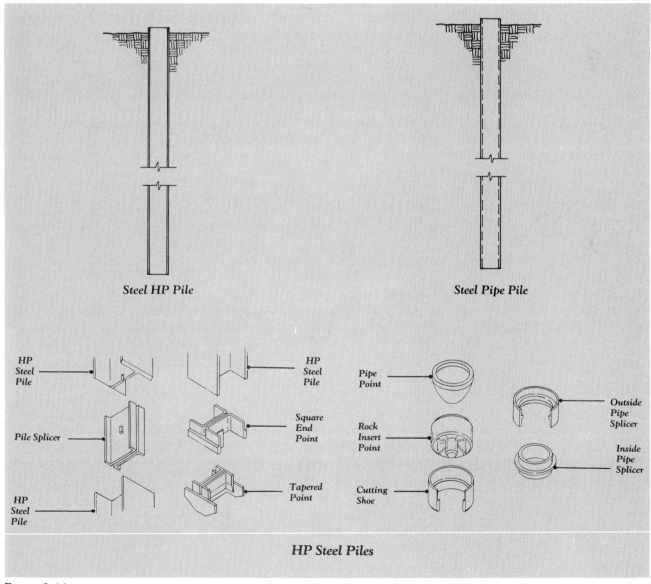

Figure 8.11

be visually inspected. Caissons are either reinforced or unreinforced, and either straight or belled out at the bearing level as illustrated in Figure 8.13.

There are three basic types of caissons: **belled caissons, straight caissons**, and **socketed** (or **keyed**) caissons.

Caissons are belled at the lower end to distribute the building load over a greater area and thus have a reduced bearing pressure on the soil. They should only be used in soils such as clays, hardpan, gravel, silt, and

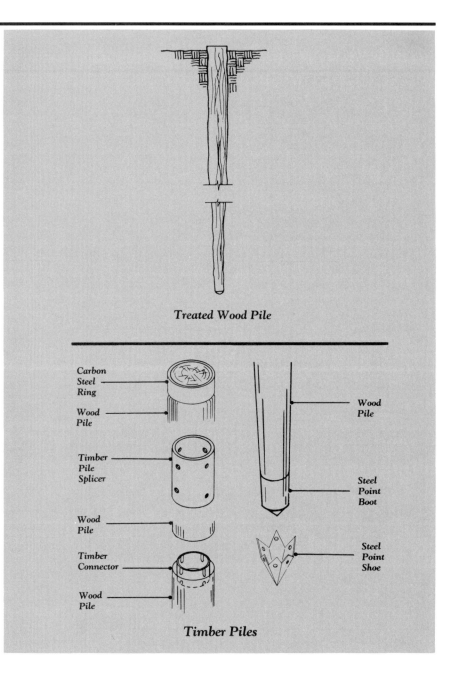

Treated Wood Pile

Carbon Steel Ring

Wood Pile

Timber Pile Splicer

Wood Pile

Timber Connector

Wood Pile

Wood Pile

Steel Point Boot

Steel Point Shoe

Timber Piles

Figure 8.12

igneous rock, and are not recommended for shallow depths or poor soils. Steel casings line the drilled shaft for caissons used in weaker soils.

Typical caissons may have a straight shaft when the supporting strata provides sufficient bearing for the end area.

Socketed caissons are used for extremely heavy loads. Installation of these piles involves sinking the shaft into rock to produce combined friction and bearing support action.

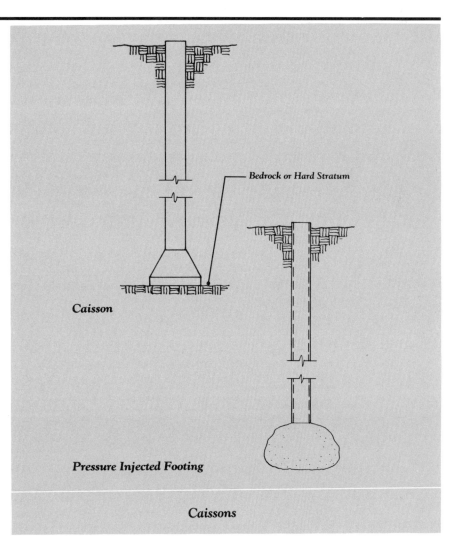

Caisson

Bedrock or Hard Stratum

Pressure Injected Footing

Caissons

Figure 8.13

Pressure Injected Footings

Pressure-injected footings or bulb end piles are placed in the same way as cast-in-place concrete piles, but differ in that a plug of uncured concrete is driven through the casing to form a bulb in the surrounding earth at the base of the pile. The bulb forms a footing with the pile acting as a column or pier. Piles of 25′ or less may have the casing withdrawn, but those of 25′ or more are usually cased with metal shells.

Chapter Nine
Superstructure

The superstructure extends above the substructure and is made up of various load-carrying (structural) systems of a building such as columns, beams, and trusses. The assembly of structural elements in the superstructure is known as framing. Materials and framing methods for constructing the superstructure of a building are described in this chapter.

Basic Materials

The superstructure is constructed from steel, reinforced concrete, masonry, or wood. **Steel superstructures** are an assembly of steel beams, girders or trusses, and columns. Steel framing is utilized in all types of buildings except residences, where it is limited to pipe columns and sometimes beams. **Reinforced concrete superstructures** utilize concrete slabs, beams, girders, columns, and/or walls to carry the loads. Like steel, concrete is rarely used in residential superstructures. Concrete is more commonly found on structures such as hotels, office buildings, warehouses, schools, industrial buildings, and apartment complexes. **Wood frame construction** is commonly used in the superstructure of single family residences and apartments, and sometimes for other commercial buildings. This type of framing uses wood joists, beams, stud walls, and sometimes trusses as structural elements. Finally, the only load-carrying systems identified with **masonry construction** are (bearing) walls and sometimes columns. Combinations of wood studs and bricks (known as **brick veneer**) may also be used in the exterior walls of residential units.

Steel Frame Construction

Although reinforced concrete is presently used to construct many tall buildings, structural steel is used exclusively for buildings over fifty stories high. Versatility of design – the potential for unlimited combinations of columns, beams, girders, and miscellaneous shapes – and the high strength of steel in comparison to other structural materials make steel a good choice for high rise buildings.

Fabrication
Steel is shop-fabricated to conform with **shop drawings** developed from a set of **structural drawings**. Structural drawings are prepared by the structural engineer to show the layout, elevation, and sizes of all the steel members that constitute the frame. These drawings, however, do not give the exact length of the members, clearances required, or details

of how they are connected or fastened to each other – necessary for assembly on the site. For this purpose, the fabricator develops a set of shop drawings. An example of a structural drawing for one floor of a multi-story building is illustrated in Figure 9.1. Most of the framing is repetitive except for the two bays in the middle of the framing plan, which are designed to admit openings for mechanical shafts, elevators, and stairways.

Subcontractors who are specialists in steel construction usually perform this portion of a project. Some general contractors subcontract one company to perform both the fabrication and the erection of the steel. In other cases, firms will use two separate companies – one for fabrication and one for erection.

The fabricator submits steel shop drawings to the contractor, showing the exact dimensions of each piece of steel, details of how the various pieces will be connected to one another, to guide assembly of the framing system. After steel shop drawings are prepared by the fabricator, it is customary to submit the drawings (through the general contractor) to the architect/engineer for review and approval. This is to ensure that they (the shop drawings) are in accordance with the contract drawings and meet the intentions of the structural design team. After the approval of the shop drawings, revisions are made where necessary prior to fabrication. When fabricated, each piece is either stenciled or painted with a code indicating exactly where it belongs in the building. Each piece is then inspected to ensure that the quality, and dimensions, conform to the shop drawings and the contract plans and specifications; and that they are painted and organized in piles according to the order in which they will be shipped to the job site. It is the fabricator's responsibility to deliver the various components of the structural steel framing to the construction site in such condition that they can be assembled without additional processing or fabrication.

Once the components are delivered to the site, the work of the fabricator ends and that of the erector begins. The task of unloading the steel at the site may be performed by the general contractor or the subcontractor hired for the erection, depending on the stipulations in the subcontract agreement. Most subcontracts require the erector to unload the steel from the delivery trucks, because it has three major advantages: it permits the erector to check the delivery to ensure that all the pieces on the material list are there and that the sizes and dimensions are correct; it permits the steel to be sorted out and stacked in the order in which they will be erected; and it also saves the general contractor the problem of renting a crane just to unload the steel. The steel erector has the responsibility of assembling the steel components furnished by the steel fabricator or supplier. This is accomplished by workers (known as **ironworkers** in the construction industry) who unload the steel with the help of a crane, sort the pieces according to the location in the building and the sequence of erection, and connect the various pieces together to form the frame of a building.

There are three common methods of connecting steel members. They are:

- Common bolting
- High strength bolting
- Welding

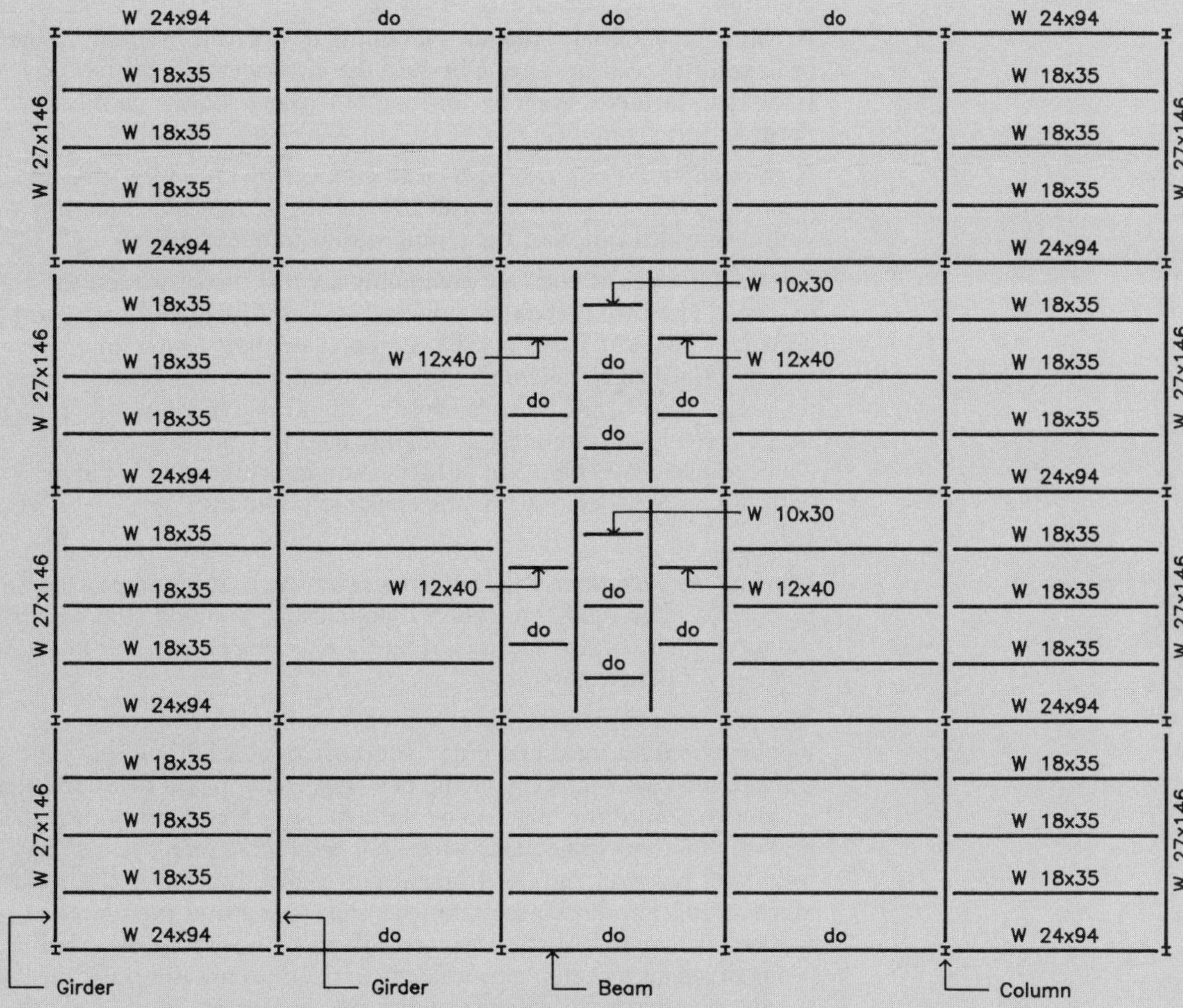

First Floor Structural Drawing of a
Multi-Story Building

Figure 9.1

Bolting

A bolt is an externally threaded fastening device with a round, square, or hexagonal head projecting beyond the circumference of the body (shank) to facilitate gripping, turning or striking. Bolted connections are illustrated in Figure 9.2.

High strength bolting can be used to connect two pieces of steel by inserting a bolt through pre-drilled holes in the members, securing it with a threaded nut, and tightening with a torque wrench.

Two major types of bolts are commonly used in the construction industry. They are **carbon steel bolts (ASTM A307)** and **high strength bolts (ASTM A325 and A490)**. Carbon steel bolts, sometimes also called unfinished or machine bolts, are usually used in secondary and temporary type connections because of their relatively low strength. High strength steel bolts are most commonly used in structural steel connections. A490 bolts are of higher strength than A325, but A325 bolts are more widely used in the construction industry.

Welding

Welding steel elements of a frame together, such as beams to columns, produces a more rigid connection than bolting. Welding is more labor-intensive than bolting and consequently more expensive, but may be required for design purposes.

The two main types of welds commonly used in the construction industry are **fillet weld** and **butt (or groove) weld.** Fillet welds are the quicker and easier to apply of the two, especially in the field, and require no preparation of the edges to be welded. They are used in most beam-to-column connections where clip angles are employed. Fillet welds are, however, not as strong as butt welds. Butt or groove welds are much stronger and are necessary when full strength of the pieces to be fastened is required, such as flange-to-flange connections on columns or beams. Examples of different welded connections are illustrated in Figure 9.3. Notice that the reference line carries the symbol of the weld and the arrow points to the weld.

Standard symbols for welded joints, as designated by the American Institute of Steel Construction (AISC), are shown in Figure 9.4. The field weld symbol in this figure is a more costly weld than the shop weld – the field weld must be accomplished with the member erected in place, as opposed to the controlled environment of the shop.

Welds (particularly those in the critical areas of a structure) must be thoroughly inspected and tested to ensure that there are no hidden defects below the surface. The three most common methods of testing welds are: **x-rays, ultrasonic tests** and the **magnetic particle test.**

In any type of weld, it is important to note that the quality of the weld depends to a large extent on the experience and qualifications of the welder. It is therefore recommended that the qualifications (certification, etc.) of welders be verified prior to the beginning of welding operations.

Cast-In-Place Concrete

Concrete structures are heavier than other types of structures, involve labor-intensive placement methods, are susceptible to variable weather conditions, and each component must be formed, poured, cured and the formwork stripped. On the other hand, concrete is versatile; it can be formed in many shapes and the exposed wall surfaces can be finished into several different types of textures.

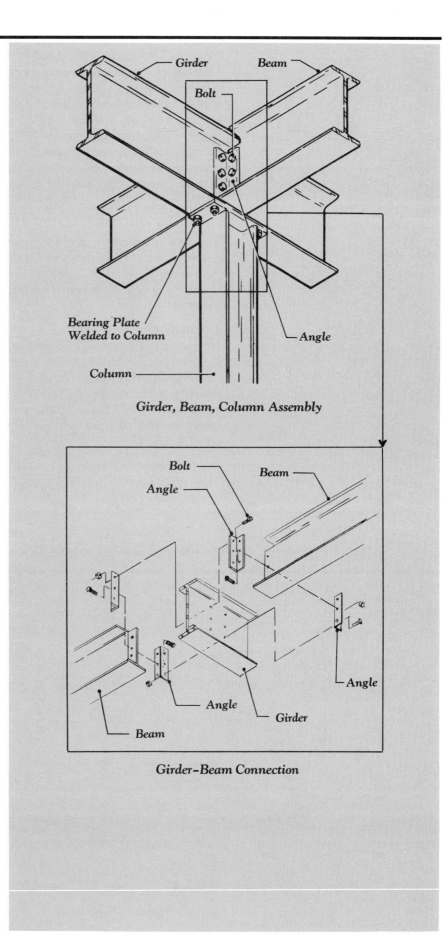

Girder, Beam, Column Assembly

Girder–Beam Connection

Figure 9.2

Concrete framing for the superstructure of a building is accomplished with either **cast-in-place concrete** (on-site) **or precast concrete.** Precast concrete is used for sections that can be prefabricated off-site. Cast-in-place concrete is selected only for fabrication of structural framing members that are too heavy to be transported from a precasting plant or when irregularities in shape and size of design cannot be accommodated in the precasting plant. Cast-in-place concrete is described in the following paragraphs of this section and precast concrete is treated in the next section of this chapter.

All cast-in-place concrete work involves the basic elements of formwork, reinforcing, concrete placement, curing and finishing.

The way in which the components relate to each other may vary for different types of structures and individual types of concrete work. Figure 9.5 illustrates the relationship and relative importance of the proportions of each concrete work component for a completely concrete-framed structure.

Formwork

Formwork is a temporary support or molding constructed to contain fresh concrete until it holds its own shape and reaches design strength. Formwork alone often accounts for about one third of the cost of overall concrete work (see Figure 9.5). For certain individual concrete framing systems where beams, columns, walls, and slabs are used, job-built formwork may even account for 50% to 60% or more of the total concrete costs.

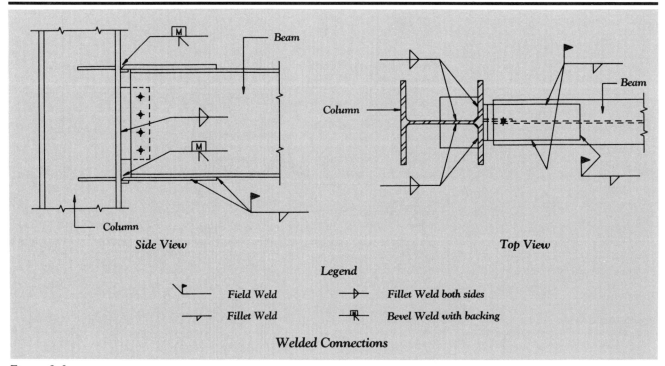

Figure 9.3

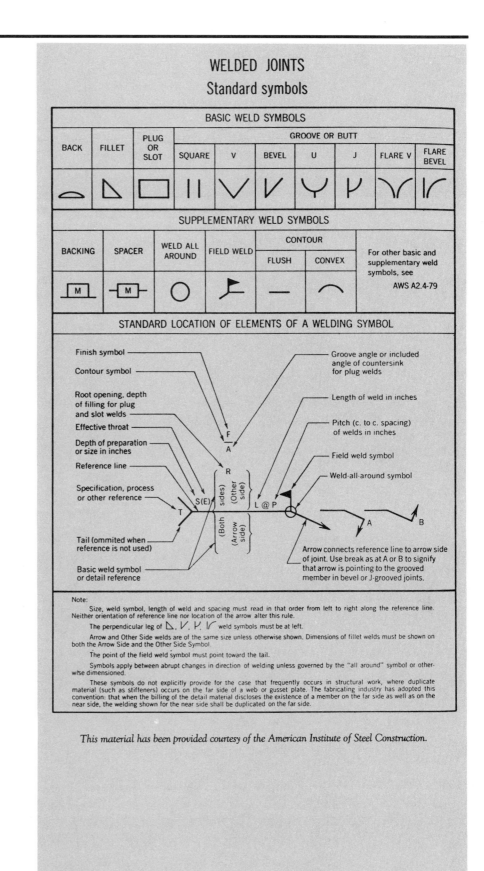

This material has been provided courtesy of the American Institute of Steel Construction.

Figure 9.4

Columns

Columns can be round, square, or rectangular. Forms for the three basic types of cast-in-place columns are illustrated in Figure 9.6.

The formwork for round columns can be made of wood or steel. However, in recent years, factory-made fibre forms and preformed casings made of laminated paper (known as sonotube) have become very popular. Unlike wood and steel forms, fibre forms and sonotubes cannot be reused.

Square and rectangular columns can be formed with wood or steel forms utilizing either bolt yokes (B in Figure 9.6) or adjustable clamps (C in Figure 9.6).

Concrete columns are subject to bending as well as axial stresses, and without reinforcing can easily crack. As a result, it is customary to reinforce concrete columns. Columns are usually found in the structural set of drawings and also may be listed in a schedule (shown in Figure 9.7).

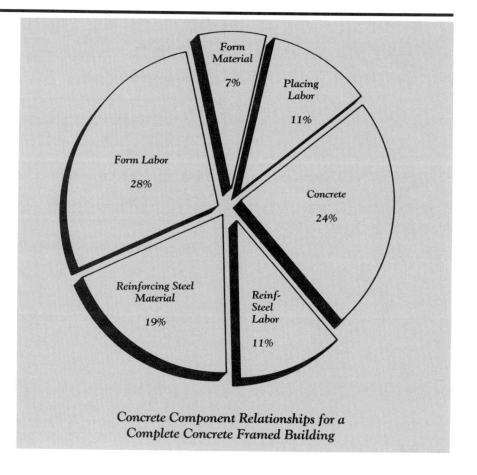

Concrete Component Relationships for a Complete Concrete Framed Building

Figure 9.5

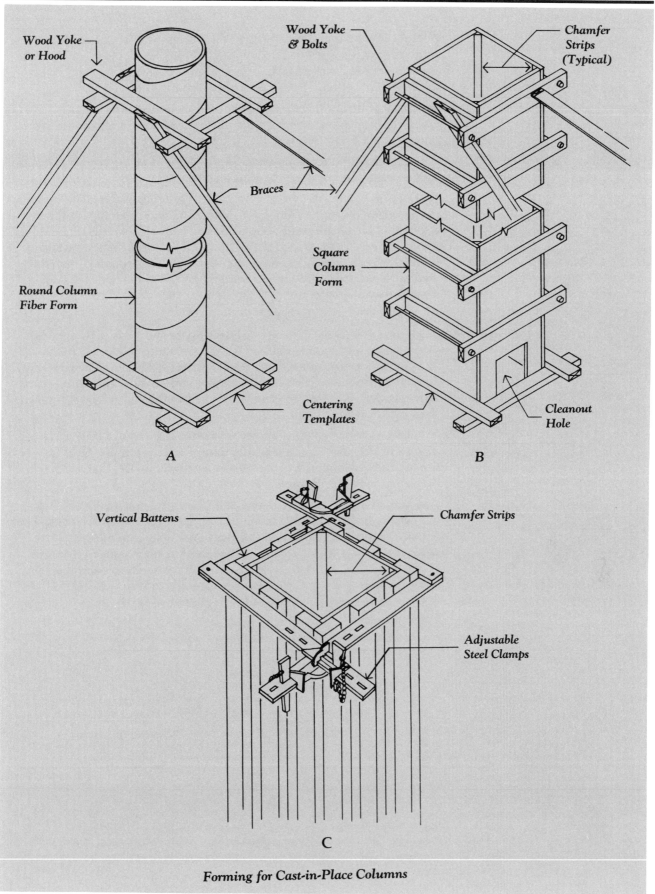

Wood Yoke or Hood

Wood Yoke & Bolts

Chamfer Strips (Typical)

Braces

Round Column Fiber Form

Square Column Form

Centering Templates

Cleanout Hole

A

B

Vertical Battens

Chamfer Strips

Adjustable Steel Clamps

C

Forming for Cast-in-Place Columns

Figure 9.6

Beams

A beam is a structural member spanning horizontally between columns or walls that is subject to bending from vertical loads. Normal beams carry floor loads, but exterior beams, known as spandrels, carry wall loads as well as floor loads and tie the floor together. Typical beam configurations are illustrated in Figure 9.8.

Concrete beams, like columns, are also found in the structural set of drawings and listed in a schedule (shown in Figure 9.9).

A reinforced concrete bond beam is often placed at the top of a masonry wall to strengthen and tie the wall together.

Beam formwork is one of the most expensive types of formwork because of the required shoring (supports), limited reuse of material, and time-consuming layout. Shoring equipment and material offer maximum reuses. However, the varied sizes of wood forms used for the sides and bottom of beams often have a single use. The most common materials used for beam forms are plywood and dimensional lumber, but steel forms are available as well.

Slabs

Suspended (elevated) concrete slabs for floors and roofs span between support members, unlike slabs-on-grade, and must be formed and shored (supported) on the bottom and sides. Formwork for elevated slabs may be fabricated with wood framing and plywood on-site, or with patented forming systems. There are several types of reinforced concrete suspended slabs based on this design.

One-way slabs are solid, reinforced cast-in-place slabs of uniform depth that carry the loads to the supports in one direction only. They may be single or multiple span and are usually supported by bearing walls or beams, as shown in Figure 9.10.

One-way concrete girders, beams and slabs are reinforced similar to one-way slabs and are solid monolithically (no joints) cast systems. They are an effective support system for heavy loads and are most effective when the span is under 20 feet. When used as floor systems, one-way concrete girders are relatively deep and the formwork is often complex and expensive. The materials usually consist of dimensional wood framing and plywood contact surfacing supported by shores or scaffolds (illustrated in Figure 9.11).

Column Schedule			
Ident.	No.	Size	Reinforcing
C-1	8	24″ x 24″ x 12′	8-#11 ties #4 @ 22″
C-2	12	20″ x 20″ x 12′	8-#9 ties #3 @ 18″
C-3	4	16″ x 16″ x 12′	8-#9 ties #3 @ 16″

Figure 9.7

Two-way concrete beams and slabs are solid slabs that are cast monolithically with support beams on columns, as shown in Figure 9.12. They are reinforced to carry the loads to the supports in two directions.

Two-way beams and slabs are more efficient for supporting heavy or concentrated loads than one-way slabs, and are most cost-effective when cast in bays that are less than 30 feet in span.

Flat concrete slabs with drop panels are solid slabs cast monolithically with a thickened area of concrete surrounding the column (known as a drop panel) where it (the column) meets the slab, as illustrated in Figure 9.13.

This type of slab is reinforced like a two-way slab, can sustain heavy loads, requires less concrete and reinforcing, requires smaller columns, and can be cast in bays with long spans.

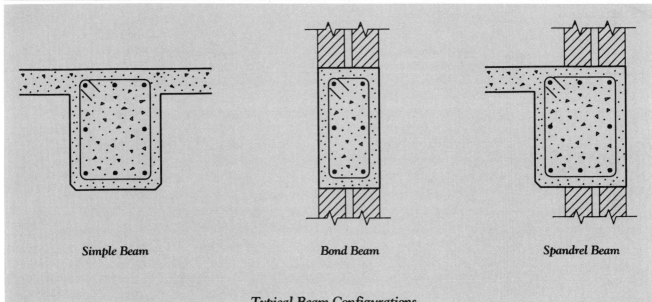

Simple Beam   Bond Beam   Spandrel Beam

Typical Beam Configurations

Figure 9.8

Beam Schedule			
Ident.	No.	Size	Reinforcing
B-1 Ext.	1	1' x 2'6" x 60"	See Re-Bar Schedule
B-2 Ext.	2	1" x 2'4" x 75'	
B-3 Ext.	2	8" x 1'6" x 60"	
B-4 Ext.	2	6" x 1'6" x 125"	

Figure 9.9

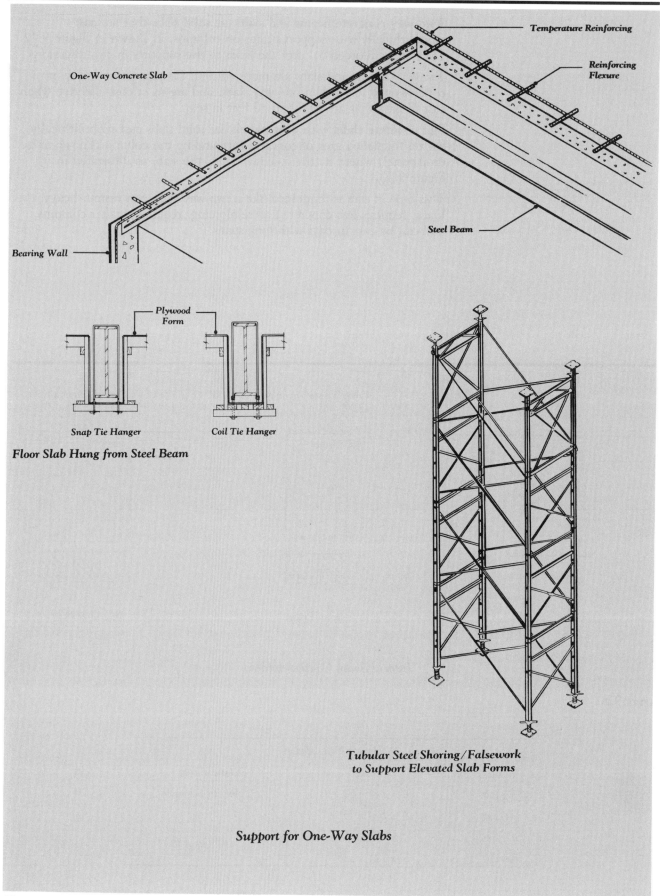

Temperature Reinforcing

Reinforcing Flexure

One-Way Concrete Slab

Steel Beam

Bearing Wall

Plywood Form

Snap Tie Hanger

Coil Tie Hanger

Floor Slab Hung from Steel Beam

**Tubular Steel Shoring/Falsework
to Support Elevated Slab Forms**

Support for One-Way Slabs

Figure 9.10

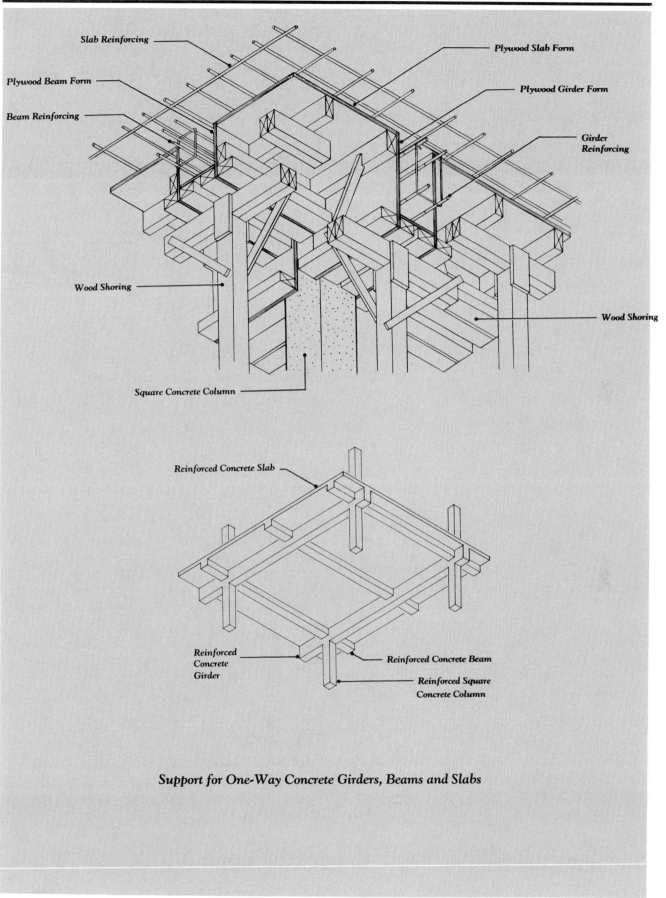

Slab Reinforcing

Plywood Beam Form

Beam Reinforcing

Plywood Slab Form

Plywood Girder Form

Girder Reinforcing

Wood Shoring

Wood Shoring

Square Concrete Column

Reinforced Concrete Slab

Reinforced Concrete Girder

Reinforced Concrete Beam

Reinforced Square Concrete Column

Support for One-Way Concrete Girders, Beams and Slabs

Figure 9.11

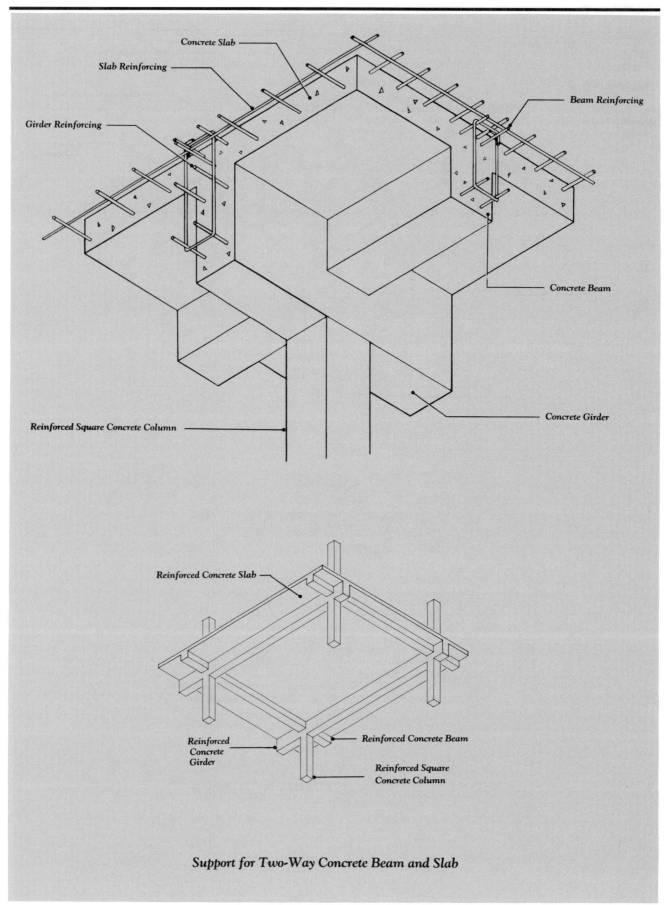

Concrete Slab

Slab Reinforcing

Girder Reinforcing

Beam Reinforcing

Concrete Beam

Concrete Girder

Reinforced Square Concrete Column

Reinforced Concrete Slab

Reinforced Concrete Girder

Reinforced Concrete Beam

Reinforced Square Concrete Column

Support for Two-Way Concrete Beam and Slab

Figure 9.12

Flat-plate concrete slabs are solid, uniform two-way slabs without drop panels or interior beams, as illustrated in Figure 9.14.

Flat-plate slabs are chosen for multi-story buildings with repetitive floors because: they provide designers flexibility in location of columns and openings through the slab, and provide contractors flexibility in the use of flying forms; are very economical and efficient when designed for moderate spans and to carry moderate uniform loads; and can provide savings by reducing the height of buildings when minimum floor depths are used.

One-way concrete joist slabs are monolithic combinations of concrete joists and thin slabs, as illustrated in Figure 9.15. Joists all span one way into beams.

The voids between the joists are created with prefabricated, void pan-shaped forms made out of metal, fiberglass, or paper.

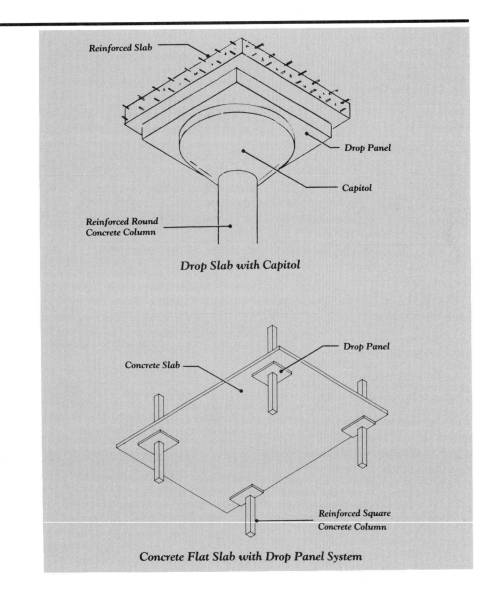

Drop Slab with Capitol

Concrete Flat Slab with Drop Panel System

Figure 9.13

One-way joist slabs are lighter in weight than one-way beams and slabs, and permit long spans. Concrete quantities for joist systems can be calculated using the table in Figure 9.16.

Volume of concrete for beams should be calculated separately and added to the figure obtained from Figure 9.16.

Concrete waffle slab construction consists of evenly-spaced joists at right angles to each other and integrated with a thin slab (illustrated in Figure 9.17). The joists are formed using standard square domes prefabricated from steel or fiberglass. Domes are omitted around the columns to form solid panels.

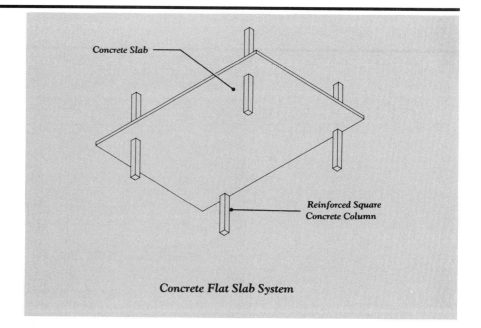

Concrete Flat Slab System

Figure 9.14

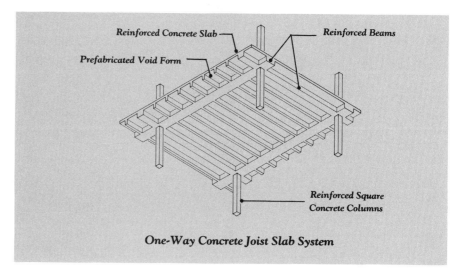

One-Way Concrete Joist Slab System

Figure 9.15

Standard domes come in two main sizes: 19 inches square, available in depths from 6 to 12 inches, and 30 inches square, available in depths from 8 to 20 inches.

Waffle slabs are considerably lighter (in weight) than solid flat-plate slabs. In addition, they can be used in longer spans and can sustain heavier superimposed loads.

Waffle slabs are aesthetically desirable for exposed ceilings because of the resulting geometrical shapes. The volume of concrete for waffle slabs is calculated by finding the total volume (as if there were no voids) from the top of the slab to the bottom of the pan, and then deducting the domes (voids). Volumes for standard domes are listed in Figure 9.18.

Flying Formwork

The high cost of supported slab formwork has led to the evolution of cost-competitive formwork systems. This is formwork for elevated slabs that is fabricated in large sections, supported on deep metal trusses, and moved from one floor to the next with a crane. This type of formwork eliminates much of the cost associated with the labor for stripping and erecting of forms.

Slipforms

This method of continuously moving wall forms is useful on circular structures (such as silos and multi-celled storage structures over 30 feet

Concrete Quantities (CF concrete/SF floor) for Single & Multiple Span Concrete Joist Construction

Depth (Rib/Slab)	Width					
	20" Forms			30" Forms		
	5" Rib 25" O.C.	6" Rib 26" O.C.	7" Rib 27" O.C.	5" Rib 35" O.C.	6" Rib 36" O.C.	7" Rib 37" O.C.
8"/3"	0.40	0.42	–	0.36	0.37	–
8"/4½"	0.53	0.55	–	0.48	0.50	–
10"/3"	0.45	0.47	–	0.39	0.41	–
10"4/½"	0.57	0.61	–	0.51	0.53	–
12"/3"	0.49	0.52	–	0.42	0.45	–
12"/4½"	0.62	0.65	–	0.55	0.57	–
14"/3"	0.54	0.57	–	0.45	0.48	–
14"/4½	0.66	0.69	–	0.58	0.61	–
16"/3"	–	0.63	0.66	–	0.52	0.55
16"/4½"	–	0.75	0.79	–	0.65	0.68
20"/3"	–	0.75	0.79	–	0.61	0.64
20"/4½"	–	0.87	0.91	–	0.74	0.77

Figure 9.16

high) as well as tall building core shear walls (such as elevator shafts, stairwells, mechanical chases, etc.). By the time the concrete has passed from the top to the bottom of the form, it has set and developed sufficient strength. Slipform systems are used to cast chimneys, towers, piers, dams, underground shafts, or other structures capable of being extruded. A slipform system is illustrated in Figure 9.19.

Slipforms are usually four feet high and are raised by jacks climbing on rods or tubes embedded in the concrete. Workers add concrete and reinforcing in a continuous upward process. The jacks are powered by hydraulic, pneumatic, or electric motors, and are available in 3, 6, and 22 ton capacities. The forms can "travel" up a structure at a rate of 6 inches to 20 inches per hour for silos and 6 inches to 48 inches per hour for shaft work.

Reinforcing

Reinforcing consists of steel bars, fabric, or wires cast into concrete to withstand bending and stretching (tensile stress). The size and quantities of reinforcing steel can vary greatly depending on the size of the loads, dimensions of the member, strength of concrete, and type of steel.

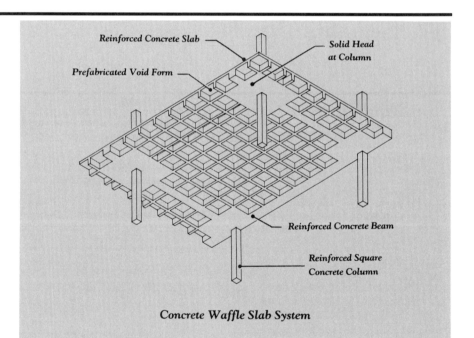

Reinforced Concrete Slab — — *Solid Head at Column*

Prefabricated Void Form —

Reinforced Concrete Beam

Reinforced Square Concrete Column

Concrete Waffle Slab System

Figure 9.17

Standard Dome Sizes and Volumes									
	19" Domes				30" Domes					
Depth	6"	8"	10"	12"	8"	10"	12"	14"	16"	20"
Volume (CF per dome)	1.09	1.41	1.90	2.14	3.85	4.78	5.53	6.54	7.44	9.16

Figure 9.18

Reinforcing steel is usually fabricated from shop drawings, cut to size, and bent in a fabrication shop. It is then shipped to the site where it is sorted and installed by workers known as "rodmen" or "rodbusters." Figures 9.20a and b show both proportionate quantities per square foot of floor area and form and reinforcing quantities per cubic yard.

The placement of reinforcing steel for slabs usually follows this order: the bottom steel, electrical conduit, mechanical pipes (and the top steel, if required).

Beam and column reinforcing may be prefabricated and placed in the forms by hand, but preferably by crane.

Precast Concrete

Precast concrete is cast in a location other than its final position in a building (usually at a precasting plant), cured, transported to the site, and then erected. Precast has the following advantages over cast-in-place concrete:

- Precast can be more economical, due to savings in labor (because casting is done at ground level) and materials (because formwork costs per unit of finished concrete is low since steel, wood or plastic forms can be used over and over again).
- Precast is usually of better quality because the casting is done in industrial plants that can be mechanized and quality-controlled.
- It is possible to obtain special or a variety of architectural appearances or textures.
- Erection of precast concrete is much faster than cast-in-place

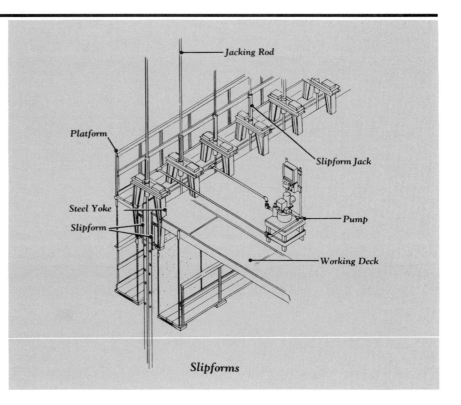

Figure 9.19

Slipforms

Proportionate Quantities

The tables below show both quantities per square foot of floor area as well as form and reinforcing quantities per cubic yard. Unusual structural requirements would increase the ratios below. High strength reinforcing would reduce the steel weights. Figures are for 3000 psi concrete and 60,000 psi reinforcing unless specified otherwise.

Type of Construction	Live Load	Span	Per sf of Floor Area				Per cu yd of Concrete		
			Concrete	Forms	Reinf.	Pans	Forms	Reinf.	Pans
Flat Plate	50 psf	15 ft	.46 cf	1.06 sf	1.71 lb		62 sf	101 lb	
		20	.63	1.02	2.4		44	104	
		25	.79	1.02	3.03		35	104	
	100	15	.46	1.04	2.14		61	126	
		20	.71	1.02	2.72		39	104	
		25	.83	1.01	3.47		33	113	
Flat Plate (waffle construction) 20″ domes	50	20	.43	1.0	2.1	.84 sf	63	135	53 sf
		25	.52	1.0	2.9	.89	52	150	46
		30	.64	1.0	3.7	.87	42	155	37
	100	20	.51	1.0	2.3	.84	53	125	45
		25	.64	1.0	3.2	.83	42	135	35
		30	.76	1.0	4.4	.81	36	160	29
Waffle Construction 30″ domes	50	25	.69	1.06	1.83	.68	42	72	40
		30	.74	1.06	2.39	.69	39	87	39
		35	.86	1.05	2.71	.69	33	85	39
		40	.78	1.0	4.8	.68	35	165	40
Flat Slab (two way with drop panels)	50	20	.62	1.03	2.34		45	102	
		25	.77	1.03	2.99		36	105	
		30	.95	1.03	4.09		29	116	
	100	20	.64	1.03	2.83		43	119	
		25	.79	1.03	3.88		35	133	
		30	.96	1.03	4.66		29	131	
	200	20	.73	1.03	3.03		38	112	
		25	.86	1.03	4.23		32	133	
		30	1.06	1.03	5.3		26	135	
One Way Joists 20″ pans	50	15	.36	1.04	1.4	.93	78	105	70
		20	.42	1.05	1.8	.94	67	120	60
		25	.47	1.05	2.6	.94	60	150	54
	100	15	.38	1.07	1.9	.93	77	140	66
		20	.44	1.08	2.4	.94	67	150	58
		25	.52	1.07	3.5	.94	55	185	49
One Way Joists 8″ x 16″ filler blocks	50	15	.34	1.06	1.8	.81 Ea.	84	145	64 Ea.
		20	.40	1.08	2.2	.82	73	145	55
		25	.46	1.07	3.2	.83	63	190	49
	100	15	.39	1.07	1.9	.81	74	130	56
		20	.46	1.09	2.8	.82	64	160	48
		25	.53	1.10	3.6	.83	56	190	42
One Way Beam and Slab	50	15	.42	1.30	1.73		84	111	
		20	.51	1.28	2.61		68	138	
		25	.64	1.25	2.78		53	117	
	100	15	.42	1.30	1.9		84	122	
		20	.54	1.35	2.69		68	154	
		25	.69	1.37	3.93		54	154	
	200	15	.44	1.31	2.24		80	137	
		20	.58	1.40	3.30		65	163	
		25	.69	1.42	4.89		53	183	
Two Way Beam and Slab	100	15	.47	1.20	2.26		69	130	
		20	.63	1.29	3.06		55	131	
		25	.83	1.33	3.79		43	123	
	200	15	.49	1.25	2.70		41	149	
		20	.66	1.32	4.04		54	165	
		25	.88	1.32	6.08		41	187	

Figure 9.20a

Proportionate Quantities (cont.)

4000 psi Concrete and 60,000 psi Reinforcing — Form and Reinforcing Quantities per cu yd					
Item	Size	Forms		Reinforcing	Minimum	Maximum
	10″ x 10″	130 sfca		#5 to #11	220 lbs	875 lbs
	12″ x 12″	108		#6 to #14	200	955
	14″ x 14″	92		#7 to #14	190	900
	16″ x 16″	81		#6 to #14	187	1082
	18″ x 18″	72		#6 to #14	170	906
	20″ x 20″	65		#7 to #18	150	1080
Columns	22″ x 22″	59		#8 to #18	153	902
(square	24″ x 24″	54		#8 to #18	164	884
tied)	26″ x 26″	50		#9 to #18	169	994
	28″ x 28″	46		#9 & #18	147	864
	30″ x 30″	43		#10 to #18	146	983
	32″ x 32″	40		#10 to #18	175	866
	34″ x 34″	38		#10 to #18	157	772
	36″ x 36″	36		#10 to #18	175	852
	38″ x 38″	34		#10 to #18	158	765
	40″ x 40″	32		#10 to #18	143	692

Item	Size	Forms	Spirals	Reinforcing	Minimum	Maximum
	12″ Diameter	34.5 lf	190 lb	#4 to #11	165 lb	1505 lb
		34.5	190	#14 & #18	—	1100
	14″	25	170	#4 to #11	150	970
		25	170	#14 & #18	800	1000
	16″	19	160	#4 to #11	160	950
		19	160	#14 & #18	605	1080
	18″	15	150	#4 to #11	160	915
		15	150	#14 & #18	480	1075
	20″	12	130	#4 to #11	155	865
		12	130	#14 & #18	385	1020
	22″	10	125	#4 to #11	165	775
		10	125	#14 & #18	320	995
Columns	24″	9	120	#4 to #11	195	800
(spirally		9	120	#14 & #18	290	1150
reinforced)	26″	7.3	100	#4 to #11	200	729
		7.3	100	#14 & #18	235	1035
	28″	6.3	95	#4 to #11	175	700
		6.3	95	#14 & #18	200	1075
	30″	5.5	90	#4 to #11	180	670
		5.5	90	#14 & #18	175	1015
	32″	4.8	85	#4 to #11	185	615
		4.8	85	#14 & #18	155	955
	34″	4.3	80	#4 to #11	180	600
		4.3	80	#14 & #18	170	855
	36″	3.8	75	#4 to #11	165	570
		3.8	75	#14 & #18	155	865
	40″	3.0	70	#4 to #11	165	500
		3.0	70	#14 & #18	145	765

Figure 9.20b

because the labor and time involved in the erection and stripping of formwork on-site is eliminated.

- Precast provides a practical alternative in situations where site conditions, design, or other considerations do not permit casting-in-place.

The major disadvantages of precast concrete include the following:

- The weight and size of precast limits what can be delivered over the roadways.
- Precast panels are subject to damage during erection.
- Precast concrete must be connected to other structural elements to form an integrated structural system.

Handling Procedures

The procedures for handling structural precast concrete are similar to those of structural steel framing. Under normal circumstances, the general contractor or the subcontractor (most general contractors hire subcontractors with the equipment, knowledge, and expertise on precast work) submits the contract drawings of the proposed project to the precast manufacturer, whose engineers, in turn, prepare shop and erection drawings for each individual member. These drawings are submitted to the architect/engineer for review to ensure that they conform to the original design intent, and to make corrections where appropriate.

After review, the shop and erection drawings are returned to the manufacturer (through the general contractor) for casting. The elements are cast, cured, marked according to their designated location in the proposed building, stockpiled at the plant, transported to the construction site at the appropriate time, and erected with a crane (or cranes) in accordance with the erection plans.

Precast Elements

Structural precast elements consist of slabs, beams, girders, columns, and wall panels. Standard details of typical units are shown in Figure 9.21.

Precast concrete planks can be quickly erected to produce a large, workable floor in a minimum amount of time (shown in Figure 9.22). Voids in the planks may be used to carry utilities. The bottom of the planks can be painted and used as the exposed ceiling for the area below.

Precast, prestressed single T beams are structural members that are supported on beams or bearing walls where the flanges alone provide the floor structure. Topping them with two inches of concrete will eliminate the visible joints. The T beam is illustrated in Figure 9.23.

Precast concrete columns, beams and double T's are reinforced or prestressed members. Figure 9.24 illustrates this system.

Columns may be one or several stories high and, in many cases, require the use of temporary adjustable shores until the remaining structural elements are in place and connected. Beams may be prestressed or reinforced rectangular, T-shaped, or L-shaped members, depending on the design or the building configuration. Double T's may be used for roof slabs without any topping, or for floors and roofs with concrete topping. Figure 9.25 shows the common shapes of precast beams.

Post-tensioning

It is possible to design slabs and beams that are reduced in size, longer in span, but capable of sustaining heavier loads through a process known as post-tensioning. This is a process by which hardened, reinforced concrete is prestressed opposite to the anticipated stresses using steel rods from working loads or strands known as tendons. Tendons are available in various sizes and lengths, with the common sizes being 0.5 and 0.6 inches. The tendons are normally tensioned by using pressure jacking equipment after the concrete has reached approximately 75% of its ultimate strength. The cableways may be grouted after tensioning to provide a bond between the steel and concrete, or the bond may be prevented by coating the tendons with anti-corrosive grease and wrapping them with waterproofing paper or plastic. The cableways are grouted by using a pressure grout pump with threaded fittings that attach to a plate at the end of the cableway, and plugging the hole at the opposite end.

			Prestressed Precast Concrete Structural Units		
Type	**Location**	**Depth**		**Span in Ft.**	**Live Load Lb. per S.F.**
Double Tee	Floor	28" to 34"		60 to 80	50 to 80
	Roof	12" to 24"		30 to 50	40
	Wall	Width 8'		Up to 55' high	Wind
Multiple Tee	Roof	8" to 12"		15 to 40	40
	Floor	8" to 12"		15 to 30	100
Plank	Roof			Roof / Floor	
		4"		13 / 12	40 for Roof
or	or	6"		22 / 18	
		8"		26 / 25	
		10"		33 / 29	100 for Floor
	Floor	12"		42 / 32	
Single Tee	Roof	28" 32" 36" 48"		40 80 100 120	40
AASHO Girder	Bridges	Type 4 5 6		100 110 125	Highway
Box Beam	Bridges	15" 27" 33"		40 to 100	Highway

Figure 9.21

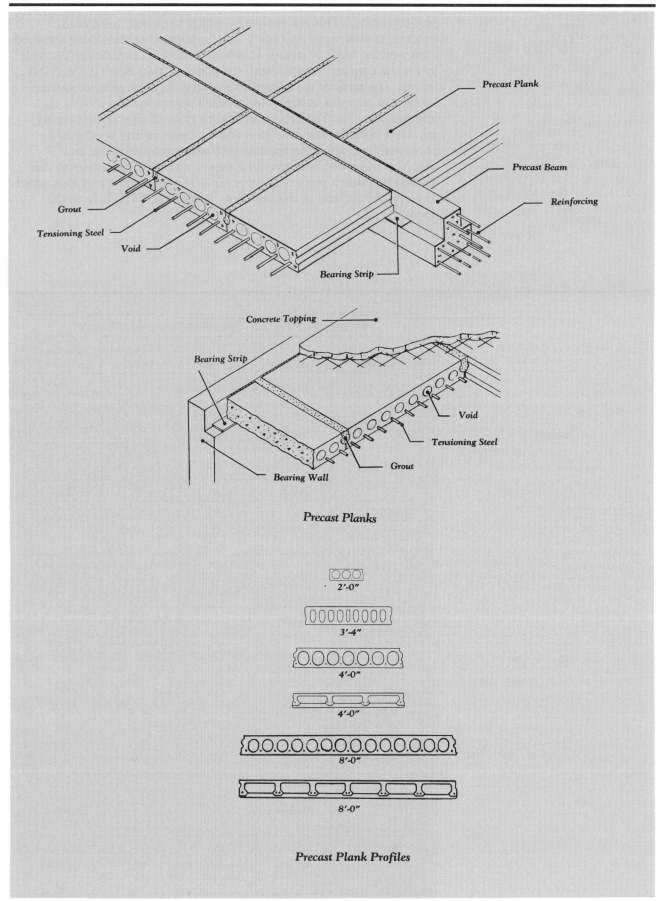

Precast Plank

Precast Beam

Reinforcing

Grout

Tensioning Steel

Void

Bearing Strip

Concrete Topping

Bearing Strip

Void

Tensioning Steel

Grout

Bearing Wall

Precast Planks

2'-0"

3'-4"

4'-0"

4'-0"

8'-0"

8'-0"

Precast Plank Profiles

Figure 9.22

Usually, post-tensioning experts and suppliers provide engineering, personnel training, and orientation services at little or no cost, and furnish the equipment (jacks, pumps, etc.) required for post-tensioning. Post-tensioning assembly and a slab are shown in Figure 9.26.

Lift-Slab Construction

This type of construction almost eliminates all the costs of labor and material associated with slab formwork. Lift-slab construction is accomplished by casting the slabs of a building in a stack on the ground and then lifting them to their final designated elevation with jacks attached to pre-erected steel columns. Lift-slab assembly is shown in Figure 9.27.

In addition to eliminating the ordinarily required flat slab formwork, this system permits post-tensioning or reinforcing, as well as the installation of mechanical and electrical items embedded at ground level prior to lifting.

Tilt-up Construction

In this method, reinforced concrete wall panels are cast horizontally into forms on a concrete slab-on-grade at a location adjacent to their eventual location. Then the panels are tilted up into their vertical position and connected. This eliminates the cost associated with wall forms.

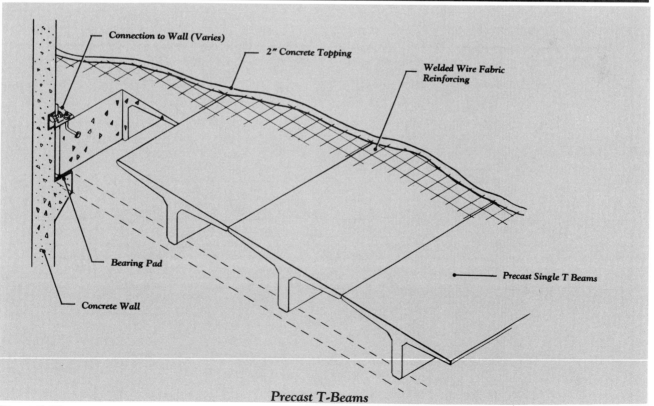

Figure 9.23

Masonry Construction

In the superstructure of a building, bearing walls of concrete blocks, bricks, or a combination of the two can be used to support floor and roof structures of steel, concrete, or wood. When compared with steel and reinforced concrete construction, masonry construction can be more economical because, in addition to their structural function, steel members also serve as the exterior closure (partitions) or interior partitions.

Reinforcing

Masonry walls can be used: to enclose buildings in order to keep out the natural elements; for partitions in order to subdivide large floor areas into usable space; to construct fire walls in order to resist the spread of fire and; to serve as barriers that resist the transmission of heat and sound.

Unreinforced masonry walls usually do not sustain as much load and stress as reinforced masonry walls, and are not recommended for locations where there are earthquakes. However, with reinforcing, masonry walls can carry heavy loads and withstand high stresses. Reinforcing may be done horizontally along the joints (as illustrated in Figure 9.28) and vertically in the cells.

Joint Reinforcing

Joint reinforcing may be either **truss type** or **ladder type.** The truss type of joint reinforcing is usually used in bearing walls because it provides better load distribution, while the ladder type is often used in light-duty non-loadbearing walls.

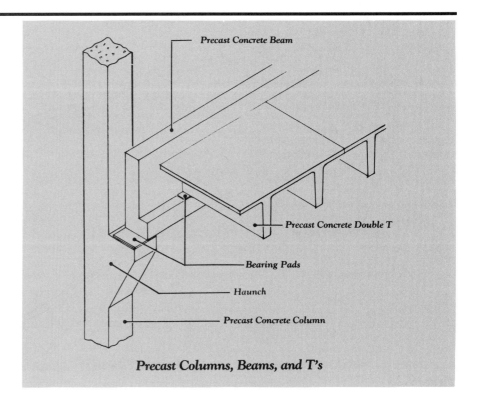

Precast Columns, Beams, and T's

Figure 9.24

Structural reinforcing is used in concrete block loadbearing walls in the form of steel bars installed vertically and grouted, as illustrated in Figure 9.29.

Fabrication

Masonry construction, in contrast to concrete and steel, does not require expensive fabrication or processing of major materials (except on projects requiring unusual sizes, shapes or stonework) before installation – most masonry units can be obtained in standardized sizes and shapes. Masonry normally requires the use of relatively inexpensive tools on-site, and the rental of equipment such as forklifts (for lifting or moving masonry units) and mortar mixing equipment. Masonry can be installed to a height of four feet, above which the work must be done from scaffolding. Masonry construction is described in more detail in Chapter 7, "Basic Construction Materials," and Chapter 10, "Exterior Closure."

Wood Construction

Structural lumber is usually dressed on all four sides (see Chapter 7 for a definition of dressing) and can be used in light frame construction for joists, posts, beams, columns and trusses. It can also be laminated into columns, beams, rigid frames, and arches. Wood may be exposed and finished for interior or exterior use and can be pressure-treated to resist moisture and rot. Wood structures are usually fastened with nails, dowels, screws, bolts, adhesives, and fabricated metal connectors (such as split rings, shear plates, and flat spiked grid connectors). Examples of some of the most common metal connectors for wood are shown in Figure 9.30.

Fabrication

Wood roof trusses are factory-fabricated with dimension lumber for high or low pitched roofs, hipped roofs, mansard roofs, and flat roofs. They

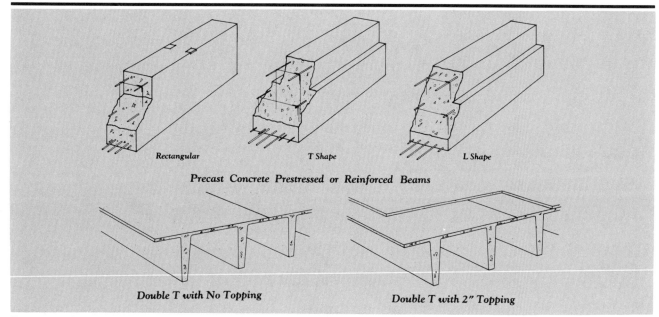

Rectangular   T Shape   L Shape

Precast Concrete Prestressed or Reinforced Beams

Double T with No Topping   Double T with 2" Topping

Figure 9.25

can be obtained from various manufacturers in several different configurations. Because of their clear span characteristics, trusses provide flexibility for interior planning and partition layout in buildings.

Wood trusses are usually fabricated by a truss manufacturer in a plant and transported to the job site, where they can be erected efficiently with a boom truck or a crane and a small crew. (Common truss configurations are illustrated in Figure 9.31).

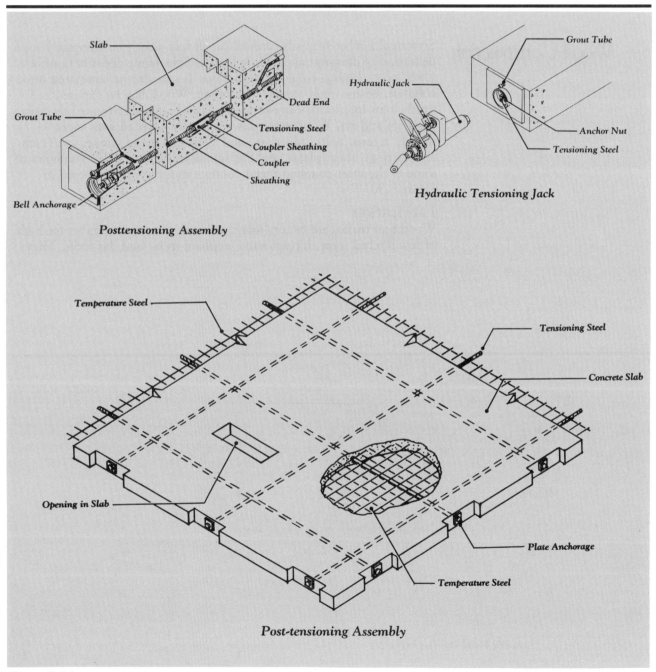

Figure 9.26

Classifications

When used in construction, wood work can be classified as **rough carpentry or finish carpentry.** Rough carpentry is wood that serves a structural function or is eventually concealed from view. Finish carpentry is visible in a completed structure and, as such, must be factory or field finished with paint or varnish. Most general contractors perform the rough carpentry and some finish carpentry, like door frames, wood sills, and paneling with their own forces. More specialized finish carpentry work, such as wood cabinets, shelving, and stair railings, is performed by and/or purchased from millwork subcontractors.

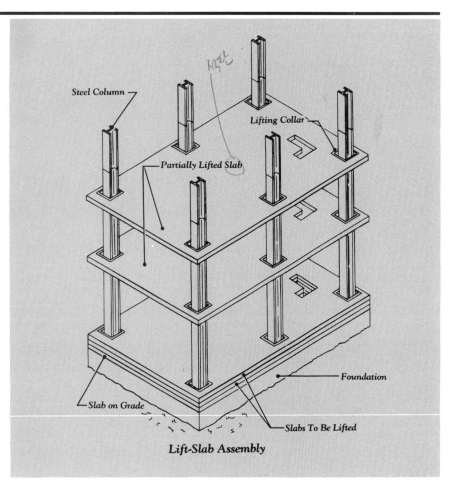

Lift-Slab Assembly

Figure 9.27

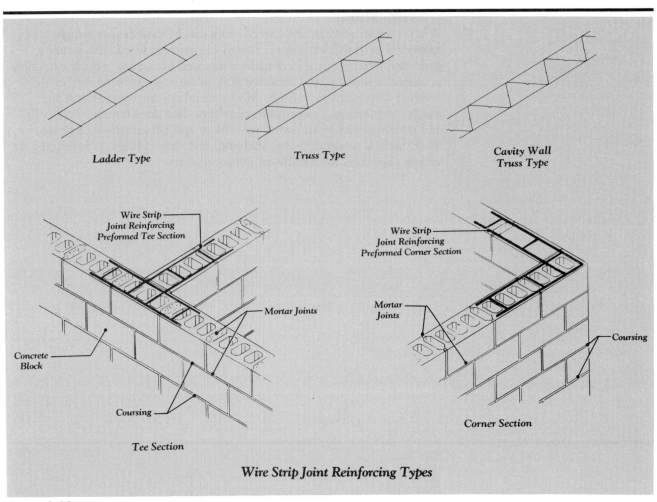

Ladder Type

Truss Type

Cavity Wall
Truss Type

Wire Strip
Joint Reinforcing
Preformed Tee Section

Mortar Joints

Concrete
Block

Coursing

Tee Section

Wire Strip
Joint Reinforcing
Preformed Corner Section

Mortar
Joints

Coursing

Corner Section

Wire Strip Joint Reinforcing Types

Figure 9.28

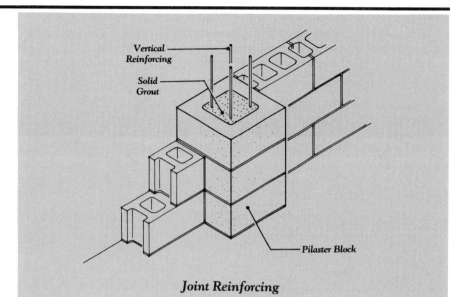

Joint Reinforcing

Figure 9.29

Split Ring Connector

4″ Shear Plate Connector

2-5/8″ Shear Plate Connector

Flat Spiked Grid Connector

Connectors, Used in Trusses Fabricated from Timbers

Figure 9.30

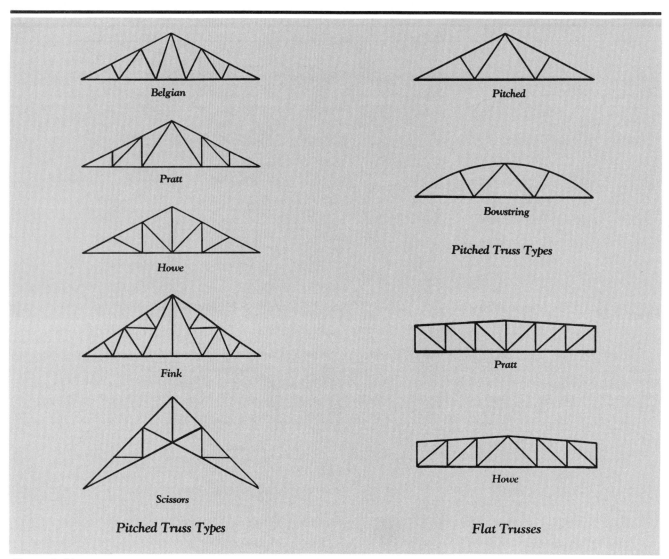

Belgian

Pratt

Howe

Fink

Scissors

Pitched Truss Types

Pitched

Bowstring

Pitched Truss Types

Pratt

Howe

Flat Trusses

Figure 9.31

Chapter Ten
Exterior Closure

The exterior closure, "building skin," or envelope is the most visible part of a building and usually constitutes the greatest share of the cost of a building. It provides security against intruders and protection from natural elements such as wind, sun, rain, and snow. In addition to forming the envelope of a building, the exterior closure may be designed to function as part of the structural component, such as bearing and shear walls. Materials most commonly employed in structural closure walls are aluminum, concrete, glass, masonry, steel, and wood.

Curtain Walls

The exterior facia may be designed as a structural element that supports a portion of the floors or as a nonsupporting curtain wall that is supported by the floor system, floor by floor. Some of the materials used in the construction of curtain walls are aluminum, concrete, glass, masonry, plastics, steel, and wood, singly or in combinations. The walls may be prefabricated and erected or placed in pieces or sections.

Examples of curtain walls are shown in Figure 10.1.

A curtain wall is held in place in a metal frame (as shown in Figure 10.2). Closure at junctions may be accomplished by the use of caulking, gaskets, or sealants.

The self-supporting curtain wall is attached by clips at each floor, whereas the supported wall is attached to girts or rails (horizontal) and mullions (vertical) which, in turn, are tied to the structural framing.

Glass may be part of the curtain wall, usually in a continuous horizontal belt at each floor, or windows at regular or irregular intervals.

Concrete

Concrete exterior closure includes cast-in-place concrete walls, precast wall panels, or tilt-up panels. In addition, concrete walls may be reinforced to resist variations in temperature, or reinforced to resist vertical or horizontal loads (if designed to carry some of the structural load of a building).

Cast-in-Place Concrete

Various types of materials are used to form cast-in-place concrete walls: job-built plywood, prefabricated plywood, modular steel framed plywood, or aluminum forms. A second function of wall forms may be architectural; to imprint textures or patterns on the concrete walls, as illustrated in Figure 10.3.

Special patterns and textures may be economically achieved with formliners made of fiberglass, or different plastics such as rigid PVC, ABS, and highly flexible elastomeric compounds such as urethane.

Abrasive methods can also create textures on concrete walls, expose the underlying aggregate, and conceal surface defects. Some of the most common finishing methods include **hand rubbing** with either a special synthetic stone or with burlap and cement paste; **surface grinding** with a power tool to expose and flatten large aggregate; **bush hammering** with a power tool or by hand to expose the aggregate and create a rough-textured surface finish; **sandblasting** to produce a mildly textured surface while exposing the aggregate at the same time; and **acid etching** to remove the superficial layer of sand and cement to expose the aggregate.

Special sealers are usually sprayed on the exposed concrete surfaces for weather protection and to minimize discoloration. The sealers require reapplication every few years. Concrete exterior closure, as part of the superstructure, is described in more detail in "Chapter 9, Superstructure – Framing."

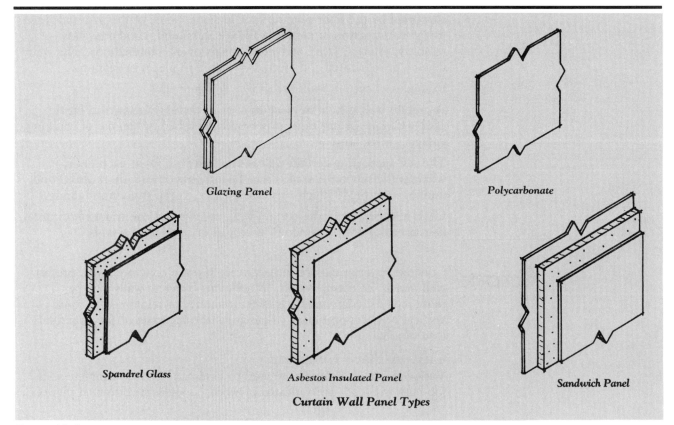

Glazing Panel

Polycarbonate

Spandrel Glass

Asbestos Insulated Panel

Sandwich Panel

Curtain Wall Panel Types

Figure 10.1

Precast Concrete

One advantage of using precast over cast-in-place concrete panels is its faster erection during all weather conditions. Consistent finishes can be produced more easily with precast because of the controlled environment at the plant. Sophisticated finishes and shapes may be produced in a plant that are difficult to achieve on the construction site. Examples of precast panel types are illustrated in Figure 10.4.

Precast wall panels may or may not act as loadbearing members, depending on how they are attached to the structural frame. (See Chapter 9, "Superstructure," for a detailed description of loadbearing concrete panels.)

Insulation

Heat loss through precast panels can be controlled by sandwiching insulating material inside the panel during casting. Another solution is to construct an additional curtain wall of drywall and metal studs behind the precast panels. The outer precast curtain wall provides the weather and security protection and the inner drywall curtain wall the heat loss protection.

Tilt-up Precast Panels

Tilt-up precast panels are cast horizontally on the permanent building slab-on-grade at designated locations and, once cured, are tilted into place with a crane. To prevent bonding of the panels to the casting slab, plastic sheeting or liquid bond breaker is applied.

Sometimes, the building slab is not available as a casting bed due to space limitations or steel delays. Under such circumstances, temporary concrete slabs (known as "casting beds") are installed at appropriate

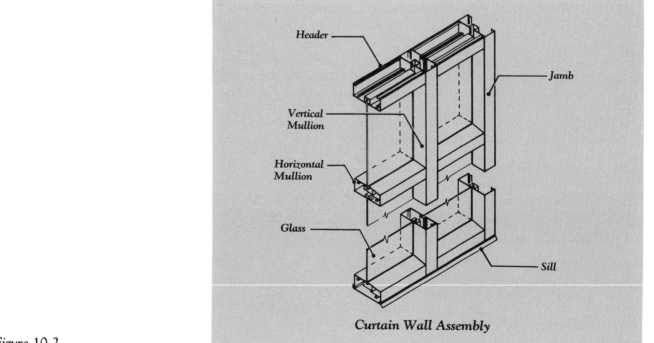

Curtain Wall Assembly

Figure 10.2

locations on the construction site, and the panels are cast on them. The panels are then lifted into position with the use of inserts cast into the panels and appropriate lifting gear as shown in Figures 10.5 and 10.6.

The locations for the lifting inserts are identified on the structural drawings. Some of the lifting plates cast into the edge of panels may be used for connection to the structural frame of the building.

After the panel is tilted into its final position with a crane, it is temporarily supported by adjustable braces (Figure 10.7) until the panel is welded and/or grouted in place.

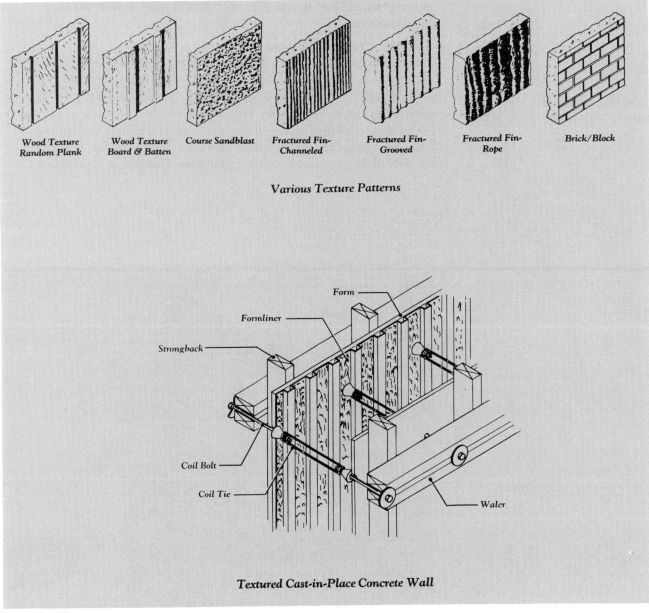

Wood Texture Random Plank   Wood Texture Board & Batten   Course Sandblast   Fractured Fin-Channeled   Fractured Fin-Grooved   Fractured Fin-Rope   Brick/Block

Various Texture Patterns

Textured Cast-in-Place Concrete Wall

Figure 10.3

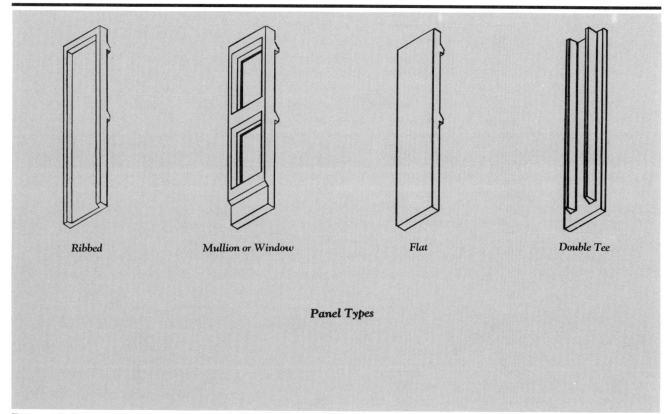

Ribbed   Mullion or Window   Flat   Double Tee

Panel Types

Figure 10.4

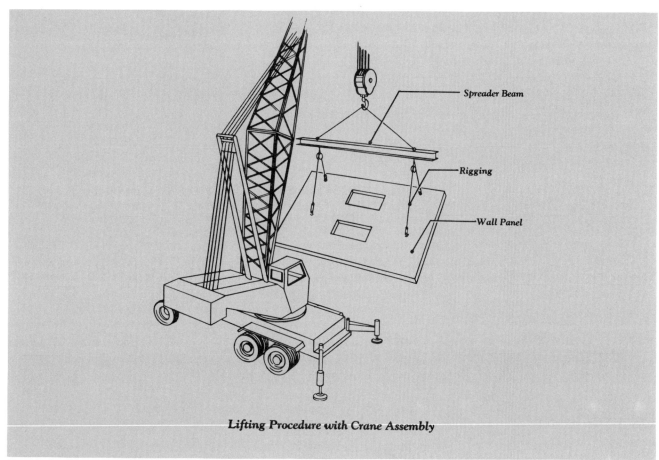

Lifting Procedure with Crane Assembly

Figure 10.5

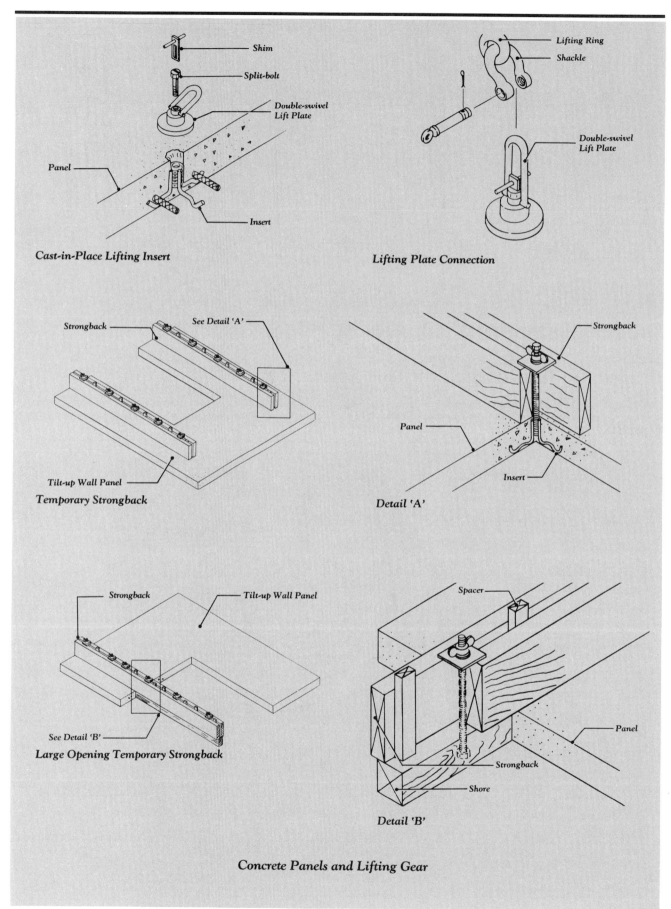

Cast-in-Place Lifting Insert

Lifting Plate Connection

Temporary Strongback

Detail 'A'

Large Opening Temporary Strongback

Detail 'B'

Concrete Panels and Lifting Gear

Figure 10.6

Casting concrete panels in one location, and then moving them to another location on the building, should be avoided. The problem is usually solved by stacking or placing one panel on top of another.

Masonry

Concrete blocks, bricks, stone, or stucco are commonly used exterior masonry materials.

Weatherproofing

Masonry walls are essentially porous and absorb water, thus these walls must be sealed. Current theory favors allowing the water to penetrate the exterior veneer and controlling it on the back-up wall. A masonry wall with a face veneer, air space (1/2″ or more), and back-up wall is known as a **cavity wall**.

Back-up walls may be masonry or drywall curtain walls. The veneer is attached to the back-up wall with ties embedded into the wall coursing. The drywall curtain wall is framed with metal or wood studs, insulated, sheathed, and finally waterproofed.

Concrete Blocks

Concrete blocks are among the most frequently used materials for the construction of masonry exterior walls because they are strong, versatile, and economical. They can be used for non-loadbearing walls, or can be

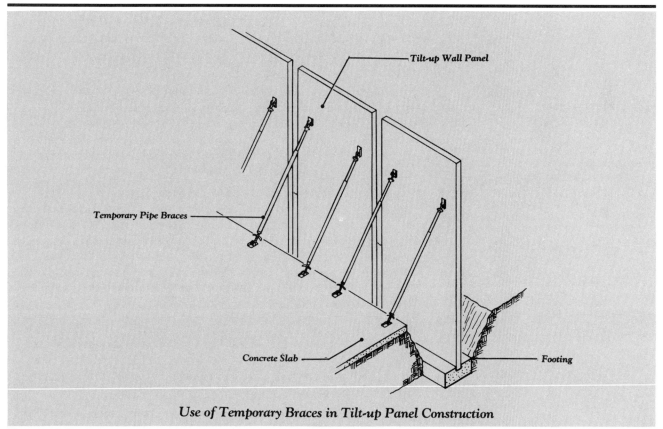

Use of Temporary Braces in Tilt-up Panel Construction

Figure 10.7

reinforced with vertical steel bars grouted in the voids and horizontal joint reinforcement to act as loadbearing walls.

When serving as the finished wall, concrete blocks can be obtained with a variety of architectural finishes and shapes such as fluted, ground face (exposed aggregate), split-ribbed, split-faced, slump, hexagonal, or deep groove, as shown in Figure 10.8.

Concrete blocks can also be used as the back-up for walls with brick or other veneer facings as in cavity walls (see Figure 10.9).

When used without facing, exterior block walls can be finished with stucco, painted, or coated with a variety of opaque and clear sealers. Insulation for single wythe block walls can be achieved by either installing insulating boards on the interior face between the furring strips (for drywall) or by using rigid foam inserts or loose perlite to fill the voids in the blocks. For cavity walls, rigid insulating boards may be attached within the cavity beneath the waterproofing to the surface of the inner wythe.

Bricks

Individual bricks, when used in wall construction, are staggered to allow them to interlock and act as one unit. A single wythe (layer) of brick is a veneer, whereas a wall consists of two or more wythes. In traditional wall construction, most of the bricks are layed in courses, flat, the long way exposed, known as **stretchers**. To tie this wythe into the other wythes, some of the bricks are turned with the long way going into the wall, called **headers**. The pattern in which the brick is layed is known as the **bond**. The most popular bonds used in construction today are: common bond, Flemish bond, English bond, and the standard running or stretcher bond. Also known as American bond, the common bond pattern has a header course every sixth course. The Flemish bond alternates headers and stretchers in each course. The English bond runs alternate courses of headers and stretchers. In the standard running or stretcher bond, the face brick are all stretchers. Brick bond patterns are illustrated in Figure 10.10.

There are a few other orientations of individual bricks in a wall. Bricks that are installed on end with the narrow sides exposed are called **soldiers**. When bricks are laid on their faces with their ends exposed, usually as caps for walls or sloping sills under windows, they are known as **rowlocks**. Bricks installed at the corner of a building with one end and one side exposed are referred to as **quoins**.

Brick walls are not waterproof, therefore, provisions must be made to limit the amount of water that may penetrate the exterior surface. Brick may be waterproofed by installing flashing at the junction of floors and walls, as well as over and under openings. Another method is the application of waterproofing material on the outside face of back-up walls in cavity walls between the wythes. Weep holes may be installed above the flashing at brick shelves and lintels to provide a means of escape for moisture that penetrates the wall.

Stone

Another masonry material commonly used for exterior closure is stone. Stone walls and veneers are made of fieldstone rubble and ashlar, which may be coursed or uncoursed, and slab stones. Types of stone used for slabs are limestone, granite, and marble, to name a few.

Rubble is a stone consisting of unsquared pieces while ashlar is made up of squared pieces. Slab panels are used as a decorative veneer attached to

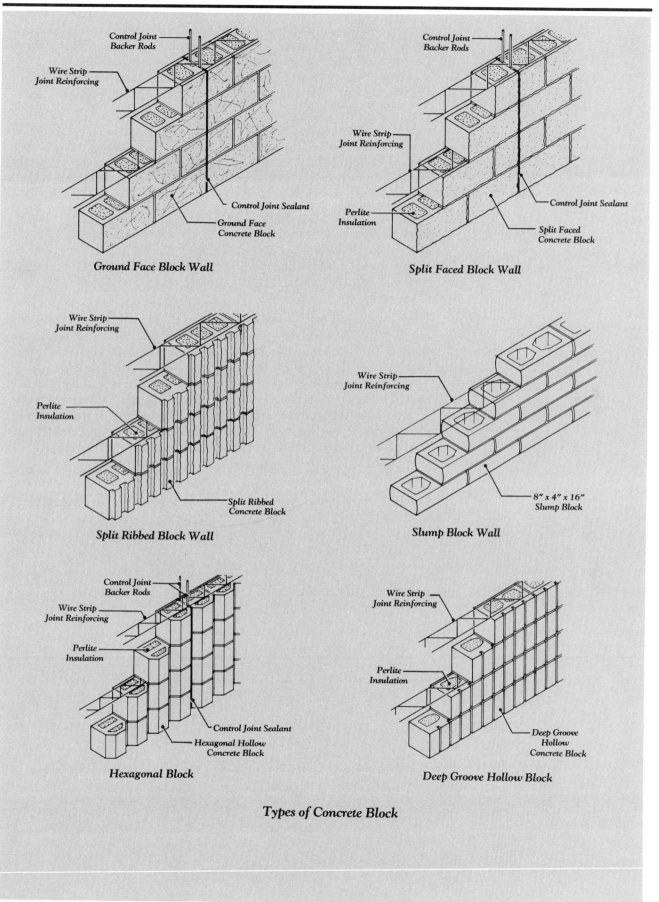

Ground Face Block Wall

Split Faced Block Wall

Split Ribbed Block Wall

Slump Block Wall

Hexagonal Block

Deep Groove Hollow Block

Types of Concrete Block

Figure 10.8

the steel frame of a building. Any of these materials may be used as a facing with concrete block or drywall curtain back-up. Coursed stone is a masonry wall that has continuous horizontal joints. Random, or uncoursed, stone is a wall with no horizontal joints. Both rubble and ashlar walls may be coursed or uncoursed. Stone panel assemblies are shown in Figure 10.11.

Rubble and ashlar stone are installed like brickwork, except that the mason carefully selects or trims each piece for the available space. Slab stone is installed like precast; it must be hoisted into place, and attached with pins, bolts, or anchors. (See Chapter 7 for more details on stone.)

Stucco

Stucco is a cement plaster that can be applied (like plaster) to a mesh or lath attached to the exterior surface of a building with a masonry or drywall curtain system, to provide a decorative and weather-resistant surface free of joints. This material may be made from a mixture of sand, cement, lime, and water; or with patented mixes and a variety of additives.

There are several methods of applying stucco. However, the two most common methods are the **open-frame method** and the **direct-application method**. In the open-frame method, waterproofed building paper is first attached directly to a wood or steel frame (usually wood or steel studs) for moisture protection. Next, galvanized metal lath is attached to the studs. On some projects, self-furring lath with integral waterproof paper is used. Then the stucco is applied to the lath, usually in three coats (like plaster). The first coat is the **scratch coat**, the second is the **brown** or **levelling coat** and the third is the **finish coat**.

In the direct-application method, plywood sheathing is attached to wood or stud systems. A bonding agent is applied before the first coat(s) of stucco. If the sheathing or the surface is unsuitable for direct stucco application, then the surface is covered with building paper, and overlaid with self-furring metal lath, before applying the stucco. On concrete or

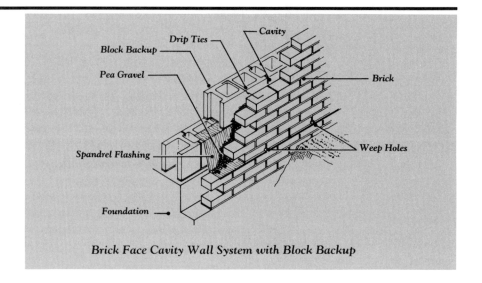

Brick Face Cavity Wall System with Block Backup

Figure 10.9

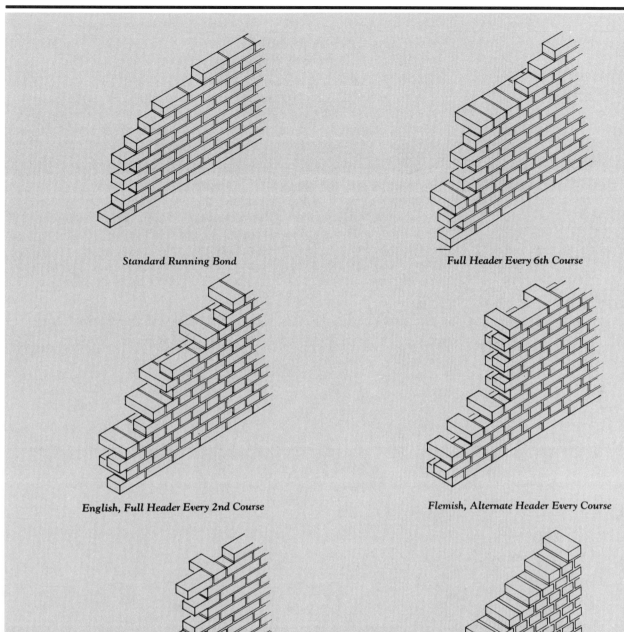

Standard Running Bond

Full Header Every 6th Course

English, Full Header Every 2nd Course

Flemish, Alternate Header Every Course

Flemish Alternate Header Every 6th Course

Brick Veneer, Full Header Throughout

Brick Bond Patterns

Figure 10.10

masonry walls, one or two coats of stucco are applied directly to the walls, alone or with wire mesh reinforcement. Figure 10.12 contains examples of both methods and the common types of metal lath.

The finished stucco coat can be painted, tinted, or treated with colorless coating material to prevent water penetration. In addition, the exterior stucco finish is highly textured and coarse in appearance, which readily conceals staining and shrinkage cracks. Overall shrinkage cracks can be minimized with control joints at regular intervals.

Glass

In construction, the words *glass* and *glazing* are often used interchangeably. For exterior closure, the distinct difference between them must be understood. Glass is made by mixing sand (silicon dioxide) with lime, soda ash (sodium carbonate) and small quantities of potassium oxide and alumina. This mixture is heated to a molten state and then cooled to form glass. Glazing is the process of setting glass in an opening.

Sizes

The most common glass is plate or float glass and the thicknesses in which it is manufactured are: 3/32-inch thick glass, known as

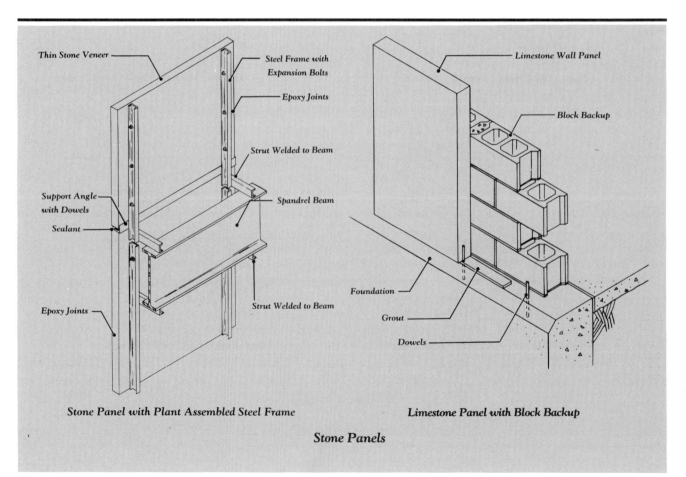

Stone Panel with Plant Assembled Steel Frame

Limestone Panel with Block Backup

Stone Panels

Figure 10.11

202

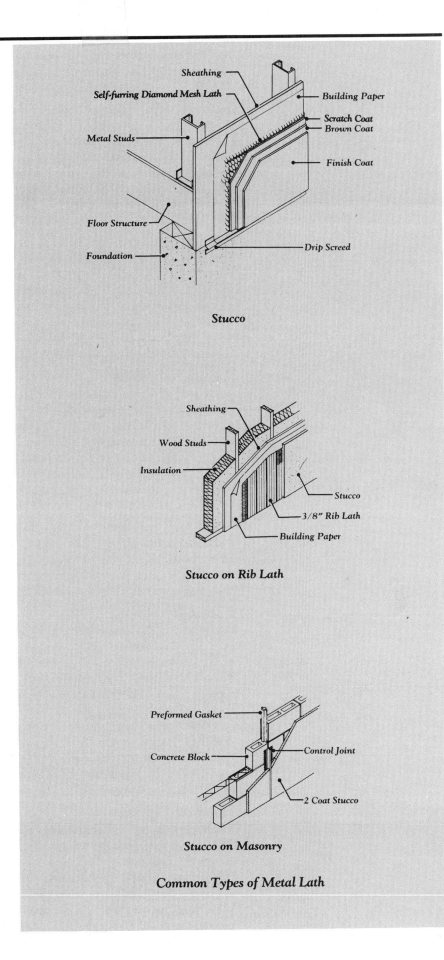

Stucco

Stucco on Rib Lath

Stucco on Masonry

Common Types of Metal Lath

Figure 10.12

single-strength glass, and 1/8-inch glass, or **double-strength glass**, most commonly 1/4-inch thick, up to 1/2-inch thick. Other thicknesses, such as 1-inch, can be obtained from glass manufacturers by special order.

The necessary thickness of exterior glass is determined by factors such as the size of each opening, the maximum wind loads expected, determined from the height of the building and geographical location, and how the glass is to be supported. Regular plate glass (known as float glass) is used for small windows in relatively low buildings such as supermarkets and strip malls, while tall buildings, which are subject to increased winds, require thicker or special types of glass.

Most applications of glass discussed below concern its use as a lite (or pane) supported in a frame whose function is to comprise a window system or a window in a curtain wall system. As such, the lite must provide the maximum viewing area while being supported solely along the edges. Glass may be placed, however, as a decorative panel in a curtain wall system, running in a bank around the building exterior below the windows, called a spandrel. Because of the opaque finish, the panel may be supported with a back-up wall and consequently not required to be as thick as window glass.

Tempered Glass

Tempered glass is about four times as strong as regular glass. It is manufactured with compressive stresses in the faces and edges, and tensile stresses in the core of the glass. This type of glass is required by code in and around doors, wherever heavy pedestrian traffic presents an increased risk of breakage. Tempered glass is also used for exterior surfaces exposed to intense heat, cold, and/or heavy wind pressures because it is resistant to impact and thermal stress. Its use is limited because it is twice the cost of float glass in a comparable thickness.

When tempered glass breaks, it is instantly reduced to small square-edged granules instead of long sharp-edged pieces characteristic of untempered glass. Thus, all drilling or cutting must be done before the glass is tempered because performing these operations on tempered glass releases the stresses in the glass and causes it to disintegrate.

Laminated Glass

Laminated glass is manufactured by inserting a layer of transparent vinyl between two sheets of glass, and then bonding all three layers together under heat and pressure. This type of glass is basically used as safety glass but is also a better barrier against the transmission of sound than other types of glass. Laminated glass is most often used in environments where there is a desire to limit the amount of noise from the outside, such as hospitals, classrooms, and homes. It is also used for overhead glazing and skylights, because when laminated glass breaks, the shards of glass are held in place in the frame by the vinyl instead of falling out of the frame and injuring people below. Like tempered glass, the high cost limits its use to where it is required.

Insulated Glass

Insulated glass is used in buildings where thermal loss must be controlled. The energy savings experienced when using insulated glass more than offsets the cost difference between insulated and plate glass (it is three times more expensive). Insulated glass is manufactured by inserting a dry, low-conductivity gas or dry air into two or three sheets of glass, fusing them together and hermetically sealing the assembly. When two sheets of glass are fused and sealed, it is called **double-glazed**, when three sheets are used, it is known as **triple-glazed**. This type of glass is an extremely good thermal insulator and is estimated to reduce the rate of heat loss to about a third of that of a single sheet of glass.

Coated Glass

All of the previously mentioned types of glass are available with a tinted or reflective coating to reduce glare and cut down on solar heat gain. The more popular colors of tinting are gold, green, bronze, gray, and blue. Reflective coated glass, from the outside of a building, appears as a mirror during the day and as dark transparent glass at night when inside lights are turned on.

Wired Glass

This type of glass is manufactured by rolling a mesh of small wires into hot sheets of glass. Wired glass is commonly used for windows in fire walls and fire doors because the wires hold the pieces of glass together when the glass breaks as a result of thermal stress.

Glass Blocks

A glass block closure wall has an advantage over masonry in that it admits light while preventing heat transmission. Glass blocks, as shown in Figure 10.13, are manufactured in units like brick or block, and can be assembled to form exterior walls.

Glass blocks are available in sizes ranging from 6″ × 6″ to 12″ × 12″, with thicknesses from 3″ to 4″. Other manufacturing options include transparency to permit vision through them, hollowness, and with inserts to reduce the transmission of solar heat into a building.

Metal

Formed metal panels may be used as siding for exterior closure, as shown in Figure 10.14. The panels can be made from steel or aluminum sheet metal, and may be ordered plain or insulated. Often a pattern, like a corrugation, is rolled into the panel, which creates a shadow line as an architectural feature. The panel is supported by horizontal girts and vertical sag rods which tie into the structure. A drywall curtain wall may function as a back up for such a wall. This closure system is often sold with a similar roofing panel and total structural frame as a pre-engineered building which can be set on the client's foundation. Finished metal panels may be used as decorative spandrel panels in a curtain wall system, similar to glass spandrel panels.

Insulation

The insulated panel can be assembled in the field or obtained prefabricated from the factory (see Figure 10.15). When assembled in the field, the interior liner panel and insulation are first attached to the girt, then the exterior face panel is installed to interlock with grooves in the interior liner panel. Factory assembled panels usually come with the insulation already sandwiched or foamed in place between the interior liner panel and the exterior face panel.

Finish

Sheet metal exterior panels can be finished with a variety of coatings for protection against corrosion. They can be manufactured with a stainless steel, galvanized, or aluminum finish. In addition, both steel and aluminum panels are available with baked enamel or porcelain finish.

Wood

Wood is commonly used for exterior closure of residential and small commercial structures. Wood siding (Figure 10.16), plywood panels

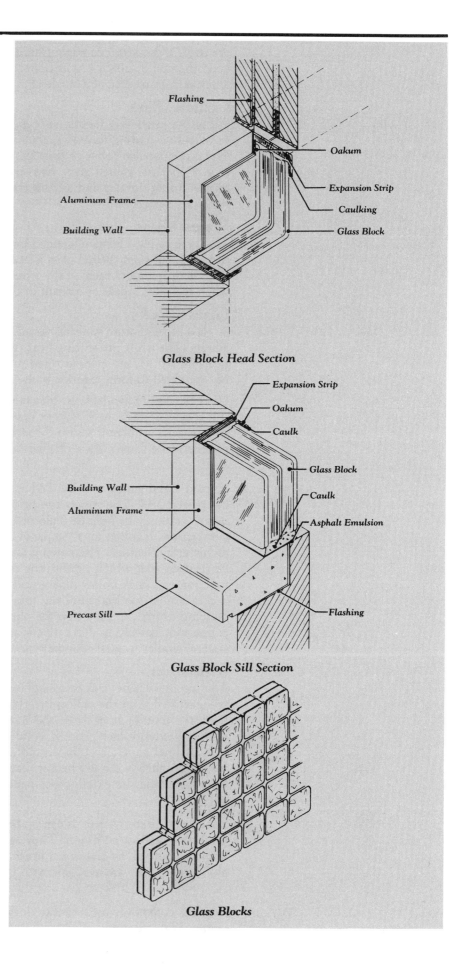

Glass Block Head Section

Glass Block Sill Section

Glass Blocks

Figure 10.13

(Figure 10.17) and wall shingles (Figure 10.18) are typical materials used for exterior closure. Advantages of using wood are the availability of materials, ease of fastening (with nails), and low cost.

Wood siding is made from timber species such as redwood and cedar; these woods resist moisture and withstand extreme variations in temperature. Other species such as pine and fir, as well as some man-made wood products, can be used for siding provided that they are finished with stain or paint for weather protection. (See Chapter 7, "Basic Construction Materials," for more information on wood.)

Installation

Proper installation of wood siding requires the attachment of plywood sheathing to the wood studs, followed by building paper, and then the exterior siding.

Plywood paneling, when used as exterior siding, is manufactured with waterproof glue to provide weather protection. Plywood siding is installed directly to the stud wall without sheathing.

Cedar shingles are installed very similar to wood siding. First plywood sheathing is nailed to the wood studs. This is followed by building paper and, finally, the shingles.

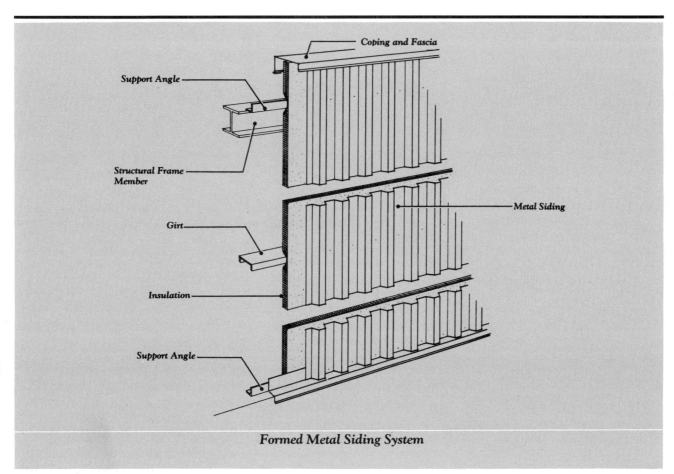

Formed Metal Siding System

Figure 10.14

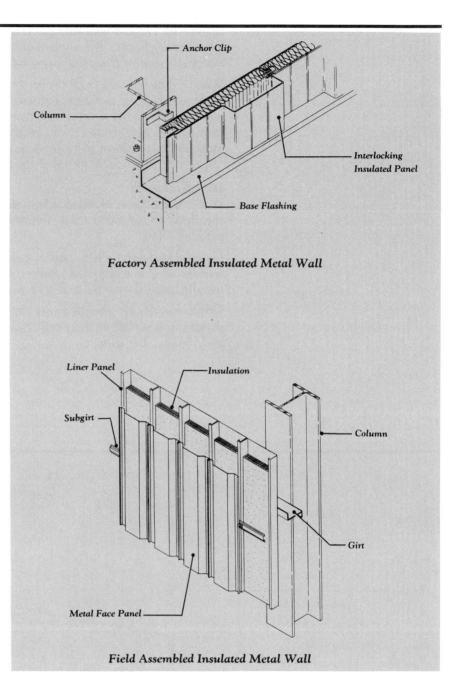

Factory Assembled Insulated Metal Wall

Field Assembled Insulated Metal Wall

Figure 10.15

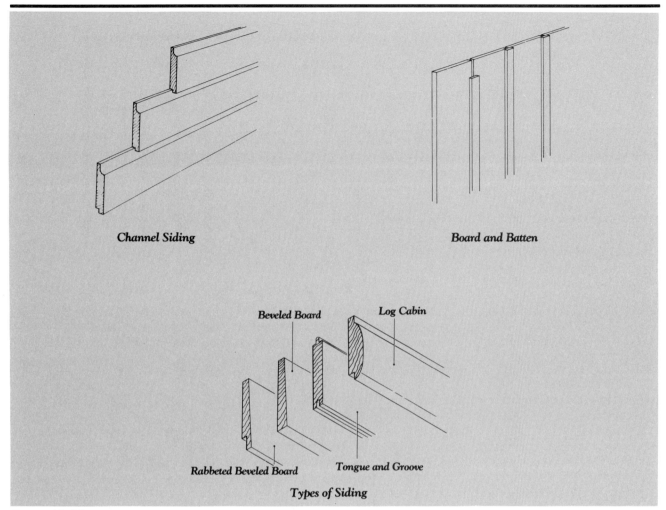

Channel Siding

Board and Batten

Beveled Board

Log Cabin

Rabbeted Beveled Board

Tongue and Groove

Types of Siding

Figure 10.16

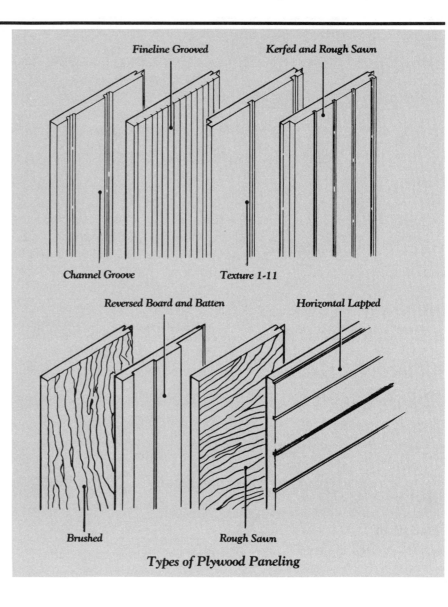

Fineline Grooved

Kerfed and Rough Sawn

Channel Groove

Texture 1-11

Reversed Board and Batten

Horizontal Lapped

Brushed

Rough Sawn

Types of Plywood Paneling

Figure 10.17

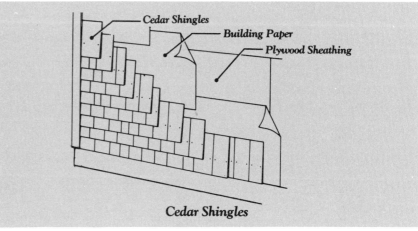

Cedar Shingles

Building Paper

Plywood Sheathing

Cedar Shingles

Figure 10.18

Chapter Eleven

Roofing

Like the exterior walls, the roof is a critical component of the building because it provides protection from the weather and insulation from extremes of heat and cold. In comparison to walls, the cost of a roof is low. However, the roof must be free from leaks that can damage expensive interior finishes. It is, therefore, important to select the right roofing system for a building, and that the roofing system be properly installed. In purchasing a roof, it is essential to require a guarantee of materials and installation as insurance against future problems.

General contractors usually subcontract the roofing work to reputable roofing contractors. The scope of subcontracted work includes the roof covering, insulation, and roofing accessories such as flashing, hatches, and skylights.

Roof Covering

There are two main categories of roofs: **pitched roofs** and **flat roofs**. Pitched roofs are sloped to drain water to the perimeter of the building, thereby providing little or no opportunity for standing water to penetrate the surface. Flat roofs are sloped to interior drains which can become blocked and allow water to accumulate that may eventually penetrate the building. The minimum slope required to achieve effective drainage on most flat roofs is 1/8" to 1/4" drop per foot of run.

Within these two main categories, there are five types of roof covering, shown in Figure 11.1 and described in the following paragraphs.

Built-up Roofing
This roofing system is used for flat roofs, and consists of three distinct elements.

- **Felt**, installed in layers and serves the same purpose as reinforcing in concrete
- **Bitumen**, of either coal-tar pitch or asphalt, which is the "glue" installed between the layers of felt to hold them together, and also serves as the waterproofing material in the system
- **Ballast**, which normally consists of gravel or slag, mineral granules, or a mineral-coated cap sheet

The most common built-up roofing systems contain 2, 3, or 4 plies of felt with either asphalt bitumen or coal-tar pitch between them. An example of a built-up roof system is shown in Figure 11.2.

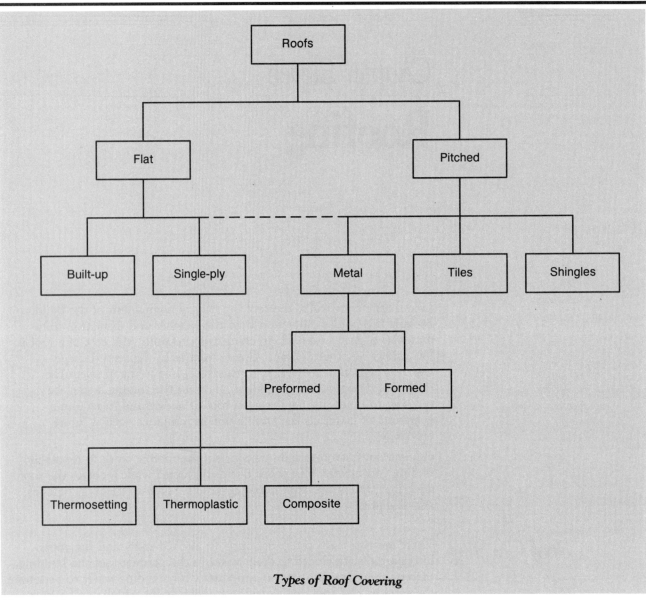

Types of Roof Covering

Figure 11.1

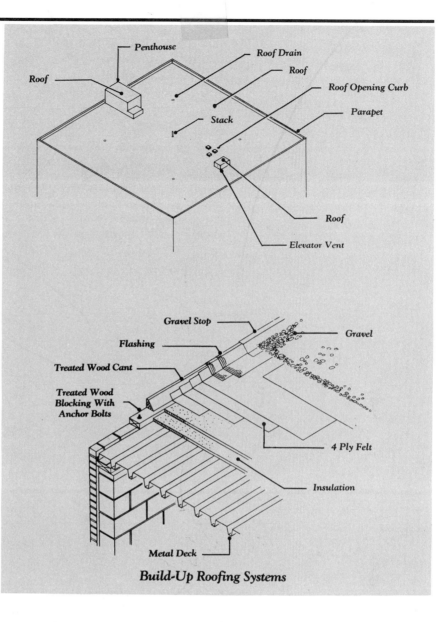

Build-Up Roofing Systems

Figure 11.2

213

Built-up roofing can be installed on rigid deck insulation or directly on a structural roof deck. Structural roof decks commonly used under flat roofs include the following:

- Plywood over wood joists
- Solid wood decking over timber framing
- Corrugated steel decking over structural steel framing

Built-up roofing is used on flat roofs of most commercial buildings.

Single-ply Roofing

Single-ply roofing systems are installed on flat roofs of commercial buildings. Also known as membrane roofing, single-ply can be categorized into three main groups. They are: thermosetting, thermoplastic, and composites. A classification, characteristics, and installation guide for the the three groups of single-ply roofing appears in Figure 11.3.

Single-Ply Roofing Membrane Installation Guide

Generic Materials (Classification)	Compatible Base						Attachment Method					Sealing Method					
	Slip-Sheet Req'd	Concrete	Exist. Asphalt Memb.	Insulation Board	Plywood	Spray Urethane Foam	Adhesive	Mechanically Fastened	Fully Adhered	Loose Laid/Ballast	Partially-Adhered	Adhesive	Hot Mopped	Hot Air Gun	Self-Sealing	Solvent	Torch Heating
Thermo Setting																	
EPDM (Ethylene, propylene)	X	X	X	X	X	X	X	X	X	X	X	X				X	
Neoprene (Synthetic rubber)	X	X		X	X		X		X	X		X					
Thermo Plastic																	
PIB (Polyisobutylene)	X	X	X	X	X	X	X	X	X		X	X				X	
CSPE (Chlorosulfonated polyethyene)	X	X		X	X	X	X	X	X	X		X	X	X	X		
CPE (Chlorinated polyethylene)	X	X		X	X			X		X				X	X		
PVC (Polyvinyl chloride)	X	X		X	X	X		X		X	X	X				X	
APP (Atactic Polypropylene)	X	X		X	X	X		X		X			X	X			X
SBS (Styrene Butadiene)	X	X		X	X	X		X		X	X		X	X	X		X
NBP (Acrylonitrile Butadiene Copolymer)	X	X		X	X	X		X		X					X		
EIP (Ethylene Interpolymer Ethyl)	X	X		X	X				X						X		
Composite																	
Glass reinforced EPDM/neoprene	X	X		X	X	X			X			X					X
Modified bitumen/polyester	X		X	X	X				X			X	X				X
Modified bitumen/polyethylene & aluminum	X	X		X	X		X		X			X					X
Modified bitumen/polyethylene sheet	X	X		X	X					X				X			X
Modified bitumen/polyethylene sheet	X	X		X	X					X				X			X
Modified CPE				X	X					X		X					
Non-woven glass reinforced PVC							X		X	X		X					
Nylon reinforced PVC		X		X	X					X				X		X	X
Nylon reinforced butyl or neoprene	X								X					X		X	X
Polyester reinforced CPE	X	X	X	X	X	X				X	X	X	X			X	
Polyester reinforced PVC	X	X		X	X	X				X	X	X	X	X		X	
Rubber asphalt/plastic sheet	X	X	X	X	X				X						X		

Figure 11.3

Single-ply roofing can be installed in five main ways – loose-laid and ballasted, partially adhered, fully adhered, mechanically fastened, or adhesive.

The loose-laid and ballasted method, the most economical and commonly used system, involves the fusing or gluing of the side and end laps of the membrane in order to form a continuous nonadhered sheet that is held in place with ballast (stones, usually about 1/4″ to 1/2″ in size).

The partially adhered system, which requires no ballast, is installed by attaching the membrane with a series of strips or plates to the supporting roof structure.

The fully adhered system, which requires no ballast, involves a uniform and continuous attachment of the membrane to the manufacturer's approved base material. This system is time-consuming and expensive to install.

The mechanically fastened system refers to attaching studs to the base material and, after the membrane is installed, screwing buttons over the draped stud to hold the membrane in place.

The base material over which the membrane is installed is rigid insulation. The "R value" (thermal resistance) can vary based on the thickness and type of insulation, which could include: isocyanurate, polystyrene, or polyurethane.

Manufacturers of membrane roofing material certify local roofers as installers of their system and provide inspection services during construction as a prerequisite to issuing their guarantee. Various single-ply installations are shown in Figure 11.4.

Metal Roofing

Metal roofing can be categorized into two main systems. They are: preformed metal roofing systems and formed metal roofing systems.

Preformed Metal Roofing

Preformed metal roofing systems are installed on pitched roofs and, like metal siding, are made from aluminum or steel. Preformed deck is supported on purlins or other framing members, and then fastened with self-tapping screws with attached neoprene washers to prevent water from leaking through. Aluminum roofs can be prepainted or left natural, while steel roofs are usually galvanized, painted, or coated with asphalt. Preformed roofing is illustrated in Figure 11.5. This roof is cost-competitive with conventional roofing systems like built-up and membrane roofs.

Formed Metal Roofing

Formed metal roofing systems are usually installed on sloped roofs that have been covered with a base of plywood and concrete. Formed metal roofing systems are made from copper, tin, lead, or zinc alloy (T-C-Z). Flat sheets of metal are joined by tool-formed batten-seam, flat-seam or standing-seam joints. Various formed roofing seams are shown in Figure 11.6.

Formed lead roofs usually change to a white color after a number of years due to a process of oxidation. Formed copper roofs, unless treated to preserve a desired color, often turn blue-green (if the building is located in a "clean air" environment) or black (if the building is located in an industrial setting with a lot of chemicals in the environment). This type of roof is more expensive than a conventional roof but it has a pleasing appearance and a long life.

Tile

Tile roofing systems consist of tiles made from clay or concrete, installed on sloping roofs in overlapping layers with staggered vertical joints. Roofing tiles are attractive, durable, fireproof, and long-lasting, but are initially expensive. However, when the life cycle costs of roofs are considered, the high initial cost of tile may be offset by lower maintenance and replacement costs than with other, less durable roofing systems.

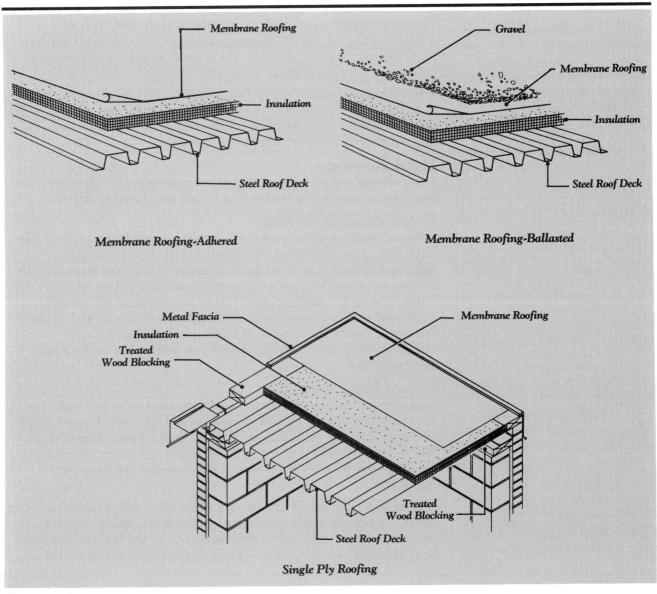

Figure 11.4

Roofing tiles are available in a variety of colors, patterns, and textures. The most popular shape is the mission tile, shown in Figure 11.7.

Because of the added load imposed by the tiles, which are heavier than other roofing materials, buildings with tile roofing require a stronger roof structure to support the additional load.

Shingle Roofing

Shingles are popularly used for covering sloped roofs, particularly in residential structures. Shingled roofs are normally designed to direct water by means of the slope. Therefore, such roofs often require a pitch of 3" or more per foot to perform effectively.

Shingles can be made from several different materials – aluminum, steel, slate, fiberglass, wood and asphalt (see Figure 11.8).

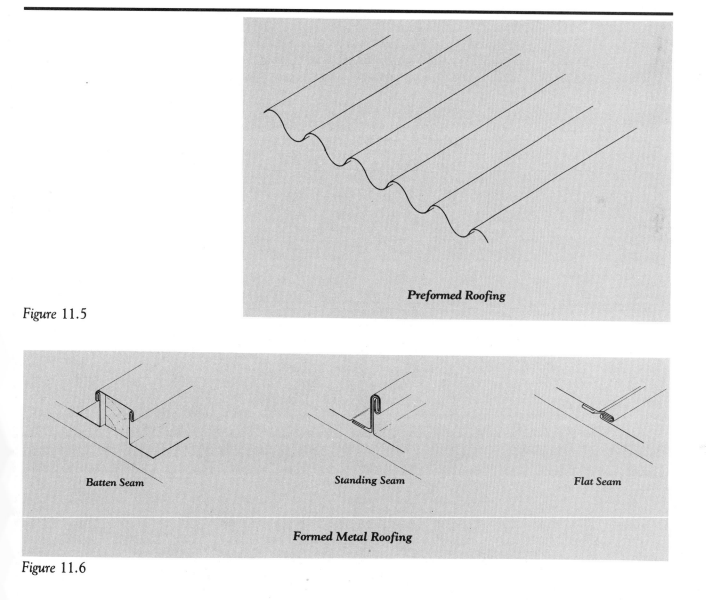

Preformed Roofing

Figure 11.5

Batten Seam   **Standing Seam**   **Flat Seam**

Formed Metal Roofing

Figure 11.6

Asphalt shingles are used on the majority of single-family homes in the United States because they are readily available, relatively inexpensive, easy to install, moderately fire-resistant, and last from 10 years to 20 years, depending on the composition, manufacturer, and the level of maintenance sustained during the life cycle of the material.

Asphalt shingles are made from heavy sheets of asphalt-impregnated felt with mineral granules on the face to act as both a decorative finish and a wearing layer. Shingles are usually installed by nailing them over roofers' felt that is applied to a plywood sheathing.

Asphalt shingles are available in a variety of weights and styles. The three-tab 240 lbs. is the most popular and economical size.

The American Society of Testing and Materials (ASTM), for building code purposes, categorizes roofing materials into four major classes.

- **Class A** includes materials that have been certified as Class A by approved testing agencies, as effective against severe fire exposure such as clay tiles, slate and concrete materials.
- **Class B** includes materials that have been certified as effective against moderate fire exposure, such as sheet metal roofing and composition shingles.
- **Class C** includes materials that have been certified as effective against light fire exposure, such as wood shingles treated with fire retardants and most asphalt shingles.
- **Unclassified** materials include untreated wood shingles used on uninhabitable structures such as storage sheds.

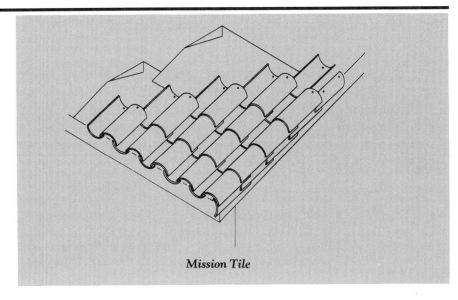

Mission Tile

Figure 11.7

Roofing Insulation

In most buildings, it is desirable to reduce both the loss of heat through the roof in the cold months and the conduction of heat from the sun through the roof into the building in the warmer months. This is the main purpose of roofing insulation.

Roofing insulation may be rigid or flexible. The four main types are: fill insulation, reflective insulation, batt insulation, and rigid insulation.

Fill Insulation

Fill insulation is blown through large tubes into spaces above the ceilings of buildings. It consists of granulated rock wool, fibrous mineral wool, or glass wool, either in the form of pellets blown in loose form into open spaces, or a fluffy noncombustible material. This type of insulation is used in residential structures and is blown or poured loose into the attic space above ceilings. Since the solar heat is allowed to be conducted through the roof, the attic space must be adequately vented.

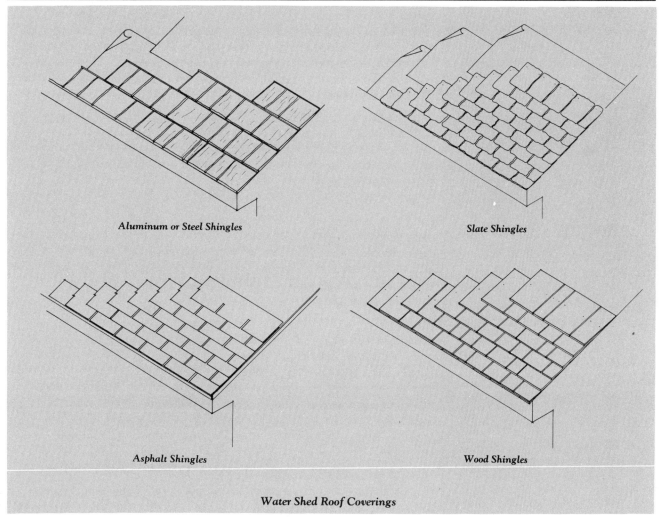

Aluminum or Steel Shingles

Slate Shingles

Asphalt Shingles

Wood Shingles

Water Shed Roof Coverings

Figure 11.8

Reflective Insulation

This type of insulation is placed in open spaces above the ceilings in a building to reflect a large percentage of the solar energy that strikes the roof. It is usually made from very thin sheets of copper or aluminum, or aluminum foil attached to the surface of rigid fiber or gypsum boards. Reflective insulation is installed between roof rafters.

Batt Insulation

Batt insulation is made from mineral fiber or glass fiber and may be in the form of "quilts" or "blankets." When used in residential buildings, it is placed above the ceiling, in the attic space. When used in commercial buildings, batt insulation is placed above the suspended ceilings, in the plenum. The attic or plenum must be vented.

Batt insulation may also be stapled between the rafters in wood framing. It may also be draped above the steel joist framing before the formed metal roof is installed in a metal building. Batt insulation is manufactured with or without a facing; kraft facing (made of heavy paper), foil facing (aluminum), and vinyl facing. The primary function of the facing is to act as a vapor barrier where condensation occurs between air at two different temperatures. A secondary function may be aesthetic.

Rigid Insulation

This type of insulation is installed on built-up and single-ply roofs between the roof deck and the roofing, for commercial buildings (illustrated in Figure 11.9). It is manufactured in sheets measuring from $2' \times 4'$ to $4' \times 8'$, in thicknesses from 1/2" to 3". The thermal resistance, "R value," of the insulation depends on the material and the thickness. Some single-ply roofing manufacturers specify a certain insulation for use with their membrane.

Isocyanurate, mineral fiberboard, fiberglass board, fiberglass and urethane composite board, foamglass sheets, perlite sheets, perlite urethane composite sheets, phenolic foam sheets, polystyrene sheets, and urethane and gypsum board composite sheets are some commonly used types of rigid insulation.

Roofing Accessories

In addition to insulation and roof coverings, there are several roofing system accessories that are of equal importance in preventing the penetration of water. These accessories waterproof the boundaries of roofs, such as edges and openings, and include flashing, expansion joints, gravel stop, gutters and downspouts, and specialties such as hatches and skylights.

Flashing

An edge condition is waterproofed by turning up flashing on a vertical surface such as a cant strip, parapet, curb, or wall. Base flashing is used to cover the exposed vertical edge of the roofing and counter flashing to terminate the base flashing. Flashings are thin impervious sheets made from metal such as aluminum, copper, lead-coated copper, lead, copper-clad stainless steel, stainless steel, zinc and copper alloy, galvanized metal, or rubber such as polyvinyl chloride (PVC) and butyl rubber.

Examples of roof flashing appear in Figure 11.10.

Typically, flashings are installed on the perimeter of the roof, around penetrations through roofs (such as pipes, vents, hatches, skylights, curbs for rooftop equipment, etc.), along roof expansion joints, and sometimes, at places on the roof where there are changes in slope.

Like insulation, flashing materials should be selected that are compatible with the roofing system and adjacent materials.

Expansion Joints

Expansion joints introduce a discontinuity into two different portions of the same building, such as between two wings or between a high rise and a low rise section. It allows the structural system of each portion to act independently of the other. In a roofing system, this is achieved by making an edge condition on either side of the joint and covering the separation with a metal or rubber closure piece. Expansion joints typically consist of job-built or prefabricated blocking material designed to raise the joint covering above the roofing material, as illustrated in Figure 11.11.

The joint may also be filled with a compressible material such as rubber, felt, or neoprene to keep it air tight.

Gravel Stop

Gravel stop is a strip or flange usually fabricated from aluminum, copper, lead-coated copper, polyvinyl chloride, galvanized steel, or stainless steel, and used at the edges of flat roofs. An example is shown in Figure 11.12.

A gravel stop serves three functions: as termination gravel at the edge of a roof, as a counter flashing, and as a decorative strip. The height of the exposed face normally varies from 4 to 12 inches or more and the flashing return is fabricated to suit the roof edge conditions. The finish on the gravel stop may be natural, painted, or in the case of aluminum, anodized.

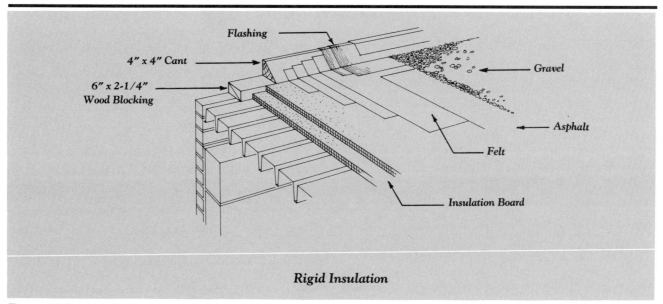

Rigid Insulation

Figure 11.9

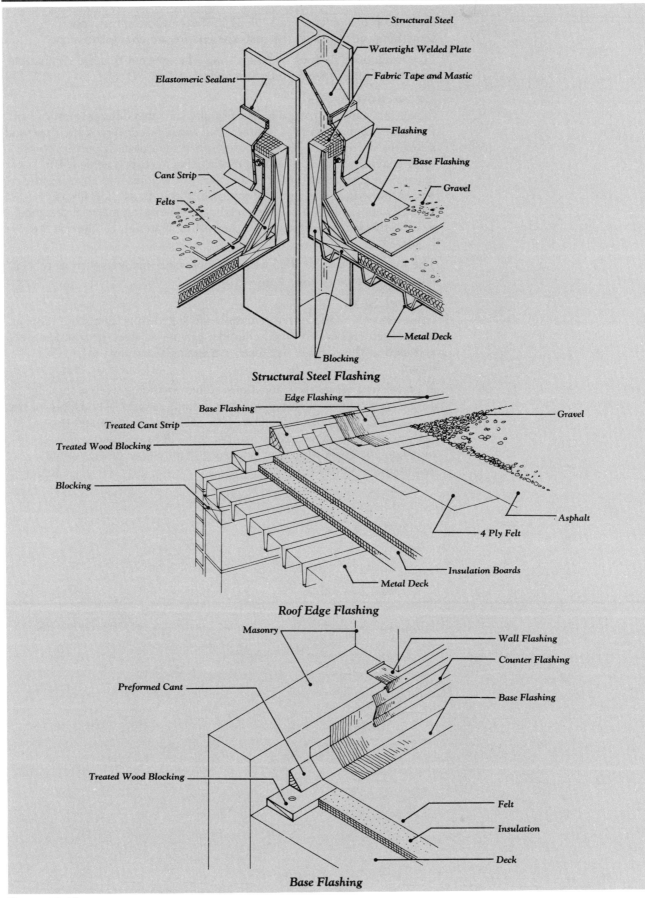

Structural Steel Flashing

Structural Steel
Watertight Welded Plate
Fabric Tape and Mastic
Flashing
Base Flashing
Gravel
Metal Deck
Elastomeric Sealant
Cant Strip
Felts
Blocking

Roof Edge Flashing

Edge Flashing
Base Flashing
Treated Cant Strip
Treated Wood Blocking
Blocking
Gravel
Asphalt
4 Ply Felt
Insulation Boards
Metal Deck

Base Flashing

Masonry
Wall Flashing
Counter Flashing
Base Flashing
Preformed Cant
Treated Wood Blocking
Felt
Insulation
Deck

Figure 11.10

222

Gutters

Gutters and downspout systems are used to collect runoff from the perimeter of a sloped roof that has no interior drainage. Examples of gutters and downspouts are shown in Figure 11.13.

Gutters may be metal, such as aluminum, copper, lead-coated copper, galvanized steel, and stainless steel, plastic, or vinyl. They are usually available in stock lengths and various cross-sectional shapes along with accessories such as mounting brackets, connectors, corners, end caps, downspout connectors and leaf guards. Round or rectangular downspouts are also available with accessories to match gutter systems.

Hatches

Roof hatches are required by many building codes to either provide access from the building to the roof or to help clear the building of smoke, in the event of fire. Examples of the two types of hatches are illustrated in Figure 11.14.

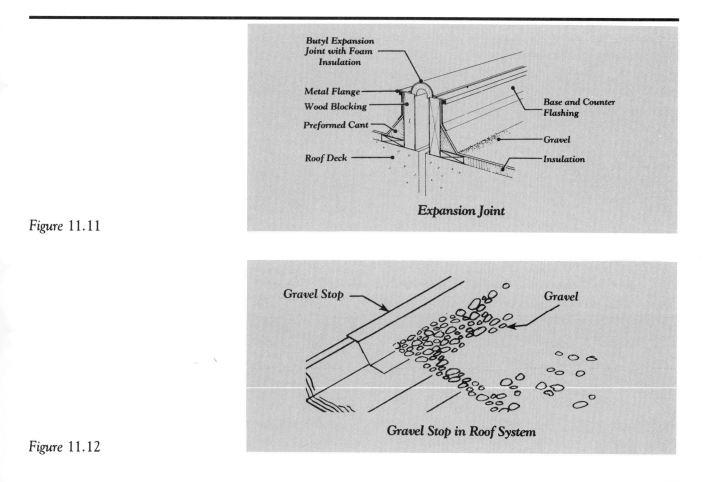

Figure 11.11

Butyl Expansion Joint with Foam Insulation

Metal Flange
Wood Blocking
Preformed Cant

Roof Deck

Base and Counter Flashing

Gravel

Insulation

Expansion Joint

Figure 11.12

Gravel Stop

Gravel

Gravel Stop in Roof System

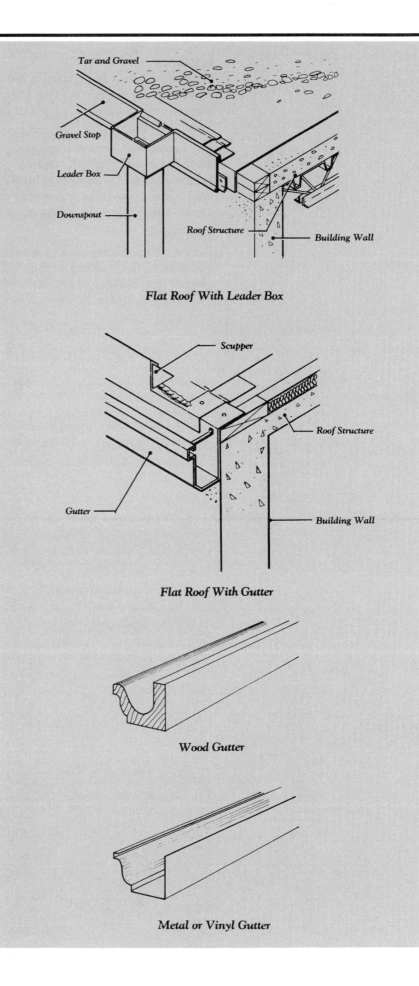

Flat Roof With Leader Box

Flat Roof With Gutter

Wood Gutter

Metal or Vinyl Gutter

Figure 11.13

Roof hatches for access are generally prefabricated from aluminum or steel and assembled with a preformed curb with counter flashing. Access to the hatch is usually provided by a ladder permanently attached to an adjacent wall inside the building. The covers are typically hinged and have operating levers, latches, and sometimes, locks. Some models may be available with an optional plexiglass cover.

Smoke hatches are also prefabricated with a preformed metal curb. The cover is usually spring-loaded and opens automatically when activated by a fusible link. Both types of hatches are secured in place on the substrate, first, then the roofing is tied into the curb with flashing.

Skylights

Skylights are mainly used to provide natural light through the roof to the interior and, if operable, provide ventilation. They can be custom fabricated to satisfy most design requirements.

Skylights are usually made from metal frames and are single or multi-glazed with acrylic or polycarbonate plastic, or laminated, tempered, wired, or insulated glass. Skylights and domes are manufactured in many sizes, shapes, and configurations as illustrated in Figure 11.15.

Summary

The roof is a very important part of a building. Therefore, care should be taken in selecting the proper system. In addition to an appropriate design and material specification, it is advisable to select a qualified and experienced roofer to install the system in accordance with the manufacturer's instructions. Appropriate materials and installation will save time and money otherwise spent in making repairs to the roof if water penetration occurs.

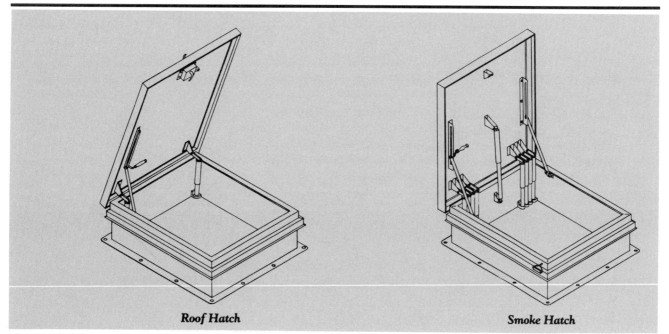

Roof Hatch　　　　　**Smoke Hatch**

Figure 11.14

225

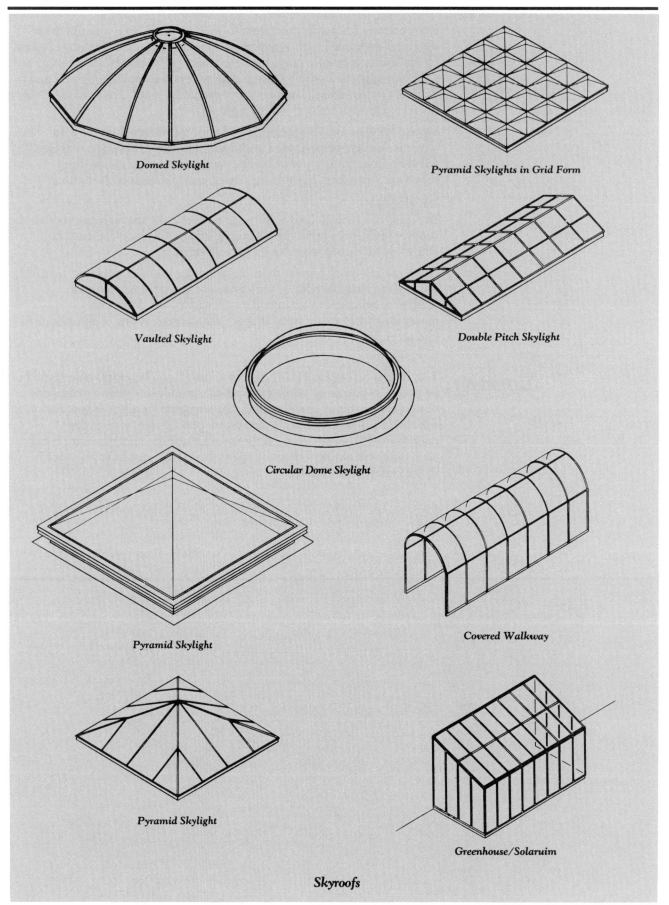

Domed Skylight

Pyramid Skylights in Grid Form

Vaulted Skylight

Double Pitch Skylight

Circular Dome Skylight

Pyramid Skylight

Covered Walkway

Pyramid Skylight

Greenhouse/Solaruim

Skyroofs

Figure 11.15

226

Chapter Twelve

Interior Construction

Most interior construction is installed after the substructure, superstructure, exterior closure, and roofing are complete enough to protect the interior of the building from the weather. Although there are variations from one building to another, the scope of work of interior construction can be generally classified into **partitions, millwork, finishes,** and **doors and hardware.** Each of these main categories has several subcategories, as shown in Figure 12.1.

Because of the specialized and varied nature of interior construction, most general contractors subcontract the interior work to specialists who perform this kind of work on a regular basis.

Partitions Interior partitions are categorized into two main groups: **stationary** and **moveable.** In addition to dividing and separating open spaces within a building, interior partitions may also serve as **fire walls, fire separation walls, shaft walls,** or **bearing walls.** Fire walls extend continuously from the foundation to the roof, to restrict the spread of fire through a building. Fire separation walls also restrict the spread of fire through a building, but unlike fire walls, do not extend from the foundation to the roof. Shaft walls are used principally to surround stair, elevator, and mechanical shafts that require specified fire ratings.

Stationary Partitions

Stationary interior partitions may be constructed from concrete or masonry which can be left unfinished or simply painted. Wood or metal can also be used to construct partitions as well, with a greater degree of finish work. (A variety of finishes are discussed in more detail in the latter part of this chapter.)

Concrete and Masonry

Concrete partitions are cast-in-place or precast. Masonry is erected in nominal sizes of 4″ to 12″ units of concrete block or bricks, or of structural glazed tile. (See Chapter 8 for more information on concrete.) These partitions add considerably to the total load on the foundations, and thus are usually used for sheer walls, fire walls, or bearing walls.

Wood

Wood stud partitions (shown in Figure 12.2) can be readily fabricated on a construction site for all partitioning requirements.

Wood stud partitions are fabricated of 2″ × 4″, or 2″ × 6″, dimensional lumber, S4S, spaced 12″, 16″, or 24″ on center and covered with a variety of finishes such as gypsum wallboard (known popularly as drywall or sheetrock), plaster, composition board, or wood panelling.

This type of partition may be used in conjunction with several layers of finishes to meet the fire rating and/or acoustical requirements. Examples of wood stud partitions of various constructions are shown in Figure 12.3.

Any applicable building codes should be consulted to determine the thickness of the partition, the required fire rating, and the material to be selected.

Metal

Metal stud partitions are commonly used for commercial construction projects in the United States. They are fabricated from light-gauge metal (usually steel) and designed to be either loadbearing or non-loadbearing.

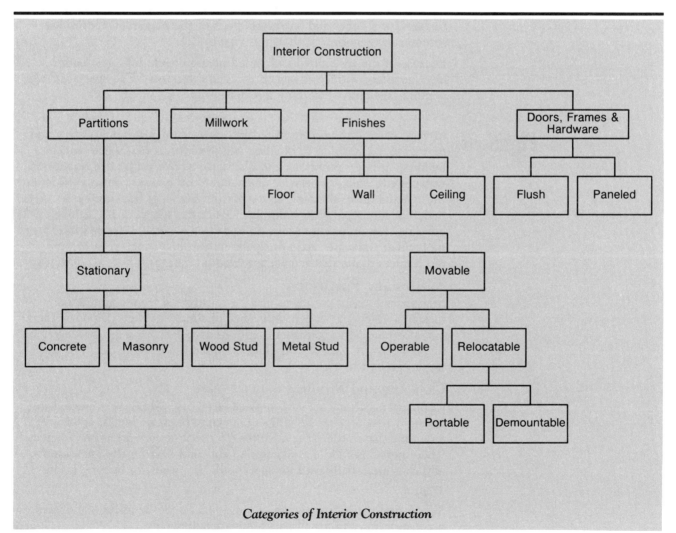

Categories of Interior Construction

Figure 12.1

Non-loadbearing studs are available in 25 and 20-gauge, and in widths of 1-1/2″ to 3-5/8″, 4″, and 6″. Loadbearing studs (also referred to as "C studs") are available in 18 to 12 gauge and in depths from 1-5/8″ to 12″.

Metal studs for interior partitions may be covered similar to wood studs, as illustrated in Figure 12.4.

Metal studs are generally manufactured with openings or "knockouts" to allow passage for plumbing pipes, electrical conduits, and wiring, and are available with matching track and bridging. The studs are available factory-painted or galvanized and may be connected to the track with self-tapping screws, drilling, or welding. Partition framing is attached to concrete with expansion bolts or power-driven fasteners, and to steel framing with power-driven fasteners.

A special type of metal stud is manufactured for fire-rated (mechanical) shaft wall construction called a CH stud, in which the panel on the shaft side is installed as the studs are erected.

Moveable Partitions

Moveable partitions include **operable walls** (folding partitions) and **relocatable partitions**, and are available in a variety of sizes, shapes, and finishes.

Operable Walls

Operable partitions are either manually or power-operated. Configurations include the folding accordion, folding leaf, or individual panel systems, as shown in Figure 12.5. These walls are usually top-track supported, but some models are available with floor supports. Track systems can be obtained in straight lengths, curves, or with right-angle layouts and switches. Provisions must be made in the ceiling finish and structure to allow for the support track.

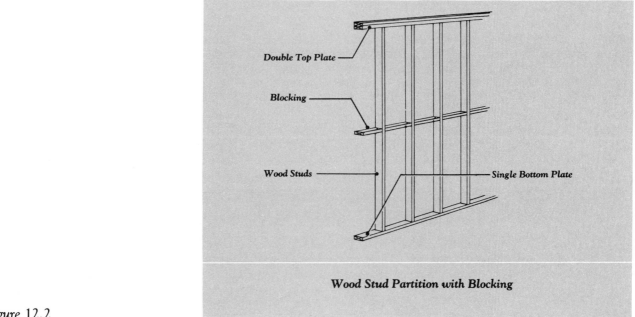

Double Top Plate

Blocking

Wood Studs

Single Bottom Plate

Wood Stud Partition with Blocking

Figure 12.2

The panels for operable partitions are usually made from wood, aluminum, or composition board filled with sound insulation and painted or covered with carpet, fabric, plastic laminate, vinyl, cork or wood panelling.

Large operable partitions are generally installed by factory specialists or authorized manufacturer's representatives after the framing and supporting members have been furnished and erected by the general contractor.

Relocatable partitions are either **portable**, designed for frequent relocation, or **demountable**, designed for infrequent relocation. An example of a relocatable partition is shown in Figure 12.6.

Relocatable partitions are manufactured of the same materials as operable partitions. However, they may be custom-fabricated to meet the designer's specifications.

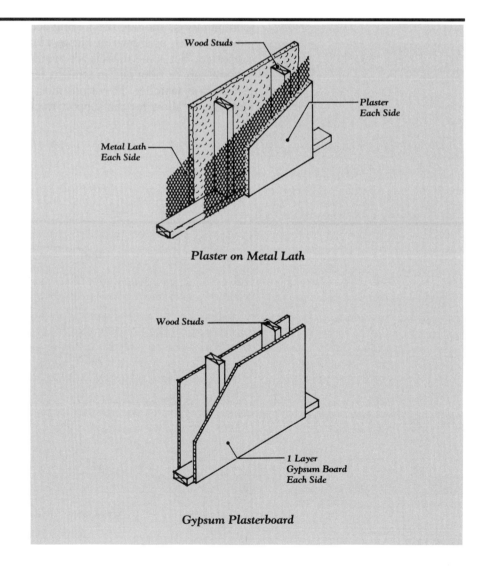

Plaster on Metal Lath

Gypsum Plasterboard

Figure 12.3

Demountable partitions are either hollow or solid, are fixed in place by tracks set into the floor and ceiling, and involve a limited amount of field assembly. The panels are modular and made of gypsum enamel and carpeting. Power is delivered to the wall switches and outlets through vertical mullions. The normally solid partition may also be ordered with partial, half, or full glass windows. These partitions are usually employed to create full private offices, with doors, within a floor plan.

Portable partitions are self-supporting by virtue of being interconnected with adjacent partitions running at right angles. They are used to define work "stations" without doors rather than full offices and are partial, not full height, partitions. The panels may contain power and are prefabricated, needing only field connections. The choice of finishes for portable partitions is similar to those for demountable partitions. A number of different accessories are available that can be mounted onto the walls, including shelves, desk tops, and drawer units.

Millwork

The term *millwork* is used to refer to manufactured products of wood or plastic that are installed as finishes on the project. Millwork items are manufactured from softwoods such as fir or pine. Certain millwork items have been minimally manufactured (shaped or surfaced), such as moldings and trim (shown in Figure 12.7). Other products that fall into this category are shelving and handrails. Most of the labor to turn this material into a finished product, like door frames and casings or base molding, is provided by finish carpenters in the field. Finish carpenters also work with minimally manufactured hardwood items to produce

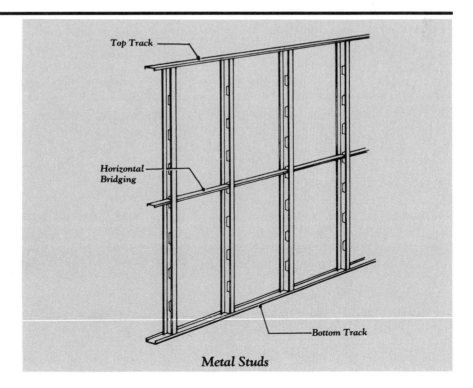

Figure 12.4

Metal Studs

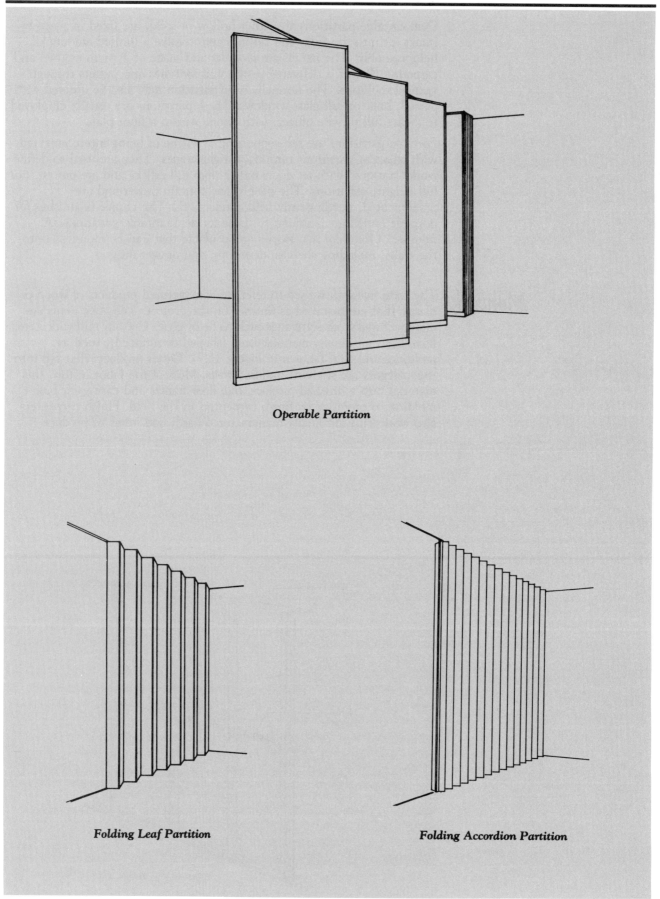

Operable Partition

Folding Leaf Partition

Folding Accordion Partition

Figure 12.5

window sills, thresholds, chair rails, and stair parts. Some stair pieces, such as baluster and starting newels (see Figure 12.7), have been turned on a lathe.

A second group of millwork items are fabricated mainly in the shop or factory, requiring only minimal assembly in the field. These include casework, cabinets, desks, countertops, special railings, panelling, doors, and windows. Stock items in this category come off an assembly line in a factory. Custom items are made in a local millworking shop.

Finishes

Interior finishes protect the interior surfaces in a building from wear and tear while providing a pleasant, comfortable, and coordinated appearance.

Floor Finishes

Although several factors are considered in the selection of floor finishes, the following represent some common considerations:

- Cost (initial and life-cycle)
- The amount and type of traffic
- The environment that the finish must withstand
- The ease and cost of maintenance
- The appearance
- The type and condition of the subfloor
- The waste factor during installation

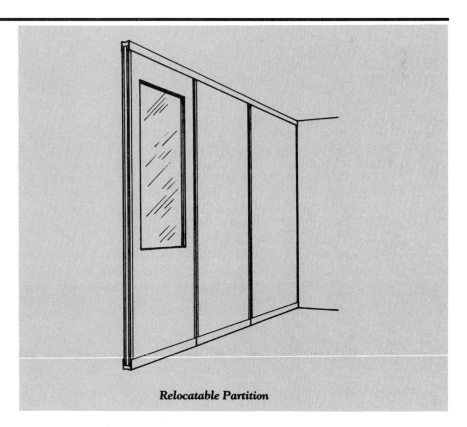

Relocatable Partition

Figure 12.6

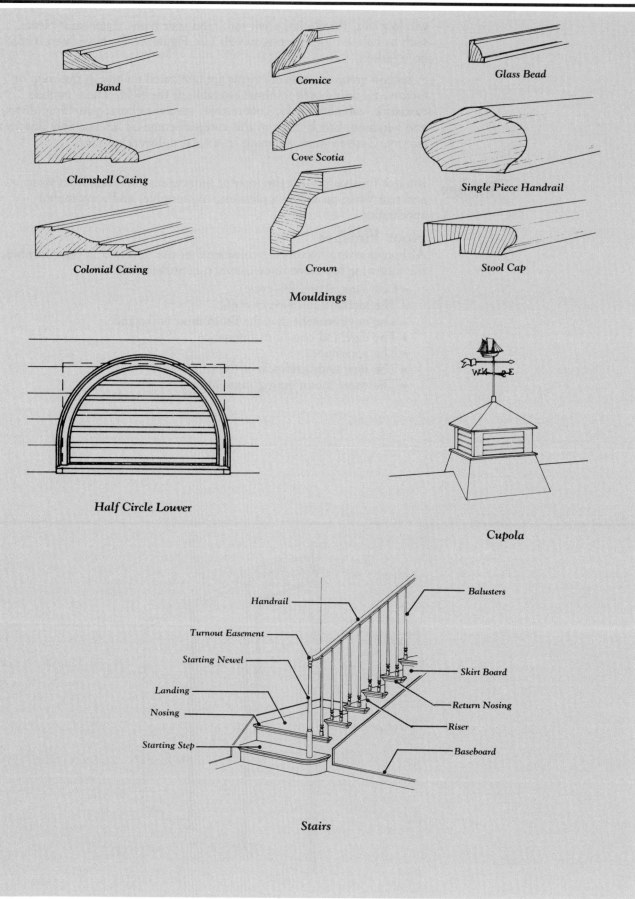

Band

Cornice

Glass Bead

Clamshell Casing

Cove Scotia

Single Piece Handrail

Colonial Casing

Crown

Stool Cap

Mouldings

Half Circle Louver

Cupola

Handrail

Balusters

Turnout Easement

Starting Newel

Skirt Board

Landing

Return Nosing

Nosing

Riser

Starting Step

Baseboard

Stairs

Figure 12.7

Along with the selection of flooring, a suitable base must be chosen. The base is the material placed between the wall and the floor. A carpentry item can be selected, but there are a variety of other flooring materials available as well.

Carpet

Carpet is preferred as flooring in both residential and priority areas of commercial buildings because it is an attractive, sound-softening covering that can be installed relatively cleanly and quickly. The surface material of carpet may be acrylic, nylon, polypropylene, and/or wool. The backing is made from jute, cotton, rayon, polyester, or polypropylene. The surface material is attached to the backing by tufting, weaving, fusion bonding, knitting, or needle punching.

Carpet is specified by its face weight in ounces per square yard, pile height, density, or stitches per inch.

Carpet is manufactured in rolls that vary in width from 12 feet to 20 feet; the width must be considered in determining the amount of waste and subsequent final cost of the materials. It is usually installed over sponge rubber, urethane, or foam pads. Some manufacturers seal carpet with an attached pad. An example of carpet laid on a pad is shown in Figure 12.8. The most common bases used with carpet are vinyl or rubber in commercial construction, and wood in residential construction. Vinyl carpet base is usually flat or straight (i.e., having a vertical leg only). It comes in heights of 2-1/2, 4 and 6 inches, all 1/8" thick, and a variety of complementary colors. Vinyl carpet is applied with adhesive and has special pieces for corners and exposed ends.

In recent years, carpet tiles have become popular on commercial projects for ease of installation. Special flat electrical cables are available for power distribution under these tiles. They are especially desirable on raised flooring (pedestal) systems for access computer cables, wiring, power, and telephone lines. The use of carpet tiles permits economical relocation or repair of any underfloor systems. It also allows worn areas to be easily replaced without having to replace the entire carpet.

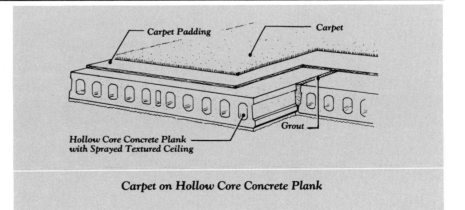

Carpet on Hollow Core Concrete Plank

Figure 12.8

Resilient Flooring

The most common material specified for this type of flooring is vinyl composition tile (VCT). However, other tile is available in the following materials: asphalt, pure vinyl, cork, and rubber. Resilient flooring is also manufactured as "sheet goods" (rolls) in polyvinyl chloride and vinyl. All of these tiles are available with or without resilient backing in a wide range of colors and designs. Preparation of the subfloor for resilient tile involves the use of steel trowels for finishing new concrete floors or a thin concrete, wood, plywood, or hardwood underlayer for irregular surfaces.

As with carpeting, vinyl or rubber bases are used with resilient floors as well. In this application, the cove shaped base (as opposed to straight) is preferred. Dimensions and color selections are similar to carpet base. Figure 12.9 shows resilient tile installed on a concrete slab.

Composition Flooring

Occasionally, certain flooring materials must be seamless to meet high sanitary standards. Composition flooring is one such material composed of colored aggregate in an epoxy, polyester, acrylic, and/or polyurethane resin base. This material is slip-proof and highly durable. In most cases, the materials combined to form composition flooring are highly specific for the intended application.

Examples of areas where composition flooring is required are beverage bottling plants, parking facilities, gymnasiums, multi-purpose rooms, locker rooms, and explosion hazard areas.

Composition flooring is made by mixing a two-part compound, which is hand-troweled by trained specialty contractors. For this type of flooring, both the slab preparation and timely application are critical to the success of the installation.

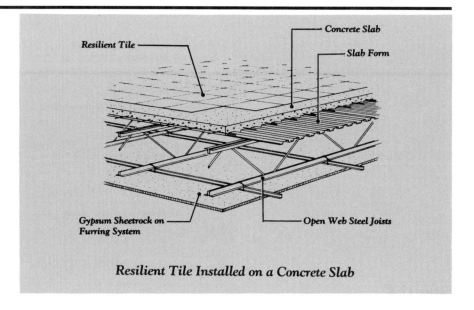

Resilient Tile Installed on a Concrete Slab

Figure 12.9

236

Wood Flooring

The most common wood flooring materials are hardwoods, oak, and maple, and for softwood, pine. Hardwoods such as ash, beech, cherry, mahogany, and pecan; exotic hardwoods such as ebony, karpa wood, rosewood, and zebra wood; and softwoods such as cedar, fir, spruce, and hemlock can also be used to create different effects.

Wood flooring is available in four common forms – strip solid or laminated planks, solid or laminated parquet, industrial wood block flooring, and fabricated wood block flooring.

Strip Flooring: Strip flooring material is available in several different milling formats and combinations including tongue-and-grooved and matched, square-edged, and jointed with square edges and splines. Strip flooring can be installed on either a wood or concrete subfloor. A typical subfloor in wood framing is made up of wood boards or plywood sheets fastened to the floor joists, as illustrated in Figure 12.10.

Parquet Flooring: Parquet floors (shown in Figure 12.11) are prefabricated in squares of various sizes milled with square edges, tongue-and-grooved edges, or splines. Parquet flooring material is available from some manufacturers with optional adhered backings that protect the wood from moisture, add comfort to the walking area, provide insulation, and deaden sound. This type of flooring is installed by attaching the squares with adhesive to firm level subfloors of

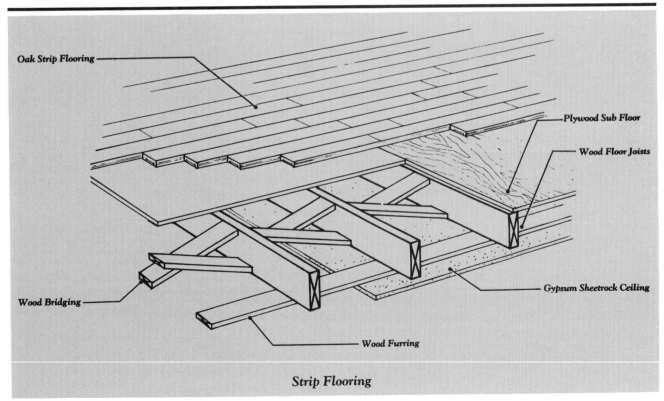

Oak Strip Flooring

Plywood Sub Floor

Wood Floor Joists

Gypsum Sheetrock Ceiling

Wood Bridging

Wood Furring

Strip Flooring

Figure 12.10

concrete, boards, plywood, particle board, or over existing floor coverings such as resilient tile and terrazzo.

Wood Block Flooring: Industrial wood blocks, also known as "end-grain blocks," are used for industrial applications. This material is manufactured from heavy pieces of wood cut into individual blocks. Typical surface dimensions of wood block are $3'' \times 6''$, $4'' \times 6''$, and $4'' \times 8''$, and have a nominal thickness ranging from 1-1/2" to 4". Wood blocks may also be purchased in preassembled strips, with the ends of the grain exposed to wear. Installation involves applying a layer of pitch to a concrete floor and then setting the wood blocks in the pitch. The finish coating of pitch or similar material is then squeezed into the joints between the blocks to provide additional fastening strength. A final sealer is applied to provide the surface finish.

Fabricated Flooring: Fabricated wood flooring consists of squares or rectangular blocks formed by fastening short pieces of strip flooring together with tongue-and-groove joints on all sides. The surfaces of fabricated flooring may be sanded, filled, waxed, and polished at the factory. This type of flooring is suitable for gymnasium or sports floors, where specialized installation methods are required because of a unique function and size.

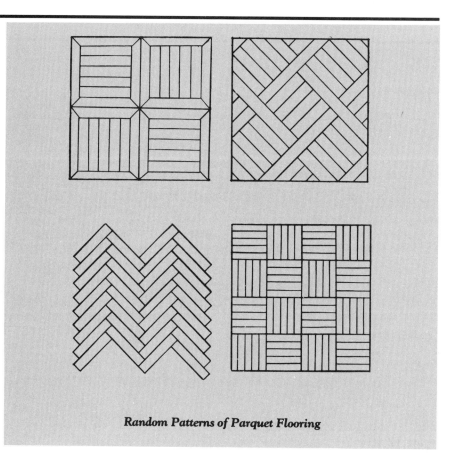

Random Patterns of Parquet Flooring

Figure 12.11

Tile Flooring

Tiles are versatile materials for creating various floor and wall finishes because of their modular installation and multi-purpose capabilities. Tiles are manufactured in a wide range of shapes, sizes, and finishes from several basic materials including clay, porcelain, cement, metal, and plastic. In addition, split brick pavers, quarry tiles, and terra cotta tiles are available. Tile shapes and sizes vary from 1″ (mosaic) squares to a variety of rectangles, mosaics, patterned combinations, hexagons, octagons, valencia, wedges, and circles. Multicolored designs, mural sets, or individual pieces embossed with special designs, logos, or pictures can be custom ordered.

Ceramic Tile: The most popular tile is ceramic tile. The most common tile sizes for walls are 4″ × 4″ and 6″ × 6″ and for floors, 1′ × 1′. Standard and custom ceramic tiles are manufactured with various surface finishes including glazed, unglazed, matte, nonslip, and textured.

There are two methods commonly used for installing ceramic tiles – the thick set method and the thin set method. For the thick set method (also known as mud set), tiles are installed in a mixture of portland cement, sand, and water, screeded to a thickness of 3/4″ to 1-1/4″. The thin set method involves installing tiles with latex or epoxy based mortars or adhesives. Tile installation is completed by grouting, which seals the joints and provides a uniform appearance. There are several appropriate mixtures to use; epoxy grout and silicone rubber grout are two commonly used sealants.

In addition to standard (flat) wall tile, there are bullnose pieces with a rounded edge for a top border and cove pieces for a base. When floor tile is used alone there are smaller surface and cove bases to complement that design.

Stone Flooring

Stone flooring is comprised of square tiles or slabs of slate, flagstone, granite, or marble 3/8″ to 1″ in thickness. Patterned or random designs are created during installation, as illustrated in Figure 12.12.

Stone floors are installed in mortar beds, mastic adhesive, or are thin set. When installed in a mortar bed, the thickness of the stone can vary inversely with the depth of mortar to produce a level surface. However, when the stone floor is thin set or laid in mastic, gauged (constant thickness) stones must be used. Installation is usually completed by grouting the joints with premixed grouting materials in various colors of mortar, and applying a coat of sealer to the surface. A flat (vertical) stone base is often used with stone flooring.

Concrete Topping

A bare concrete floor serves a dual purpose: it supports the structural load while providing a wearing surface. When concrete is used for interior floors, a **topping** may be applied to the floor. Concrete topping is a mixture of portland cement, fine aggregate (sand), water and, in some cases, small coarse aggregate (1/2″ maximum in size). The thickness of the topping varies from 3/4″ to 2″. Various admixtures or hardeners are added to the topping to improve its wearing properties, and coloring additives to improve its appearance. In some cases, three coats of paint are applied in place of a coloring additive. A monolithic base is usually formed in conjunction with the topping.

Although concrete toppings are not as comfortable as some of the other floor coverings, they are relatively inexpensive, easily cleaned, and very durable if constructed properly. Bare concrete floors, if finished with steel trowel machines and sealed, make excellent floor finishes.

Terrazzo Flooring

Terrazzo flooring is exceptionally durable, easy to clean and maintain, and is available in many colors.

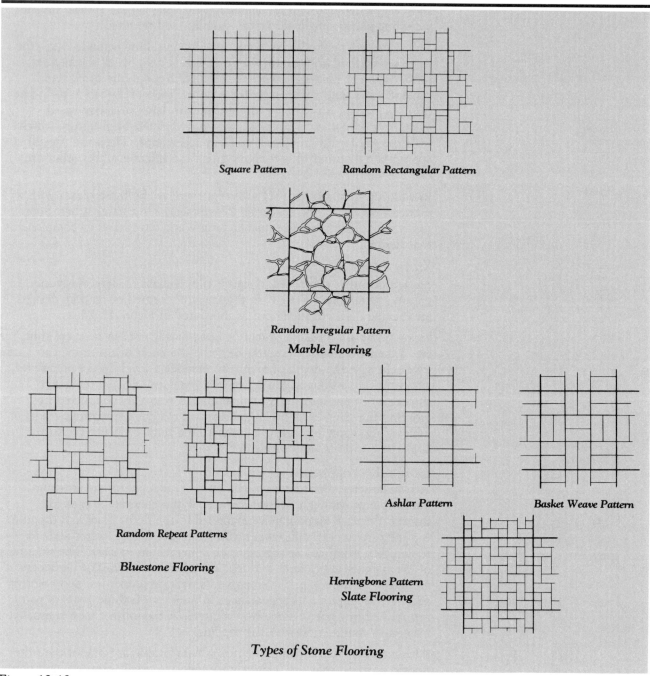

Square Pattern   Random Rectangular Pattern

Random Irregular Pattern
Marble Flooring

Random Repeat Patterns

Bluestone Flooring

Ashlar Pattern   Basket Weave Pattern

Herringbone Pattern
Slate Flooring

Types of Stone Flooring

Figure 12.12

Terrazzo is made from a colored epoxy cement concrete (matrix) containing aggregate chips of granite, marble, glass, and onyx. The finished surface is then ground and polished to highlight the colorful aggregate material within. In some cases, well-graded gravel or other stone materials are added to the mix to create different textures. Terrazzo flooring is illustrated in Figure 12.13.

Terrazzo flooring is installed in a 5/8" thick layer: on a concrete underbed; over sand as sand-cushioned terrazzo; bonded terrazzo; monolithicly applied on a concrete slab; or in a thin (1/8") layer directly on the concrete slab. Sand-cushioned terrazzo consists of three layers of material: a 1/4" sand cushion placed on a concrete slab and covered by an isolation membrane; an approximately 2-1/8" thick mesh-reinforced concrete underbed; and a 5/8" thick terrazzo topping. Bonded terrazzo consists of two layers: a 1-1/8" thick concrete underbed placed on the slab and a 5/8" thick terrazzo topping. Monolithic terrazzo topping can only be applied to a properly prepared concrete slab. First, control joints are saw-cut and divider strips grouted into place. The divider strips are manufactured from zinc, brass, or colored plastic. The strips serve several purposes: to control shrinkage; as leveling guides; as dividers to permit changes in aggregate mix; and as a design to separate one section from another. Once positioned, the 5/8" layer of terrazzo can be placed and ground.

Wall Finishes

The most commonly used wall finishes are painting and wall covering, which vary considerably with respect to sequence in the construction, surface preparation, application, waste calculations, and maintenance.

Painting

Painting protects interior wall surfaces against moisture, stain, and wear, and provides a neat, coordinated, pleasant appearance. Paints are readily available in a wide range of colors and sheens (gloss, semi-gloss, and flat). Varnishes and urethanes can also be used on wood surfaces. A breakdown of paint types by usage is shown in Figure 12.14.

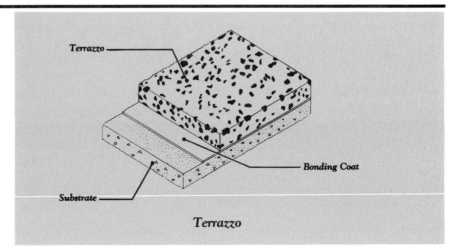

Terrazzo

Bonding Coat

Substrate

Terrazzo

Figure 12.13

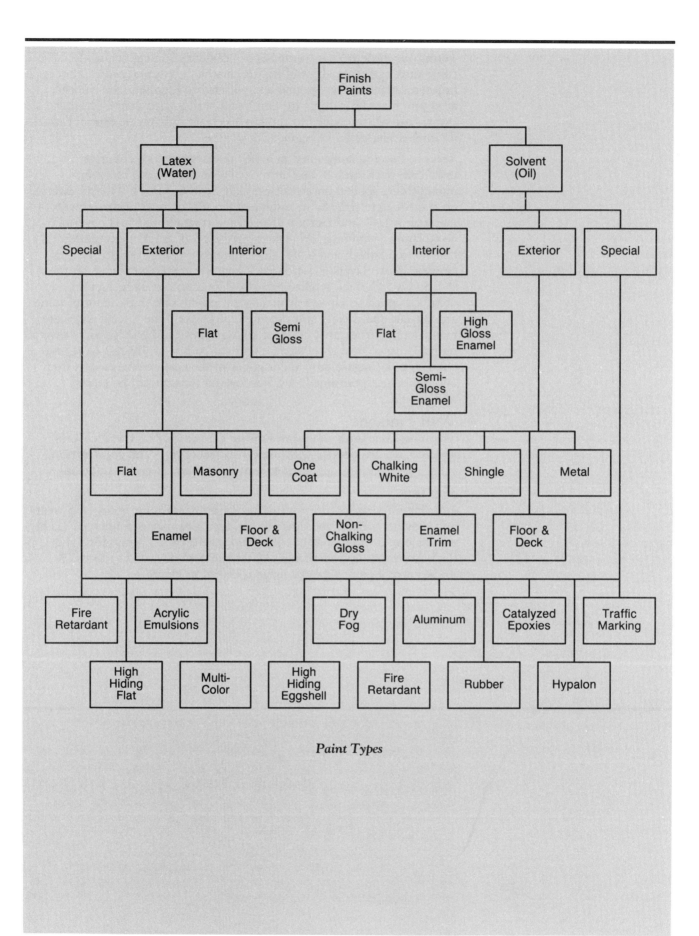

Paint Types

Figure 12.14

The four main groupings for painting and coating are: transparent finishes, primers, undercoating, and finish coats.

Transparent Finishes: The first group includes shellac, lacquer, and varnish, primarily to protect natural wood used in finishes such as floors, stairs, doors, and furniture.

Primers: The two main types of primers are oil-based primer and latex. Oil-based primer is compatible with both oil (solvent) and latex-based finish paints, but latex primer can only be used with latex finish paint. A primer's functions are to seal the substrate and give the surface a uniform opacity. Other primers have been developed for highly specific substrates such as masonry, metal, or previously varnished surfaces. Concrete block surfaces must be filled, rather than primed, prior to painting.

Undercoating: Undercoating is the preferred first coat under enamel paint finish coats.

Finish Coats: The two main formulations for finish paint are latex (water) or solvent (oil) based. Latex paints are emulsions and dry through the evaporation of water. Drying is fast under normal conditions and in hot climates may be so rapid as to inhibit brushing. Latex paints do not penetrate the surface, so surface preparation is critical to a good bond. Mechanical methods such as wire brushing are employed to remove chalk, flaking paint, and loose dirt. Chemical methods such as bleach and detergents are used to remove oil, grease, and mildew.

Solvent paints dry through the solvent evaporation. Neither formulation is good for immersion in water, but solvent paints develop a tighter film than latex paints and are superior in abnormally wet environments. Solvent paint surfaces deteriorate through oxidation which a film of fresh solvent paint can arrest. A latex paint film is "breathable," however, under which old solvent painted surfaces will continue to oxidize and peel.

Paints get their color through pigments and their spreadability through the "vehicle." The vehicle component in latex paint is a man-made resin and in solvent paint is oil. Enamels are solvent-based paints in which the pigments are more finely ground and the vehicle is varnish, a combination of resins and oil. This premium finish spreads much smoother than paint, is self-leveling, and has considerable hiding power. The resulting film has a high gloss and retains the gloss for the extended period.

Special Paints: Special paints have been developed for as many specific applications as there are surfaces or conditions, some of which bear mentioning. Paints with improved "hiding" power, that of obscuring the undercoat, are referred to as "one coat" and "high hiding." These paints can be applied in thick coats, without sagging (running), and are used for exterior, rapid interior and acoustical repainting.

Solvents in dry fog paint are used for spraying interior walls and ceilings. These paints dry before they fall to the floor, eliminating damage caused by overspray.

Fire retardant paints have been developed in several formulations, both latex and solvent, which significantly reduce flame spread through swelling (intumescence), to form a honeycomb structure to protect the surface.

A few paints have been developed for immersion in water (for swimming pools and exterior masonry), among them cement and rubber-based types. Rubber-based paints, when used along with aluminum paints, are excellent for protecting metals in roofing, window, railing, and heating systems.

Several paints develop films of extreme hardness that are very dense, which protect surfaces from harsh chemicals. Such compounds are the result of catalytic reaction of epoxy materials, used on tanks, pipes, and structural steel. These are applied in layers much thicker (20 mils) than paint (4 mils) and are more properly called coatings.

Most paint coatings are applied with brushes, rollers, or spray guns of which there are two types; air and airless. The number of coats applied depends on factors such as the type of material to be coated and the intended use of the building, and is indicated in the specifications or finishes schedule.

Costs: There are minimal mobilization (set-up) costs associated with painting operations; the compressors in an air spray situation account for a large percentage of set-up costs. Other set-up costs involve protection of other finishes, drop cloths, scaffolding, and daily cleanup of tools. Cleanup costs are reduced with the use of latex paints because they drip less and are water soluble.

Application: Obviously, the fastest rate of application with the least amount of control is by spraying, but this method is limited to large surfaces. Because overspray is hard to control, there is a 10 to 20% material loss. Some paints are formulated for spray application only, such as high hiding and catalyzed types. For others, such as fire retardant and aluminum paints, the desired coating thickness is better controlled with spray guns. Usually, paints are thinned somewhat to facilitate spraying.

Roller application is the next fastest painting method but it is also limited to larger surfaces because splattering is hard to control. Extensions of the handle can sometimes eliminate the need for scaffolding.

Brush work is used for most types of painting and is the method over which the worker has the most control. It is required for narrow surfaces, accent stripping, curved and irregular surfaces such as piping and millwork, and ornamented work. Some paints, like machinery enamel, must be brush-applied.

Wall Coverings

Wall coverings may be manufactured, printed, or woven. The selection of materials is enormous and includes burlaps, jutes, weaves, grasses, paper, leather, vinyl, silks, corks, aluminum foil, copper sheets, cork tiles, wood panelling, and mirrors. Wallpaper, vinyl coverings, and woven fabric coverings are the most popular and are available in different weights, backings, colors, and quality. Wood coverings usually come from the factory in the form of panels or strips.

Surfaces to receive wallcovering must be prepared by sizing or preluding the surface. Mildew must be treated with bleach. "Hot spots," or highly alkaline concentrations on the surface, will discolor the wallpaper and must be treated with zinc sulfate. Holes and cracks must be filled and the surface should be left uniformly smooth.

The roll is cut into strips, paste is brushed on the back (or if the wall covering is prepasted, water), and strips hung butting up to each other, being careful to match the pattern along the common edge. The simple or plain papers, solid colors, and grasscloths are the quickest to install and involve only 10% material waste. The patterned papers involve between 25% and 30% waste and more. Bold patterns are the most time-consuming and may result in as much as 60% material waste.

Ceiling Finishes

The function of the ceiling finish is to hide the structural, mechanical, and electrical systems from view, and provide an attractive surface that is easily maintained and sometimes sound-absorbing. These finishes fall into three main types: exposed structural, adhered, and suspended.

Exposed Ceilings

Rather than hide the structural system, it can be left exposed and painted in a warehouse, mechanical, or utility area, where aesthetics are not a consideration. In commercial areas, the structure may still be left exposed, obscured or muted by a flat black or dark paint that contrasts with bright wall colors. Another tactic is to draw attention to ceiling systems by decorating them in bright colors.

Adhered Ceilings

An adhered ceiling may be attached directly to the structure above with fasteners or adhesive. Ceilings in residential construction, for example, are often drywall nailed to the joists directly or first to furring, to create a level nailing surface.

Plaster can be applied directly on self-furring strips (leveling) or metal lath. Examples of directly attached gypsum board and plaster are shown in Figure 12.15. Each of these can be further finished with paint, trowel, or spray-on textured finish.

Ceiling tiles, 12" × 12", can be mounted on a flat substrate with adhesive. These are usually an acoustical (sound absorbing) material made of mineral fiber, sometimes having plastic or metal facing (see Figure 12.16).

Ceiling tiles are commonly found in sizes from 1' square to 2' × 4' rectangles and almost always are acoustical. The exposed face may be

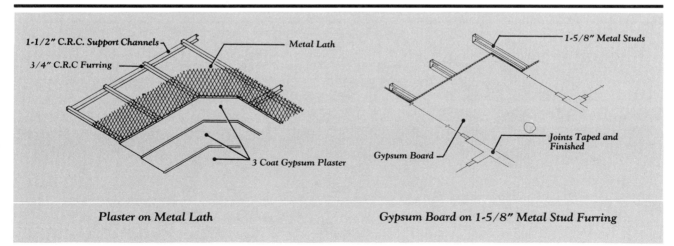

Plaster on Metal Lath   Gypsum Board on 1-5/8" Metal Stud Furring

Figure 12.15

perforated, fissured, textured, or plastic covered. Acoustical ceiling tiles (shown in Figure 12.16) are available in mineral fiber tiles with many patterns and textures.

Suspended Ceilings

Suspended ceilings consist of a ceiling board or tile and/or a suspension system. One component of the suspension system is the main runner, consisting of a 1-1/2" channel, spaced 2 to 3 feet apart and hung from the supporting structure. From the main runner, cross members are supported by clips, 1 to 2 feet apart, to suit the modular tile size. For a concealed spline ceiling, with 1 foot square tiles, the spline is, in turn, supported by the cross members.

Suspended ceiling boards can be sealed in place to create an isolated air space between then and the next level, called a plenum, which acts in the heating system as a return air reservoir. This design saves on return air ductwork costs. However, most building codes require that a plenum ceiling contain fire-rated components.

Installation of the suspension system or ceiling grid is usually coordinated with several subcontractors whose work is related to the ceiling finishes. First, the ceiling grid must be centered within the perimeter partitions of the individual room. Next, the sprinkler heads are centered, in rows, in the individual ceiling tiles. The light fixtures are usually the same size (modular) as the ceiling tiles and the layout is as symmetrical as their positioning will allow. Finally, the diffusers for the heating system are placed in rows occupying full or half modules within the grid. Although the ceiling drawings in the architectural set addresses some of these problems, the final layout is a result of the coordination of several subcontractors' shop drawings.

Doors, Frames, and Hardware

Interior doors are made of wood or metal, and "hung" by carpenters on wood or metal frames with hinges.

Doors can be hung singly or in pairs, with the exception of commercial entrance doors that open into the room they are serving. The way a

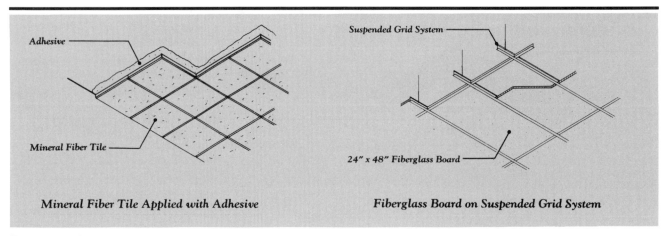

Mineral Fiber Tile Applied with Adhesive   **Fiberglass Board on Suspended Grid System**

Figure 12.16

door opens is described as its "swing" and the various swings are right hand, left hand, right hand reverse, and left hand reverse.

Doors can be made with solid faces or partial faces to full glass windows, as well as louvers to permit air transmission.

Door frames are fabricated to suit the opening (door) size and are reinforced to receive hinges and other hardware. Door frames are rabbeted to create a door stop or the stop is applied as a separate piece. The thickness (depth) of the frame coincides with the wall thickness.

Wood Doors

Wood doors are available in two basic designs: flush and panel, illustrated in Figures 12.17 and 12.18, respectively.

Flush wood doors have two smooth faces and are manufactured as hollow core, particle board core, or solid core. Flush facings are single sheets of lauan mahogany, birch, other hardwood veneers, or synthetic veneers created from a medium-density overlay and high-pressure plastic laminate. These veneers are attractive and require only a clear finish. The core materials used for flush doors depend, to a certain extent, on the quality of the interior finishes and the sound proofing provided by the denser cores. This design is the most common, having universal appeal to commercial as well as residential owners.

Paneled wood doors are manufactured from pine or fir. This type of door typically has a solid wood stile (vertical edge member) and rail (cross-membrane), and a one-, two-, five-, six-, and eight-panel design. Simulated six-panel doors with hollow cores and molded hardboard facings are also available. These doors are painted, and their use is limited in residential construction.

Wood doors are classified into three main grades: architectural or commercial grade, residential grade, or decorative grade.

Residential Grade

Residential wood doors are the least costly and have thin face veneers that are interior-glued and unmatched in their grain pattern, softwood stiles, and cores made from low density materials. Residential wood doors can be purchased and pre-hung in frames which need only be nailed in place. These doors are specified for interior use in areas not requiring a great degree of security.

Architectural Grade

Architectural doors are the wood doors specified exclusively in commercial construction. This type of door is very durable; it features thick face veneers that are exterior-glued and matched in their grain pattern, hardwood stiles, and hot-bonded dense cores.

Decorative Grade

Decorative wood doors may be hand carved and are manufactured from solid wood. They tend to be much more expensive than architectural and residential doors because of the exotic wood used (oak, mahogany, etc.), and the special craftsmanship required to produce them.

Hollow Metal Doors

The most common hollow metal (steel) doors are flush design, but residential doors are available in several decorative patterns that are embossed into or applied onto the face sheets. Metal doors can be galvanized and primed, or factory-finished with enamel in a variety of colors.

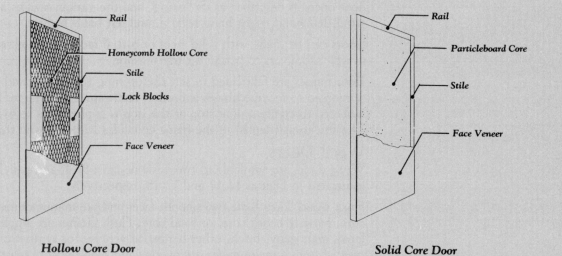

Rail
Honeycomb Hollow Core
Stile
Lock Blocks
Face Veneer

Hollow Core Door

Rail
Particleboard Core
Stile
Face Veneer

Solid Core Door

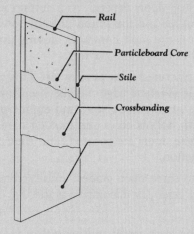

Rail
Particleboard Core
Stile
Crossbanding

Solid Core Door With Crossbanding

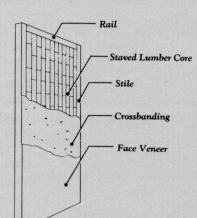

Rail
Staved Lumber Core
Stile
Crossbanding
Face Veneer

Staved Wood Core Door

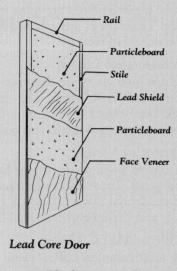

Rail
Particleboard
Stile
Lead Shield
Particleboard
Face Veneer

Lead Core Door

Flush Doors

Figure 12.17

248

Like wood, hollow metal doors come with hollow cores which may optionally be filled with thermal or sound insulation. The face sheets of commercial doors can range from 20 to 14 gauge and residential doors are thinner at 24 gauge. Hollow metal frames are made of thicker material than the door faces, starting at 18 gauge but more commonly at 16 gauge. Depths can vary to suit the wall from 4-3/4" (drywall and studs) to 8-3/4" (drywall and concrete block). Frames may be field-assembled (knock down) or shop welded. The section which is used for the frame includes the casing (trim), which returns to the wall to suit either a drywall or masonry finish.

Fire Ratings

Both wood and hollow metal doors may carry a label with a fire rating by a certified agency – Underwriters' Laboratories (UL) or Factory Mutual (FM). The ratings are usually represented by letters (A through E), or hour ratings (3 through 3/4) based on the value of the temperature rise

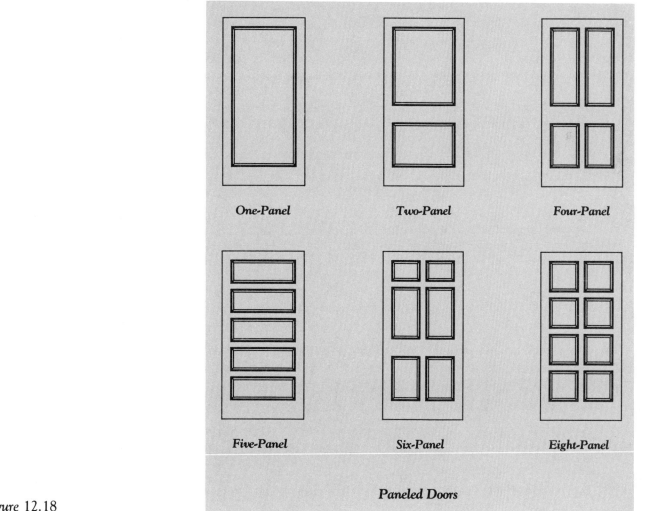

One-Panel   Two-Panel   Four-Panel

Five-Panel   Six-Panel   Eight-Panel

Paneled Doors

Figure 12.18

on the opposite side of the door, from the source of the heat (fire), as illustrated in Figure 12.19a and 12.19b.

Manufactured door sizes range from 2 to 4 feet wide and from 6'8" to 8'0" high. Entrance doors may be 2'8" or wider. Typical commercial doors are wider, 3'0" usually, and thicker by 1-3/4". Corridor and exit doors are required to be 7'0" by code.

Hardware

Hardware for construction relates to hanging and operating doors and includes: hinges, locksets, handles, panic devices, push plates, closers, and weatherstripping. The amount of hardware on a project is considerable and can easily exceed the cost of the doors in commercial construction. The hardware is identified in a schedule in the specifications describing the type, model number, and finish of each item which comprises the total "set" for a given door. There can easily be one to two dozen sets for the total job. Door hinges, measured in pairs, usually one and one-half per door, are required to permit the doors to swing.

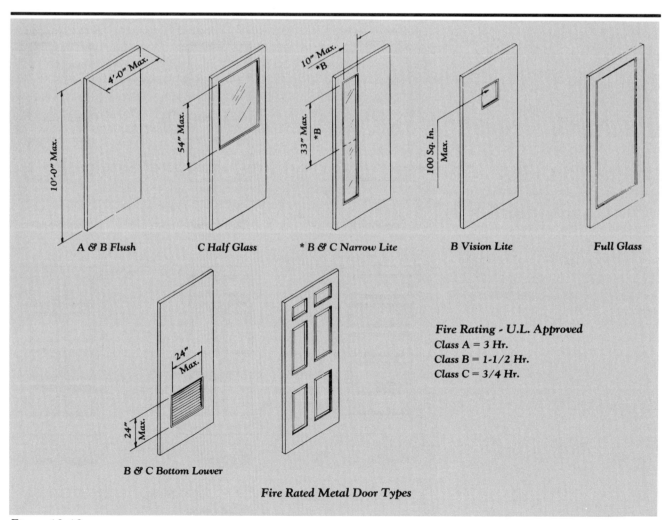

Fire Rated Metal Door Types

Figure 12.19a

Cylindrical locksets require a hole roughly 2″ in diameter in the face of the door, whereas mortise locksets are set in a recess notched in the edge of the door, a more costly installation. In a cylindrical lockset, the door is locked with a key by making the handle (and latch) inoperable, while a mortise lockset has a lock cylinder separate from the handle by which the key operates a dead bolt. Both cylindrical and mortise locksets may be non-keyed, either with or without the ability to be locked. Lockable doors are known as "privacy type" doors, while doors without locks are known as "passage type" doors.

Fire Door

Classification	Time Rating (as Shown on Label)		Temperature Rise (as Shown on Label)	Maximum Glass Area
3 Hour fire doors (A) are for use in openings in walls separating buildings or dividing a single building into the areas.	3 Hr.	(A)	30 Min. 250°F Max	None
	3 Hr.	(A)	30 Min. 450°F Max	
	3 Hr.	(A)	30 Min. 650°F Max	
	3 Hr.	(A)	*	
1-1/2 Hour fire doors (B) and (D) are for use in openings in 2 Hour enclosures of vertical communication through buildings (stairs, elevators, etc.) or in exterior walls which are subject to severe fire exposure from outside of the building. 1 Hour fire doors (B) are for use in openings in 1 Hour enclosures of vertical communication through buildings (stairs, elevators, etc.)	1-1/2 Hr.	(B)	30 Min. 250°F Max	100 square inches per door
	1-1/2 Hr.	(B)	30 Min. 450°F Max	
	1-1/2 Hr.	(B)	30 Min. 650°F Max	
	1-1/2 Hr.	(B)	*	
	1 Hr.		30 Min. 250°F Max	
	1-1/2 Hr.	(D)	30 Min. 250°F Max	None
	1-1/2 Hr.	(D)	30 Min. 450°F Max	
	1-1/2 Hr.	(D)	30 Min. 650°F Max	
	1-1/2 Hr.	(D)	*	
3/4 Hour fire doors (C) and (E) are for use in openings in corridor and room partitions or in exterior walls which are subject to moderate fire exposure from outside of the building.	3/4 Hr.	(C)	**	1296 Square
	3/4 Hr.	(E)	**	720 square inches per light
1/2 Hour fire doors and 1/3 Hour fire doors are for use where smoke controls is a primary consideration and are for the protection of openings in partitions between a habitable room and a corridor when the wall has a fire-resistance rating of not more than one hour.	1/2 Hr.		**	No limit
	1/3 Hr.		**	

*The labels do not record any temperature rise limits. This means that the temperature rise on the unexposed face of the door at the end of 30 minutes of test is in excess of 650°F.
**Temperature rise is not recorded.

Figure 12.19b

There are several grades of hardware: light duty or residential, standard duty, and heavy duty. For hinges, this is expressed in terms of usage: low, average, and high frequencies.

Most general contractors order doors, frames, and hardware from various suppliers or manufacturers and then install them with their own carpenters. The door frame schedule and supplier must be closely coordinated with the hardware schedule and supplier. For example, templates are transmitted to hollow metal suppliers immediately following approval of the door schedule. In this case, time can be a critical factor; custom hollow metal frames, doors, and hardware are long lead items that can be hard to obtain on time.

Chapter Thirteen
Mechanical

Almost every building requires a supply of water, a means of discharging waste, and a means of heating, cooling, and venting air. Although this portion of construction is accomplished by highly specialized subcontractors, the general contractor or anyone administering a project should be familiar with the fundamentals of mechanical work. Basic knowledge of the scope of work involved in mechanical installations will enhance communications with the specialty contractors who perform it.

The mechanical portion of construction involves three main categories of work: **plumbing**, **fire protection**, and **HVAC** (heating, ventilating, and air conditioning). These three divisions and their subcategories are illustrated in Figure 13.1.

Components

There are several components that all mechanical systems have in common: piping, valves, fixtures, and equipment. These components are described in the next few sections, followed by descriptions of each mechanical system they comprise.

Piping
Piping is necessary to connect any source point to its final distribution point. For example, hot water heaters are connected to faucets and pumps to the storage tanks. The type of pipe materials used depends on the mechanical system.

Piping systems consist of more than just straight lengths of pipe. There are couplings to connect adjacent lengths together. Other fittings are used when pipe changes direction, known as elbows, or where piping branches, known as tees or wyes.

Horizontal runs of pipe, when they are not buried, must be supported from the ceiling by hangers (either adjustable yoke and threaded rod type, or fabricated steel trapeze type).

Vertical pipes are run in spaces, and called chases. The individual pipe is referred to as a riser.

Small diameter pipe that is thinner walled is called tubing. With the exception of flexible tubing, most pipe is furnished in hard straight lengths.

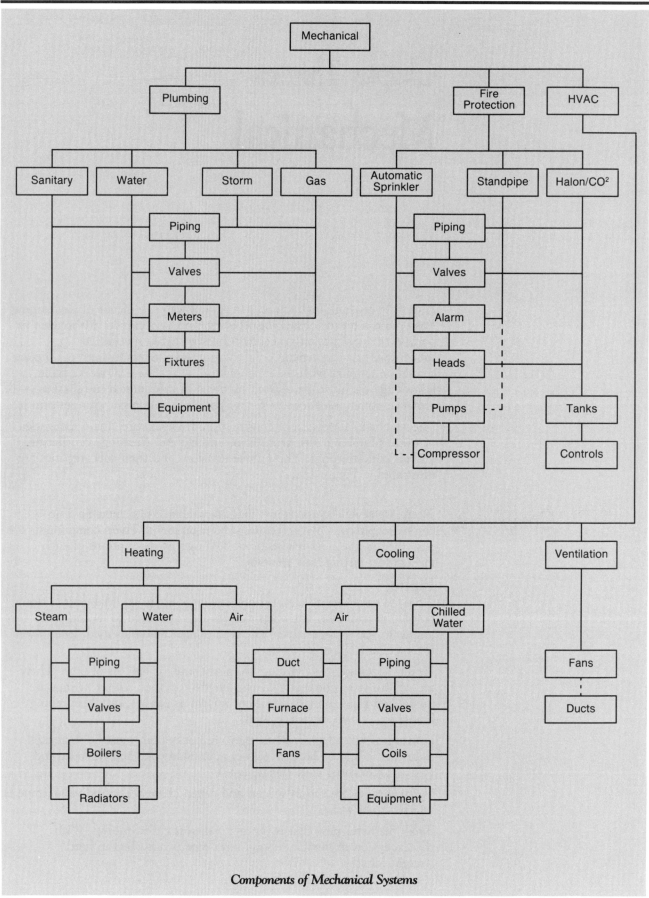

Components of Mechanical Systems

Figure 13.1

Pipes can be designed to handle fluid either under pressure (such as water and gas) or gravity flow (such as storm or waste). In laying out piping systems on a floor plan, gravity flow pipe locations take priority over pressure pipe locations.

Classification

Pipe is classified by the material, the type of pressure it can withstand, types of services used, type of connection, and inside diameter (I.D.) or outside diameter (O.D.). Schedule 40 pipe is the standard weight pipe suitable for carrying either water under street pressure or waste not under pressure.

Types of Piping

Cast iron pipe, synonymous with soil pipe, transports waste from plumbing fixtures into local sewer mains. It also is used in "stacks" for venting waste piping, as well. Soil pipe is connected with bell and spigot joints or no-hub couplings. Fittings for cast iron piping are available in several configurations (see Figure 13.2).

Copper pipe is used in water supply systems. There are five classes of copper pipe and tubing – types K, L, M, DWV, and ACR. Type K is relatively thick-walled and is utilized for underground or interior applications where the use of more durable or higher pressure tubing is desired. Type L is medium-walled and used for interior plumbing, heating, and cooling systems. Type M is light-walled and used mostly in low-pressure applications such as heating, cooling, drainage lines, or sprinkler systems in construction. DWV, the thinnest-walled of all the copper tubing, is used for non-pressurized applications such as drainage waste and venting systems. ACR is used for refrigerant piping. Copper pipe is joined by threaded connections and copper tubing by soldered connections. Fitting materials can be either wrought copper or cast bronze (see Figure 13.3).

Plastic piping is manufactured of both rigid or flexible plastic. Polyvinyl chloride (PVC), chlorinated PVC (CPVC), Acrylonitrile Buradiene Styrene (ABS), and reinforced fiberglass are materials used for rigid plastic pipe, utilized in waste and water systems. Flexible plastic pipe, called tubing, includes polybutylene and polyethylene. The former is utilized in ambient water systems, while the latter is utilized in hot water and gas systems. Water service, gas, site drainage, heating, cooling, electrical conduit, and telephone ducts utilize other types of plastic piping.

There are numerous methods for joining plastic pipe, as shown in Figure 13.4. There are similar connections to other pipe materials, such as threaded, flanged, compression, clamps, and gas heated. Unique to plastic pipe are solvent welded and fusion type connections.

Steel piping, commonly referred to as "black steel," connects gas, steam, and water supply to their respective terminal units. This pipe may be galvanized, and is manufactured either welded or seamless, in accordance with American Society of Testing Materials (ASTM) specifications. Welded pipe is used for low pressure applications normally found in plumbing, heating, cooling, and fire protection systems. Seamless pipe is intended for higher temperatures and pressure and is flexible (can be bent or coiled).

American Standards Association (ASA) classifies steel pipe by the wall thickness, Schedule 40 representing the standard weight steel pipe. Extra

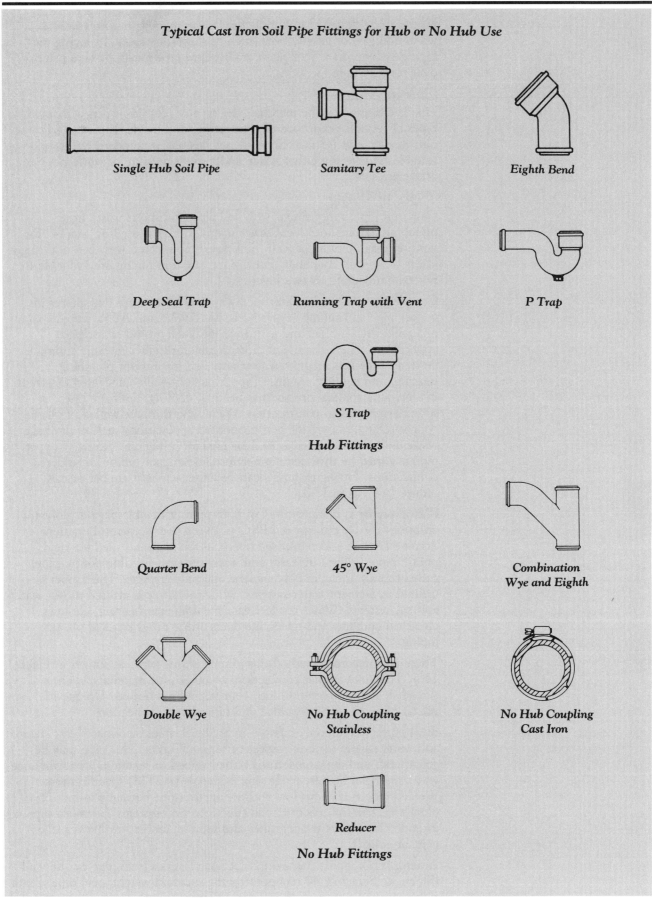

Typical Cast Iron Soil Pipe Fittings for Hub or No Hub Use

Single Hub Soil Pipe

Sanitary Tee

Eighth Bend

Deep Seal Trap

Running Trap with Vent

P Trap

S Trap

Hub Fittings

Quarter Bend

45° Wye

Combination
Wye and Eighth

Double Wye

No Hub Coupling
Stainless

No Hub Coupling
Cast Iron

Reducer

No Hub Fittings

Figure 13.2

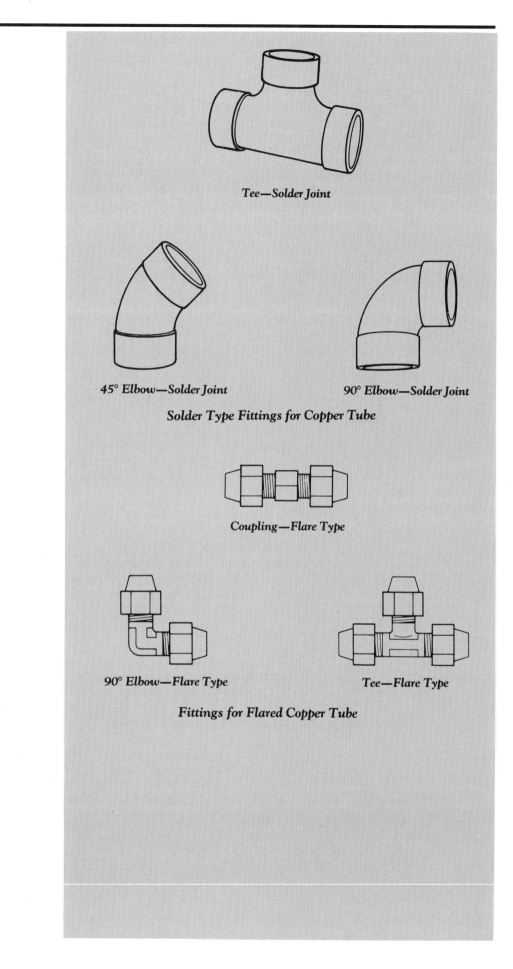

Tee—Solder Joint

45° Elbow—Solder Joint   90° Elbow—Solder Joint

Solder Type Fittings for Copper Tube

Coupling—Flare Type

90° Elbow—Flare Type   Tee—Flare Type

Fittings for Flared Copper Tube

Figure 13.3

Quarter Bend-Socket Joint

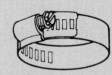

Stainless Steel Clamp Ring

Eighth Bend—Socket Joint

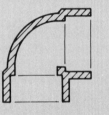

90° Elbow—Acetal Flare Type

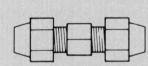

Coupling—Acetal Flare Type

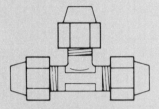

Tee—Acetal Flare Type

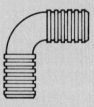

90° Elbow—Fusion Type

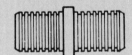

Coupling—Fusion Type

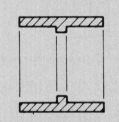

Tee—Fusion Type

90° Elbow—Brass Insert Type

Coupling—Brass Insert Type

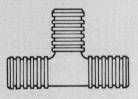

Tee—Brass Insert Type

90° Elbow—Acetal Insert

Coupling—Acetal Insert

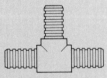

Tee—Acetal Insert

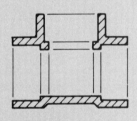

90° Elbow—Nylon Insert

Coupling—Nylon Insert

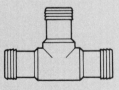

Tee—Nylon Insert

Fittings for Various Plastic Piping Methods

Figure 13.4

strong (XS) pipe is classified as Schedule 80, and thin wall pipe (comparable to plastic and copper tubing) is Schedule 10.

Steel pipe fittings are made from several materials; cast, malleable, and ductile iron, and forged, black, and carbon steel. They are connected in a variety of ways; threaded and coupled, threaded flanged, butt welded, weld-on flanged, and mechanical joints. Fittings for steel pipe are shown in Figure 13.5.

Valves

Valves control fluids in piping systems by starting and stopping the pressure or flow within the system. The valve can be operated manually or automatically. An automatic valve can be operated pneumatically or electrically. There are six main types of valves – gate, globe, check, ball, butterfly, plug, and relief valves (see Figure 13.6).

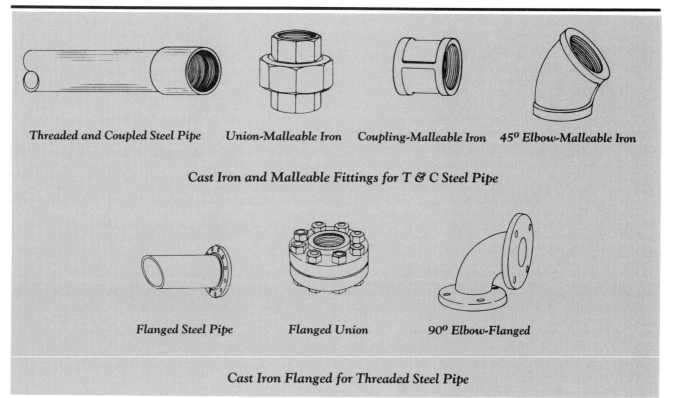

Threaded and Coupled Steel Pipe *Union-Malleable Iron* *Coupling-Malleable Iron* *45° Elbow-Malleable Iron*

Cast Iron and Malleable Fittings for T & C Steel Pipe

Flanged Steel Pipe *Flanged Union* *90° Elbow-Flanged*

Cast Iron Flanged for Threaded Steel Pipe

Figure 13.5

Gate valves are used to provide full flow of fluids, minimize pressure drop and, on rare occasions, allow shut off control. Globe valves are used where operation is infrequent and close flow control is desired and are often applied as throttling valves. Check valves are one-way valves designed to prevent back-flow when the direction of fluid is reversed. Ball valves are less common and are specified where frequent operation is required, such as the control of medical gasses. Butterfly valves can be used for both shut-off and throttling applications, particularly in situations where frequent operation is required. It is light weight and suitable for automation. Plug valves are normally used to control fluids

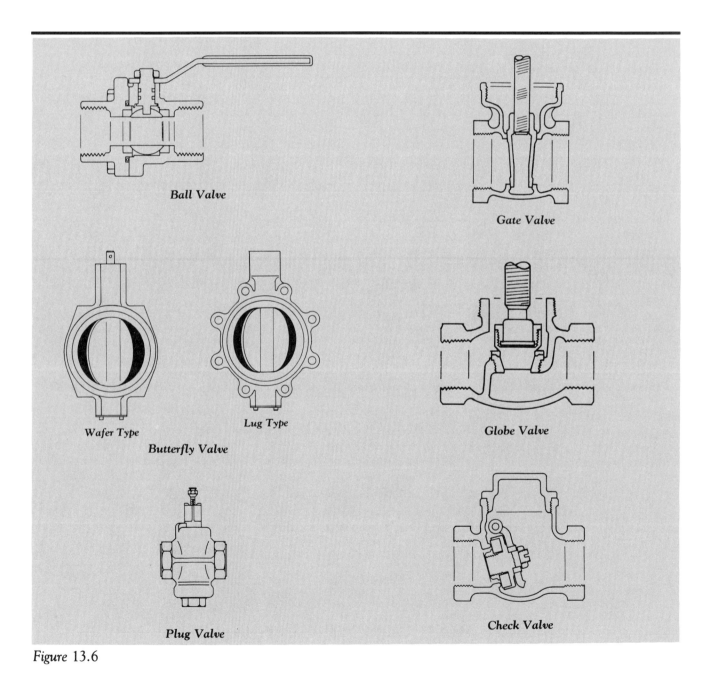

Ball Valve

Gate Valve

Wafer Type   **Lug Type**

Butterfly Valve

Globe Valve

Plug Valve

Check Valve

Figure 13.6

similar to ball and butterfly valves except that their reliability makes them ideal with gritty suspensions or corrosive chemical solutions. Relief valves are used to open at high temperatures and pressures to prevent rupture of tanks or water flashing to steam.

Fixtures

Supply piping often terminates in plumbing fixtures which, in turn, are the origin of waste piping. Lavatories, sinks, urinals, water closets (toilets), bathtubs, shower stalls, and drinking fountains are typical plumbing fixtures.

The most common materials used for fixtures have been vitreous china and porcelain enamels, which can be produced in a variety of colors on a metal base. This base was traditionally cast iron but steel and aluminum are suitable replacements. Stainless steel requires no additional finishing and has been employed in the fabrication of sinks and drinking fountains. Fiberglass has a finish that resembles porcelain, has the strength of steel, and is considerably lighter in weight than other materials. It has gained wide acceptance in residential construction.

Fixtures can either be floor mounted or wall hung, the latter being supported on carriers, built into the wall. Multiple water closets in separate men's and women's toilets are usually gang (groups) mounted back to back sharing a common chase and rough-in piping.

Fixtures are common components in sanitary and water systems but elements in other mechanical systems can be thought of as fixtures as well. Appliances are like fixtures at the end of the gas and/or water supply piping and some even generate sanitary water. Sprinkler heads are located at the end of of fire protection piping and, like fixtures, are ready to disperse water on demand. Radiators are terminal units in heating systems transferring heat from the steam or hot water supply piping to the air and discharging condensate or cooled water back to the boiler.

Equipment

There are several types of equipment associated with mechanical systems. Hot water heaters are one type, found in plumbing systems. Hot water heaters may be oil fired, gas fired, or electric (illustrated in Figure 13.7). The number of heaters and the capacity of each are usually indicated on the Equipment Schedule in the plumbing drawings. These units are sized by the number of occupants and the anticipated consumption per occupant. Hot water requirements may not always be ideal on some light commercial projects and office buildings, and individual tenants may prefer to provide their own hot water heating equipment rather than share a common unit. Small ceiling or under-sink mounted heaters are designed for such situations. Hot water heaters may be assigned to either the heating or electrical contractor, and care should be exercised to prevent duplication of orders.

Pumps

Pumps have many uses in the mechanical systems, most commonly drawing water from supply wells or boosting street water pressure for protection systems. Less common pump applications are circulating water for heating or cooling; transferring heating oil; draining sumps (low points) in wet basements; and ejecting sewage from pits or collection tanks. Some commonly used pumps are illustrated in Figure 13.8. There are a variety of pump designs with characteristics that make each desirable for a certain situation. The manufacturer's performance data must satisfy the requirements in the specifications before it can be installed on the project.

Plumbing Systems

There are four types of plumbing systems – water, sanitary, storm, and gas – all of which are included in most buildings. Water systems supply potable water to the building. Sanitary plumbing systems collect the waste for discharge into a septic tank or sanitary sewer system. The third type, storm systems, collect water from storm drains and discharge it into a storm sewer system. Gas plumbing systems supply gas to the heating equipment that burns it for fuel.

Water Systems

Water supply for a building can be taken from street mains that make up a delivery system throughout a municipal water district. The mains under existing roads are pressurized and must be tapped without shutting them off. A separate line may be required for domestic (potable) water and water for fire protection systems. A valve is usually placed near the main on the (buried) supply line, which can be operated above ground to shut off the water to the entire building. The meter is often placed inside where the supply enters the building, but on larger commercial projects it is located in a (precast) concrete pit. Since water systems are kept under pressure, there must be a means of isolating separate branches in the event of leaks. This is accomplished with shut-off valves accessible under floor systems, behind access panels, or under base cabinets. Branch lines also terminate in valves which are known under various names: faucets at fixtures, flush valves at water closets, mixing valves

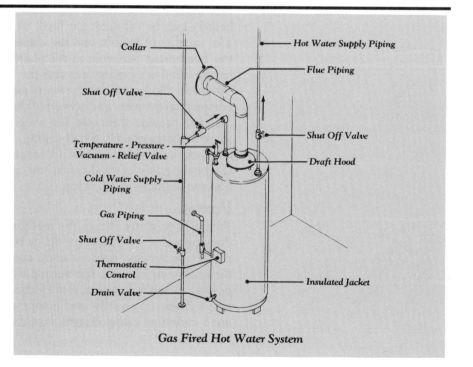

Gas Fired Hot Water System

Figure 13.7

in showers, and sillcocks for yard watering. Water lines are often insulated either due to condensation (cold water) or thermal (hot water) considerations.

Sanitary Systems

Sanitary systems are almost always gravity flow systems. They originate in open drains in sinks, bathtubs, floors, and submerged drains under water closets. (Protection from noxious odors associated with sanitary waste is provided by traps just below the drains, which retain a small amount of water as a seal.) Gravity flow lines are installed at a slope to give adequate velocity to the wastes.

Once the sanitary piping has exited the building it is laid in straight lengths to the nearest street main. Manholes are placed at required intervals or at changes in vertical or horizontal alignment (bends), to provide access for maintenance.

Storm Systems

Like sanitary systems, storm systems originate in open drains as well, only storm drains are located on the exterior of a building. Roof drains are placed at low points in a flat roof. Where rain is collected in a gutter system, storm risers are located to receive the downspouts where they meet the ground. On roads and parking areas, rainwater flows by gravity to low points, where drains are located.

Storm and sanitary wastes were once collected in a common piping system, and simply discharged into a major body of water. When it

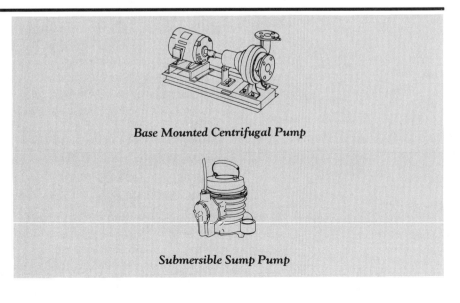

Base Mounted Centrifugal Pump

Submersible Sump Pump

Figure 13.8

became necessary to treat the sanitary waste (imposed by regulations) storm water (which is not treated) and sanitary waste were separated.

Gas Systems
Gas flows in piping mains under pressure.

Plumbing Installation
Plumbing is installed in two phases, known as **rough plumbing** and **finish plumbing**. Rough plumbing, commonly referred to as "roughing in", involves all plumbing work that is eventually hidden from sight by floors, walls, and ceilings. Finish plumbing includes all the plumbing work that is exposed to the human eye upon completion of the project, the most obvious being the plumbing fixtures.

Fire Protection Systems

Fire protection in buildings is provided by two types of systems – **automatic sprinkler systems** and **fire standpipes**. Special systems utilizing Halogen-type extinguishing agents, foam, or carbon dioxide are used where applicable.

Automatic Sprinkler Systems
Automatic systems are either wet pipe systems or dry pipe systems. In the wet pipe system, water is constantly maintained in the piping, regardless of whether there is a fire or not. In contrast, the piping of dry pipe systems is kept empty; water is admitted only when the system is activated by heat or smoke.

The **wet pipe system** is the most popular of the two because of its quick response and relatively low cost. It consists of a system of pipes, as shown in Figure 13.9. This system contains preset thermal elements and a number of sprinkler heads, usually installed below the ceiling.

The pipes in a wet pipe system are filled with water under pressure. Heat will melt a fusible element and open the affected sprinkler head. The system will continue to operate until the main valve is manually closed which releases water immediately to suppress the fire. Once opened, the heads must be replaced before the system can be repressurized.

The number of sprinkler heads that are required is based on delivering the required gallons of water per minute to the remote areas of the building. Sometimes adding heads is not enough and a booster pump is required to augment the flow pressure.

The **dry pipe system** is used in unheated areas of a building where winter temperatures would cause water to freeze and break the pipes. Rather than water, the piping is filled with compressed air (see Figure 13.10). Heat opens the head as before, which causes the pressure to drop, opening a water valve. Water then enters the piping system and is released through the open sprinkler heads. Dry pipe system installation is comparatively more costly than wet system installation due to the requirement for compressed air equipment and special sprinkler heads. Another disadvantage of a dry system is that response time is slower than that of a wet system. An advantage is that damage from leaks in the piping is eliminated.

Three variations of dry pipe systems are: **preaction systems**, **deluge systems**, and **firecycle systems** (shown in Figure 13.11).

Piping in a preaction system is left empty and is only filled with water when heat is detected by a thermostatic release. The release is so highly sensitive that the sprinkler heads do not open until a much greater temperature rise is detected. The release also activates an alarm which provides an early warning to building occupants to evacuate, and notifies the local fire department in advance. The advantage is that the response to the fire is much faster.

A deluge system is a version of the preaction system in which the sprinkler heads are open type nozzles. When the thermostatic release opens the deluge valve, water is immediately discharged through the open nozzles. This system is often used for hazardous material storage, due to its ability to prevent the spread of fire by instantly wetting down the entire protected area. The advantage of open type nozzles is that they do not have to be replaced once they are used.

A firecycle system is a dry system with electrical detectors that sense both when a fire starts and when it is out. These detectors operate solenoid switches that are capable of opening or closing flow control valves, thus allowing water to be discharged from open nozzles (or not). The same results can be achieved using an automatic "on-off" sprinkler head in a wet pipe system.

The disadvantage of a standpipe system is that the fire must be humanly detected rather than detected by automatic sensors, and the hose nozzle must be brought to the source of the fire. One advantage is the cost savings in eliminating the sprinkler piping. Another is that the water in the system can be concentrated at the point where it is most effective.

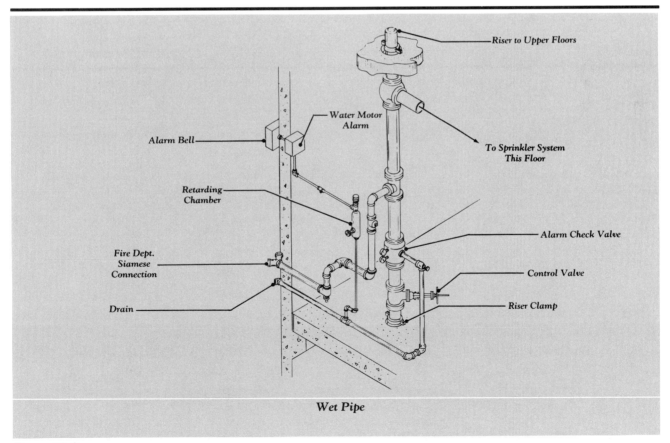

Wet Pipe

Figure 13.9

The pressure in the street water main is usually sufficient to satisfy the flow requirements for most projects. On high rise buildings, booster pumps or roof tanks may be required to supplement this pressure.

Fire Standpipes

Fire standpipes can be used to deliver water for fighting fires to the upper stories of tall commercial buildings and interiors of large malls. Rather than running hoses from the street, the fire department attaches their equipment to hose connectors on the specific floor or area of the building. Smaller hoses may be provided with the standpipe to permit the tenants to fight the fire in advance of the fire department. Each of these aspects saves considerable time in getting the fire under control. Fire standpipes are made of steel pipe with fittings, as shown in Figure 13.12. These systems fall under one of three user classes as follows:

- **Class I** is for use by fire departments and personnel with special training for heavy hose; it has 2-1/2″ hose connections.

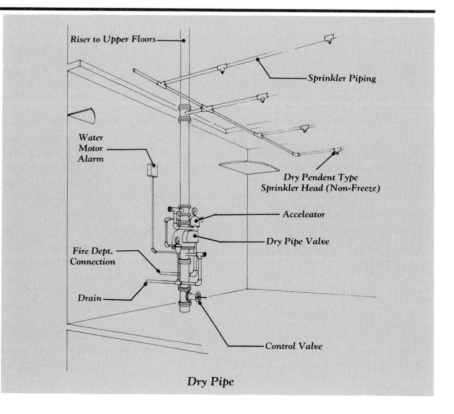

Figure 13.10

Dry Pipe

- **Class II** is for use by building occupants until the arrival of the fire department, with 1-1/2″ hose connector with hose.
- **Class III** is for use by either fire departments and trained personnel or by the occupants of a building – it has both 2-1/2″ and 1-1/2″ hose connections or one 2-1/2″ hose valve with an easily removable 2-1/2″ by 1-1/2″ adapter.

These are several variations of standpipe systems just as these were for sprinkler systems and they are listed by type as follows:

- **Type 1** refers to a wet standpipe system with the supply valve opened and water pressure maintained at all times.

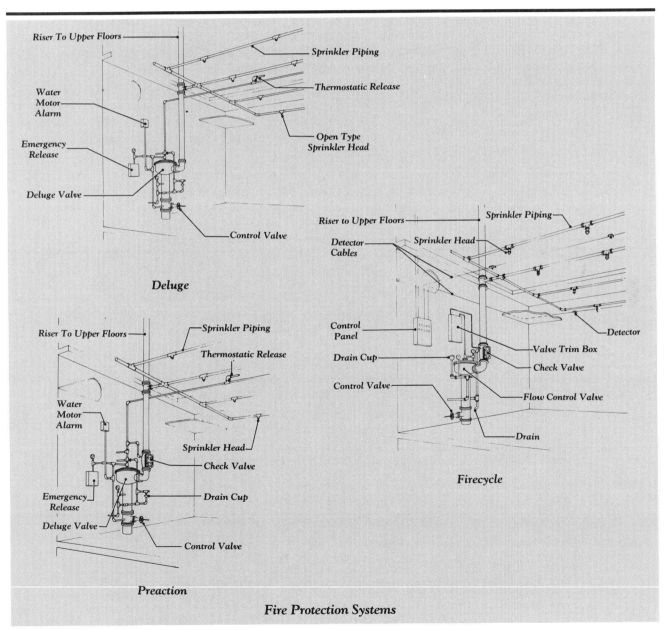

Figure 13.11

- **Type 2** systems are designed with approved devices to automatically admit water to the system when a hose valve is opened.
- **Type 3** system configurations permit water to be admitted through approved remote controlled devices that are located at hose stations.
- **Type 4** refers to dry standpipe systems with no fixed water supply.

Halon Systems

Halon fire suppression systems can be installed in buildings in the form of portable extinguishers, strategically located cylinders, or a centrally located battery of storage cylinders connected to a piping distribution system with discharge nozzles (as shown in Figure 13.13).

Halon is a colorless gas capable of penetrating places where water and chemicals are unable to penetrate because it is several times heavier than air. The toxicity of Halon gas ranges from nontoxic to low toxicity, depending on the concentration used. **Halon 1301** is commonly used to achieve a concentration of 5 to 7 percent, because it has no adverse effects on the occupants of a building for brief (4 to 5 minute) exposures. A concentration of 7 to 10 percent requires the evacuation of building occupants within one minute of exposure, while concentrations above 10 percent require evacuation prior to discharge.

A Halon system contains a series of photoelectric or ionization type fire and smoke detectors, strategically located in the areas of a building to be protected. These detectors are wired to a control panel that activates the alarm systems, verifies or proves the existence of combustion, and

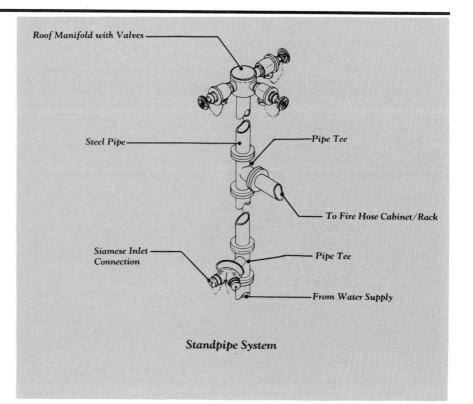

Roof Manifold with Valves

Steel Pipe

Pipe Tee

To Fire Hose Cabinet/Rack

Siamese Inlet Connection

Pipe Tee

From Water Supply

Standpipe System

Figure 13.12

releases the Halon gas, all in a matter of seconds. While expensive, Halon systems are desirable in some applications because they are fast, effective, and clean; there is no residue that can damage or contaminate documents, records, electronic equipment, or other contents of a building.

HVAC Systems

Heating, ventilation, and air conditioning systems consist of the components described earlier in this chapter, along with the equipment (including the delivery method), and the terminal units. All three systems are usually installed by one contractor who employs pipefitters, sheet metal workers, and mechanics.

Heating

The most common types of heat are steam or hot water, forced warm air, and electric. Less common types are solar, radiant and gas, or electric infra red. Selection of any heating system is governed by factors such as the availability, efficiency of operation, cost of maintenance, and cost of fuel. For purposes of organization, electric heat is described briefly here and is described in more detail in Chapter 14, "Electrical."

Steam and Forced Hot Water

Hot water or steam is generated in a boiler system that is either prefabricated or assembled in the field. This equipment is manufactured

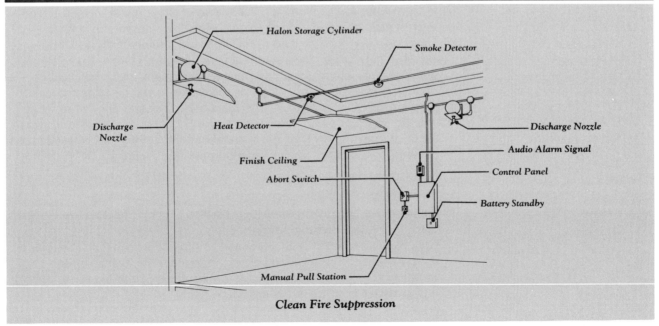

Clean Fire Suppression

Figure 13.13

from cast iron or steel with internal tubes of steel or copper. Boilers use one or a combination of the following sources for energy: gas, coal, oil, electricity, or wood. Typical boilers, illustrated in Figure 13.14, are the mainstay of this type of system.

Additional equipment may be required for certain fuels. Heating oil must be stored in a tank in a heated area and is pumped to the boiler. Forge storage tanks remain outside but the delivery piping to the boiler must be heat traced. Coal and wood require storage areas and large coal systems need conveyors for delivery to the equipment.

Heat is delivered under pressure to the hot water or steam (hydronic) terminal units by piping. Some common hydronic units are radiators, convectors, or coils. Most common radiators are freestanding cast iron, but wall hung or baseboard units are available. Fin tube radiators are a common type of convector. Coil units are mounted in duct (forced air) systems or in floor or ceiling cabinets with blower fans, called fan oil units.

The spent hot water is returned to the boiler under pressure in forced hot water systems, whereas steam becomes condensate in the radiator and is returned to the boiler by gravity flow in the steam systems.

Forced hot water heat has entirely replaced steam heat in residential construction. Radiators are sized for the given room, corridor, or other areas they serve and are placed where air circulation will stop downdrafts, such as beneath windows. Ceiling hung fan coil units are placed in warehouses near loading docks or receiving areas for supplemental heat when doors are open for extended periods. Steam or hot water piping may be connected to air curtains at mall entrances and loading docks, which create a barrier to drafts and dust with a constant stream of blown air.

Forced Warm Air

Forced warm air systems (shown in Figure 13.15) usually consist of a direct-fired heating unit such as a furnace, with either a gravity ventilator or a blower, and a system of ducts. The furnace can be gas, coal, or oil-fired, or electric.

Ductwork for forced warm air is a system of sheet metal or rigid fiberglass ducts which transport heated air just as piping transports hot water. Ducts may be round or rectangular in shape, usually fabricated from sheets of galvanized steel, aluminum, or fiberglass boards. In environments where corrosive elements are present, stainless steel or plastics may be used. The ducts distribute air in the building through supply registers and diffusers, that direct the flow and amount of air to specific rooms or areas. A separate system of ducts can be used to return air to the heating unit, or the space above the ceiling can be treated as a plenum, or reservoir, for the same purpose (see Figure 13.16).

Supplemental furnaces to augment heated air may be placed within the ductwork system itself.

Forced warm air systems are widely used to generate heat for residential, commercial, and some industrial buildings, because air cooling equipment can be easily incorporated to provide a year-round system. A variety of filters (either cleanable or disposable) are available for installation in the return air plenum, just ahead of the blower to remove dust particles from the air being circulated.

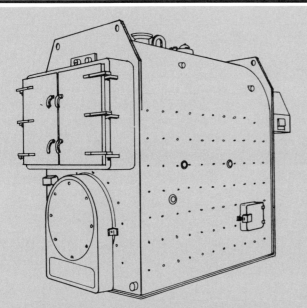

High Firebox, Steel, Fire Tube Boiler-Commercial

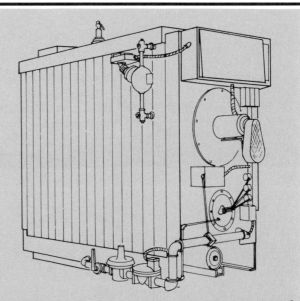

Packaged, Gas Fired, Steel, Watertube Boiler-Commercial

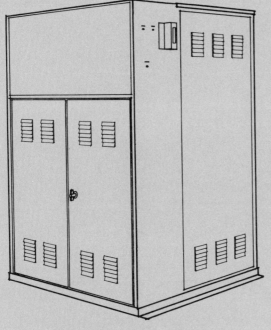

Electric Steel Boiler, Commercial

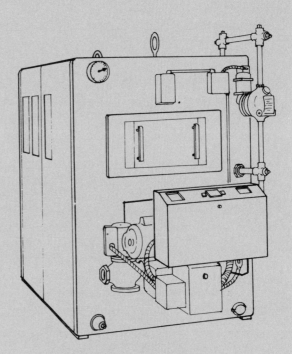

**Packaged, Cast Iron Sectional,
Gas/Oil Fired Boiler-Commercial**

Boilers

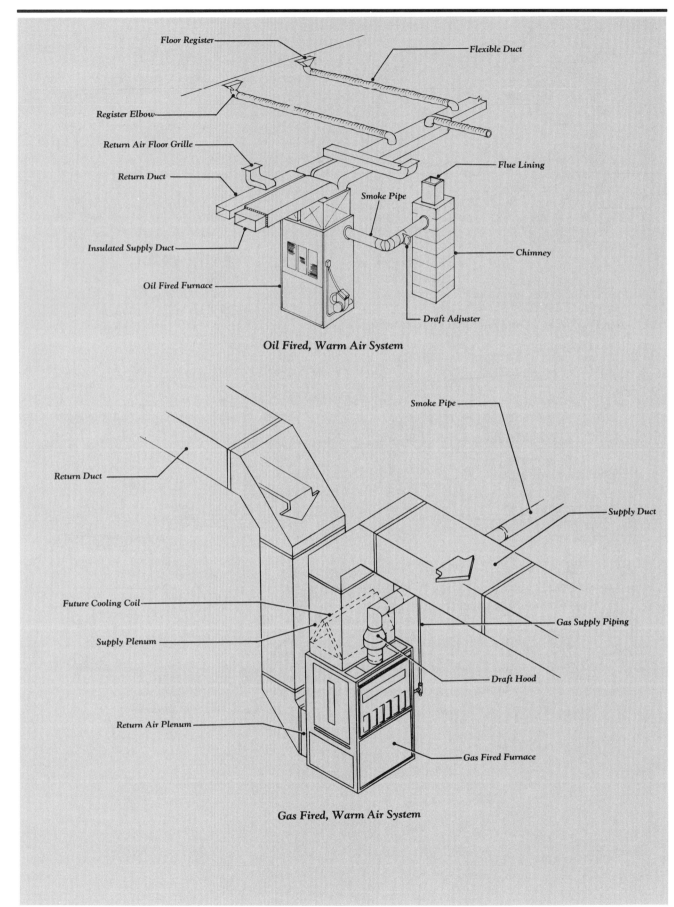

Oil Fired, Warm Air System

Gas Fired, Warm Air System

Figure 13.15

Electric

Electricity can be the type of heat used for duct coils or baseboard radiators or the source of energy for boilers or furnaces in forced hot water and warm air systems. It can also be used to operate heat pumps. Heat pumps are reportedly very efficient because they use ambient outside air to heat or cool a building. During the summer the heat pump draws the hot air out of a building, whereas in the winter, heat pumps collect natural heat from the outside air, the earth, or water, and pump it inside.

Solar

Solar heating systems (illustrated in Figure 13.17) use energy from the sun to provide heat and hot water to buildings. Solar collectors, heat exchangers, pipes, a storage system, and controls make up the solar heating system. Although solar heating systems have been installed and used successfully in many parts of the United States, they are usually supplemented by conventional heating systems.

Cooling

The two types of cooling are chilled water and cool air. The components of cooling systems are similar to heat, namely, equipment, delivery systems, and terminal units. Cooling equipment is rated by tons, which refers to the amount of heat that is absorbed in melting a ton of ice (i.e., 12,000 BTU per hour, for 24 hours).

Chilled Water

Chilled water cooling systems involve three distinct piping systems. First, coils in the terminal unit transfer heat from the room to the chilled water piping system which brings it to the chiller. Second, coils in the evaporator section of the chiller transfer heat from the chilled water to the refrigerant piping system, which brings it to the condenser section.

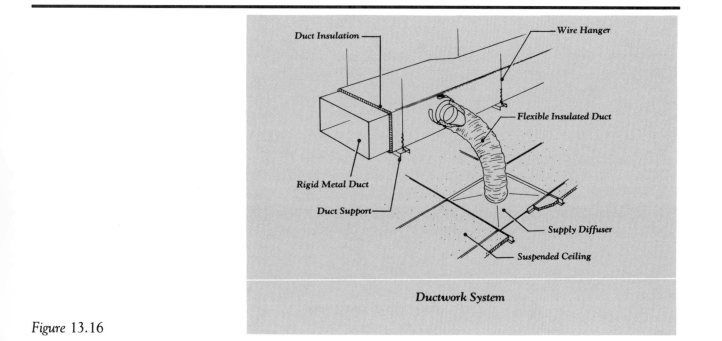

Ductwork System

Figure 13.16

Third, the condenser transfers heat from the refrigerant to the condenser water piping which releases it to an available body of water.

There are two types of chiller designs: **compression type** and **absorption type.** The compression type operates on electric energy and the absorption type depends on available solar or low cost steam. The major pieces of equipment in the compression type are the compressor and the condenser. The most common compressor utilized is the reciprocating piston type. There are three types of condensers. From smallest to largest they are air cooled, water cooled, and cooling tower type. Where an

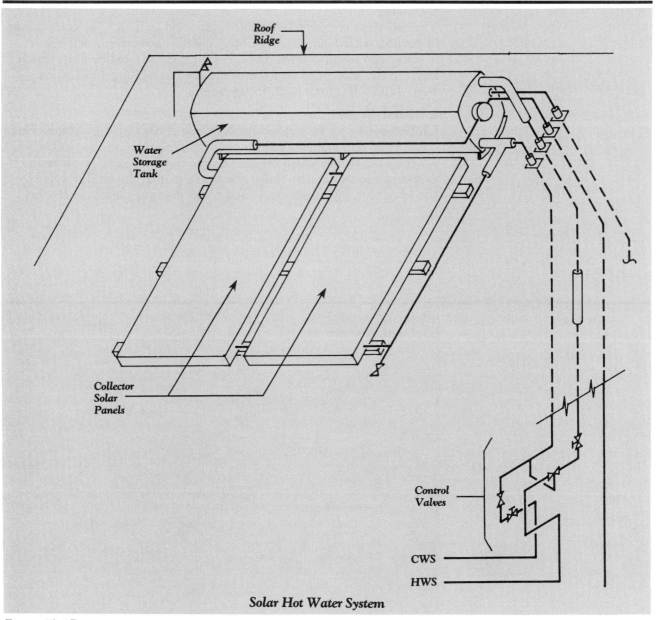

Solar Hot Water System

Figure 13.17

abundant water supply is not available, as in cities, a cooling tower is used in conjunction with a condenser to recycle the condenser discharge.

The major pieces of equipment in the absorption type are the absorber and the condenser. An absorber is a large tank of water containing spray heads.

Cool Air Systems

Cool air systems consist of a chiller and an air handling unit or other heat exchanger. A ductwork distribution system is optional. The air handling unit (AHU) can consist of only three sections: filter, fan, and coil. Rather than purchasing a separate chiller, however, all or some of the chiller components (evaporator, compressor, and condensor) can be incorporated into the air handling unit. A common packaged cool air unit contains an evaporator and compressor requiring only a condenser to be mounted separately. Both computer room and direct expansion cooling units contain all of the chiller components. The standard wall hung or window mounted "air conditioner" is a type of direct expansion cooling unit. Some typical cool air systems are shown in Figure 13.18.

Combined Systems

Central station air handling units contain the same three basic elements as the cooling units with the coil section separated into heating and cooling subsections (see Figure 13.18). Additional features may be to condition the air by removing or adding moisture (humidification), introducing make up (outside) air, and reheating the air.

A package unit can contain the refrigeration equipment (chiller) and the heating equipment together. This is usually rooftop mounted with the condenser section, often the air cooled type (see Figure 13.18).

Rooftop units are commonly specified for low-rise commercial and industrial buildings because installation, operations, and maintenance costs are relatively low. Rooftop air conditioning units can be purchased as self-contained units that can be shipped completely assembled, wired, piped, charged with refrigerant, and factory-tested to the jobsite. Factory-fabricated curbs for mounting these units on the roof are available from most manufacturers. Rooftop units are most often powered by electricity for cooling and gas for heating. (A rooftop unit is shown in Figure 13.18.)

To minimize the size of the openings cut for supply and return ductwork to the rooftop units, and to reduce the load on the roofing structure, split systems are used. The air handling section can be pad mounted within the building with only the air cooled condenser mounted on the roof. The openings in the roof are cut for condenser piping.

Fans and Ventilators

Fans supply, circulate, or exhaust air in buildings. With the exception of the paddle fan, that has to be located in the area or space being served, fans may be located either in the space being served, or at another (remote) area (connected by ductwork to the space being served). Fans and ventilators are illustrated in Figure 13.19.

The function of roof ventilators is to move air from the interior of a building to the outside, often without the aid of motor-driven fans.

The air removal process may be accomplished when warm air rises, being displaced by denser or heavier colder air, or by the action of wind siphoning air through the ventilator.

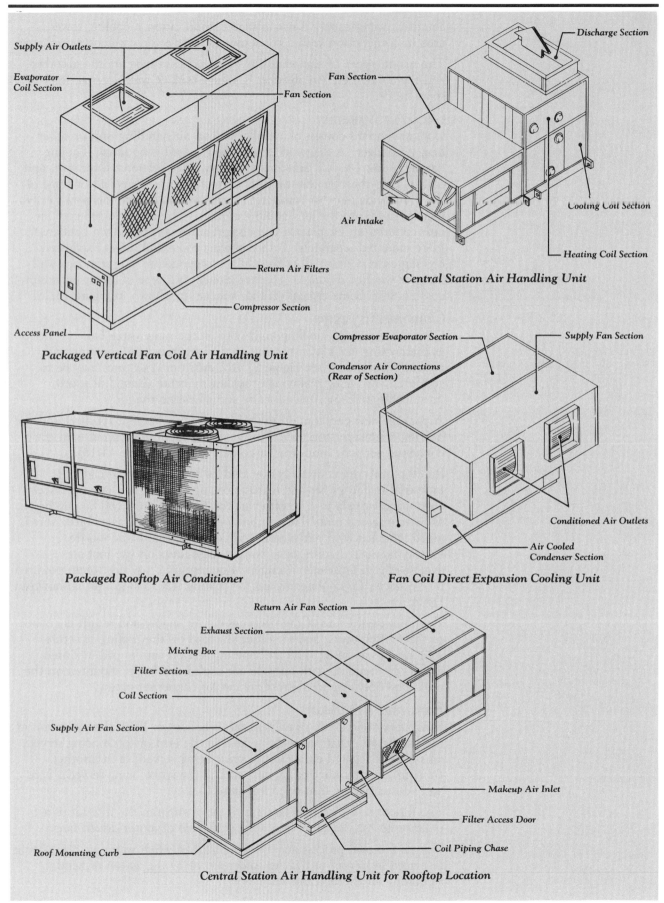

Supply Air Outlets

Evaporator
Coil Section

Fan Section

Return Air Filters

Compressor Section

Access Panel

Packaged Vertical Fan Coil Air Handling Unit

Discharge Section

Fan Section

Air Intake

Cooling Coil Section

Heating Coil Section

Central Station Air Handling Unit

Packaged Rooftop Air Conditioner

Compressor Evaporator Section

Supply Fan Section

Condensor Air Connections
(Rear of Section)

Conditioned Air Outlets

Air Cooled
Condenser Section

Fan Coil Direct Expansion Cooling Unit

Return Air Fan Section

Exhaust Section

Mixing Box

Filter Section

Coil Section

Supply Air Fan Section

Makeup Air Inlet

Filter Access Door

Coil Piping Chase

Roof Mounting Curb

Central Station Air Handling Unit for Rooftop Location

Figure 13.18

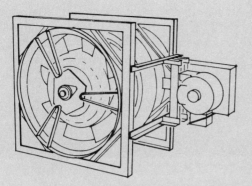

Axial Flow, Belt Drive, Centrifugal Fan

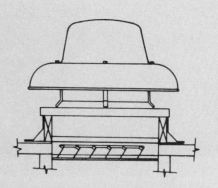

Centrifugal Roof Exhaust Fan

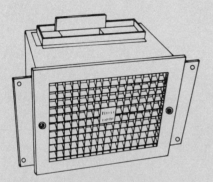

Ceiling Exhaust Fan

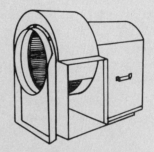

Belt Drive, Utility Set

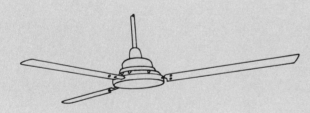

Paddle Blade Air Circulator

Belt Drive Propeller Fan with Shutter

Fans and Ventilators

Figure 13.19

Exhaust fans are used for removing air from toilets, kitchens, and ducts, and can be mounted on the roof or exterior wall of the building. The fan may draw air directly from a room or from exhaust ductwork. Bathroom exhaust fans can be ceiling mounted and their low pressure output limits the length of duct to between 10 and 20 feet.

Chapter Fourteen
Electrical

Electrical systems in building construction fall into four major groups: lighting, power, motor control centers, and special systems. These systems and their components are illustrated in Figure 14.1.

As with mechanical work, electrical installation has a "roughing-in" phase and a finished phase. Electrical rough-in includes hidden work such as the installation of conduits, wire, and boxes. The finish portion includes the installation of fixtures, equipment, devices, breakers, and switches.

Components

There are several components that all electrical systems have in common: raceways, conductors, devices, switches, panelboards, and fixtures. These electrical components are described in the following sections.

Raceways

Raceways are channels installed to house and protect electrical conductors (wires). They consist of: conduit, which carries wiring; cable tray which carries cables; duct (such as under floor and trench type) which is embedded in the concrete slab; or surface metal raceways, such as bus duct used where it is not possible to embed conduit in a wall. These raceways (some of which are shown in Figures 14.2 and 14.3) can be grouped in a multitude of combinations to house wiring systems. Each of these types of raceways is manufactured with fittings and accessories that enable them to be assembled into networks for distribution throughout the structure.

Conduit in trench is used for power distribution, communications, and outdoor lighting applications such as roadways or parking lots. The conduit installation may be either direct burial or concrete encased. Rigid galvanized steel and rigid PVC conduit are usually used in trenches. For corrosive soil applications, PVC-coated rigid steel may be specified. Fiber duct or PVC (plastic) conduit may also be used for the installation of a concrete duct bank.

Conduit in concrete slab is used for both branch circuit piping and power distribution where the locations of end use will not change. Embedded conduit is usually a very cost-effective method of raceway installation because of savings in support costs and reduced run lengths. The most common types of pipe used in embedded concrete raceways, or

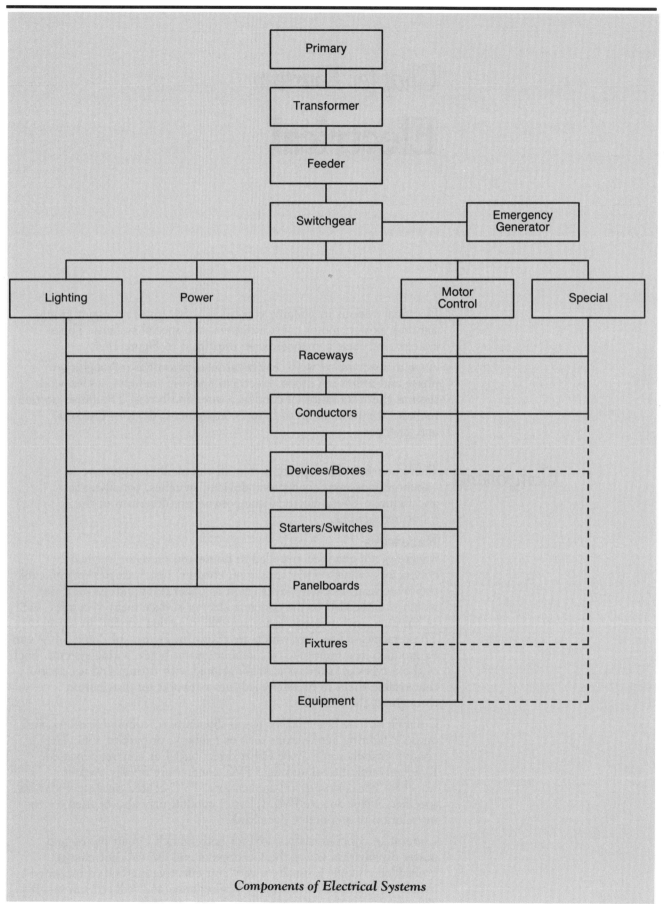

Components of Electrical Systems

Figure 14.1

"slab work" are PVC schedule 40 (plastic), rigid galvanized steel, and intermediate metallic conduit (IMC). These types of conduit are most resistant to corrosion and oxidation. Aluminum conduit is not recommended for use in concrete that contains chloride due to its potential for oxidation and expansion.

Conductors

A conductor is a wire or metal bar with a low level of resistance to the flow of electric current. Conductors are fed through the raceway systems to deliver the electrical power. They are made of copper or aluminum wire enclosed in a jacket of insulation. Conductors are designated by wire gauge (diameter) and type of insulation or protective jacket. Wire is rated by its voltage capacity. Typical types and designations are shown in Figure 14.4.

Cable refers to conductors made up of heavy or multiple wires, contained in a common jacketing. Cable may be run in conduit or in certain applications, by itself.

Cable run by itself is protected by sheathing which is either non-metallic or metallic (armored). Non-metallic sheathed cable (Romex) is available

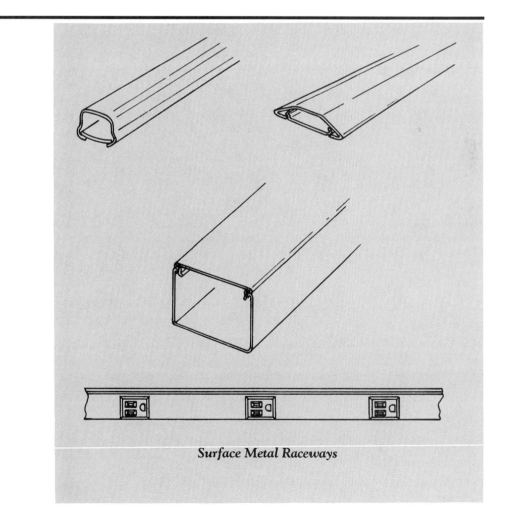

Surface Metal Raceways

Figure 14.2a

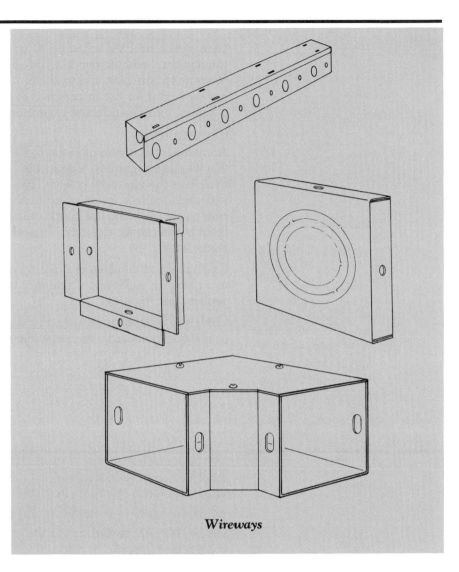

Wireways

Figure 14.2b

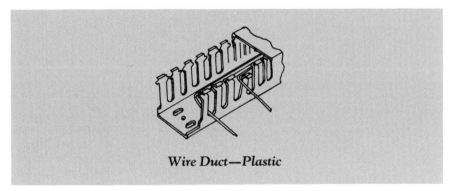

Wire Duct—Plastic

Figure 14.2c

in 2, 3, and 4 wire configurations and is installed in certain types of non-rated construction, such as residences. It is available in different gages of insulated wire.

Armored cable (one type is designated BX cable) is used in situations where physical protection is needed and conduit is not practical. Armored cable is not installed in conduit, underground, or in wet locations.

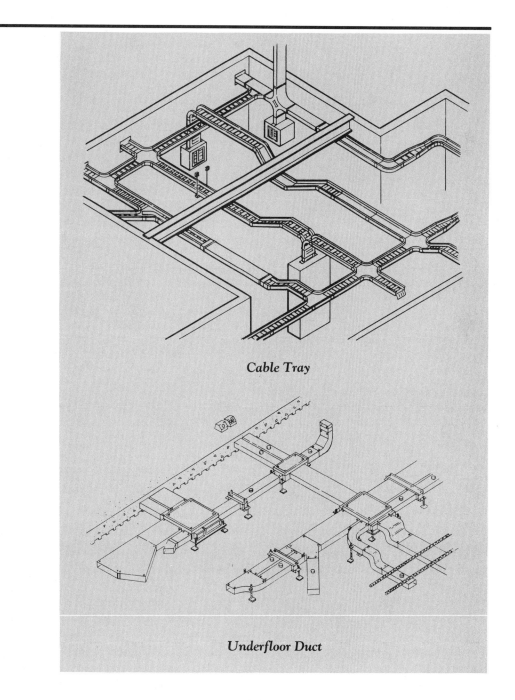

Cable Tray

Underfloor Duct

Figure 14.3

These two types of conductors are shown in Figure 14.5. It should be noted that individually insulated conductors (wires) are only used when installed in other types of protective raceways.

Other types of conductors are used for special purposes: high voltage shielded cable, flat wire for undercarpet installations, low voltage wires for telephone, and coaxial cable for data transmission. Some of these are illustrated in Figure 14.6.

Minimum Copper and Aluminum Wire Sizes Allowed for Various Types of Insulation

	Minimum Wire Sizes								
	Copper		Aluminum			Copper		Aluminum	
Amperes	THW THWN or XHHW	THHN XHHW *	THW XHHW	THHN XHHW *	Amperes	THW THWN or XHHW	THHN XHHW *	THW XHHW	THHN XHHW *
15A	#14	#14	#12	#12	195		2/0		
20	#12	#12			200	3/0			
25			#10	#10	205			250MCM	4/0
30	#10	#10			225		3/0		
40			# 8		230	4/0		300MCM	250MCM
45				# 8	250			350MCM	
50	# 8		# 6		255	250MCM			300MCM
55		# 8			260		4/0		
60				# 6	270			400MCM	
65	# 6		# 4		280				350MCM
75		# 6	# 3	# 4	285	300MCM			
85	# 4			# 3	290		250MCM		
90			# 2		305				400MCM
95		# 4			310	350MCM		500MCM	
100	# 3		# 1	# 2	320		300MCM		
110		# 3			335	400MCM			
115	# 2			# 1	340			600MCM	
120			1/0		350		350MCM		500MCM
130	# 1	# 2			375			700MCM	
135			2/0	1/0	380	500MCM	400MCM		
150	1/0	# 1		2/0	385			750MCM	600MCM
155			3/0		420	600MCM			700MCM
170		1/0			430		500MCM		
175	2/0			3/0	435				750MCM
180			4/0		475		600MCM		

Notes:
*Dry locations only
1. Size #14 to 4/0 is in AWG units (American Wire Gauge).
2. Size 250 to 750 is in MCM units (Thousand Circular Mils).
3. Use next higher ampere value if exact value is not listed in table.

Figure 14.4

Grounding protects persons from injury in the event of an insulation failure within equipment; it also stabilizes the voltage with respect to ground and prevents surface potentials between equipment, which could harm both people and equipment (in a hospital, for example). Grounding is accomplished by the placement of a conductor between electrical equipment or a circuit and the earth. In most distribution systems, one conductor of the supply is grounded. This conductor is known as "neutral wire." In addition, the National Electric Code (NEC) requires that a grounding conductor be supplied to connect non-current-carrying, conductive parts of an electrical system to ground.

Boxes and Devices

A wiring device is a component that controls or conducts, but does not consume, electricity. Wiring devices include such items as receptacles,

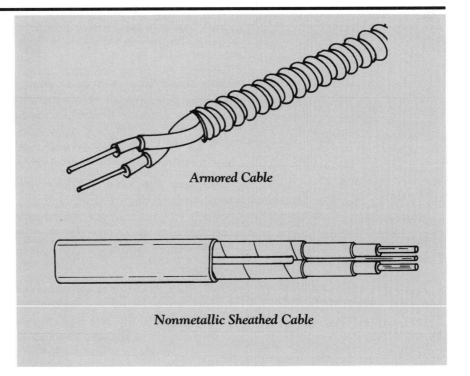

Armored Cable

Nonmetallic Sheathed Cable

Figure 14.5

wall switches, pilot lights, and wall plates. A box is used in electrical wiring at each junction point or device. Boxes provide access to electric connections and serve as a mounting for fixtures or switches. Pull boxes are inserted in a long run of conduit to facilitate the pulling of wire. They are also used where conduits change direction or wires divide into different directions. Cabinets are used to receive panelboards where wire terminates. Both come in various types to match the requirements of a given environment. Types of boxes are shown in Figure 14.7.

Boxes are usually made of galvanized steel, epoxy painted steel, stainless steel, or aluminum. Outlet boxes made of steel or plastic are used to hold wiring devices, such as switches and receptacles. They are also used as a mount for lighting fixtures.

Receptacles (commonly called "outlets") are a convenient means of connecting portable equipment and appliances to power. Receptacles are available in voltage ratings ranging from 125 to 600, and in amperages from 10 to 400. A wide variety of prong configurations is used to avoid having a plug or cap with a certain voltage and ampere rating inserted into a receptacle or another rating. Some typical prong configurations are shown in Figure 14.8.

Starters, Boards, and Switches

Starters are electric controllers that accelerate a motor from rest to running speed; they are also used to stop the motor. Boards serve as a mounting for electric components and/or controls. Switches are devices used to open, close, or change the condition of an electric circuit. Various types of starters, boards, and switches, and their purposes, are described below.

Circuit Breakers

Wiring (conductors) delivers electricity to fixtures and receptacles organized into networks called circuits. Circuit breakers are used in general distribution and in branch circuits to protect the wires and equipment downstream from current overload. Circuit breakers are rated in amperes and are capable of interrupting their rated current at their rated voltage. There are several types of circuit breakers: magnetic trip only, molded case, current-limiting (which includes three coordinated current-limiting fuses), and electronic trip.

Fuses

Fuses are used to interrupt a circuit in the event of overload. Fuses have a fusible link through which the current must flow. If too much current flows, the resulting heat melts the link. This stops the flow of current. There are many different types of fuses, such as plug, cartridge, and bolt-on. Fuses are designed with fast-acting or time-delay links. Both types will have the ability to react quickly to short-circuit currents.

Some plug fuses have an Edison screw base, which is the same as a medium base lamp. Others have a type "S" base, which requires an adapter screwed into the medium base socket. The purpose of these adapters is to discourage the use of fuses larger than the size appropriate to the existing wiring.

Starters

Starters are available in several different types and configurations— motor-starting switches, single-throw, across-the-line switches, and magnetic across-the-line starting switches. It is important to identify not only the types of starters, but also the type of enclosure for each starter.

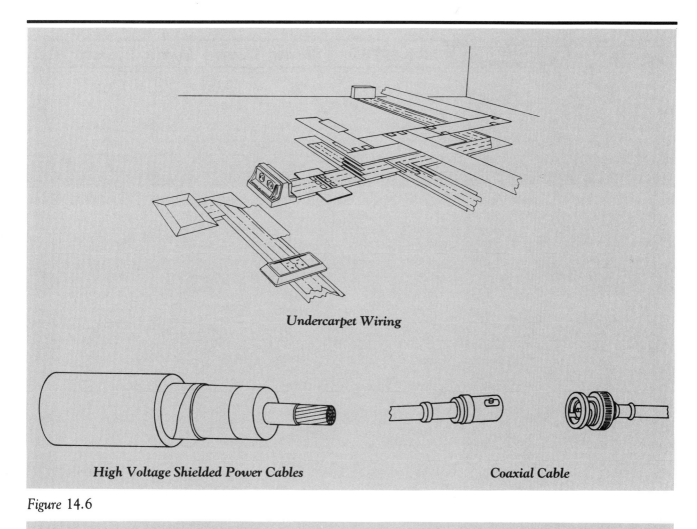

Undercarpet Wiring

High Voltage Shielded Power Cables

Coaxial Cable

Figure 14.6

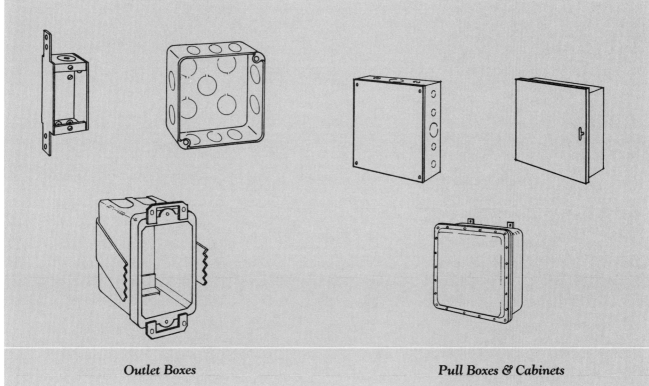

Outlet Boxes

Pull Boxes & Cabinets

Figure 14.7

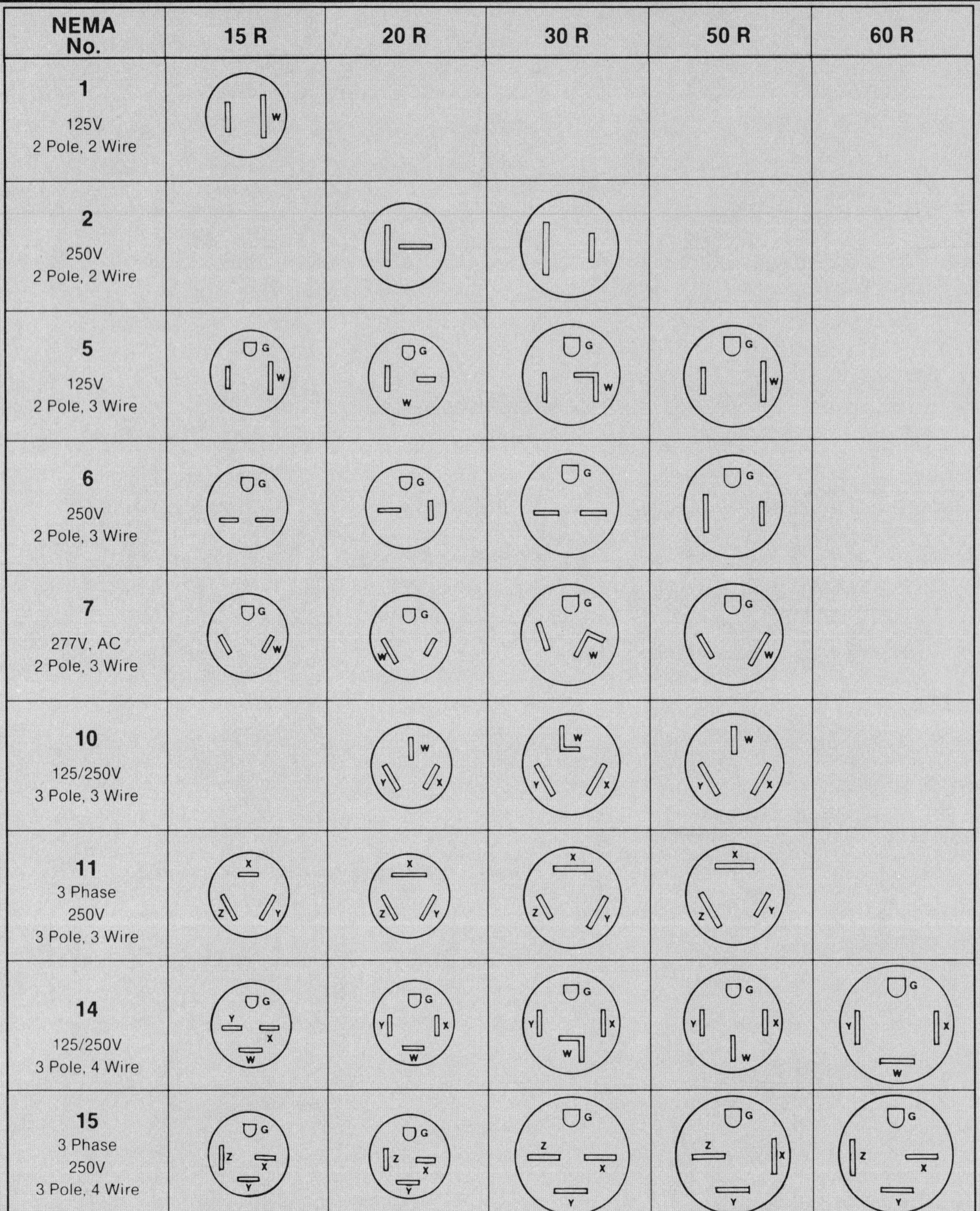

NEMA No.	15 R	20 R	30 R	50 R	60 R
1 125V 2 Pole, 2 Wire					
2 250V 2 Pole, 2 Wire					
5 125V 2 Pole, 3 Wire					
6 250V 2 Pole, 3 Wire					
7 277V, AC 2 Pole, 3 Wire					
10 125/250V 3 Pole, 3 Wire					
11 3 Phase 250V 3 Pole, 3 Wire					
14 125/250V 3 Pole, 4 Wire					
15 3 Phase 250V 3 Pole, 4 Wire					
18 3 Phase 208Y/120V 4 Pole, 4 Wire					

Figure 14.8

Relays

A relay is a control device that takes one input to a coil and operates a number of isolated circuit contacts in a control scheme. An electromagnetic coil is used to operate an armature, which holds the contacts. The relays contacts may be set up in several configurations: open at rest (normally open) and closing when energized; or closed at rest (normally closed) and opening when energized. A relay may have from 1 to 12 or more poles (contacts).

Magnetic Contactor

A relay with heavy-duty contacts is known as a magnetic conductor. In this type of relay, an electromagnetic coil is energized to close the contacts and hold them closed. Magnetic contactors are used to switch heating loads, capacitors, transformers, or electric motors. They do not have overload protection, are available with from 1 to 5 poles (separate circuits), and are usually controlled by a wall switch or push-button station.

Meter Sockets and Centers

Meter sockets are enclosures designed to receive the plug-in utility watt meters that monitor a customer's power usage (see Figure 14.9). For multiple tenants in commercial or residential buildings, meter centers may be used to monitor and distribute a single service entrance cable to two or more different users. A meter center may have a main breaker or some other protection device.

Switches

Safety switches (as opposed to "light switches") are intended for use in general distribution and in branch circuits. They provide an assured means of manually disconnecting a load from its source. The salient feature of a safety switch is that its operating handle is capable of being padlocked in the "OFF" position. This feature protects those working on the equipment from the possibility that someone might inadvertently energize the circuit. This is critical for some devices, such as fans, where not only is a switch required by code, but the switch must be installed within sight of the fan.

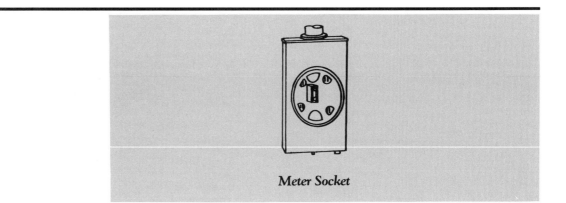

Meter Socket

Figure 14.9

Control switches provide manual input to the control circuits of relays or magnetic starters. These switches are used for equipment such as valves, fans, pumps, conveyors, and air conditioners. Control switches are assembled, or "built-up" using three components: 1) the legend plate, 2) the operator mechanism, and 3) the contact blocks. Each of these is available in a multitude of styles and types which can be combined in nearly endless variations to suit the particular application. See Figure 14.10 for illustrations of control and safety switches.

Boards

Panelboards are used to group circuit switching and protective devices into one enclosure. Panelboards consist of an assembly of bus bars and circuit protective devices housed in a metal box enclosure. Load centers are a specialized type of panelboard used principally for residential applications containing circuit breakers.

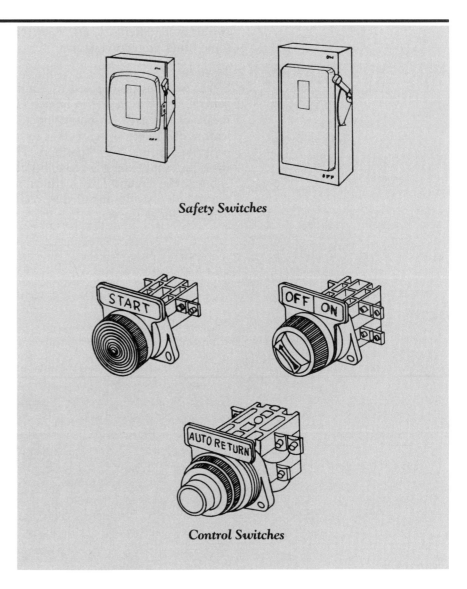

Safety Switches

Control Switches

Figure 14.10

Switchboards are used in buildings that have larger load requirements than can be served by a single load center panelboard and its disconnect device. This modular assembly of functional components or parts includes a service section, auxiliary section, metering component, and distribution sections.

Boards are illustrated in Figure 14.11.

Substations

A substation, or secondary unit substation, is an assembly consisting of a high-voltage incoming line section, a step down, three-phase power transformer, and a secondary low-voltage distribution section. Substations have two principal applications, both of which are industrial. The first is as an incoming service center; the second is a power center with dense, high power requirements. A substation is illustrated in Figure 14.12.

Transformers and Bus Duct

Transformers are devices with two or more coupled windings, with or without a magnetic core. They introduce mutual coupling between circuits and are used to convert a power supply from one voltage to another. Bus duct, or "busway", is a prefabricated unit that contains and protects one or more busses. These devices are illustrated in Figure 14.13 and described in the following paragraphs.

Transformers

Transformers are used in Alternating Current (AC) systems to convert from one voltage to another. They cannot be used in Direct Current (DC) systems. They are often used in construction to step down the primary "street" voltage to the secondary voltage required by fixtures and equipment in the project.

Transformers are used for four basic applications: 1) instrument transformers, 2) control transformers, 3) isolating transformers, and 4) power transformers. For example, isolating panels are used in hospitals, where they serve as added protection – to patients and sensitive monitoring equipment – from the effects of ground potentials. This kind of protection is particularly important in a hospital environment because of the numerous electrical instruments and appliances with wet systems.

Bus Duct

Bus duct provides a flexible distribution system for power in industrial and commercial buildings. The busway itself consists of copper or aluminum bars mounted in a sheet metal enclosure. There are several types available. The most common are feeder-type (indoor), plug-in type (indoor), and weatherproof feeder-type.

In some styles of bus ducts, branch taps can be readily changed to conform to new locations of motors and equipment. This system is widely used in industrial plants where equipment is continually changed to meet new manufacturing conditions.

Feeder-type bus duct is used primarily in industrial buildings to connect the service entrance to the main switchboard, or for high-capacity feeders to distribution centers, including feeder risers. Plug-in bus ducts are used for indoor systems where flexibility is needed for power over a wide area. Weatherproof feeder-type bus duct performs the same function as feeder type busway, but it is enclosed in a weatherproof casing for use outdoors or in damp, indoor areas.

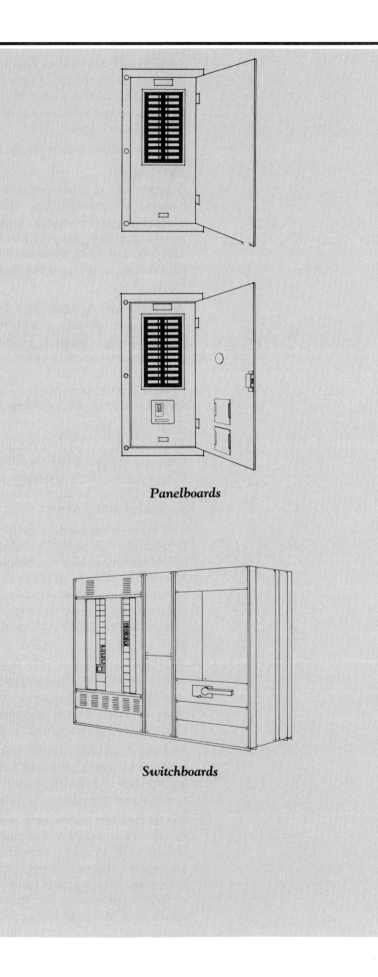

Panelboards

Switchboards

Figure 14.11

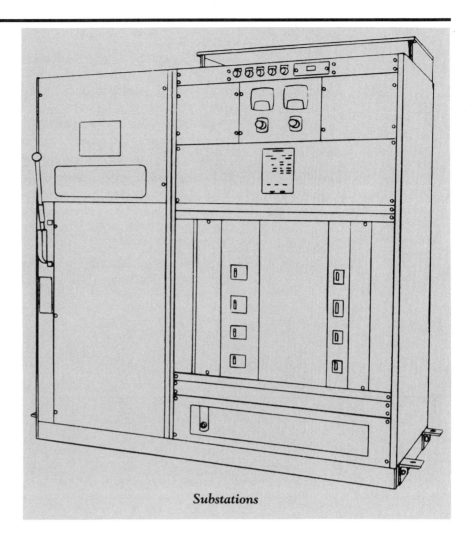

Substations

Figure 14.12

Fixtures

By far the most elemental portion of electrical construction is lighting. The first commercial use of electricity was for lighting. Today, virtually every building, industrial plant, house, bridge, and roadway sign makes extensive use of lighting fixtures. In building construction, lighting is still the largest single electrical cost center.

Interior Lighting Fixtures

Fixture styles for interior building lighting can be either surface-mounted or recessed in a wall or ceiling (shown in Figure 14.14). Other options are pendant or hanging fixtures. There are, of course, numerous variations of all of these styles. Certain designs take into account the ceiling system, such as the modular lay-in fixtures that match the ceiling grid spacing.

Lamps for interior lighting fixtures can be incandescent, fluorescent, or high-intensity discharge (HID).

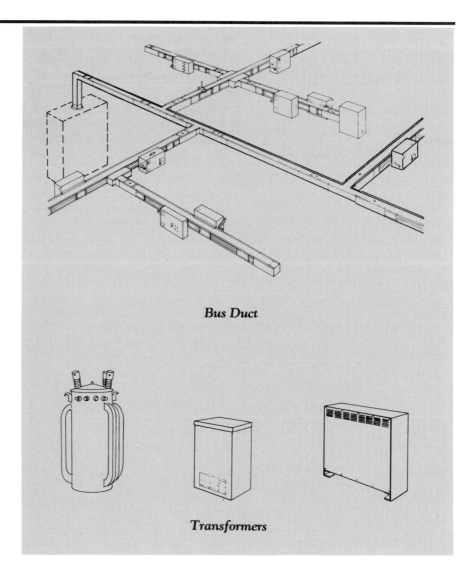

Bus Duct

Transformers

Figure 14.13

Incandescent lamps are the least efficient of the above, but their low initial cost keeps them attractive. Also, their "warm" (high red content) color spectrum is pleasing for many applications. One significant advantage of incandescent bulbs is that they light up instantly.

Fluorescent lamps require the use of ballast coils, which makes initial fixture costs somewhat higher than the cost of incandescent fixtures. Fluorescent lamps are, however, more efficient, and their color spectrum can more closely recreate natural daylight. A few different fluorescent lamp constructions are available that offer trade-offs among efficiency, color spectrum, and lamp cost. Fluorescents find their widest application in office buildings where people spend long periods of time reading and/or working with documents. Fluorescent fixtures are available with a rapid-start requiring only a couple of seconds to light.

HID (High Intensity Discharge) lamps generally are more efficient than fluorescent but do not generate the same broad light spectrums. HID lamps require special ballasts and require several minutes to warm up before full output is reached. Types of HID lighting include metal halide, mercury vapor, and high pressure sodium.

Exit and Emergency Fixtures

Exit lights are available with mounting arrangements for walls or ceilings and with or without directional arrows. Explosion-proof enclosures can

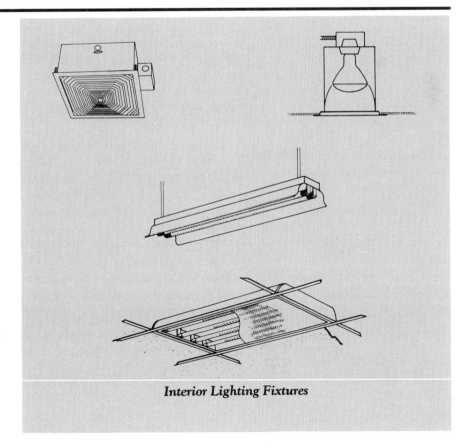

Interior Lighting Fixtures

Figure 14.14

be obtained for these lights. Exit signs have either incandescent or fluorescent lamps. Six-inch "EXIT" letters are standard.

Battery-operated emergency lights are available with either battery-mounted or remote heads. Several different types of batteries and voltages are available. Emergency lights are usually surface-mounted. (A special lamp pack is available for use in fluorescent fixtures; it mounts either in the ballast channel or on top of the fixture.)

Exterior Fixtures

The same assortment of lamps used for interiors (discussed previously) is also available for exterior use. Low-pressure sodium (LPS) is an additional option for exterior fixtures. Low-pressure sodium lamps generate an almost monochromatic, yellow light and are highly efficient. They require 7 to 15 minutes to reach full output.

Fluorescent lamps require special considerations when used outdoors. They are sensitive to low temperatures and require more starting energy in cold weather.

Exterior fixtures can be mounted on poles or attached directly to the building. These fixtures are available in vandal proof models where such construction is required.

Lighting

Lighting is designed to provide a certain level of illumination to the specific building area, specified in **footcandles**. A corridor in an office building may require only 30 footcandles, whereas a work area requires 100 footcandles. The illumination measurement is based on type and density of light fixtures, the ceiling height, and the reflectance value of the walls and ceilings.

Lighting circuits are made up of groups of common fixtures and wall (toggle) switches serving one or more rooms. Two toggle switches operating the lights for a single room are designated as three-way switches. In commercial areas, selected fixtures within a circuit may be connected to a second circuit for night or emergency lighting. Switches may be set on timers that automatically turn on and off at preset intervals or they may have a delay feature that would allow an individual enough time to exit the building after the switch had been thrown.

Power

Power involves the distribution of receptacles or plugs throughout a building to make electricity available to portable equipment such as copy machines, refrigerators, or window air conditioning units. These circuits may or may not be switched and are commonly 110 volt. The placement and quantity of these outlets is usually dependent on partition or work station layout. Circuit breakers for power wiring are kept in a separate panel from those for lighting on commercial projects.

When higher voltages are required for equipment and appliances, a single circuit is dedicated for that function alone. The plugs are configured in these receptacles to receive only plugs for equipment requiring the added voltage.

Situations involving stationary motors and equipment (without plugs) may be wired directly without any receptacles. Examples of this type of power distribution are air conditioning units and elevators.

Service

Service includes the excavation and structures for bringing power to the building and the actual installation of the primary cables. Figure 14.15 illustrates typical methods by which power is carried to the project.

This category covers the distribution methods used to route power, control, and communications cables onto a facility's property and between its buildings and structures. There are three basic options: 1) direct burial cables, 2) underground in duct banks, and 3) overhead on poles.

Direct Burial Cables

Direct burial cables are the least versatile; they are generally used for residential applications where aesthetics are a more important factor than flexibility or an allowance for future changes. Occasionally, direct burial is used in commercial and industrial facilities to route a branch feeder to unique equipment, such as a well pump or roadway lighting.

Duct Banks

Duct banks are a group of two or more underground raceways (conduits) usually encased in concrete. Although more costly than direct burial systems, duct banks offer three advantages. First, the cables are far better

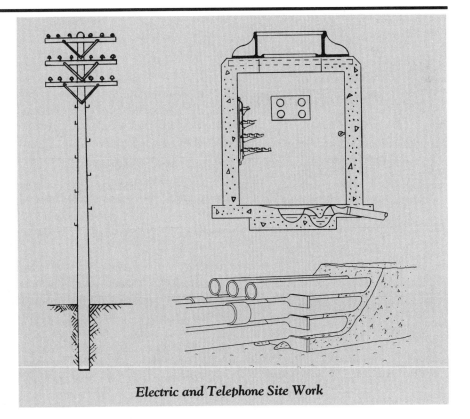

Electric and Telephone Site Work

Figure 14.15

protected from hazards and the elements. Secondly, groups of several cables can be pulled though each conduit (and many conduits may be installed in each duct bank). Finally, new cables may be pulled (or failed cables replaced) quickly and economically to meet future needs.

For duct banks that cover long distances, access must be provided to the run for pulling cables. When only a few conduits are installed, a hand-hole meets this requirement. For multiple conduit banks and for large conduits, a manhole is installed. Hand-holes and manholes may also serve to change the direction of a run or to split up a run.

The most common duct bank conduit material was formerly asbestos cement. In recent years, however, asbestos has been discontinued entirely in favor of plastic (PVC) and fiber duct. Galvanized steel may also be used, especially when power cables and instrumentation will be pulled into separate conduits in close proximity to each other.

Poles

Poles and overhead routing represent the most conventional method of distributing power and communication cables. Many cables are built and rated for aerial service. Some cables include "strength members" to carry the tensions of the stretched cables. Still other types of cables, such as service drops and telephone lines, will be supported by a steel messenger wire. Code requirements may dictate certain minimum heights for suspended cable.

Motor Control Centers

Many commercial buildings and process plants maximize efficiency by grouping electrical motor controls into centralized locations, motor control centers (MCC's). MCC's, illustrated in Figure 14.16, provide a structure for mounting a variety of motor starters, auxiliary controls, and feeder tap units. Some MCC's allow for mounting starters on both the front and back panels. Some commonly used components in MCC's are combination starters with either circuit breakers or fused disconnects; reversing and two-speed motor starters; feeder circuit breakers; main circuit breakers; lighting panelboards; and transformers.

Special Systems

Special systems include unique control or monitoring equipment used for specialized applications in residential, commercial, and industrial construction. Included are electric heating and residential wiring, television, public address, and sound, doorbell and paging systems.

Detection Systems

Fire alarm systems and burglar alarm (intrusion detection) systems are similar in both their principles of operation and their installation techniques. Nevertheless, they are two separate and distinct installation components. Rarely do they share any hardware or wiring (see Figure 14.17).

Burglar alarm systems consist of control panels, indicator panels, various types of alarm devices, and switches. The control panel is usually line powered with a battery backup supply. Some systems have a direct connection to the police or protection company, while others have auto-dial telephone capabilities. Most, however, simply have local control monitors and an annunciator. The sensing devices are various pressure switches, magnetic door switches, glass break sensors, infrared beams, infrared sensors, microwave detectors, and ultrasonic motion detectors. The alarms are sirens, horns, and/or flashing lights.

Fire alarm systems consist of control panels, annunciator panels, battery with rack and charger, various sensing devices, such as smoke and heat detectors, and alarm horn and light signals. Some fire alarm systems are very sophisticated and include speakers, telephone lines, door closer controls, and other components. Some fire alarm systems are connected directly to the fire station. Requirements for fire alarm systems are generally more closely regulated by codes and by local authorities than are intrusion alarm systems.

Lightning Protection

Lightning protection for the rooftops of buildings is achieved by a series of lightning rods or air terminals joined together by either copper or aluminum cable (as shown in Figure 14.18). The cable size is determined by the height of the building. The lightning cable system is connected through a downlead to a ground rod that is a minimum of 2' below grade and 1-1/2' to 3' out from the foundation wall.

Television Systems

Master T.V. antenna systems are used in schools, dormitories, and apartment buildings. Each system consists of the antenna, lightning arrester, amplifier, splitters, and outlets. The signal is received by the antenna and increased by the amplifier. It then goes through the main cable to the splitter. Here, the signal is split among several branch circuit cables. Figure 14.19 shows the layout of a T.V. system.

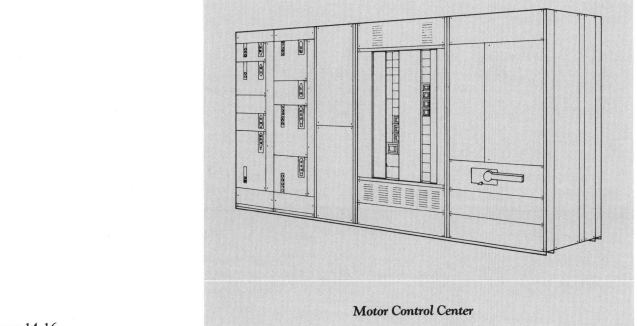

Motor Control Center

Figure 14.16

Residential Wiring

Residential wiring can be organized into six defined systems, which comprise all electrical components needed for a complete residential electrical installation:

- Service
- Branch circuit wiring
- Appliances
- Heating and A/C
- Intercom and/or doorbell systems

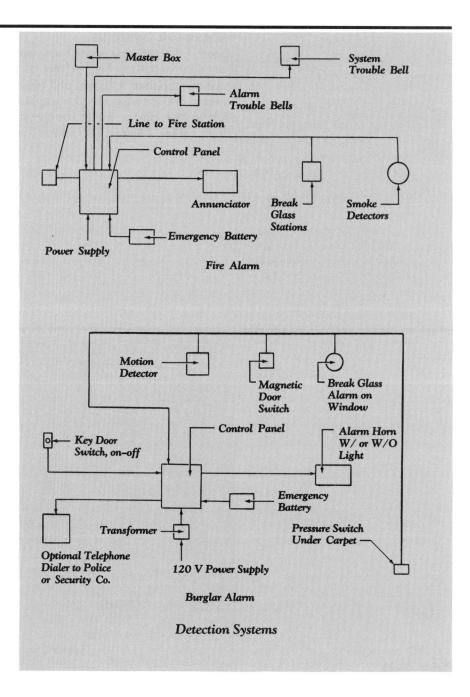

Figure 14.17

- Light fixtures
- Special needs

Branch circuits are circuits that contain any combination of receptacles, switches, and light outlets.

Appliance circuits are defined as specific needs, or direct-connected outlets. Examples are range circuits, water heater circuits, exhaust fans, disposal wiring, and dryer circuits. These circuits are run to, but do not include, the appliance itself. There is little variation in the voltage and amperage requirements of appliances.

Residential intercom systems consist of a master station (most commonly located in the kitchen area), up to 8 remote speakers, and associated low-voltage wiring. The transformer steps voltage down from 110V to 24V. Remote speakers are interconnected with #18 gauge nonmetallic sheathed cable.

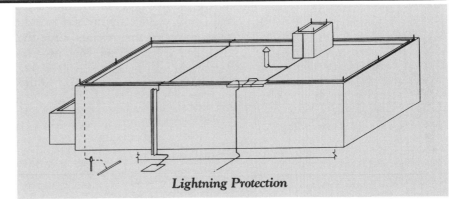

Figure 14.18

Lightning Protection

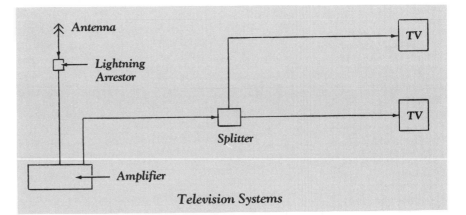

Figure 14.19

Television Systems

Heating and air conditioning circuits are direct, or "home runs." Most estimating standards do not include the equipment, which is instead supplied and installed by the mechanical contractor; the circuit and tie-in are done by the electrical contractor.

The raceways used in residential wiring vary according to specifications as well as state, local, and national electrical codes. Because of the wide variations in cost, it is important to note the type of raceway material being used. Some of the more common types are listed below:

- Nonmetallic sheathed cable (Romex)
- BX cable
- EMT conduit
- Aluminum or steel conduit may also be used.

Electric Heating

Electric heating has a wide range of equipment and applications. Electric space heat may be provided with a baseboard arrangement, wall-mounted units, or ceiling-hung heaters. The baseboard heaters are usually convection types. They are classed in terms of watts per foot (i.e., watt density). Low watt density models produce approximately 175 W/L.F., while high watt density units 257 W/L.F. (This number suggests the operating temperature of the element.) Baseboard heaters are available in sizes that increase in 2' increments—from 2' to 12' long. They may be rated for operation on 120, 240, or 277 volts.

Unit space heaters generally operate with forced air (fans) blowing across an electric coil. These units are rated in terms of their heat output in kilowatts (KW). Sizes run from 10 KW to 50 KW. Although 208 to 240-volt single-phase units are used, 240 and 480-volt three-phase units are far more common.

There are two types of thermostat controls for heater circuits. The first is full (line) voltage thermostat switches. The second is low-voltage, relay-equipped thermostats. Line thermostats are not suited for more than 240 volts, nor are they used for large heaters at lower voltages. Minimum wall insulation values must be met when electric heating is installed in residences. Figure 14.20 shows electric heating equipment.

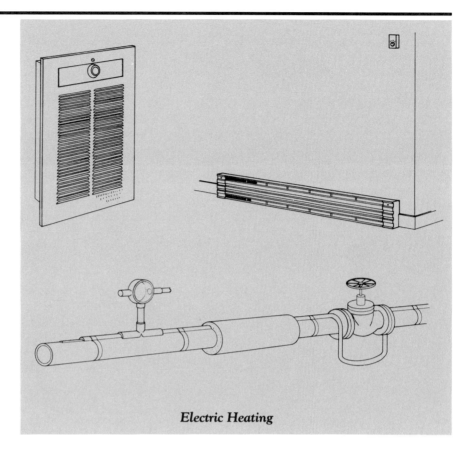

Electric Heating

Figure 14.20

Part Three

Project Management

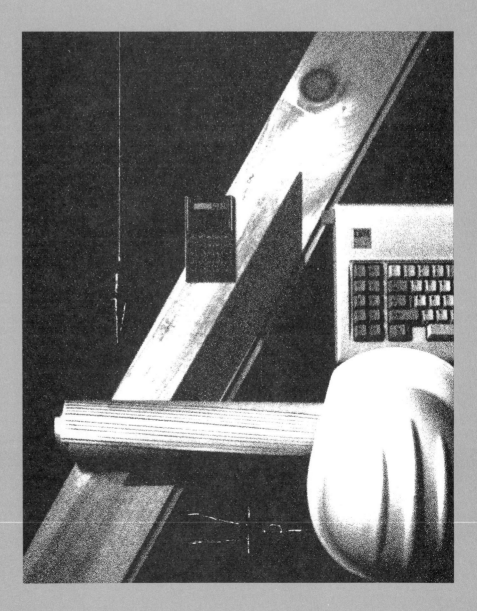

Chapter Fifteen

Project Administration

The management and control of a building project are two of the most critical functions in the construction process. Much effort, time, and emphasis is placed on the acquisition of a contract (estimating, bidding, and negotiation). However, all that effort may be wasted unless the resources of the firm are effectively directed and controlled to complete the project successfully – in accordance with the contract documents, within budget, on time, and safely. The following are some of the key elements that lead to successful project management.

Organization
The establishment of an effective organization constitutes one of the key ingredients of successful project management. For any organization to be effective, it must recognize the aims and objectives of the firm, show defined lines of authority, supervision, and communication, and must have employees who are experienced and qualified so that authority can be delegated.

Although most construction firms tend to lean towards a matrix type of structure (an organizational structure in which the horizontal and vertical lines of authority are combined to permit the flow of authority both down and across the structure), there is no one single type of organizational structure that definitively "works." Each construction firm establishes an organizational structure suited to its specific needs and resources depending on its size, annual overhead costs, annual volume of contracts, and geographic location, as well as economic, technical, operational and other considerations.

Organizational Structure
Organizational structures in construction range from a one-man organization (as illustrated in Figure 15.1) to ones that include hundreds of people.

Small Organizations
A one-man organization (not a corporation) consists of an owner, or sole proprietor, who "wears many hats" and performs all the required functions (estimating, project management, and bookkeeping), perhaps with the help of consultants or part-time employees. A typical owner of such an organization may have worked for a contractor in the past, and now wishes to start his/her own firm. Because of the ever-increasing

complexity and sophistication of the construction process, one person rarely can handle all of the roles and responsibilities required of today's construction firms.

For a small contractor, a three or four-man operation, as shown in Figure 15.2, can often be more practical and efficient. In this type of structure, the president handles all or most of the administrative duties, with other areas handled by "specialists" (e.g., estimator, bookkeeper, project manager).

It is not unusual to find other variations of this type of structure. For instance, the president may hire an assistant to perform all of the administrative work so he/she can perform the tasks of sales, estimating or project management.

Figure 15.3 illustrates the basic organizational structure of a large or sophisticated construction firm. It is also possible to have several variations of this type of structure. For instance, some firms combine the

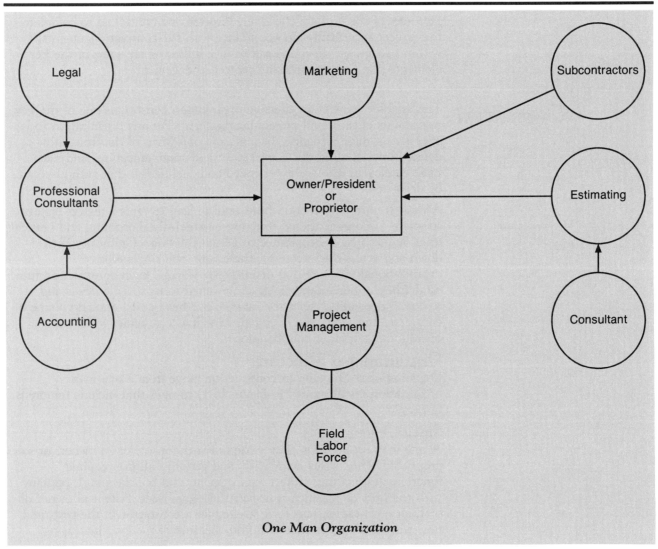

One Man Organization

Figure 15.1

estimating and project management groups under one department, and the estimators also act as project managers. Other firms keep the two groups in separate departments where each project manager has a one- or multi-project responsibility, as illustrated in Figure 15.4. In this type of organization, there is usually a separate estimating group headed by a chief estimator who reports to either the construction manager or the vice-president for construction operations.

Large Organizations

Larger and more sophisticated firms that handle several different types of projects usually retain several division directors or assistant vice-presidents, each reporting to the vice-president of construction operations, as illustrated in Figure 15.5.

Large size construction firms have increased specialization within each division. For instance, each division may have several groups or subdivisions such as estimating, or project management. Within each subdivision, there can be further specialization. For example, the

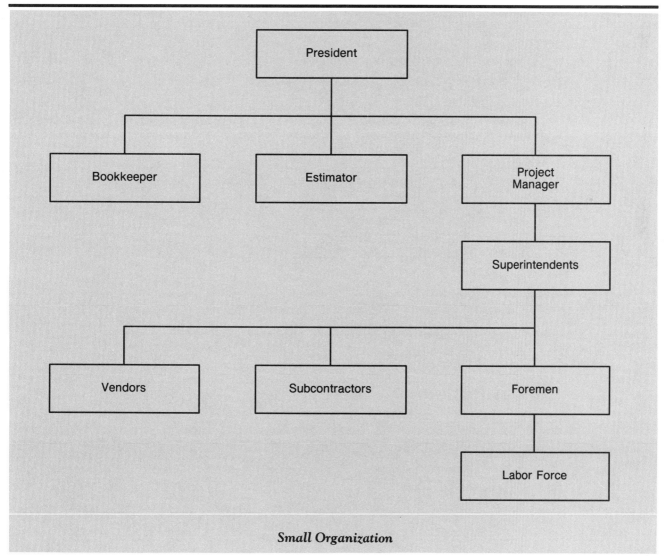

Small Organization

Figure 15.2

estimating group may have estimators who specialize in civil work, architectural work, mechanical work, and electrical work.

Field vs. Office

Although the organizational structure of construction firms varies considerably from one firm to the other, all firms can be broken down into two main parts – office organization and field organization (see Figure 15.6).

Costs for the office ("home office") organization are often included as part of the firm's general overhead. Such costs are usually applied as an overall percentage of construction costs based on projected annual volume. The field office costs are included as part of the field overhead (general conditions) and as a construction cost applicable to a specific project. The field organization is directed by a project superintendent. However, on large projects, it is not uncommon for construction firms to place a project manager, an on-site office manager, and an assistant superintendent in the field as well. The project manager supervises the

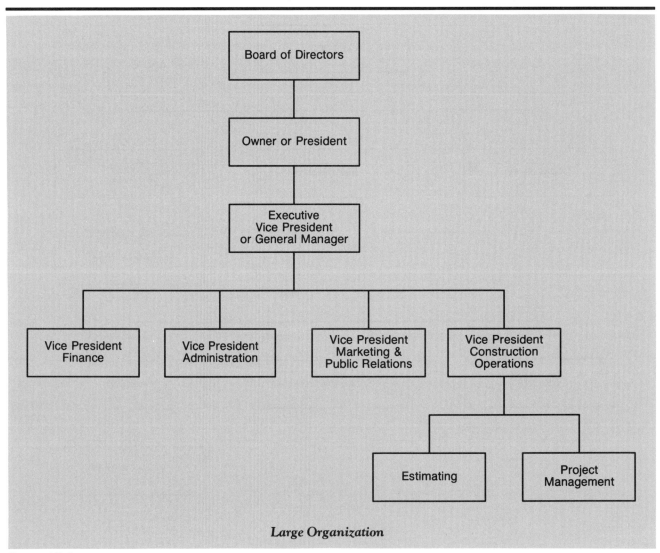

Large Organization

Figure 15.3

field organization and facilitates on-site management, handles all communication with the owner or his/her representative and the architect/engineer, and provides the control of subcontractors and suppliers. The on-site office manager handles all matters related to general administration, accounting, purchasing, and cost control. The assistant superintendent helps oversee quality control and safety aspects of the project.

The level of sophistication of a contractor's organization and the costs involved are management decisions. A firm can easily become ineffective and lose profits by increasing its overhead costs unnecessarily. A common mistake is to have too large an office staff. On the other hand, a lack of qualified and adequate personnel can also cause a firm to fail. A balance must be struck between the two.

Communication

In addition to the intercommunication between the various entities shown in Figure 15.7, there is also intra-communication within each one. Effective communication is critical in the management of a construction project. When there is a lack of communication between two or more key players in the construction process (such as between the owner's site representative and the contractor's superintendent), conflicts can easily occur. These conflicts can be damaging, expensive, and can hinder the progress of the project. Misguided communications lead to

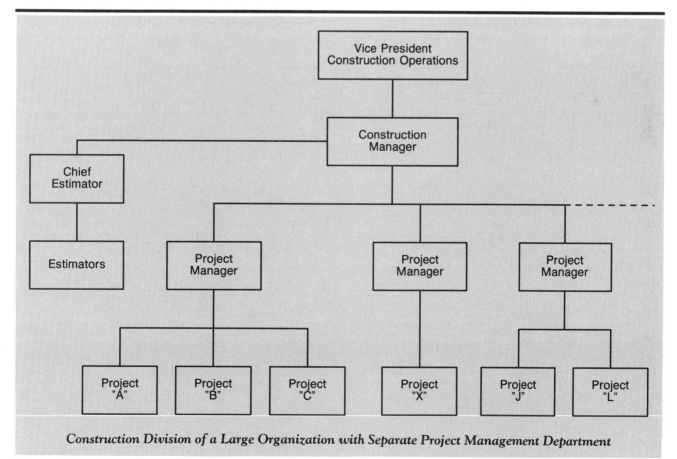

Construction Division of a Large Organization with Separate Project Management Department

Figure 15.4

311

serious problems such as job delays, cost overruns and, possibly, construction claims. Some examples of scenarios depicting effective and ineffective communication, with possible outcomes, are illustrated in Figure 15.8.

The following techniques can be used to avoid conflicts and arguments resulting from poor communication.

- **Avoid talking when another person is talking.** One cannot listen well to what the other person is saying if both are talking at the same time. It is better to be patient and allow the other person plenty of time to talk without interruption, and then get a message across when he/she is finished.
- **Avoid doing other things such as** reading or looking elsewhere while the other person is talking. Listen to understand and not just to oppose.
- **Avoid raising your voice or talking in a loud tone.** Always remember that the fact or the truth of the subject of discussion will not be altered by the loudness of your voice.

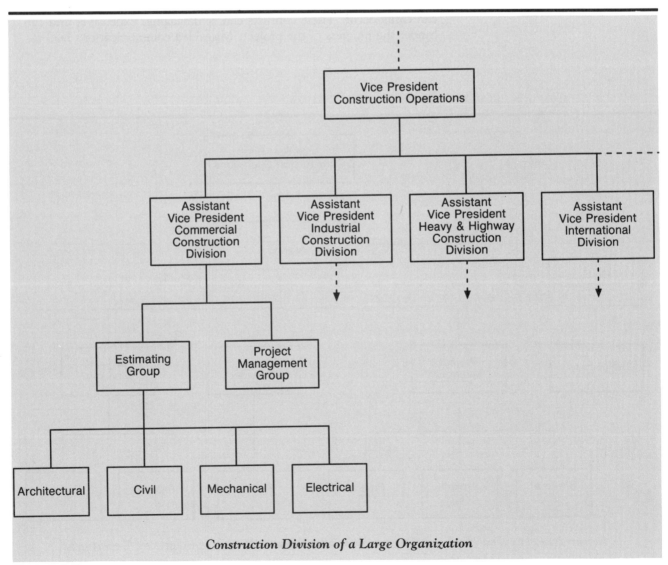

Construction Division of a Large Organization

Figure 15.5

- **Avoid getting angry.** Every effort should be made to control angry outbursts, since most people tend to misinterpret the meaning of statements made by other people when they are angry.

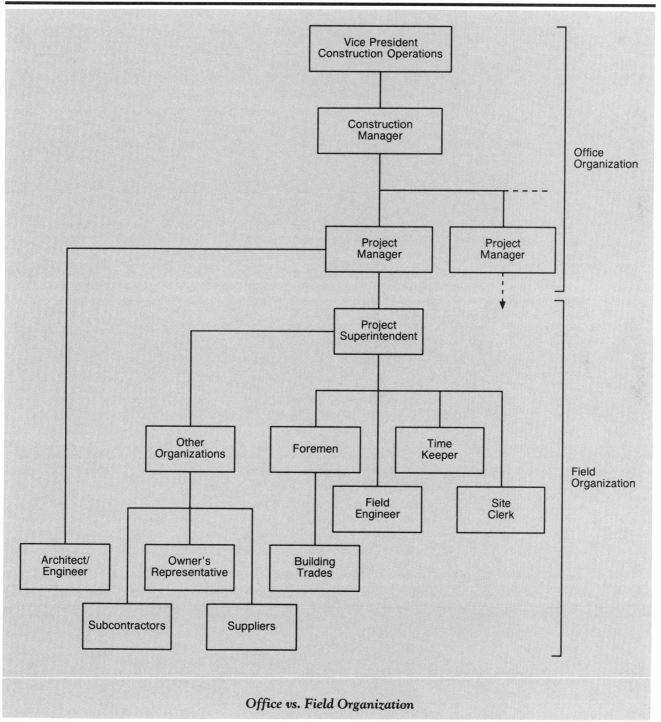

Office vs. Field Organization

Figure 15.6

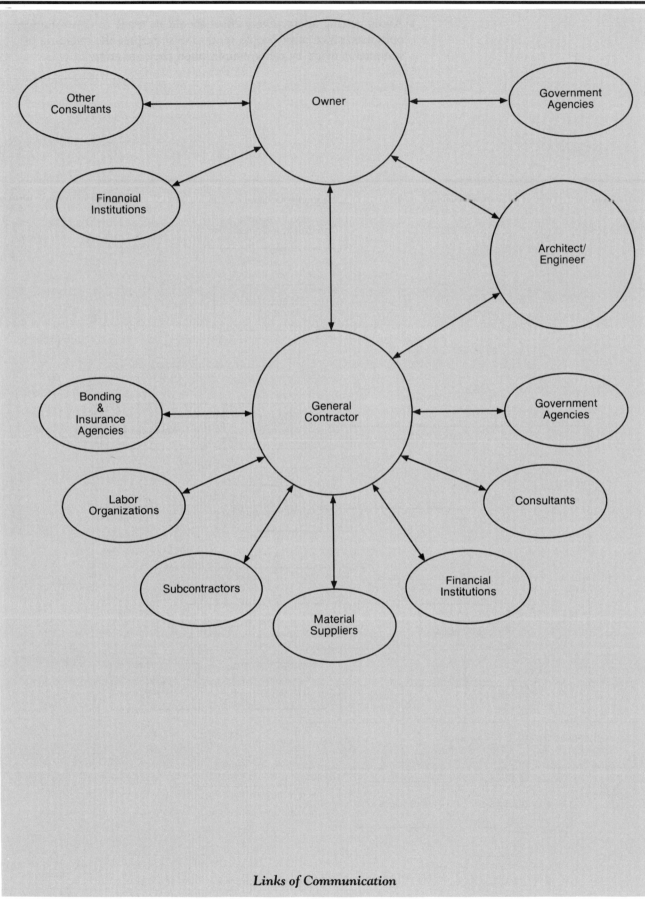

Links of Communication

Figure 15.7

- **Avoid criticism.** Most people become defensive and angry when criticized publicly.
- **Avoid making the other person tense.** Put the other person at ease when you sense any tension. This may be accomplished by interjecting some humor, telling a funny story that can be related to the subject of discussion, or changing the topic for a brief moment. In other situations, it may be effective to request a short break or even a postponement of the meeting to a later time or another day.

These techniques should be treated as goals. It may not be possible to be in control of every situation, but considering these techniques and using them appropriately can help minimize and avoid potential conflicts and arguments.

Procurement

In project management, procurement, also referred to as "buy out", is the process of negotiating subcontracts and issuing the agreements, negotiating for materials and supplies, and issuing purchase orders. The procurement phase begins after award of a general contract, once a decision has been made on which portions of the project will be

---

Communication Scenarios

Scenario	Result	Possible Reaction
1. Owner's representative to contractor: "Will you be kind enough to go over your estimate for this modification once again? I did not quite understand it the first time."	Understanding	Contractor goes over the estimate again very calmly, and slowly. He/she may even check at a certain point to ensure that the clarification is adequate.
2. Owner's representative to contractor: "I don't understand your estimate and I am not going to accept it."	Anger and Frustration	Contractor gets angry and an argument ensues.
3. In negotiating a change order, a supervising architect/engineer states to a contractor: "Our engineers' estimate is much lower than yours and I can only go by that estimate."	Disgust	Contractor is disgusted because the architect/engineer is not considering the rationale behind his/her estimate, and is only pushing for the engineers' estimate, which is only to the owner's advantage. Negotiations break down and nothing is accomplished.
4. Architect/engineer to contractor: "Our engineers' estimate and your estimate are far apart. Would you mind going over your estimate and the plans with our engineers to determine why we have such a large difference?"	Cooperation	The contractor may review the plans and his/her estimate with the engineers to resolve their differences.

Figure 15.8

performed by the contractor's own forces, and which ones will be subcontracted. In most firms, the project manager performs the procurement function.

Usually the project manager, after carefully studying a set of the contract documents, prepares a list of all the work activities for which materials or services must be procured. This is known as the **procurement list.** It may help to use a preprinted form, as shown in Figure 15.9, to prepare and record this list.

Following are some suggestions that, if used, can facilitate the procurement process.

- The project estimator may arrange all bids and quotations received in order, starting with the lowest price to the highest price, by trade or service proposed.
- The project manager schedules several meetings as needed with the project estimator to clarify the scope of work and any exceptions, and to review all bids and quotations.
- The estimator (along with the project manager) may or may not attend negotiations with subcontractors or vendors.
- Items or work required for the early stages of the project, or "rush items," – such as sitework, reinforcing steel, metal inserts for the concrete foundation and slab, metal door frames – should be procured first. The next items to procure are "long lead items," such as elevators, switchgear, etc.
- The scope of work should be fully discussed with each subcontractor or vendor during negotiations to ensure that they can meet the plans and specifications, fit the needs of that particular project, and meet scheduled delivery dates.
- Subcontract agreements, purchase agreements, or purchase orders are prepared and sent out to the respective subcontractor or vendor for execution immediately after negotiations are completed. Considerable time can be saved in this effort if the project manager prepares "master agreements" containing the "boiler plate" information (standard information such as project description and number, name of general contractor, architect/engineer, and owner). In this way, only specific information (subcontractor name, scope, and price) needs to be filled in for each subcontractor or vendor.
- The project manager should not sign any subcontract or purchase agreements until they are returned signed by the recipient with the appropriate insurance certificates and surety bonds, where required.

Change Orders

A change order is written when a change or modification to the scope of the contract, as represented in the contract documents (contract drawings or specifications), is requested by the owner or the architect/engineer after the award of the contract. In the ideal situation, all parties to the contract agree on all aspects of a change – scope, price, time extensions – prior to the work being done. Unfortunately, job conditions and other factors do not always make this feasible. As a result, on some projects, alternate arrangements and negotiations during or after the completion of change order work remain the only viable alternative.

Types of Change Orders

All changes to construction contracts fall into one of two main categories:

Procurement List

Project No:	Project Manager:			Contract No:					
Specification Number	Item Description	Subcontractor (Labor Only)		Supplier (Material/Equipment-No Labor)		Subcontractor (Labor/Material-Turn-key)			
		Date	Name and Comments	Date	Name and Comments	Date	Name and Comments		

Figure 15.9

- **Changes with no cost impact:** Changes in the scope of the contract that do not increase or decrease the original or revised contract price.
- **Changes with cost impact:** Changes in the scope of the contract that increase or decrease the original or revised contract price.

Time extensions and other variations from original planning may be necessary in either of these two categories.

Sources of Change Orders

Following are the three main entities that initiate change orders.

- The owner or an authorized owner's representative such as the resident engineer, inspector, or on government projects, the contracting officer
- The architect/engineer
- The general contractor

A flow chart of a "typical" change order process is illustrated in Figure 15.10.

Under ordinary circumstances (when the change is not an emergency or will not delay the project), a potential change is identified by one of the listed sources, and then sent to the owner through his authorized representative. The owner may request input from the project architect/engineer. The architect/engineer reviews the proposed change and examines its merit, develops the scope, specifications, and drawings as needed, and provides a cost estimate for the change order work. The contractor is provided a copy of the drawings and specifications, and is requested to submit his own cost proposal. The contractor's price proposal is reviewed by the owner or his representative and, if it is determined to be acceptable with respect to cost and time, a change order is issued. Preprinted standard forms are available for the issuance of change orders, as shown in Figure 15.11.

If the contractor's proposal is not accepted, negotiations are held to determine a mutually satisfactory price before the contractor can proceed to work on the change.

In emergency or critical situations, where the change order process described above may delay the project or result in an additional claim, the owner or his authorized representative may direct the contractor to proceed with the work associated with the change. The issue of cost and time may be delayed, to be resolved at a more appropriate time.

Very few plans and specifications are "perfect" when they leave the architect/engineer's office – there is no "perfect set of plans and specifications." Sometimes mistakes are inevitable (by all parties) in the tremendous effort to meet tight schedules and deadlines. Job conditions, availability of materials and equipment, and user requirements may change after the award of a contract. Change orders are, therefore, common on most construction projects. Most importantly, change orders must be handled properly, or they can "snowball" into serious disputes, excessive delays, damage to previously installed work, or additional contractor claims. If and when changes do occur, every effort must be made to process and resolve them promptly to minimize the potential complications.

Claims and Disputes

Claims and disputes have always created serious problems in most industries, and the construction industry is no exception. It is, therefore, extremely important that people who manage construction projects fully

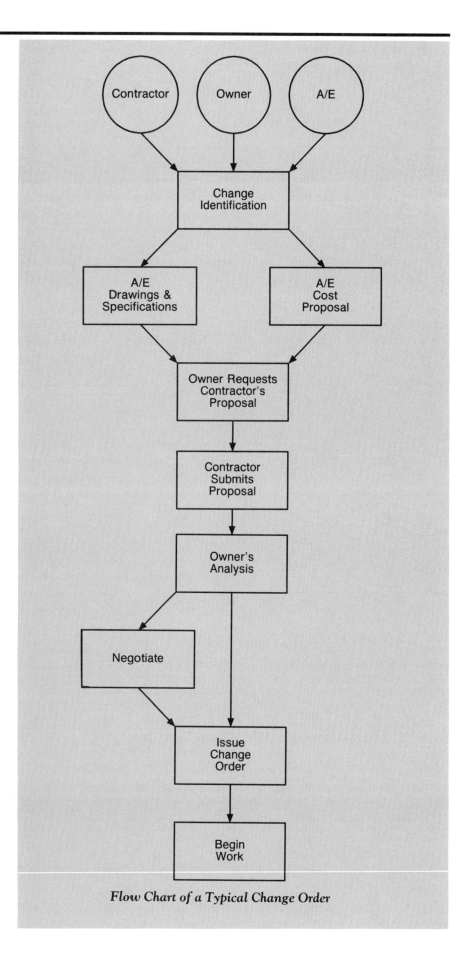

Flow Chart of a Typical Change Order

Figure 15.10

⚓ Means Forms

CONTRACT CHANGE ORDER

FROM:

_____

_____

_____

_____

TO:

_____

_____

_____

_____

CHANGE ORDER NO.		
DATE		
PROJECT		
LOCATION		
JOB NO.		
ORIGINAL CONTRACT AMOUNT	$	
TOTAL PREVIOUS CONTRACT CHANGES		
TOTAL BEFORE THIS CHANGE ORDER		
AMOUNT OF THIS CHANGE ORDER		
REVISED CONTRACT TO DATE		

Gentlemen:

This CHANGE ORDER includes all Material, Labor and Equipment necessary to complete the following work and to adjust the total contract as indicated;

☐ the work below to be paid for at actual cost of Labor, Materials and Equipment plus _____ percent (_____ %)

☐ the work below to be completed for the sum of _____

_____ dollars ($ _____)

_____

_____

_____

_____

_____

_____

_____

_____

_____

_____

_____

_____

_____

_____

_____

_____

_____

_____

_____

_____

CHANGES APPROVED

The work covered by this order shall be performed under the same Terms and Conditions as that included in the original contract unless stated otherwise above.

By _____

By _____

Signed _____

By _____

Figure 15.11

understand the sources, causes, and consequences of claims. A thorough understanding can help to prevent claims and minimize the antagonism that often accompanies claims.

Sources of Claims

On construction projects, nearly all claims and disputes can be traced to one or a combination of the following sources:

- The architect/engineer
- The owner
- The contractor, including subcontractors and suppliers
- Job conditions

The Architect/Engineer

The three main causes of claims that can be traced to the architect/engineer on most construction projects are:

- Ambiguous specifications or drawings
- Design errors
- Conflicts and omissions

Ambiguities may occur in a set of plans and specifications when there are words, illustrations, statements, or sentences that may have more than one reasonable interpretation and/or are susceptible to misinterpretation by others.

Design errors may occur due to inexperience, the specification of old products that are no longer available being applied in new or unsuitable situations, the use of "boiler-plate" specifications from previous projects (often referred to as a "cut and paste" job) for a new project without the proper adjustments or appropriate revisions, and the specifications of newer products to which the construction industry has not been exposed.

Conflicts and omissions may occur when there is a lack of proper coordination between the different disciplines of the design team (architects, structural engineers, civil engineers, mechanical engineers, and electrical engineers) by the responsible party. On most projects, the architect procures the services of several design disciplines; each prepares the design for its area of expertise independently. It is the duty of the responsible architect during the design process to coordinate, review, and ensure that the designs and specifications of the different disciplines will fit and work together with no conflicts. Sometimes this effort suffers because of time constraints, unrealistically tight schedules, or the lack of adequate personnel. A breakdown in coordination can result in conflicts between specifications and drawings; between the different sections of a set of specifications; between different parts of a set of drawings; or between a set of drawings, specifications, and the proposed site. The majority of these problems can be eliminated through close coordination and communication between all the disciplines throughout the design process. Conflicts resolved during the design phase are considerably less costly (often at no cost) than those occurring during the construction phase.

The Owner

The three main causes of claims that can be attributed to the owner are:

- Improper actions or lack of action
- Requested changes after final design and/or contract award
- Delays

Examples of improper actions by the owner (or the owner's representative) that can result in claims are:

- Improper or overzealous inspection
- Technically inexperienced and/or unqualified site representatives of the owner
- Untimely payment to a contractor
- Improper termination procedures
- Changes in the method of operation of owner's site representative
- Unfair interpretation of plans, specifications, policies, and regulations
- Furnishing of incorrect, misleading or ambiguous information by the owner's authorized representatives
- Failure to act or undue delay in acting on administrative or other matters

Changes: Change orders can and do occur on most construction projects because the owner has the right to make changes at any time, provided that he is aware of the associated costs and time extensions. However, changes can result in claims due to the failure of the owner or his authorized representative and the contractor to agree on the terms of the change (i.e., scope of the change, dollar amount, time extension, etc.). "Evidence of constructive changes" is another type of claim which can arise when an action or statement by the owner or his authorized representative leads a contractor to believe that a change to the scope of the contract is being requested, wanted, or needed by the owner.

Delays: Delays initiated by an owner can lead to claims because construction contracts have a set time limit and contractors allocate specific resources (funds, personnel, equipment, overhead costs, surety bonding lines, and lines of credit) to each job. Therefore, owner initiated delays that cause a contract to extend beyond the stipulated time limit will cost the contractor money. If an equitable settlement is not reached for the additional costs of such delays, a claim may be made by the contractor for damages. Examples of owner-caused delays are: taking too long (longer than the period stipulated in the contract documents) to approve submittals such as shop drawings and samples; failure to make decisions in a timely fashion on items such as changes or change order proposals; delaying the award of contract, notice to proceed, or progress payments to a contractor; interference with the operations of the contractor or his subcontractors; and refusal to accept materials or completed work that meet the contract plans and specifications.

The Contractor

Causes of claims that can be traced to contractors include:

- Financial and management problems
- Technical and other problems

Management Problems: Examples of a contractor's financial and management problems that can lead to claims include: personnel problems such as overworked, inexperienced, or otherwise unqualified personnel who can make mistakes; failure to meet financial obligations such as payroll, subcontractor, and supplier payments, on a regular or timely basis; lack of proper management tools or skills; or failure to respond in a timely fashion to contractual matters such as a correspondence or an owner's request for proposal.

Technical Problems: Examples of technical problems that can result in claims include:

- Inadequate site investigation prior to the submittal of a cost proposal or bid

- Failure to read and understand contract documents properly
- Failure to have all ambiguities cleared up prior to bidding or negotiating a contract
- Relying solely on past trade or industry practices without regard for the peculiarities of a specific project
- Failure to make contract submittals in a timely manner
- Poor or unacceptable workmanship
- Failure to order materials, equipment, and supplies needed for a project on time to meet critical delivery dates
- Failure to properly coordinate the work of subcontractors
- Failure to follow plans and specifications
- Unrealistic scheduling
- Unrealistic or inaccurate cost estimates
- The anticipation of reduced profits or potential loss

Job Conditions

Claims caused by job conditions can be classified into two groups. They are:

- Acts of God
- Changed site conditions

Acts of God: Acts of God include direct, sudden, and irresistible action of natural forces, that cannot be reasonably foreseen or prevented, such as floods, hurricanes, earthquakes, and other natural catastrophes. Claims result when the contractor and owner cannot agree on the actual effects of acts of God on the project.

Changed Site Conditions: Claims on changed conditions are initiated when there is a disagreement between an owner and a contractor as to: whether or not conditions at the proposed site have changed since the time of the contractor's cost estimate; and whether or not the changed conditions, when established, have an impact on the execution of the work. Changed conditions occur when the conditions specified in the contract documents, or reasonably anticipated in the plans, specifications, or the proposed site, turn out to be different from what is actually encountered by the contractor at the time physical construction begins. The presence of rock, water, and/or unsuitable earth that differ from what was represented in the contract documents are examples of changed site conditions.

Minimizing Claims and Disputes

Claims and disputes are inevitable in construction, due to the fragmented nature and complexity of the building process. Because of the high costs and time associated with litigation, efforts should be made to anticipate and resolve claims and disputes through alternate mechanisms such as negotiations or arbitration. The American Arbitration Association has been successful in resolving many construction disputes and its services should be seriously considered. Litigation should be used only as a last resort.

The following are suggested tips that can help minimize the likelihood and impact of construction claims and disputes:

- Develop internal mechanisms for minimizing the likelihood of disputes before they occur by anticipating and resolving potential construction problems as quickly as possible.
- Develop strategies to ensure that construction proceeds while disputes are being resolved (whenever possible), such as keeping lines of communication open, and finding ways to resolve the disputes instead of pushing them towards even more disputes.

- Avoid delays in communication or in taking action. Damages for delays are often severe, because the impact of a short delay can cause a ripple effect throughout a project.
- Confirm all oral agreements or changes, in writing, as soon as possible after reaching them.
- The superintendent or his field engineer and the owner's site representative should all maintain a daily record of work in progress, including items such as the precise date and time of arrival of materials, equipment, or subcontractors on-site. This can be done using a standard form as shown in Figure 15.12.
- Maintain a comprehensive file for each major construction phase. Properly supported documentation (by all parties) can help clarify misunderstandings and act as an incentive for the parties to settle the dispute.

Litigation is time-consuming and disruptive, and should only be a "last resort," as it can increase the final cost of a project tremendously, delay the completion of a project, lead to damage of previously completed work, and prejudice contractors against performing for an owner. Negotiated settlements and, if that fails, arbitration, are the preferred mechanisms for settling disputes, because they save time and money for all parties.

Value Engineering

Value Engineering (VE) is defined as an organized, creative, and systematic effort used to analyze the function of an item in order to determine if another item can perform the same function at a lower possible life-cycle cost without sacrificing quality, safety, reliability, maintainability, interchangeability, and longevity. In short, VE is a study of how construction costs can be reduced by substituting different materials or equipment that will perform the same function at a lower cost, thereby obtaining top value for every dollar spent. This process is a system of analyzing other alternatives for a specific item. The system can be broken down into four major sequential phases – data gathering, speculation, evaluation, and proposal.

Data Gathering

In the data gathering phase, the basic function of the item is defined by asking questions such as:
- What is the item?
- What does it do?
- What does it cost?
- What is it worth?
- What is the cost/worth ratio?

Usually, the lower the cost-to-worth ratio, the better the value of the dollar spent.

Speculation

The VE team is assembled to "brainstorm," or generate alternative items that will perform the same function as the item being analyzed. During this phase, all ideas, no matter how ridiculous they may seem, are written down – all alternatives and ideas generated during the brainstorming session are not judged or evaluated in this phase. The speculation phase ends with the preparation of a list of alternative items and the determination of a price for each one.

Means Forms

DAILY CONSTRUCTION REPORT

PROJECT **R.S. Means Office Building**
ARCHITECT **C. Linde Assoc**   WEATHER **Clear**

JOB NO. **86-1**
DATE **6-10-89**
SUBMITTED BY **R.V.G.**
TEMPERATURE **55°** AM **75°** PM

CODE NO.	WORK CLASSIFICATION	FOREMEN	MECHANICS	LABORERS	SUBCONTR'S	TOTAL HOURS	DESCRIPTION OF WORK
01-10	General Conditions	1					Superintendent
	Site Work: Demolition						
	Excavation & Dewatering						
	Caissons & Piling						
	Drainage & Utilities						
	Roads, Walks & Landscaping						
03-36	Concrete: Formwork		1			8	Form & place base slab @
	Reinforcing		1			8	Northwest Corner
	Placing		2	3		40	
	Precast						
	Masonry: Brickwork & Stonework						
04-10	Block & Tile				6	48	East Wall
	Forklift Operator		1			8	
	Metals: Structural						
	Decks						
	Miscellaneous & Ornamental						
06-50	Carpentry: Rough		2			16	Set H.M. Door Frames for Masons
	Finish						
	Moisture Protection: Waterproofing						
07-10	Insulation			2		16	Finish Rigid Insul @ Fndn Wall
	Roofing & Siding						
	Doors & Windows						
	Glass & Glazing						
	Finishes: Lath, Plaster & Stucco						
	Drywall						
	Tile & Terrazzo						
	Acoustical Ceilings						
	Floor Covering						
	Painting & Wallcovering						
	Specialties						
	Equipment						
	Furnishings						
	Special Construction						
	Conveying Systems						
15-10	Mechanical: Plumbing				2	16	Rough-In Underground
	HVAC						
16-20	Electrical				1	4	Conduit for Masons

Page 1 of 2

Figure 15.12

EQUIPMENT ON PROJECT	NUMBER	DESCRIPTION OF OPERATION	TOTAL HOURS
Texas Screed	310	Screed Conc. Slab	6
Forklift	110	Rented To Masons	8

EQUIPMENT RENTAL - ITEM	TIME IN	TIME OUT	SUPPLIER	REMARKS
2- Power Buggies	8:00	4:00	Equip Co.	

MATERIAL RECEIVED	QUANTITY	DELIVERY SLIP NO.	SUPPLIER	USE
H.M. Door Frames	20	7754	Hard-Ware Co.	
Bar Joists	1 Lot	86-100	Builders Supply	Roof Framing

CHANGE ORDERS, BACKCHARGES AND/OR EXTRA WORK

None

VERBAL DISCUSSIONS AND/OR INSTRUCTIONS

Masons told to watch schedule
Coordinated Electrician & Mason for Conduit Installation

VISITORS TO SITE Architect & Owner - 1 Hr. in P.M.

JOB REQUIREMENTS Tomorrow - Finish Floor Slabs

Page 2 of 2

Figure 15.12 (cont.)

Evaluation

In this phase, the alternatives listed in the speculation phase are evaluated and rated using criteria such as: initial cost, performance, durability, maintenance, life-cycle costs, and aesthetic qualities. From the ratings, the best alternatives are selected for further investigation and comparison.

Proposal

The proposal phase involves the preparation and submittal of a proposal to an owner for review. An example of the VE proposal is shown in Figure 15.13.

Although the format of a VE proposal varies throughout the construction industry, most usually include all or part of the following:

- Project identification (name and number)
- Date of proposal
- Description of item being analyzed
- Summary of the proposed change – usually showing the original item with its cost on one side and the proposed alternative item with its cost on another side
- Estimated cost summary, showing the:
    Cost of the original item
    Cost of the proposed item
    Initial savings
    Life-cycle costs (annual savings)
    Life-cycle costs (gross savings)
    Percent of instant savings
    Percent of life-cycle savings
- Other supporting documents (sketches and manufacturer's literature)

The Why's of Value Engineering

Most people wonder how savings can be achieved with value engineering and why the original designer does not anticipate such savings. The main reasons why savings can be achieved through value engineering are: rapid advances in technology, excessive costs of originally specified items, historical cost data, and design concerns. Often a reason for better alternatives is simply an objective viewpoint, seeing options not obvious to those close to the project.

Advances in Technology

New materials, methods, and equipment are developed and made available continually. It is not always possible for designers to be aware of every new innovation that can cost-effectively replace "boiler-plate" specified items.

Excessive Costs

A designer may specify the "best" item that he/she is aware of. In other words, the item specified may be a "Cadillac," even though a "Chevrolet" may serve the same function. However, an alternative must be analyzed in a careful VE study to determine its merits.

Historical Cost Data

In some cases, the VE team may have access to feedback and actual data collected after the implementation of similar, previous VE proposals. This kind of data may not always be available to designers during the design of a project.

A Sample Value Engineering Proposal Form

Project <u>Bentil Square Condominiums</u> Date <u>31 July 1989</u>

Item <u>Exterior Covering</u>   Project No. <u>KKB/XQT-1990</u>

Summary of Change (Description)

Before $ <u>95,155</u>   After $ <u>58,835</u>

First floor
   8" Brick Veneer

First floor
   7/8" Cement Stucco on metal
   lath, colored and brushed

Second floor
   19/32" textured III Exterior
   Champion Masonite siding

Second floor
   8" wide Vinyl siding
   textured and colored

Estimated Cost Summary (see attached cost estimates)

	SF of Units	Unit Cost/SF	Total $
A. Original	22,252	4.28	95,155
B. Proposed	22,252	2.65	58,835
C. Initial savings			36,320
D. Life-cycle costs annual savings (1 year) ...			2,391
E. Life-cycle costs gross savings (40 years) ...			154,123
F. Total (Annual)			38,711

Percent Savings Instant   38.2%

Percent Savings Life-cycle   30.1%

Figure 15.13

Design Concerns

Recently, some contracts have included VE incentive clauses, whereby the contractor gets a share (usually a percentage) of the savings achieved through any value engineering efforts. In such cases, an owner may prefer that the contractor perform a VE study on items that appear to be design concerns before they go through the change order route. In such situations, the owner saves money by offering incentives to the contractor (sharing in the savings) as opposed to requesting a change order.

The value engineering concept is most effective when applied during the design phase of a project. However, it can be used during the construction phase, with the following benefits.

- The potential to reduce the overall cost of a project
- An owner can share in cost savings
- Design problems that may otherwise take the form of costly claims and change orders by the contractor can be amicably resolved
- The owner obtains the optimum value for every dollar spent

Safety

Accidents on construction sites cost the construction industry an estimated $8 billion every year. In addition to economic aspects, there is also the human factor – when there is an injury or fatality, there is pain and suffering, not only by the injured, but also their families and relatives. Injury can also affect job productivity indirectly by reducing the morale of other workers. Therefore, safety should be one of the most important concerns of all the parties involved in a construction project. When there is an accident, everyone loses. The injured worker suffers; the contractor suffers economic losses and faces increases in the premiums of his Workers' Compensation Insurance; the owner pays more for his project, because the increase in the contractor's Workers' Compensation Insurance premium is passed on to the owner as part of the contractor's general overhead.

A safety program is more than fancy slogans. Emphasis on safety should be directed by top management to the superintendent, who should implement the safety program effectively at all times. The supervisor ensures that safety guidelines are followed by all who visit and work at that site – visitors, the contractor's own personnel, the owner's personnel and representatives, subcontractors, suppliers, and delivery personnel.

Safety standards have been established by the Occupational Safety and Health Administration (OSHA) and guidelines for safety exist in most standard national and local building codes. The acronym OSHA also stands for the Occupational Safety and Health Act which was passed by the Congress of the United States in 1970 and went into effect in April, 1971. The main function of the Occupational and Safety and Health Administration is to set safety and health standards for all workers. In the construction and other industries, the Department of Labor and OSHA compliance officers enforce the OSHA standards in various locations throughout the country. Specific details of OSHA standards as they pertain to the construction industry can be obtained in a manual published by the U.S. Department of Labor entitled *Safety and Health Regulations for Construction*.

Although safety is every worker's responsibility, it is the direct responsibility of the contractor's management personnel and the project superintendent. The following are suggestions that can help avoid accidents on construction sites:

1. Before starting each project, the contractor should prepare a safety plan based on potential hazards that may be encountered at the various phases of the project.
2. The contractor should hold a safety indoctrination meeting prior to the start of each project, and whenever new workers are hired, or new subcontractors come to the site.
3. Project management personnel – project managers and superintendents – should hold regular safety meetings for all personnel at the site.
4. All site personnel should be advised to report all safety hazards promptly.
5. The project superintendent and his foremen must be firm, alert, and forceful in ensuring that all personnel, methods, equipment, and practices comply with safety regulations.
6. Site personnel who violate, ignore, or refuse to follow safety regulations and practices must be dealt with promptly and severely.
7. The contractor should have a safety incentive system or reward for workers who follow safety practices and regulations, and work for long periods without an accident.

Project Completion

The main objective of a contractor, after contract award, is to complete the project according to the plans and specifications, on time, and to make the expected or more profit. Therefore, the completion of a project is very important both to the owner and the contractor.

In the construction industry there are three types of completion.
- Partial Completion
- Substantial Completion
- Final Completion

Partial Completion

Partial completion is where a portion or portions of the work have been completed and can be inspected and evaluated by the owner or his representative. Upon inspection and acceptance, the owner makes a partial payment to the contractor for the work completed. Usually a retainer – 5% to 10% of the partial payment amount – is withheld by the owner until final payment.

Substantial Completion

Substantial completion is the point at which a construction project is habitable, or suitable for occupancy, with only a few work items to be completed. Usually the owner pays the contractor in full, less the amount required to complete the remaining work items. For example, an office building may be said to be substantially complete if every item is completed, inspected, accepted, and a certificate of occupancy has been obtained, except for the grass required as part of the landscaping. In such a case, an owner can begin leasing office space, or permit tenants to take occupancy, and pay the contractor the remainder of the contract amount less the cost of the landscaping work.

Final Payment

When the project is fully completed in accordance with the contract documents, the contractor receives the final payment. At this point, the whole work has been inspected and accepted by the owner or his representative. The contractor must also furnish the owner with a waiver of lien for all labor and material used on the project. A waiver of lien is a legal document with certain legal implications. An attorney should be consulted regarding its use. Figure 15.14 is an example of a waiver of lien form.

It is often said that "the most difficult and critical stages of a construction contract are starting it and finishing it." Others in the construction industry have also made the observation that "most construction projects progress well until they are about 85% to 90% complete, then they seem to take forever to complete." Several reasons have been given for the apparent "slowdown" towards the end of a project, such as: contractor delays, weather delays, owner delays, and lack of incentive on the part of contractor's personnel (who may be worried about their job security – whether or not the contractor will have another job after this one). A project closeout procedure is, therefore, a very important aspect of contract administration, even for an owner. The following is a contract closeout checklist that can serve as a memory jogger for experienced contract administrators of both an owner and a contractor, and a guide for novices, upon the completion of a project, but before final payment is made to the contractor.

1. **Submittals.** Make sure that all outstanding, required submittals have been received, especially items such as reports and certificates.
2. **As-built drawings.** All as-built drawings should be received, checked, and approved by the architect/engineer for completeness. All changes made after contract award and during construction should be clearly marked. Contractors should be encouraged to work on the as-builts as the project progresses, when changes are made and approved, instead of waiting until the end of the project.
3. **Training Session.** If required by the specifications, make sure training sessions are conducted for the owner's maintenance personnel by the contractor and his subcontractors, consultants, etc.
4. **Test Results.** Make sure that the results of all tests performed by the contractor or independent laboratories have been received. These usually include:
   Soil tests
   Concrete tests
   Structural steel tests (such as a welding test)
   Mechanical tests (HVAC balancing results and piping tests)
   Electrical tests
5. **Book of Instructions for submittal material.**
6. **Warranties.** Ensure that the manufacturer's instructions, warranties and guarantees have been received and comply with the requirements of the specifications, paying attention to items such as the required warranty period.
7. **Permanent keys.** All permanent keys, properly identified and labelled, must be received and checked to ensure that they fit their respective locks and operate properly.
8. **Punch list.** Make sure that all items on the punch list have been completed and accepted.
9. **Adequate contractor personnel.** Reach an understanding with the contractor to employ an adequate number of personnel to finish the punch list items and complete the job. If possible, a time-table or schedule should be established for the completion of remaining items.

Means Forms

WAIVER OF LIEN
MATERIAL OR LABOR

STATE OF _MASS_   _1 MAY_   19 _89_

COUNTY OF _PLYMOUTH_

To All Whom It May Concern:

Whereas the undersigned _EXCAVATION, INC._

has been employed by _OFFICE BUILDERS, INC._
                         General Contractor/Owner

to furnish labor and/or materials for _BUILDING EXCAVATION AND BACKFILL_
                                           Nature of the Work

for the Building and Premises known as _R.S. MEANS OFFICE BUILDING_

At _100 CONSTRUCTION PLAZA_   In _KINGSTON, PLYMOUTH_
          Address   City, County, State
MASSACHUSETTS

Lot No. _1_   Section _1_   Township _1_   Range _1_

Now, Therefore, Know Ye, That _EXCAVATION, INC._   the undersigned

for and in consideration of the sum of _SEVENTY-FOUR THOUSAND_   Dollars

and other good and valuable considerations, the receipt whereof is hereby acknowledged, do hereby waive and release any and

all lien, or claim or right to lien on said above described building and premises under the Statutes of the State of _MASSACHUSETTS_

relating to Mechanics' Liens, on account of labor or materials, or both, furnished or which may be furnished, by the undersigned

to or on account of the said firm or individual therein named for said building or premises.

Given under _____ hand _____ and seal this _1ST_ day of _MAY_ A.D. 19 _89_

Witness: _R.S. Means_   _____ (SEAL)

Witness: _____   _____ (SEAL)

                                           By _____

                                           Title _____

Subscribed and sworn to before me this

_1ST_ Day Of _MAY_ 19 _89_

My Commission Expires _6-1-91_

_____
Notary Public

Figure 15.14

332

10. **Certificate of occupancy.** Make sure that all tests and inspections required by local or national authorities have been successfully completed and a certificate of occupancy, where applicable, has been issued by the appropriate authority.
11. **Final release.** Make sure that the contractor has properly executed a final release or waiver of liens prior to releasing the final check.

Chapter Sixteen

Computer Applications

As the construction industry becomes more and more complex, its management requirements begin to change. With this change arises the need for an effective management tool to collect, organize, report, store, and retrieve information in a timely, accurate, and coordinated manner. Computers have satisfied this need since the evolution of construction-oriented software in the late sixties. Today, these high-powered systems and their software have great capabilities. With the advent of microcomputers, this resource has become affordable and usable for individuals at all levels.

Today, computers are being used in the construction industry in a wide array of administrative, technical, financial, and other applications. Some examples include:

- Design and graphics
- Electronic takeoff
- Construction cost estimating
- Data management and word processing
- Accounting and cost control
- Planning and scheduling
- Construction cost control

Computer Graphics and Design

One of the most welcome applications is known commonly as a **Computer-Aided drafting and Design System (CADD)**. With the aid of a computer and the appropriate software, architects and engineers can prepare construction drawings quickly and accurately. Some advantages of using the CADD system in place of the traditional method of designing are:

- **Flexibility**: Several architects/engineers can work together and still produce uniform sets of construction drawings by using the same CADD software.
- **Alternatives**: CADD allows architects/engineers to quickly review several alternate designs.
- **Speed**: CADD systems allow greater speed in producing a design than do traditional drafting methods.

Future CADD Applications

The wave of the future in drafting software is to eliminate the need for printed documents and to produce an estimate directly from the CADD information. Some products are available and more are being developed that will allow the estimator to work directly with drawings stored in the computer. Two approaches are being developed. One is to supply an estimating module that will work within the CADD program to produce the estimate. This method has the potential of providing a quick and accurate cost control system that designers can use without leaving the CADD environment. Such a system could also be used by contractors.

The alternate approach is a program that will interact with the CADD drawing files to prepare estimates. Because the designer would have to leave the CADD environment to use this type of program, this second method is more appropriate for use by contractors.

Both packages would provide some type of cost data file, or the ability to create one, and report capabilities. The hardware requirements will probably include a fast microprocessor, a math coprocessor, extended machine memory, and a high capacity hard drive. The challenging aspect about the development of these programs is how to deal with the interaction between architects and estimators and vice versa. It will be interesting to see how the dynamics of this interaction will affect the development and subsequent success of these programs.

Electronic Takeoff

Within the past decade, tools have become available for automating the takeoff process. In electronic takeoff, information from architectural plans and drawings is "read" by an electronic sensing or "digitizing" device (either a pen-like stylus or a "mouse") and input into a microcomputer which then calculates the length, area, or volume of each individual item based on the location of the input points. Electronic takeoff speeds the takeoff process to a fraction of the time traditionally required for manual takeoff.

Electronic takeoff is faster, more accurate and precise, consistent, and can be used for most types of buildings. In addition, takeoff information can be stored in the computer for future use.

Electronic takeoff can be performed using the following three types of systems:
- Sonic digitizer
- Electromagnetic Digitizing Table
- Mouse

Sonic Digitizer

A sonic digitizer uses sound to measure distance. This device is composed of an aluminum board with two banks of microphones along its side. The quantity estimator lays the drawings on the board and taps a stylus on the endpoints of the item to be measured. The microphones pick up the sound, register their location, and record this information in the computer. The computer in turn, calculates the distance information to compute linear, area, and volume quantities.

The sonic digitizer is portable, and can be carried from site to site. However, this system is useful only for simple takeoffs, such as linear dimensions. It is less accurate for more complex reads or irregular shapes. The sonic digitizer is also sensitive to interferences, which can result in inaccuracies.

Electromagnetic Digitizing Table

Introduced in 1983, the electromagnetic digitizing table is a table with a copper wire grid beneath the surface that is capable of measuring 1,000 points per inch. A stylus is also used in this system to record coordinates in the computer. The computer uses these coordinates to calculate the length, area, or volume of the item in the drawing. Because of its size, this system is not portable. However it is faster and far more reliable than the sonic digitizer.

R.S. Means Company, Inc. produces a software package for quantity takeoff using the electromagnetic digitizing table. This software package, called GALAXY, is essentially an electronic data entry program designed for use with ASTRO, Means' estimating program. Once a designated quantity is taken off and entered, ASTRO supplies the item description and costs from the Means cost data base or from a user-created cost data file. Once the quantity and corresponding cost code are entered, ASTRO calculates the extension. The cost item is then added to a project data file. When the takeoff is complete, the results can be printed in any of over 20 standard report formats. Two reports that are used quite often are the *Job Summary Report* (shown in Figure 16.1) and the *Itemized Job Report* (shown in Figure 16.2).

The *Job Summary Report* provides the cost of the job, including a percentage markup, based on the 16 divisions of the CSI Code. The *Itemized Job Report* is an itemized estimate; every item on the quantity estimate is listed in division order by description, cost, and unit of measurement.

The ASTRO system alone can generate these reports, but without the GALAXY takeoff program, all of the quantities in these reports would have to be calculated manually and keyed into the computer by hand.

Digitizing Using a Mouse

The third and newest method of electronic takeoff utilizes an electronic mouse. The mouse, which is connected to a computer, is moved over various points on the plans. The quantity estimator presses a button on the mouse and the coordinates are registered and used by the computer to calculate dimensions and quantities.

Professionals in both the construction and the computer industries see this device as the wave of the future, since it eliminates the need for additional hardware (a digitizing board), yet offers the estimator a comparable level of accuracy. Furthermore, the mobility of this device enables every computer to become a potential takeoff center.

R.S. Means Company, Inc. currently offers a software package called PULSAR that, at present, is used as a project management tool and performs estimating and scheduling functions. Within a year of this printing, Means will incorporate a takeoff function for use with both the electromagnetic digitizing table and the mouse as part of its PULSAR software package.

Cost Estimating

Estimating is a formidable task that can be extremely time-consuming. Since computers can perform several calculations in fractions of a second, an estimator can reduce the time spent on mathematical calculations on the calculator and also eliminate the potential for gross mathematical errors. It is, therefore, used commonly in estimating to perform tasks such as:

- making spread sheet calculations (such as the addition, subtraction, division, or multiplication) of rows and/or columns of data which have several applications in estimating.

```
===================================================================================================
NO. No. 2010              UNBURDENED JOB REPORT SUMMARY              04-24-1989  13:26:06  PAGE  1
---------------------------------------------------------------------------------------------------

PROJECT    : R.S. Means Expansion Project        LOCATION : Kingston, Ma
ARCH/ENGR  : Best Architect Co., Inc             OWNER    : First National Bank
QUANTITIES BY: R.W.                              ENTERED BY: R.G

===================================================================================================
NO. DIVISION                                        MATERIAL    LABOR    EQUIP      SUB
                                                                                 CONTRACT
---------------------------------------------------------------------------------------------------
 1 GENERAL REQUIREMENTS                                 1802     3954        0        0
---------------------------------------------------------------------------------------------------
 2 SITEWORK                                           346337   114541   115782        0
---------------------------------------------------------------------------------------------------
 3 CONCRETE                                           576751   513045    40213        0
---------------------------------------------------------------------------------------------------
 4 MASONARY                                           249232   129080     1139        0
---------------------------------------------------------------------------------------------------
 5 METALS                                             388477   181850   113800        0
---------------------------------------------------------------------------------------------------
 6 WOOD & PLASTICS                                      2547     5373      309        0
---------------------------------------------------------------------------------------------------
 7 MOISTURE PROTECTION                                237418   116876    23008        0
---------------------------------------------------------------------------------------------------
 8 DOORS, WINDOWS, & GLASS                            151554    28139      191        0
---------------------------------------------------------------------------------------------------
 9 FINISHES                                           288572   213783    10584        0
---------------------------------------------------------------------------------------------------
10 SPECIALTIES                                         62261     6375      881        0
---------------------------------------------------------------------------------------------------
11 EQUIPMENT                                           19632      770        0        0
---------------------------------------------------------------------------------------------------
12 FURNISHINGS                                         66107     7584        0        0
---------------------------------------------------------------------------------------------------
13 SPECIAL CONSTRUCTION                                32641     2476        0        0
---------------------------------------------------------------------------------------------------
14 CONVEYING SYSTEMS                                   23600     6587      767        0
---------------------------------------------------------------------------------------------------
15 MECHANICAL                                        1314654   634948     1275        0
---------------------------------------------------------------------------------------------------
16 ELECTRICAL                                        1398346   525823      708        0
---------------------------------------------------------------------------------------------------
                              JOB TOTAL             5159931  2491204   308657        0
---------------------------------------------------------------------------------------------------
                  SALES TAX            5.00%   257997
                  MATERIAL MARK-UP    10.00%   515993
                  LABOR MARK-UP       43.00%            1071218
                  EQUIPMENT MARK-UP   10.00%                      30866
                  SUBCONTRACTOR MARK-UP 0.00%                                        0
                                             -----------------------------------------------
                                             5933921  3562422   339523              0
                                             -----------------------------------------------
                  TOTAL BEFORE PROFIT                                          9835865
                  PROFIT              5.00%                                     491793
                  BOND                0.00%                                          0
                                                                           ==========
                  JOB TOTAL PROFIT & BOND INCLUDED                        $  10327658
---------------------------------------------------------------------------------------------------
```

Figure 16.1

338

NO. No. 2010 UNBURDENED ITEMIZED JOB REPORT 04-24-1989 13:43:48 PAGE 1

PROJECT : R.S. Means Expansion Project
ARCH/ENGR : Best Architect Co., Inc
QUANTITIES BY: R.W.

LOCATION : Kingston, Ma
OWNER : First National Bank
ENTERED BY: R.G.

8 DOORS, WINDOWS, & GLASS

8.5 METAL WINDOWS

DESCRIPTION / LINE NO. / ASMBLY#	RENUMBER1	TAG / RENUMBER2	PER1	PER2	CREW	QUANTITY	UNIT	D/O	MATERIAL	LABOR	EQUIP	TOTAL	SUB
STL WNDW,STOCK UNT,COMMERICAIL PROJECTED 3'9"X5'5"													
085 104 1500 00 M					SSWK2	5.00	EA.	10.00	625.00	32.00	0.00	657.00	
-	Renov	General	100%	100%					3125.00	160.00	0.00	3285.00	
MTL WNDW,CUSTOM AL SASH, NO GLZ,MAX													
085 202 2100 00 M					SSWK2	2000.00	S.F.	85.00	26.30	3.76	0.00	30.06	
-	Renov	General	100%	100%					52600.00	7529.41	0.00	60129.41	
ALUM.WINDW,AWNING TYPE, 4' X 5'-4" OPENING STD. GLASS													
085 204 3950 00 M					SSWK2	10.00	EA.	9.00	295.00	35.56	0.00	330.56	
-	Renov	General	100%	100%					2950.00	355.56	0.00	3305.56	
							SUB TOTAL :		58675	8045	0	66720	0

8.8 GLAZING

DESCRIPTION / LINE NO. / ASMBLY#	RENUMBER1	TAG / RENUMBER2	PER1	PER2	CREW	QUANTITY	UNIT	D/O	MATERIAL	LABOR	EQUIP	TOTAL	SUB
FLOAT GLASS, 1/4" THICK, CLEAR, PLAIN													
088 118 0600 00 M					GLAZ2	850.00	S.F.	120.00	2.50	2.00	0.00	4.50	
-	Renov	General	100%	100%					2125.00	1700.00	0.00	3825.00	
							SUB TOTAL :		2125	1700	0	3825	0
							DIVISION TOTAL :		60800	9745	0	70545	0

Figure 16.2

- storing a vast amount of historical and/or new project cost data that can be recalled and/or updated instantaneously and used in estimating.
- preparing timely cost estimates in a neat, standardized, and presentable format.
- using a data base for integrating functions in construction management such as accounting, estimating, job cost control, etc.

At the time of this writing, three basic types of estimating software are available. These are general application programs such as spreadsheet and data base packages, estimating programs with pricing and reporting capabilities such as Means ASTRO system, and estimating programs that incorporate digitizer/mouse takeoff capabilities such as Means GALAXY system.

General Applications Programs

The general applications programs that can be used in conceptual and cost estimating include spreadsheets, such as Lotus 1-2-3 (Lotus Development Corporation), and data base programs, such as dBase III + (Ashton-Tate). Each of these programs offers the capability of entering and pricing estimates, but each performs the task in a different way.

Spreadsheets

A spreadsheet is a grid of intersecting columns and rows that resembles an accountant's ledger sheet. Like the ledger sheet, the "cells," or intersections of rows and columns, are used to enter information. Spreadsheet cells may contain numerical data, alphabetical data, symbols, or mathematical formulas. Calculations can be performed using the formulas in one cell and the numbers from other cells.

A spreadsheet provides flexibility by creating templates, the equivalent of a printed form, for the entry, storage, and manipulation of data in any column/row format that the user finds beneficial. The spreadsheet template offers an advantage over a printed form in that the formulas stored in the cells automatically perform their computations when data is entered or changed.

For conceptual cost estimating, spreadsheet templates are created to convert quantities into costs. Takeoff quantities and cost data can be entered into the spreadsheet or imported from an estimating program. Formulas built into the template automatically multiply quantities by prices to obtain costs. Individual costs for each section are totalled, and the section totals added to get a building subtotal. The building subtotal is then adjusted for sales tax, general conditions, overhead and profit, bid conditions, and inflation.

One drawback of using spreadsheets for estimating is that users must enter and maintain their own data. This proves to be time consuming and may be costly if an entry error goes unnoticed. One way to reduce the amount of keypunching done and the possibility of errors is to import data and quantities from an outside program. For example, all of Means' estimating programs provide a conversion utility through ASCII format (American National Standard Code for Information Interchange). Figure 16.3 is a standard report generated from Means PULSAR program. Through the ASCII conversion program, the same information can be transferred to and displayed in a spreadsheet program (Figure 16.4).

Once the information is in the spreadsheet, the user can modify or create templates to display the data in whatever format they choose

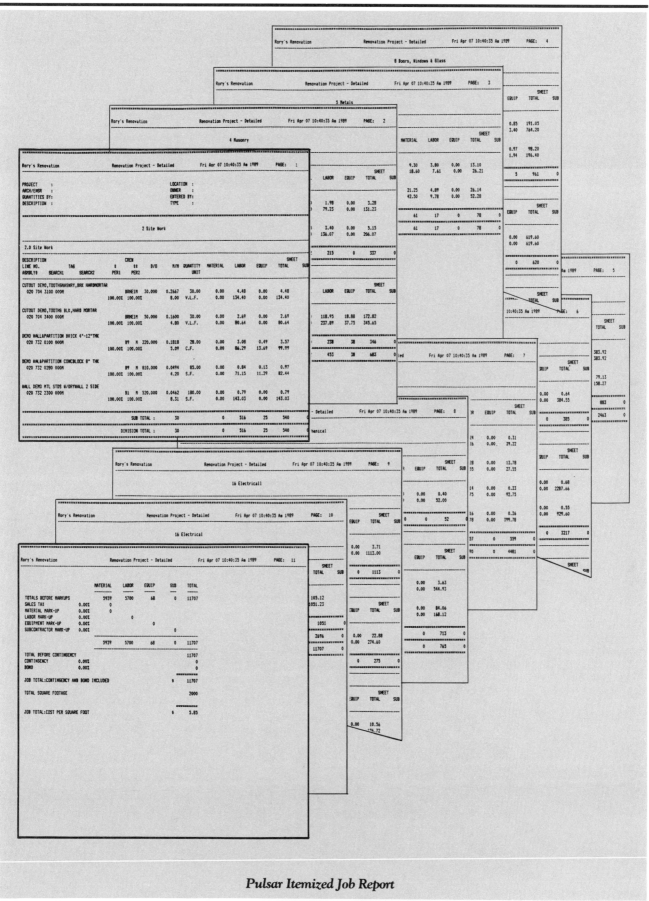

Pulsar Itemized Job Report

Figure 16.3

Line #	Description	Assem Code	Quantity	U/M	Material Cost	Labor Cost	Equip Cost	Total Cost with O&P	Prod in M/Hrs	Duration	I#	J#
020 704 3100	CUTOUT DEMO,TOOTHGMASNRY,BRK HARDMORTAR	00-0000	30	V.L.F.	0	4.48	0	6.98	0.27	1	0	16
020 704 3400	CUTOUT DEMO,TOOTHG BLK,HARD MORTAR	00-0000	30	V.L.F.	0	2.69	0	4.19	0.16	0.6	0	17
020 732 0100	DEMO WAL&PARTITION BRICK 4i-12iTHK	00-0000	28	C.F.	0	3.08	0.49	5.42	0.18	0.13	0	14
020 732 0280	DEMO WAL&PARTITION CONCBLOCK 8i THK	00-0000	85	S.F.	0	0.84	0.13	1.47	0.05	0.1	0	15
020 732 2300	WALL DEMO MTL STDS W/DRYWALL 2 SIDE	00-0000	180	S.F.	0	0.79	0	1.26	0.05	0.35	0	6
042 216 1150	CONCRETE BLOCK, BACK-UP, REINF., ALT/COUR	00-0000	40	S.F.	1.3	1.98	0	4.52	0.1	0.1	0	21
042 554 2000	BRICK VENEER SELECT COMMON, 8iX2-/3iX4i	00-0000	40	S.F.	1.75	3.4	0	7.23	0.17	0.17	0	20
045 240 0800	NEDDLE MASONRY, BRICK, 4i THICK WITH 8i B	00-0000	2	EA.	35	118.95	18.88	247.78	7.02	0.35	0	13
051 232 2100	LINTELS FORM STL 3-1/2i 12GA.4'-6iL	00-0000	2	EA.	9.3	3.8	0	16.16	0.18	0.04	0	18
051 232 2700	LINTELS FORM STL 4-1/2i 96A 9'-0iLG	00-0000	2	EA.	21.25	4.89	0	31	0.23	0.06	0	19
081 103 1160	COMRCL ST DOOR,FLUSH HOLLW CORE 1-3/8i T	06-5540	4	EA.	169	21.2	0.85	220.44	1	0	0	37
081 118 4840	ST.FRAME,KNOCK DWN,16 GA.DRYWALL,UP TO 3-	06-5540	2	EA.	73	24.23	0.97	119.77	1.14	0	0	0
083 604 2600	OVHD COM DRS STEEL SEC MANUAL 8X8	00-0000	1	EA.	450	169.6	0	763.8	8	0.5	0	38
087 116 0010	HINGES, FULL MORTISE, AVG. FREQUENCY, STL	00-0000	3	PR.	19	0	0	20.9	0	0	0	0
087 120 1400	CYL.LCKSET,HEAVY DUTY W/SECTL.TRM,KEY,SNG	00-0000	2	EA.	125	16.96	0	164.38	0.8	0.2	0	0
087 127 0200	PANIC DEVICE,WIDE STILE BAR&VERTICAL ROD,	00-0000	1	EA.	350	33.92	0	438.76	1.6	0.2	0	0
087 304 0100	THRESHOLD,3'LNG DR SADDLS,ALUM,MAX	00-0000	2	EA.	65	14.13	0	93.9	0.67	0.17	0	0
091 304 0300	T BAR SUSPENSION SYSTEM 2'X 2' GRID	06-9086	600	S.F.	0.38	0.26	0	0.83	0.01	0	0	34
092 608 2150	DRYWALL, GYPSUM, 5/8i THICK ON WALLS, FIR	06-1530	3360	S.F.	0.32	0.36	0	0.92	0.02	0	0	0
092 612 2350	METAL STUDS 25 GA. N.L.B., 3-5/8i WIDE 24	06-1530	1680	S.F.	0.2	0.35	0	0.78	0.02	0	0	0
095 104 3720	SUSPEND ACOUSTIC CEILING BRD MINRL FIB2X2	06-9086	600	S.F.	0.25	0.28	0	0.72	0.01	0	0	35
099 106 0800	SIDING ST SIDING OIL BASE PTD 2 COAT BRUS	00-0000	128	S.F.	0.07	0.24	0	0.44	0.01	0.09	0	45
099 216 1000	DOOR&WINOW,FLSH DOOR&FRM PER SIDE,OIL BS	00-0000	2	EA.	1.5	12.28	0	20.74	0.62	0.15	0	44
099 224 0840	WALL&CEILING,CONC DRYWALL OR PLAS.OIL BAS	00-0000	400	S.F.	0.09	0.14	0	0.32	0.01	0.36	0	42
099 224 2800	WALL&CEIL MASONRY/CONC BLK OIL BASE PAINT	00-0000	1540	S.F.	0.1	0.16	0	0.36	0.01	1.54	0	43
155 651 3060	HTGINSL DUK BLKT 1iFBLS 1.5#DENSE	00-0000	130	S.F.	0.4	0	0	5	0	0	0	26
157 250 0300	DUCTWORK, GALVANIZED STEEL, UNDER 400 LB	00-0000	150	LB.	1.35	2.28	0	100.85	0.1	0.64	0	24
157 450 0600	AC&V DIFFUSRS AL PERF 24X24-18X18i	00-0d00	2	EA.	64.9	19.16	0	5.04	0.8	0.2	0	25
160 205 1770	RIGID GALV STEEL, CONDUIT TO 15'H, 3/4i D	00-0000	300	L.F.	1.35	2.36	0	32.15	0.1	3.75	0	8
161 165 0030	WIRE 600 VOLT, TYPE @T8H8W, COPPER, SOLID	00-0000	12	C.L.F.	5.72	17.16	0	15.46	0.73	1.09	0	30
162 110 0150	STEEL OUTLET BOX 4i SQUARE	00-0000	12	EA.	1.12	9.44	0	16.82	0.4	0.6	0	31
162 320 0600	WIRING DEVICE SWITCH 3 WAY 15 AMP	00-0000	2	EA.	4.05	8.21	0	14.5	0.35	0.09	0	0
162 320 2470	WIRING DEVICE RECEPTACLE DUPLEX 120 VOLT	00-0000	10	EA.	3.6	6.99	0		0.3	0.37	0	0
166 130 1400	SUR FLUOR 2X4' W 3 40W LAMP & LENS	00-0000	10	EA.	72	33.12	0	129.11	1.4	1.75	0	32

Lotus 123 Spreadsheet with Imported Pulsar/ASCII File

Figure 16.4

(16.5 and 16.6). The formulas and functions of the spreadsheet can now be used to total and subtotal rows and columns, sort by specific characters, and to apply job-related percentages.

Spreadsheet programs are among the most widely used applications programs in the PC environment. There are several major brands, all similar in function, and relatively low priced. The ease of use, programming flexibility, and calculation ability make spreadsheets a valuable software tool. When applied properly, the benefits that spreadsheets provide can be successfully applied to estimating.

Data Base Programs

Data base programs provide another way in which to enter, store, and manipulate data. Rather than forcing the data into a column and row format, the user is, in this case, free to design the entry and report forms in a way that more closely meets his needs. Many data base programs have the further capability of creating specific applications with an internal programming language. For example, a program can be designed to prompt the user to enter project, estimates, and percentage information; and to enter cost code, item description, and quantity data for each estimate entry. The program can then automatically insert the costs; calculate extensions, totals, and adjustments; and print an estimate report.

Data base programs are readily available and priced similar to spreadsheet programs (leaning to the high side). Although not considered as "user friendly" as spreadsheet programs, data base programs are more powerful when applied properly. Storage, retrieval, and manipulation of data is handled more efficiently by data base programs. Again, the data must be entered by the user unless it is imported from an estimating program, such as the ASCII conversion provided by Means estimating software systems. When the extra time is taken to learn how to use the data base programs, the results can be quite rewarding.

Pricing and Report Programs

Current pricing and report programs are easy to use, powerful, and most can be used on microcomputers. Means ASTRO System is an example of a currently available pricing/report estimating software package. It has the ability to extend and summarize quantity takeoff, and can also do pricing, make adjustments, and provide a wide variety of reports.

Using the ASTRO System, takeoff items in the form of a cost code and quantity are entered into the computer through the keyboard. ASTRO supplies the item description and costs from the Means *Building Construction Cost Data*, *Mechanical*, or *Electrical* cost data files, (or any Means unit price files), or from a user-created cost data file. Each of the cost items includes a description, unit of measure, crew, productivity, bare material unit price, bare installation (labor and equipment) unit price, total bare unit price, and a total price including the contractor's overhead and profit. Adjustment percentages may be added to each takeoff entry, and each entry can be changed to more accurately reflect project conditions. Cost items may be combined to create assemblies costs.

Once the cost code and quantity are entered, ASTRO calculates the extension. The cost item is then added to a project data file. When the takeoff is complete, the results may be reported in a variety of ways. Among the reports offered are burdened (bare costs) and unburdened (with overhead and profit) *Itemized Job Reports*. This report lists all cost lines by CSI MASTERFORMAT division and subdivision. Burdened and

Line #	Descripti	Assem Code	Quantity	U/M	Material Cost	Labor Cost	Equip Cost	Total Cost with O&P	Prod in M/Hrs	Duration
020 704 3100	CUTOUT DE	00-0000	30	V.L.F.	0	4.48	0	6.98	0.27	1
020 704 3400	CUTOUT DE	00-0000	30	V.L.F.	0	2.69	0	4.19	0.16	0.6
020 732 0100	DEMO WALL	00-0000	28	C.F.	0	3.08	0.49	5.42	0.18	0.13
020 732 0280	DEMO WALL	00-0000	85	S.F.	0	0.84	0.13	1.47	0.05	0.1
020 732 2300	WALL DEMO	00-0000	180	S.F.	0	0.79	0	1.26	0.05	0.35
042 216 1150	CONCRETE	00-0000	40	S.F.	1.3	1.98	0	4.52	0.1	0.1
042 554 2000	BRICK VEN	00-0000	40	S.F.	1.75	3.4	0	7.23	0.17	0.17
045 240 0800	NEDDLE MA	00-0000	2	EA.	35	118.95	18.88	247.78	7.02	0.35
051 232 2100	LINTELS F	00-0000	2	EA.	9.3	3.8	0	16.16	0.18	0.04
051 232 2700	LINTELS F	00-0000	2	EA.	21.25	4.89	0	31	0.23	0.06
081 103 1160	COMRCL ST	06-5540	4	EA.	169	21.2	0.85	220.44	1	0
081 118 4840	ST.FRAME,	06-5540	2	EA.	73	24.23	0.97	114.77	1.14	0
083 604 2600	OVHD COM	00-0000	1	EA.	450	169.6	0	763.8	8	0.5
087 116 0010	HINGES, F	00-0000	3	PR.	19	0	0	20.9	0	0
087 120 1400	CYL.LCKSE	00-0000	2	EA.	125	16.96	0	164.38	0.8	0.2
087 127 0200	PANIC DEV	00-0000	1	EA.	350	33.92	0	438.76	1.6	0.2
087 304 0100	THRESHOLD	00-0000	2	EA.	65	14.13	0	93.9	0.67	0.17
091 304 0300	T BAR SUS	06-9086	600	S.F.	0.38	0.26	0	0.83	0.01	0
092 608 2150	DRYWALL,	06-1530	3360	S.F.	0.32	0.36	0	0.92	0.02	0
092 612 2350	METAL STU	06-1530	1680	S.F.	0.2	0.35	0	0.78	0.02	0
095 104 3720	SUSPEND A	06-9086	600	S.F.	0.25	0.28	0	0.72	0.01	0
099 106 0800	SIDING ST	00-0000	128	S.F.	0.07	0.24	0	0.44	0.01	0.09
099 216 1000	DOOR&WIND	00-0000	2	EA.	1.5	12.28	0	20.74	0.62	0.15
099 224 0840	WALL&CEIL	00-0000	400	S.F.	0.09	0.14	0	0.32	0.01	0.36
099 224 2800	WALL&CEIL	00-0000	1540	S.F.	0.1	0.16	0	0.36	0.01	1.54
155 651 3060	HTGINSL D	00-0000	130	S.F.	0.4	0	0	0	0	0
157 250 0500	DUCTWORK,	00-0000	150	LB.	1.35	2.28	0	5	0.1	0.64
157 450 0600	AC&V DIFF	00-0000	2	EA.	64.9	19.16	0	100.85	0.8	0.2
160 205 1770	RIGID GAL	00-0000	300	L.F.	1.35	2.36	0	5.04	0.1	3.75
161 165 0030	WIRE 600	00-0000	12	C.L.F.	5.72	17.16	0	32.15	0.73	1.09
162 110 0150	STEEL OUT	00-0000	12	EA.	1.12	9.44	0	15.46	0.4	0.6
162 320 0600	WIRING DE	00-0000	2	EA.	4.05	8.21	0	16.82	0.35	0.09
162 320 2470	WIRING DE	00-0000	10	EA.	3.6	6.99	0	14.5	0.3	0.37
166 130 1400	SUR FLUOR	00-0000	10	EA.	72	33.12	0	129.11	1.4	1.75

Lotus/Quattro Report

Figure 16.5

Line #		Descripti	Quantity	Units	Material	Labor	Equipment	Total Cost	Productiv	Duration
020 704 3100	CUTOUT DE	30	V.L.F.	0	4.48	0	6.98	0.27	1
020 704 3400	CUTOUT DE	30	V.L.F.	0	2.69	0	4.19	0.16	0.6
020 732 0100	DEMO WALL	28	C.F.	0	3.08	0.49	5.42	0.18	0.13
020 732 0280	DEMO WAL&	85	S.F.	0	0.84	0.13	1.47	0.05	0.1
020 732 2300	WALL DEMO	180	S.F.	0	0.79	0	1.26	0.05	0.35
042 216 1150	CONCRETE	40	S.F.	1.3	1.98	0	4.52	0.1	0.1
042 554 2000	BRICK VEN	40	S.F.	1.75	3.4	0	7.23	0.17	0.17
045 240 0800	NEDDLE MA	2	EA.	35	118.95	18.88	247.78	7.02	0.35
051 232 2100	LINTELS F	2	EA.	9.3	3.8	0	16.16	0.18	0.04
051 232 2700	LINTELS F	2	EA.	21.25	4.89	0	31	0.23	0.06
081 103 1160	COMRCL ST	4	EA.	169	21.2	0.85	220.44	1	0
081 118 4840	ST.FRAME,	2	EA.	73	24.23	0.97	119.77	1.14	0
083 604 2600	OVHD COM	1	EA.	450	169.6	0	763.8	8	0.5
087 116 0010	HINGES, F	3	PR.	19	0	0	20.9	0	0
087 120 1400	CYL.LCKSE	2	EA.	125	16.96	0	164.38	0.8	0.2
087 127 0200	PANIC DEV	1	EA.	350	33.92	0	438.76	1.6	0.2
087 304 0100	THRESHOLD	2	EA.	65	14.13	0	93.9	0.67	0.17
091 304 0300	T BAR SUS	600	S.F.	0.38	0.26	0	0.83	0.01	0
092 608 2150	DRYWALL,	3360	S.F.	0.32	0.36	0	0.92	0.02	0
092 612 2350	METAL STU	1680	S.F.	0.2	0.35	0	0.78	0.02	0
095 104 3720	SUSPEND A	600	S.F.	0.25	0.28	0	0.72	0.01	0
099 106 0800	SIDING ST	128	S.F.	0.07	0.24	0	0.44	0.01	0.09
099 216 1000	DOOR&WIND	2	EA.	1.5	12.28	0	20.74	0.62	0.15
099 224 0840	WALL&CEIL	400	S.F.	0.09	0.14	0	0.32	0.01	0.36
099 224 2800	WALL&CEIL	1540	S.F.	0.1	0.16	0	0.36	0.01	1.54
155 651 3060	HTGINSL D	130	S.F.	0.4	0	0	0	0	0
157 250 0500	DUCTWORK,	150	LB.	1.35	2.28	0	5	0.1	0.64
157 450 0600	AC&V DIFF	2	EA.	64.9	19.16	0	100.85	0.8	0.2
160 205 1770	RIGID GAL	300	L.F.	1.35	2.36	0	5.04	0.1	3.75
161 165 0030	WIRE 600	12	C.L.F.	5.72	17.16	0	32.15	0.73	1.09
162 110 0150	STEEL OUT	12	EA.	1.12	9.44	0	15.46	0.4	0.6
162 320 0600	WIRING DE	2	EA.	4.05	8.21	0	16.82	0.35	0.09
162 320 2470	WIRING DE	10	EA.	3.6	6.99	0	14.5	0.3	0.37
166 130 1400	SUR FLUOR	10	EA.	72	33.12	0	129.11	1.4	1.75

Modified Lotus/Quattro Spreadsheet

Figure 16.6

unburdened *Division Summary Reports* (providing subdivision and division totals), and *Job Report Summaries* (listing only the division totals) can also be produced. Other possible reports include summaries of the crews used, cost items modified, and adjustment percentages used.

ASTRO has an update feature that allows an old estimate to be adjusted to reflect new prices. This update can be performed for material costs only, installation costs only, or both. An additional feature of ASTRO is the previously mentioned ability to "download" project costs and quantities into spreadsheet and data base programs.

Pricing/report software is more expensive than most spreadsheet programs, partly due to its requirement for a hard drive (10 megabyte). Nevertheless, the software is quick and accurate and the available cost files reduce data entry to a minimum, reducing the opportunity for error. Furthermore, the extensive customizing options allow the package to be tailored to reflect the conditions of the local market.

Electronic Data Entry Programs

The data entry programs have the potential to significantly boost estimating productivity by increasing the speed of the quantity takeoff. The takeoff devices include any of a variety of "mice" or digitizer stylus, and digitizer tables. A stylus or "mouse" can be used to enter dimensions into the computer as it is moved over the plans in the manner of a plan measure. A digitizer table is a plan table with an electronic grid. Plan sheets are placed on the table and the stylus enters dimensions by pinpointing locations on the table grid. These dimensions provide accurate readings of the lengths, perimeters, areas, volumes, and numbers needed in the quantity takeoff. One such program is the Means GALAXY System.

The Means GALAXY System uses a digitizer table to enter the data into the computer. Just as with ASTRO, a cost code number is supplied by the estimator for the takeoff item. GALAXY can also access the Means *Building Construction*, *Mechanical*, and *Electrical* cost data files and any other Means or user-created files, to supply item descriptions and costs. GALAXY provides the same customizing and support features as ASTRO. In addition, GALAXY provides an *Estimate Checklist*, a *Trade Report* listing all trades and total hours required for a project, and a *Labor Cost Report* listing the bare and burdened hourly labor and equipment rates. A scheduling module is also available for use with GALAXY or ASTRO.

The data entry programs are more expensive than either the spreadsheet programs or the pricing/report programs. Since a mouse or digitizer table must be included in the computer system, the hardware cost is also significantly higher. The major advantage of the data entry program is the increase in productivity and accuracy afforded by entering data directly from the plans into the computer.

Data Management

In order to effectively manage construction contracts, one must be able to rapidly collect, store, access, and retrieve numerous types of data. Since the computer has an almost infinite memory for storing data and has the capability to access this data instantaneously, it can be used to manage data such as:

- historical labor productivity data for various types of construction work under varying conditions.

- historical data on a firm's general or job overhead for various types and sizes of construction projects.
- historical data of prices submitted by a firm's competitors during bid openings to be used in bidding strategy.

Computers are also used for word processing, data management, correspondence, equipment management, and other functions to manage the administrative workload more efficiently. Systems for data management include dBase by Ashton-Tate. (For more comprehensive treatment of data management on the computer, refer to *Construction Paperwork: An Efficient Management System*, Edward J. Grimes, R.S. Means Company, Inc., 1989.)

Accounting and Cost Control

Construction firms have been known to have weak accounting practices. Some of the blame has been traditionally placed on the uniqueness of the industry and its dependence on numerous crafts, subcontractors, material suppliers, and time pressures.

Today, computers have helped resolve this problem and are used to perform several accounting functions, including:

- Payroll
- Accounts payable
- Accounts receivable
- General ledger
- Financial statements
- Preparation of tax returns

Two of the most critical tasks that influence the success of a construction project are the preparation of an **accurate cost estimate** at the onset and the implementation of a **good cost control system** during construction. The cost estimate usually serves as the basis for cost control.

Cost Control

In the past, cost control has proven to be very time-consuming and costly when done manually. With a computer, it can be implemented very quickly and economically. Job cost control can be managed by utilizing a specific job cost control program or a spreadsheet set-up to display job cost information. In both cases, an estimating program should be applied first to provide the quantities and costs as the basis of comparison for subsequent actual costs.

The computer can be used extensively in cost control for functions such as:

- tracking labor, material, equipment, subcontractor, and other costs.
- tracking both current unit costs and cost to date as well as current total cost and total cost to date.
- comparing estimated costs versus actual cost.
- comparing estimated quantities versus actual quantities.
- comparing estimated man-hours versus actual man-hours expended by trade, work item, etc.
- producing historical cost data that can be conveniently stored and easily accessed for use in pricing estimates.

Although cost control should be carried over to the design function, designers are not estimators and vice versa. Currently, there are no computer programs to combine the design and estimating function.

Planning and Scheduling

Traditionally, some construction firms have not utilized a manually prepared project schedule effectively mainly because of their lack of understanding of the use and benefit of the schedule; the belief that the time and cost expended in the preparation of a schedule far outweigh the benefits to be derived from its use; and the belief that the unique nature and uncertain characteristics of a construction project make a schedule obsolete before it is even implemented.

Computers have provided solutions to some of these concerns because:

- schedules can be prepared quickly and accurately with relative ease.
- contractors can review several options and find solutions to potential problems before they occur.
- contractors can use scheduling techniques to prepare for and/or circumvent uncertain events before they occur.
- periodic updating of schedules is less cumbersome and faster.

R.S. Means Company, Inc., has recently developed a product with the Computerline Corporation, that combines the Means estimating function with the PLANTRAC scheduling function, known as PULSAR. This system is a PC based program that eliminates keyboard input errors by utilizing information input at the estimating level (done before the scheduling function) to develop a project schedule.

By giving the user the ability to input activity sequences while doing the estimate, the accuracy of schedules is enhanced and the possibility of failing to schedule activities is reduced. The estimating module of PULSAR provides PLANTRAC with an activities cost, duration, description, sequence number (either I-J or precedence) and associated CSI line or assembly numbers, depending on how the activity was quantified and entered into the estimate. Once the preliminary schedule is loaded into PLANTRAC, activities and sequences can be updated or modified and a variety of bar charts and reports generated. Sample schedules produced by PULSAR are shown in Figure 16.7.

(For more detailed information on scheduling techniques, refer to *Project Planning and Control for Construction*, by David R. Pierce Jr., and *Means Scheduling Manual*, by F. William Horsley, R.S. Means Company, Inc.)

Summary

The computer will never replace a competent designer, estimator, or quantity surveyor. However, with the continual development of increasingly sophisticated and yet user-friendly software specifically designed for the construction industry, it may be safely predicted that the future will bring new and varied uses of the computer that will help reduce costs, improve communications, and speed up the designing, estimating, scheduling, and data management functions.

PLANTRAC
========
PLANTRAC (c) TIME NOW = 1 NOV 85 NETWORK = DEMO SELECTION 2 SEQUENCE 4 VERSION 5 PAGE NO. 2
C.M. PROCESS DIAGRAM   04/27/89   08:46:54

```
T    ACT. DURA-    1    8    15   22   29    6   13   20   27    3   10   17   24   31
Y    NUMBER TION  NOV85 NOV85 NOV85 NOV85 NOV85 DEC85 DEC85 DEC85 DEC85 JAN86 JAN86 JAN86 JAN86 JAN86
                  !....!....!....!....!....!....!....!....!....!....!....!....!....!....!
                  *    !    !    !    !    !    !    !    !    !    !    !    !    !    !
    1012  1.0     !    !    !    !    !    !    !    !    !    !    !    !    !    !    !
ASSIST APPROVAL PROCESS   !...!...C..!    !    !    !    !    !    !    !    !    !    !
ZONING-REVIEW BOARDS-ETC  !
                  *    !    !    !    !    !    !    !    !    !    !    !    !    !    !
```

PLANTRAC
========
PLANTRAC (c) TIME NOW = 1 NOV 85 NETWORK = DEMO SELECTION 2 SEQUENCE 4 VERSION 5 PAGE NO. 1
C.M. PROCESS DIAGRAM   04/27/89   08:46:01

```
T    ACT. DURA-    1    8    15   22   29    6   13   20   27    3   10   17   24   31
Y    NUMBER TION  NOV85 NOV85 NOV85 NOV85 NOV85 DEC85 DEC85 DEC85 DEC85 JAN86 JAN86 JAN86 JAN86 JAN86
                  !....!....!....!....!....!....!....!....!....!....!....!....!....!....!
-----------------------------------------------------------------------------------
                  *    !    !    !    !    !    !    !    !    !    !    !    !    !    !
S   1000  1.0     !    !    !    !    !    !    !    !    !    !    !    !    !    !    !
OWNER SELECTS RUHLIN CO.  C.....!....!....!....!    !    !    !    !    !    !    !    !
AS CONSTRUCTION MANAGER   !
                  *    !    !    !    !    !    !    !    !    !    !    !    !    !    !
    1001  0.0     !
PREPARE PROJECT SCHEDULE  Bnn++++nn+++++nn++++nn+++++nn+++++nn+...!    !    !    !    !
WORKNG BACK FROM END DATE  !
                  *    !    !    !    !    !    !    !    !    !    !    !    !    !    !
    1002  1.0     !
PREPARE AN AREA + VOLUME  !..B++++nn++++nn+++++nn++++nn++++!    !    !    !    !    !
BUDGET            !
                  *    !    !    !    !    !    !    !    !    !    !    !    !    !    !
    1003  1.0     !
ASSIST IN SELECTION OF AN  !..C...!....!....!....!    !    !    !    !    !    !    !    !
ARCHITECT AND ENGINEER    !
                  *    !    !    !    !    !    !    !    !    !    !    !    !    !    !
    1004  1.0     !
ASSIST IN ARCHITECTURAL   !....C...!....!    !    !    !    !    !    !    !    !    !
PROGRAMING OPTIONAL       !
                  *    !    !    !    !    !    !    !    !    !    !    !    !    !    !
    1005  1.0     !
DEVELOP PROJECT PLAN WITH  !.....B+!....!    !    !    !    !    !    !    !    !    !
OWNER DEFINING EACH ROLE  !
                  *    !    !    !    !    !    !    !    !    !    !    !    !    !    !
    1006  1.0     !
ASSIST IN SITE SELECTION  !.....C.!....!    !    !    !    !    !    !    !    !    !
                  *    !    !    !    !    !    !    !    !    !    !    !    !    !    !
    1007  1.0     !
ASSIST WITH AGENCY        !.....C!....!    !    !    !    !    !    !    !    !    !
APPLICATIONS      !
                  *    !    !    !    !    !    !    !    !    !    !    !    !    !    !
    1008  1.0     !
COORDINATE FIELD SERVICES  !.....C...!    !    !    !    !    !    !    !    !    !
SURVEYS-MAPS-STUDIES      !
                  *    !    !    !    !    !    !    !    !    !    !    !    !    !    !
    1009  1.0     !
SCHEMATIC DESIGN REVIEW   !.....!..C..!    !    !    !    !    !    !    !    !    !
WITH SCHEDULE + PROGRAMS  !
                  *    !    !    !    !    !    !    !    !    !    !    !    !    !    !
    1011  1.0     !
UPGRADE PROJECT BUDGET    !......!...B+++nn+++++nn++++nn+++++....!    !    !    !    !
                  *    !    !    !    !    !    !    !    !    !    !    !    !    !    !
-----------------------------------------------------------------------------------
```

CRITICAL = C; NON-CRITICAL = B; IN PROGRESS = A; POS. FLOAT = +; NEG. FLOAT = -
NON WORKING DAYS = n; HOLIDAYS = H; TIME NOW = *

FLOAT = +; NEG. FLOAT = -

Plantrac (Easy Plan) Bar Chart

Figure 16.7

PLANTRAC
========

PLANTRAC (c) TIME NOW = 1 NOV 85 NETWORK = DEMO SELECTION 2 SEQUENCE 4 VERSION 5 PAGE NO. 3
C.M. PROCESS DIAGRAM   04/27/89   08:31:26

T Y	ACT. NO.	DESCRIPTION	DURA-TION (D)	RESP CODE	COST CODE	EARLIEST START	EARLIEST FINISH	LATEST START	LATEST FINISH	TOTAL FLOAT (D)	D I	RC T	RESOURCES QTY.	FROM	FOR
	1059	COMPLETE PROJECT CLOSEOUT	1.0	-	-	12/11/85	12/11/85	12/11/85	12/11/85	0.0					
E	1060	PROVIDE CONTINUING OWNER	1.0	-	-	12/12/85	12/12/85	12/12/85	12/12/85	0.0					

PLANTRAC
========

PLANTRAC (c) TIME NOW = 1 NOV 85 NETWORK = DEMO SELECTION 2 SEQUENCE 4 VERSION 5 PAGE NO. 2
C.M. PROCESS DIAGRAM   04/27/89   08:30:31

T Y	ACT. NO.	DESCRIPTION	DURA-TION (D)	RESP CODE	COST CODE	EARLIEST START	EARLIEST FINISH	LATEST START	LATEST FINISH	TOTAL FLOAT (D)	D I	RC T	RESOURCES QTY.	FROM	FOR

PLANTRAC
========

PLANTRAC (c) TIME NOW = 1 NOV 85 NETWORK = DEMO SELECTION 2 SEQUENCE 4 VERSION 5 PAGE NO. 1
C.M. PROCESS DIAGRAM   04/27/89   08:29:53

T Y	ACT. NO.	DESCRIPTION	DURA-TION (D)	RESP CODE	COST CODE	EARLIEST START	EARLIEST FINISH	LATEST START	LATEST FINISH	TOTAL FLOAT (D)	D I	RC T	RESOURCES QTY.	FROM	FOR
S	1000	OWNER SELECTS RUHLIN CO. AS CONSTRUCTION MANAGER	1.0	-	-	11/ 1/85	11/ 1/85	11/ 1/85	11/ 1/85	0.0					
	1001	PREPARE PROJECT SCHEDULE WORKNG BACK FROM END DATE	0.0	-	-	11/ 1/85	11/ 1/85	12/ 9/85	12/ 9/85	26.0					
	1002	PREPARE AN AREA + VOLUME BUDGET	1.0	-	-	11/ 4/85	11/ 4/85	12/ 5/85	12/ 5/85	23.0					
	1003	ASSIST IN SELECTION OF AN ARCHITECT AND ENGINEER	1.0	-	-	11/ 4/85	11/ 4/85	11/ 4/85	11/ 4/85	0.0					
	1004	ASSIST IN ARCHITECTURAL PROGRAMING OPTIONAL	1.0	-	-	11/ 5/85	11/ 5/85	11/ 5/85	11/ 5/85	0.0					
	1005	DEVELOP PROJECT PLAN WITH OWNER DEFINING EACH ROLE	1.0	-	-	11/ 6/85	11/ 6/85	11/ 7/85	11/ 7/85	1.0					
	1006	ASSIST IN SITE SELECTION	1.0	-	-	11/ 6/85	11/ 6/85	11/ 6/85	11/ 6/85	0.0					
	1007	ASSIST WITH AGENCY APPLICATIONS	1.0	-	-	11/ 7/85	11/ 7/85	11/ 7/85	11/ 7/85	0.0					
	1008	COORDINATE FIELD SERVICES SURVEYS-MAPS-STUDIES	1.0	-	-	11/ 8/85	11/ 8/85	11/ 8/85	11/ 8/85	0.0					
	1009	SCHEMATIC DESIGN REVIEW WITH SCHEDULE + PROGRAMS	1.0	-	-	11/11/85	11/11/85	11/11/85	11/11/85	0.0					
	1011	UPGRADE PROJECT BUDGET	1.0	-	-	11/12/85	11/12/85	12/ 6/85	12/ 6/85	18.0					
	1012	ASSIST APPROVAL PROCESS ZONING-REVIEW BOARDS-ETC	1.0	-	-	11/12/85	11/12/85	11/12/85	11/12/85	0.0					
	1010	DESIGN DEVELOPMENT AND PREP.MODELS + RENDERINGS	1.0	-	-	11/13/85	11/13/85	11/13/85	11/13/85	0.0					
	1013	UPGRADE PROJECT BUDGET	1.0	-	-	11/14/85	11/14/85	12/ 9/85	12/ 9/85	17.0					
	1014	ESTABLISH EQUIPMENT LISTS W/LEAD TIMES-AND COSTS	1.0	-	-	11/14/85	11/14/85	11/15/85	11/15/85	1.0					
	1016	PREPARE ANY PRESS RELEASE WITH OWNER APPROVAL	1.0	-	-	11/14/85	11/14/85	11/18/85	11/18/85	2.0					
	1017	ESTABLISH BIDDER LISTS AND PRE-QUALIFY BIDDERS	1.0	-	-	11/14/85	11/14/85	11/14/85	11/14/85	0.0					
	1015	OBTAIN APPROVAL OF EQUIP. AND PRE-PURCHASE	1.0	-	-	11/15/85	11/15/85	11/18/85	11/18/85	1.0					
	1018	ESTABLISH BIDDING REQUIRMENTS WITH OWNER	1.0	-	-	11/15/85	11/15/85	11/15/85	11/15/85	0.0					
	1019	ESTABLISH BID PACKAGES	1.0	-	-	11/18/85	11/18/85	11/18/85	11/18/85	0.0					
	1020	REVIEW WORKING DRAWINGS SCHEDULES-BUDGET-ETC.	1.0	-	-	11/19/85	11/19/85	11/19/85	11/19/85	0.0					
	1022	UPDATE SCHEDULE	1.0	-	-	11/20/85	11/20/85	12/10/85	12/10/85	14.0					
	1024	MOVE IN FIELD OFFICES AND EQUIPMENT	1.0	-	-	11/20/85	11/20/85	12/ 9/85	12/ 9/85	13.0					
	1023	ASSIST IN REGULATORY AGENCY APPROVALS	1.0	-	-	11/20/85	11/20/85	11/20/85	11/20/85	0.0					
	1025	HOLD PRE-BID CONFERENCES	1.0	-	-	11/20/85	11/20/85	11/20/85	11/20/85	0.0					
	1036	MONITOR CRITICAL PATH SCHEDULE	1.0	-	-	11/21/85	11/21/85	12/11/85	12/11/85	14.0					
	1021	UPDATE BUDGET	1.0	-	-	11/21/85	11/21/85	12/10/85	12/10/85	13.0					
	1027	ARRANGE GROUNDBREAKING CEREMONIES	1.0	-	-	11/21/85	11/21/85	11/21/85	11/21/85	0.0					

Plantrac Tabular Schedule Report

Figure 16.7 (cont.)

Abbreviations

A/C = Air Conditioning
A/E = Architect/Engineer
Al = Aluminum
Arch. = Architect

Bf = Board Foot
Bldg. = Building
Blk. = Block
B.M. = Bench Mark
Bm. = Beam

Carp. = Carpenter
Cf = Cubic Foot
CIP = Cast-in-place
Clg. = Ceiling
Cm = Cubic Meter
CM = Construction
    Management
Col. = Column
Conc. = Concrete
Const. = Construction
Cont. = Continuous
C.T. = Ceramic Tile
CWT. = Hundred-Weight
Cy = Cubic Yard

Demo. = Demolition
Dim. = Dimension
Dr. = Door
Dwg. = Drawing

Ea. = Each
Elev. = Elevation
Exc. = Excluded
Excav. = Excavation
Exp. Jt. = Expansion Joint
Exstg. = Existing
Ext. = Exterior

Fdn. = Foundation
Flr. = Floor
Ft. = Foot

Gal. = Gallon

Ht. (Hgt.) = Height
HVAC = Heating, Ventilating
    and Air Conditioning

ID = Inside Diameter
In. = Inch
Ins. = Insulation
Int. = Interior

Lab. = Labor
Lb. = Pound (weight)
Ls = Lump Sum

M = Thousand
Max. = Maximum
Mbf = Thousand Board Feet
Mech. = Mechanical
Min. = Minimum

N.I.C. = Not in Contract
NTS = Not to Scale
No. = Number

OC = On Center

Plumbg. = Plumbing
Psf = Pounds Per Square Foot
Ptn. = Partition

Q.T. = Quarry Tile

Rad. = Radius
Reinf. = Reinforcing
Rev. = Revision (Revised)

Sf = Square Foot
Sht. = Sheet
Specs. = Specifications
Struct. = Structural
Std. = Standard
Stl. = Steel
Sq. = Square

Temp. = Temperature
Typ. = Typical

U.O.N. = Unless Otherwise
    Noted

V.A.T. = Vinyl Asbestos Tile
V.C.T. = Vinyl Composition
    Tile

Wt. = Weight

Mathematical Tables and Conversion Factors

Decimal Equivalents of Inches in Feet

Inches	Feet
1	0.08
2	0.17
3	0.25
4	0.33
5	0.42
6	0.50
7	0.58
8	0.67
9	0.75
10	0.83
11	0.92
12	1.0

Note: To convert inches to decimal equivalent, divide the inches by 12.

Table of Square and Cubic Measure

I. Square Measure

144 square inches	=	1 square foot
9 square feet	=	1 square yard
30 1/4 square yards	=	1 square rod
160 square rods	=	1 acre
43,560 square feet	=	1 acre
4,840 square yards	=	1 acre
640 acres	=	1 square mile

II. Cubic Measure

1,728 cubic inches	=	1 cubic foot
27 cubic feet	=	1 cubic yard
128 cubic feet	=	1 cord

Major Sub-Divisions of CSI Format

Division 1—General Requirements

01010 SUMMARY OF WORK
01100 ALTERNATIVES
01200 PROJECT MEETINGS
01300 SUBMITTALS
01400 QUALITY CONTROL
01500 TEMPORARY FACILITIES
01600 MATERIAL AND EQUIPMENT
01700 PROJECT CLOSEOUT

Division 2—Site Work

02010 SUBSURFACE EXPLORATION
02100 CLEARING
02110 DEMOLITION
02200 EARTHWORK
02250 SOIL TREATMENT
02300 PILE FOUNDATIONS
02350 CAISSONS
02400 SHORING
02500 SITE DRAINAGE
02550 SITE UTILITIES
02600 PAVING AND SURFACING
02700 SITE IMPROVEMENTS
02800 LANDSCAPING
02850 RAILROAD WORK
02900 MARINE WORK
02950 TUNNELING

Division 3—Concrete

03100 FORMWORK
03150 EXPANSION AND CONTRACTION JOINTS
03200 REINFORCEMENT
03300 CAST-IN-PLACE CONCRETE
03350 SPECIALLY FINISHED CONCRETE
03360 SPECIALLY PLACED CONCRETE
03400 PRECAST CONCRETE
03500 CEMENTITIOUS DECKS

Division 4—Masonry

04100 MORTAR
04150 ACCESSORIES
04200 UNIT MASONRY
04400 STONE
04500 RESTORATION AND CLEANING
04550 REFRACTORIES

Division 5–Metals

05100 STRUCTURAL METAL
05200 STEEL JOISTS
05300 METAL DECKING
05400 LIGHTGAGE FRAMING
05500 METAL FABRICATIONS
05700 ORNAMENTAL METALS

Division 6–Wood & Plastics

06100 ROUGH CARPENTRY
06150 TRESTLES
06170 PREFABRICATED STRUCTURAL WOOD
06200 FINISH CARPENTRY
06300 WOOD TREATMENT
06400 ARCHITECTURAL WOODWORK
06500 PREFABRICATED STRUCTURAL PLASTICS
06600 PLASTIC FABRICATIONS

Division 7–Thermal & Moisture Protection

07100 WATERPROOFING
07150 DAMPPROOFING
07200 INSULATION
07300 SHINGLES AND ROOFING TILES
07400 PREFORMED ROOFING AND SIDING
07500 MEMBRANE ROOFING
07600 FLASHING AND SHEET METAL
07800 ROOF ACCESSORIES
07900 CAULKING AND SEALANTS

Division 8–Doors and Windows

08100 METAL DOORS AND FRAMES
08200 WOOD AND PLASTIC DOORS
08300 SPECIAL DOORS
08500 METAL WINDOWS
08600 WOOD AND PLASTIC
08700 HARDWARE AND SPECIALTIES
08800 GLAZING
08900 WINDOW WALL/CURTAIN WALL

Division 9–Finishes

09100 LATH AND PLASTER
09250 GYPSUM WALLBOARD
09300 TILE
09400 TERRAZZO
09500 ACOUSTICAL TREATMENTS
09550 WOOD FLOORING
09650 RESILIENT FLOORING
09680 CARPETING
09700 SPECIAL FLOORING
09800 SPECIAL COATINGS
09900 PAINTING
09950 WALL COVERINGS

Division 10–Specialties

10100	CHALKBOARDS/TACKBOARDS
10150	COMPARTMENTS/CUBICLES
10250	FIREFIGHTING DEVICES
10300	FIREPLACES
10400	INDENTIFYING DEVICES
10500	LOCKERS
10600	PARTITIONS
10650	SCALES
10670	STORAGE SHELVING
10700	SUN CONTROL DEVICES
10750	TELEPHONE ENCLOSURES
10800	TOILET AND BATH ACCESSORIES
10900	WARDROBE SPECIALTIES
10950	WASTE DISPOSAL UNITS

Division 11–Equipment

11100	BANK AND VAULT EQUIPMENT
11150	COMMERCIAL EQUIPMENT
11170	CHECKROOM EQUIPMENT
11180	DARKROOM EQUIPMENT
11300	EDUCATIONAL EQUIPMENT
11400	FOOD SERVICE EQUIPMENT
11500	ATHLETIC EQUIPMENT
11600	LABORATORY EQUIPMENT
11630	LAUNDRY EQUIPMENT
11650	LIBRARY EQUIPMENT
11700	MEDICAL EQUIPMENT
11800	MORTUARY
11830	MUSICAL EQUIPMENT
11850	PARKING EQUIPMENT
11880	PRISON EQUIPMENT
11900	RESIDENTIAL EQUIPMENT
11970	THEATER EQUIPMENT

Division 12–Furnishings

12100	ARTWORK
12200	BLINDS AND SHADES
12300	CABINETS/FIXTURES
12500	DRAPERY/CURTAINS
12600	FURNITURE
12670	RUGS AND MATS
12700	SEATING

Division 13–Special Construction

13010	AIR SUPPORTED STRUCTURES
13050	ACCESS FLOORING
13100	AUDIOMETRIC ROOM
13250	CLEAN ROOM
13300	GREENHOUSE
13400	INCINERATORS
13440	INSTRUMENTATION

13450 INSULATED ROOM
13500 INTEGRATED CEILING
13540 NUCLEAR REACTORS
13550 OBSERVATORY
13650 PREFABRICATED STRUCTURES
13700 RADIATION PROTECTION
13750 SOUND/VIBRATION CONTROLS
13800 STORAGE VAULTS
13850 SWIMMING POOLS

Division 14–Conveying Systems

14100 DUMBWAITERS
14200 ELEVATORS
14300 HOISTS AND CRANES
14400 LIFTS
14500 MATERIAL HANDLING SYSTEM
14600 MOVING STAIRS/WALK
14700 PNEUMATIC TUBE SYSTEM

Division 15–Mechanical

15100 BASIC MATERIALS AND METHODS
15180 INSULATION
15200 WATER SUPPLY AND TREATMENT
15300 WASTE WATER DISPOSAL AND TREATMENT
15400 PLUMBING
15550 FIRE PROTECTION
15600 POWER OR HEAT GENERATION
15650 REFRIGERATION
15700 LIQUID HEAT TRANSFER
15800 AIR DISTRIBUTION
15900 CONTROLS AND INSTRUMENTATION

Division 16–Electrical

16100 BASIC MATERIALS AND METHODS
16200 POWER GENERATION
16300 OUTSIDE POWER TRANSMISSION AND DISTRIBUTION
16400 SERVICE AND DISTRIBUTION
16500 LIGHTING
16600 SPECIAL SYSTEMS
16700 COMMUNICATIONS
16850 HEATING AND COOLING
16900 CONTROLS AND INSTRUMENTATION

A

accepted bid
The proposal or bid prepared by a contractor and accepted by an owner or the owner's representative as the basis for entering into a construction contract.

access
The means of approach to a building, area, or room. Also a port or opening through which equipment may be inspected or repaired.

access door or panel
A means of access for the inspection, repair, or service of concealed systems, such as air conditioning equipment.

access flooring
A raised flooring system with removable panels that allows access to the area below. This type of flooring is frequently used in computer rooms and provides easy access to cables.

acoustical barrier
A building system that restricts sound transmission.

acoustical ceiling
A ceiling system constructed of sound-control materials. The system may include lighting fixtures and air diffusers.

acre
A common unit of land-area measurement equal to 160 square rods of 43,560 square feet.

activity
In CPM (Critical Path Method) scheduling, a task or item of work required to complete a project.

activity arrow
In CPM (Critical Path Method) scheduling, a graphic representation of an activity.

activity duration
In CPM (Critical Path Method) scheduling, the estimated time required to complete an activity.

addendum, addenda (pl.)
Alteration or clarification of the plans or specifications provided to the bidder by the owner or by the owner's representative prior to bid time. An addendum becomes part of the contract documents when the contract is executed.

additive
A substance that is added to a material to enhance or modify its characteristics, such as the curing time, plasticity, or color of concrete, or the volatility of diesel fuel.

adjusted base cost
The total estimated cost or estimated unit cost for a project after adding or deducting addenda or alternatives.

adobe
An aluminous clay used to make unfired brick.

advertisement for bids
The published, public notice soliciting bids for construction. Usually, it is required by law that the advertisement be published in newspapers of general circulation in the area, when public funds are to be used for construction.

aggregate
Granular material such as sand, gravel, crushed gravel, crushed stone, slag, and cinders. Aggregate is used in construction for the manufacturing of concrete, mortar, grout, asphaltic concrete, and roofing shingles. It is also used for leaching fields, drainage systems, roof ballast, landscaping, and as a base course for pavement and grade slabs. Aggregate is classified by size and gradation.

A-grade wood
A plywood surface that is smooth and paintable. Neatly executed patches are permitted.

agreement

(1) A meeting of the minds.
(2) A promise to perform,
between signatories of a
document. (3) In construction,
the specific documents setting
forth the terms of the contracts
between architect, owner,
engineer, construction manager,
contractor, and others.

agreement form

A standard printed form used
by the signatories to an
agreement with blank spaces to
fill in the specific information
pertinent to a particular
contract.

air change

The volume of air in an
enclosure that is being replaced
by new air. The number of air
changes per hour is a measure of
ventilation.

air conditioner

A system that may control
temperature, humidity, and/or
the cleanliness of air within an
enclosure.

air conditioning

The process of controlling the
temperature, humidity, and
cleanliness of air and of
distributing it within an
enclosure.

air diffuser

An outlet in an air-supply duct
for distributing and blending air
in an enclosure. Usually, a
round, square, or rectangular
unit mounted in a suspended
ceiling.

air distributing ceiling

A suspended ceiling system with
small perforations in the tiles for
controlled distribution of the air
from a pressurized plenum
above.

air entraining agent

An admixture for concrete or
mortar mixes which causes
minute air bubbles to form
within the mix. Air entrainment
is desirable for workability of
the mix and prevention of
cracking in the freeze/thaw
cycle.

air make-up unit

A system for introducing fresh
conditioned air into an
enclosure from which air is
being exhausted.

alkyd paint

A paint, using an alkyd resin
base, and producing a quick-
drying, hard surface.

**allowable bearing value,
allowable soil pressure**

The bearing capacity of a soil, in
pounds per square foot (psf),
determined by its characteristics
such as shear, compressibility,
water content, and cohesion.
The higher the allowable bearing
value of a soil, the smaller the
footing required to support a
structural member.

allowance

(1) In bidding, an amount
budgeted for an item for which
no exact dollar amount is
available. (2) A contingency for
unforeseen costs. (3) The
classification of connected parts
or members according to their
tightness or looseness.

alternate bid

An amount stated in a bid
which can be added or deducted
by an owner if the defined
changes are made to the plans or
specifications of the base bid.

aluminum

A silver-colored, nonmagnetic,
lightweight metal used
extensively in the construction
industry. It is used in sheets,
extrusions, foils, and castings.
Aluminum is usually used in
alloy form for greater strength.
Sheets are often anodized for
greater corrosion resistance and
surface hardness. Because of its
light weight and good electrical
conductivity, aluminum is used
extensively for electrical cables.

anchor bolt, foundation bolt, hold-down bolt

A threaded bolt, usually embedded in a foundation, for securing a sill, framework, or machinery.

angle iron, angle bar

An L-shaped steel structural member classified by the thickness of the stock and the length of the legs.

anodize

The process of creating electrolytically a hard, noncorrosive film of aluminum oxide on the surface of a metal. This film can be either clear or colored.

appliance panel

An electrical service panel with circuit breakers or fuses specifically designed for service to appliances.

appraisal

An estimate of the value of a property generally made by a professional. The estimate is developed from market value, replacement cost, income produced, or a combination of these.

approved

In construction, materials, equipment, and workmanship in a system, or a measurable portion thereof, which have been accepted by an authority having jurisdiction. Usually, the term refers to approval for payment, approval for continuation of work, or approval for occupancy.

approved equal

Material, equipment, or method of construction which has been approved by the owner or the owner's representative as an equivalent to that specified in the contract documents.

apron

(1) A piece of finished trim placed under a window stool. (2) A slab of conrete extending beyond the entrance to a building, particularly at an entrance for vehicular traffic. (3) The piece of flat wood under the base of a cabinet. (4) Weather protection paneling on the exterior of a building. (5) A splashboard at the back of a sink. (6) At an airport, the pavement adjacent to hangars and appurtenant buildings.

arbitration

A method of settling disputes between parties of a contract by presenting information to recognized authorities. Parties agree in advance to binding arbitration of disputes, either as a clause in the contract or at the occurrence of a dispute. This method of avoiding litigation can save both time and money.

architect

Designation reserved, usually by law, for a person or orgnaization professionally qualified and duly licensed to perform architectural services, including but not necessarily limited to analysis of project requirements, creation and development of the project design, preparation of drawings, specifications, and bidding requirements, and general administration of the construction contract.

architect's approval

Permission granted by the architect, acting as the owner's representative, for actions and decisions involving materials, equipment, installation, change orders, substitution of materials, or payment for completed work.

architect-engineer

An individual or firm offering professional services as both architect and engineer. The term is generally used in federal government contracts.

architectural millwork, custom millwork

Millwork manufactured to meet specifications of a particular job, as distinguished from stock millwork.

armored cable, metal-clad cable

An electrical conduit of flexible steel cable wrapped around insulated wires.

arrow diagram

A CPM (Critical Path Method) diagram where arrows represent activities in a project.

article

A subdivision of a document such as a contract document.

asbestos, asbestos fiber

A flexible, noncombustible, inorganic fiber used primarily in construction as a fireproofing and insulating material. Because the airborne fibers associated with asbestos have been demonstrated to constitute a health hazard, many new controls have been placed on its use. Great care should be exercised in the use of asbestos, and local and state building codes should be consulted before installing or removing this material.

ashlar

(1) Any squared building stone. The term usually refers to thin stone used as facing. If the horizontal courses are level, it is called "coursed ashlar," and, if they are broken, it is called "random ashlar." (2) Short vertical studs between the ceiling joists and the rafters.

asphalt

A dark-brown to black bitumen pitch that melts readily. It appears in nature in asphalt beds and is also produced as a by-product of the petroleum industry.

asphalt base course

A bottom paving course consisting of coarse aggregate and asphalt.

asphalt pavement

Any pavement made from one or more layers of asphaltic concrete.

asphalt prepared roofing

A roof covering that comes in rolls and is manufactured from asphalt impregnated felt with a harder surface of asphalt applied to the surface. All or part of the weather side may be covered with aggregate of various sizes and colors. Also known as asphaltic felt, cold-process roofing, prepared roofing, rolled roofing, rolled strip roofing, roofing felt, sanded bituminous felt, saturated felt, self-finished roofing felt.

asphalt shingles, composition shingles, strip slates

Roofing felt, saturated with asphalt and coated on the weather side with a harder asphalt and aggregate particles, which has been cut into shingles for application to a sloped roof.

asphalt surface course

The top or wearing course of asphaltic concrete pavement.

assessment

(1) A tax on property. (2) A charge for specific services, such as sewer or water, by a government agency.

assignment

A document that is supplemental to the contract, stating that payment (for work completed or materials delivered) must be made to someone other than the company or person specified in the contract.

astragal

A molding attached to one of a pair of doors or casement windows to cover up the joint between two stiles.

automatic fire pump
A pump in a standpipe or sprinkler system that turns on when the pressure drops below a predetermined minimum.

automatic fire vent
A device in the roof of a building that operates automatically to control fire or smoke.

automatic operator
A remote operating device. The term usually refers to the opening and closing of doors by electronically actuated switches.

automatic sprinkler system
A system that is designed to provide instant and continuous spraying of water over large areas in the event of fire.

automatic transfer switch
In an electrical system, a switch that automatically transfers the load to another circuit when the voltage drops below a predetermined level.

award
The format of communication for accepting a bid or proposal for services, construction, materials, or equipment.

B

backfill
Earth, soil, or other material used to replace previously excavated material, often around a newly constructed foundation wall.

backfilling
(1) The process of placing backfill. (2) Rough masonry laid behind a facing or between two faces. (3) Brickwork laid in spaces between structural timbers.

backflow preventer
A device or means to prevent backflow into the potable water system.

backhoe
A powered excavating machine used to cut trenches with a boom-mounted bucket drawn through the ground toward the machine. The bucket is raised and swung to either side to deposit the excavated material.

backing
(1) The bevel applied to the upper edge of a hip rafter. (2) Positioning furring onto joists to create a level surface on which to lay floorboards. (3) Furring applied to the inside angles of walls or partitions to provide solid corners for securing wallboard. (4) The first coat of plaster on lath. (5) The unseen or unfinished inner face of a wall. (6) Coursed masonry applied over an extrados of an arch. (7) Interior wall bricks concealed by the facing bricks. (8) The wainscoting between a floor and a window. (9) The material under the pile or facing of a carpet. (10) The stone used for random rubble walls.

backing board
(1) In a suspended acoustical ceiling, gypsum board to which acoustical tiles are secured. (2) Gypsum wallboard or other material secured to wall studs prior to paneling to provide rigidity, sound insulation, and fire resistance.

backing brick
A lower quality of brick used where it will be concealed by face brick or other masonry.

back pressure
Hydraulic or pneumatic pressure in a direction opposite the normal and intended direction of flow through a pipe, conduit, or duct; usually caused by a restriction to the flow.

backsplash

A protective panel, apron, or sheet of waterproof material positioned on a wall behind a sink, counter, or lavatory.

backup

(1) The part of a masonry wall behind the exterior facing. (2) Any material or substance placed into a joint to be sealed to reduce its depth and/or to inhibit sagging of the sealant. (3) An overflow due to a blockage in a piping system.

backwater valve, blackflow valve

A check valve in a drainage pipe which prevents reversal of flow.

balanced earthwork

Cutting and filling in which the amount of one is equal to the amount of the other after swelling and compaction factors are applied.

balancing

(1) Adjusting the mass distribution of a rotor to diminish journal vibrations and control the forces on the bearings from eccentric loading. (2) In an HVAC system, adjusting the system to produce the desired level of heating and cooling in each area of a building.

ballast

(1) A layer of coarse stone, gravel, slag, etc., over which concrete is placed. (2) The crushed rock or gravel of a railroad bed upon which ties are set. (3) The transformer-like device that limits the current flowing through the gas within a fluorescent lamp or a high intensity discharge lamp, and that provides the lamp with the proper starting voltage.

ball-bearing hinge

A butt hinge with ball bearings positioned between the knuckles to reduce friction.

balloon framing, balloon frame

A style of wood framing in which the vertical structural members, i.e., the posts and studs, are single, continuous pieces from sill to roof plate. The intermediate floor joists are supported by girts spiked to or let into the studs. The elimination of cross grains in the studding reduces differential shrinkage.

baluster, banister

(1) One of a series of short, vertical supporting elements for a handrail or a coping. (2) Any vase-shaped supporting member or column. (3) The roll on the side of an Ionic capital.

bank cubic yard

A unit designating the volume of bank material measured or calculated before removal from the bank.

bank material

Soil or rock in its natural position before excavation or blasting.

bank-run gravel, bank gravel, run-of-bank gravel

Granular material excavated without screening, scalping, or crushing. This type of gravel is a naturally occurring aggregate comprised of cobbles, gravel, sand, and fines.

bar joist

A light steel joist of open web construction with a single zig-zagged bar welded to upper and lower chords at the points of contact and used as floor and roof supports.

bar support, bar chair

A rigid device of formed wire, plastic, or concrete, used to support or hold reinforcing bars in proper position during concreting operations.

base bid

The amount of money stated in the bid as the sum for which the bidder offers to perform the work described in the bidding documents, prior to adjustments for alternate bids which have been submitted.

base bid specifications

The specifications listing or describing only those materials, equipment, and methods of construction upon which the base bid must be predicated, exclusive of any alternate bids.

base course

(1) A layer of specified selected material of planned thickness constructed on the subgrade or sub-base of a pavement to serve one or more functions such as distributing loads, providing drainage, or minimizing frost action. (2) The lowest course of masonry in a wall, pier, foundation, or footing course.

base flashing

(1) In roofing, the flashing supplied by the upturned edges of a watertight membrane. (2) The metal or composition flashing used with any roofing material at the joint between the roofing surface and a vertical surface, such as a parapet or wall.

batten seam

In metal roofing, a seam fabricated around a wood strip.

batter boards

Pairs of horizontal boards nailed to wood stakes adjoining an excavation. This assembly is used with strings as a guide to elevations and to outline a proposed building. The strings strung between boards can be left in place during the excavation.

batt insulation

Thermal or sound insulating material, such as fiberglass or expanded shale, which has been fashioned into a flexible, blanket-like form. It often has a vapor barrier on one side. Batt insulation is manufactured in dimensions which facilitate its installation between the studs or joists of a frame construction.

bay

(1) In construction, the space between two main trusses or beams. (2) The space between two adjacent piers or mullions, or between two adjacent lines of columns. (3) A small, well-defined area of concrete laid at one time in the course of placing large areas, such as floors, pavements, or runways. (4) The projecting structure of a bay window.

bead

(1) Any molding, stop, or caulking used around a glass or panel to hold it in position. (2) A stop or strip of wood against which a door or window sash closes. (3) Strip of sheet metal which has been fabricated so as to have a projecting nosing and two perforated or expanded flanges. A bead is used as a stop at the perimeter of a plastered surface or as reinforcement at the corners. (4) A narrow, half-round molding, either attached to or milled on a larger piece. (5) A square or rectangular trim of less than one inch in width and thickness. (6) A choker ferrule, the knob on the end of a choker.

beam

(1) A structural member transversely supporting a load, as a girder, rafter, or purlin. (2) The graduated horizontal bar of a weighing scale. (3) A ray of light.

beam anchor, joist anchor, wall anchor

A metal tie for securing a beam, joist, or floor firmly to a wall.

beam-and-girder construction

A type of floor construction in which slabs are used to distribute the load to spaced beams and girders.

beam-and-slab-floor

A type of floor construction in which reinforced concrete beams are used to support a monolithic concrete floor slab.

bearing

(1)That section of a structural member, such as a beam or truss, which rests on the supports. (2) A device used to support or steady a shaft, axle, or trunnion. (3) In surveying, the horizontal angle between a reference direction, such as true north, and a given line. (4) Descriptive of any wall which provides support to the floor and/or roof of a building.

bearing capacity

The maximum unit pressure which a soil or other material will withstand without failure or without excessive settlement.

bearing wall

Any wall which supports a vertical load as well as its own weight.

bed

(1) The mortar into which masonry units are set. (2) Sand or other aggregate on which pipe or conduit is laid in a trench. (3) To set in place with putty or similar compound, as might be performed in glazing. (4) A supporting base for engines or machinery. (5) To level or smooth a path into which a tree is to be felled.

bedding

(1) A prepared base for masonry or concrete. (2) The lath or other support(s) upon which pipe is laid. (3) See **bed, def. 2.** (4) Any material used to **bed, def. 3.**

bedrock

Solid rock which underlies the earth's surface soil and which can provide, by its very existence, the foundation upon which a heavy structure may be erected.

benching

(1) A half-round channel cast in the concrete in the bottom of a manhole to direct discharge when the flow is low. (2) Concrete laid on steeply sloping fill to prevent sliding. (3) Concrete laid on the side slopes of drainage channels where the slopes are interrupted by manholes, etc. (4) Concrete laid on a trench for a pipeline to provide firmer support.

bench mark

A marked reference point on a permanent object, such as a metal disc set in concrete, whose elevation as referenced to a datum is known. A bench mark is used in surveying to determine the elevation of other points.

berm

(1) An artificially placed continuous ridge or bank of earth, usually along a roadside. Also called "a shoulder". (2) A ridge or bank of earth placed against a masonry wall. (3) A ledge or strip of earth placed so as to support pipes or beams. (4) Earthen dikes or embankments constructed to retain water on land which will be flood-irrigated. (5) Earthen or paved dike-like embankments for diverting runoff water.

bid

A complete and properly signed proposal to do the work, or designated portion thereof, for the amount or amounts stipulated therein. A bid is submitted in accordance with the bidding documents.

bid bond

A form of bid security executed by the bidder or principal and by a surety to guarantee that the bidder will enter into a contract within a specified time and furnish any required performance bond, and labor and material payment bond.

bid opening
The opening and tabulation of bids submitted within the prescribed bid time and in conformity with the prescribed procedures. Bid opening is preferable to bid letting.

bidder
A person or entity who submits a bid, generally one who submits a bid for a prime contract with the owner, as distinct from a sub-bidder who submits a bid to a prime bidder. Technically, a bidder is not a contractor on a specific project until a contract exists between the bidder and the owner.

bidding documents
The advertisement or invitation to bid, instructions to bidders, the bid form, other sample bidding and contract forms, and the proposed contract documents, including any addenda, issued prior to receipt of bids.

bidding period
The calendar period beginning at the time of issuance of bidding documents and ending at the prescribed bid time.

binder
(1) Almost any cementing material, either hydrated cement or a product of cement or lime and reactive siliceous materials. The kinds of cement and the curing conditions determine the general type of binder formed. (2) Any material such as asphalt, resin, or other materials forming the matrix of concretes, mortars, and sanded grouts. (3) That ingredient of an adhesive composition that is principally responsible for the adhesive properties which actually hold the two bodies together. (4) In paint, that non-volatile ingredient, such as oil, varnish, protein, or size, which serves to hold the pigment particles together in a coherent film. (5) A stirrup or other similar contrivance usually of small-diameter rod, which functions to hold together the main steel in a reinforced concrete beam or column.

binder course, binding course
(1) A succession of masonry units between an inner and outer wall to bind them. (2) An intermediate course used in asphaltic concrete paving between the base and the surfacing material and comprising bituminously bound aggregate of intermediate size.

bitumen
Any of several mixtures of naturally occurring or synthetically rendered hydrocarbons and other substances obtained from coal or petroleum by distillation. Bitumen is incorporated in asphalt and tar as used in road surfacing and waterproofing operations.

bituminous
Composed of, similar to, derived from, relating to, or containing bitumen. The term "bituminous" is descriptive of asphalt and tar products.

B-labeled door
A door carrying a certification from Underwriters' Laboratories that it is of a construction that will pass the standard fire door test for the length of time required for a Class B opening; and that it has been prepared (cuts and reinforcement) to receive the hardware required for a Class B opening.

blister

Usually an undesirable moisture and/or air-induced bubble or bulge which often indicates that some kind of delamination has taken place. Blisters can occur between finish plaster and the basecoat, between paint or varnish and the surface to which it has been applied, between roofing membranes or between membrane and the substrate, between reinforcing tape and the gypsum board to which it has been adhered, etc. (2) A tree disease characterized by the seeping of pitch onto the bark surface.

block

(1) A usually hollow concrete masonry unit or other building unit, such as glass. (2) A solid, often squared, piece of wood or other material. (3) A piece of wood nailed between joists to stiffen a floor. (4) Any small piece of wood secured to the interior angle joint to strengthen and stiffen it. (5) A pulley and its enclosure. (6) Usually one of several small rectangular divisions within a city, bounded on each side by successive streets. (7) A solid piece of wood or other material used to fill spaces between formwork members.

blocking

(1) Small pieces of wood used to secure, join, or reinforce members, or to fill spaces between members. (2) Small wood blocks used for shimming. (3) A method of bonding two parallel or intersecting walls built at different times by means of offsets whose vertical dimensions are not less than 8 inches (20 centimeters). (4) The sticking together of two painted surfaces when pressed together. (5) An undesired adhesion between touching layers of material, such as occurs during storage.

blueprint

Negative image reproduction having white lines on a blue background and made either from an original or from a positive intermediate print. Today the term almost always refers to Diazo Prints, which are architectural or working drawings having blue or black lines on a white background.

board and batten

A method of siding in which the joints between vertically placed boards or plywood are covered by narrow strips of wood.

board foot

The basic unit of measurement for lumber. One board foot is equal to a 1-inch board 12 inches in width and 1 foot in length. Thus, a 10-foot long, 12-inch wide, and 1-inch thick piece would contain 10 board feet. When calculating board feet, nominal sizes are assumed.

board sheathing

A sheathing made of boards, usually tightly spaced, except that open spacing may be used in some roofs.

boiler

A closed vessel in which a liquid is heated or vaporized either by application of heat to the outside of the vessel, by circulation of heat through tubes within the vessel, or by circulating heat around liquid-filled tubes in the vessel.

bolt

(1) An externally threaded cylindrical fastening device fabricated from a rod, pin, or wire, and having, at one end, a round, square, hexagonal, etc., head which projects beyond the

circumference of the shank to facilitate gripping, turning, and striking. The unit is inserted through holes in fabricated or assembled parts and is secured by a corresponding, internally threaded nut and tightened by the application of torque. (2) That protruding part of a lock which prevents a door from opening. (3) Raw material used in the manufacture of shingles and shakes. A wedge-shaped split from a short length log, taken to a mill for manufacturing. (4) Short logs to be sawn for lumber or peeled for veneer. (5) Wood sections from which barrel staves are made. (6) A large roll of cloth material of a given length, just as it comes from the loom. (7) A single package containing two or more rolls of wallpaper.

bond

The adhesion and grip of concrete or mortar to reinforcement or to other surfaces against which it is placed, including friction due to shrinkage and longitudinal shear in the concrete engaged by the bar deformations. (2) The adhesion of cement paste to aggregate. (3) Adherence between plaster coat or between plaster and a substrata produced by adhesive or cohesive properties of plaster or supplemental materials. (4) The arrangement of, or pattern formed by, the exposed faces of laid masonry units. (5) The layer of glue in a plywood joint.

bonding agent

A substance applied to a suitable substrate to create a bond between it and a succeeding layer, as between a subsurface and a terrazzo topping or a subsequent application of plaster.

bonding capacity

The maximum total contract value a bonding company will extend to a contractor in performance bonds. The total contract value is the sum of all contracts being bonded.

bonding company

A firm providing a surety bond for work to be performed by a contractor payable to the owner in case of default of the contractor. The bond can be for work performance or for payment for materials and labor.

bonus and penalty clause

A provision in the contract for payment of a bonus to the contractor for completing the work before a stipulated date, and a charge against the contractor for failure to complete the work by this date.

boom crane

A crane with a long slender boom, usually of lattice construction.

borrow

In earth moving, fill acquired from excavation from a source outside the required cut area.

borrow pit

An excavation site, other than a designated cut area, from which material is taken for use nearby.

box out

To make a form that will create a void in a concrete wall or slab when the concrete is placed.

box sill

A common method of frame construction using a header nailed across the ends of floor joists where they rest on the sill.

brace

(1) A diagonal tie that interconnects scaffold members. (2) A temporary support for aligning vertical concrete formwork. (3) A horizontal or

inclined member used to hold sheeting in place. (4) A hand tool with a handle, crank, and chuck used for turning a bit or auger.

branch

A term used in plumbing to define an inlet or outlet from the main pipeline, usually at a right angle to the main pipeline. The pipe may be a water supply, drain, vent stack, or any other pipe used in any mechanical piping system.

branch circuit

A portion of the electric wiring system which extends beyond the fuse or other circuit protection device protecting that circuit.

branch drain

A drain pipe from the plumbing fixtures or soil line of a building that runs into a main line.

branch duct

In HVAC, a smaller duct branching from the main duct. At each branch duct, the cross sectional area of the main duct is reduced.

branch sewer

A sewer that receives sewage from a relatively small area and is connected to a main sewer or manhole.

brick

A solid masonry unit of clay or shale, formed into a rectangular prism while plastic, and then burned or fired in a kiln.

brick anchor

Corrugated fasteners designed to secure a brick veneer to a structural concrete wall.

brick veneer

A brick facing wall laid against a structural wall but not structurally bonded to the wall and bearing no load other than its own weight.

bridging

A system of lateral braces placed between joists to distribute the load and keep them in position.

broom finish concrete

Concrete that has been brushed with a broom when fresh in order to improve its traction or to create a distinctive texture.

buck

(1) The wood or metal subframe of a door, installed in a wall to accommodate the finished frame. Also called a "door buck."
(2) One of a pair of four-legged supporting devices used to hold wood as it is being sawed. Also called a "sawbuck" or a "sawhorse."

bucket

A scoop-shaped attachment for an excavating machine that digs and transports loose earth materials, often outfitted with opening and closing mechanisms to facilitate unloading.

builder's risk insurance

A special form of property insurance to cover work under construction.

building area

The sum of the horizontal projected area of all buildings on a site. Terraces and uncovered porches are excluded, unless the stipulations of a mortgage lender or governmental program require their inclusion.

building code

The legal minimum requirements established or adopted by a governmental unit pertaining to the design and construction of buildings.

building envelope

The elements of a building which enclose conditioned areas and through which thermal energy may be transferred to or from the outside environment.

building height

Generally the greatest vertical distance measured from curb or grade level to the highest level of a flat or mansard roof or to the average height of a pitched, gabled, hip, or gambrel roof. Penthouses and the like are usually excluded if they do not exceed a specified height or their projected area is less than a specified percentage of the main roof.

building paper

A heavy, asphalt-impregnated paper used as a lining and/or vapor barrier between sheathing and an outside wall covering or as a lining between rough and finish flooring.

built-up

(1) Fabricated of two or more pieces or sheets which are laminated. (2) Assembled by fastening a number of pieces or parts to each other.

built-up beam

(1) A metal beam made of beam shapes, plates, and/or angles which are welded or bolted together. (2) A concrete beam made of precast units connected through shear connectors. (3) A timber beam made of smaller pieces which are fastened together.

built-up roofing, composition roofing, felt-and-gravel roofing, gravel roofing

A continuous roof covering made up of various plies or sheets of saturated or coated felts, cemented together with asphalt. The felt sheets are topped with a cap sheet or a flood coat of asphalt or pitch which may have a surfacing of applied gravel or slag.

bulkhead

(1) A horizontal or inclined door providing outside access to a cellar or shaft. (2) A partition in concrete forms to separate placings. (3) A structure on the roof of a building to provide headroom over a stairwell or other opening. (4) A low structure on a roof, covering a shaft or protruding service equipment. (5) A retaining structure which protects a dredged area from earth movement.

bullnose, bull's-nose

(1) A rounded outside corner or edge. (2) A metal bead used in forming a rounded corner on plaster walls.

bus, bus bar

An electric conductor, often a metal bar, that serves as a common connection for two or more circuits. A bus usually carries a large current.

bus duct, busway

A prefabricated unit containing one or more protected busses.

business agent

An official of a trade union who represents the union in negotiations and disputes, and checks jobs for compliance with union regulations and union contracts.

butt hinge

A common form of hinge consisting of two plates, each with one meshing knuckle edge and connected by means of a removable or fixed pin through the knuckles.

butt joint

(1) A square joint between two members at right angles to each other. The contact surface of the outstanding member is cut square and fits flush to the surface of the other member. (2) A joint in which the ends of two members butt each other so only tensile or compressive loads are transferred.

C

cable duct

A rigid, metal protective enclosure through which electric conductors are run. For underground installations, concrete or plastic pipes are usually used.

cable tray

An open, metal framework used to support electric conductors in a manner similar to cable duct. The primary difference is that the cable tray has a lattice type construction and an open top.

caisson

(1) A drilled, cylindrical foundation shaft used to transfer a load through a soft strata to a firm strata or bedrock. The shaft is filled either with reinforced or unreinforced concrete. (2) A watertight box or chamber used for construction work below water level.

cantilever

A beam, girder, or supporting member which projects beyond its support at one end.

cant strip

A three-sided piece of wood, one angle of which is square, used under the roofing on a flat roof where the horizontal surface abuts a vertical wall or parapet. The sloped transition facilitates roofing and waterproofing.

cap

The top piece, often overhanging, of any vertical architectural feature or wall. A cap may be external, as on an outside wall or doorway, or internal, as on the top of a column, pilaster, molding, or trim.

capital

The uppermost member of a column, pilaster, etc., crowning the shaft and taking the weight of an entablature.

casement window

A window assembly having at least one casement or vertically hinged sash.

cash allowance

An amount of money established in the contract documents for inclusion in the contract sum to cover the cost of prescribed items not specified in detail, with a provision that variations between such amount and the finally determined cost of the prescribed items will be reflected in change orders appropriately adjusting the contract sum.

casing

(1) The exposed millwork enclosure of cased beams, posts, pipes, etc. (2) The exposed trim molding or lining around doors and windows. (3) The pipe liner of a hole in the ground as for a well, caisson, or pile.

cast-in-place concrete

Concrete placed in forms at its final location.

catalyst

(1) A substance that accelerates chemical reactions. (2) The hardener that accelerates the curing of adhesives, such as synthetic resins.

catch basin

A receptor or reservoir that receives surface water run-off or drainage. Typically, a catch basin is made of precast concrete, brick, or concrete masonry units and has a cast iron frame and grate on top.

caulk

To fill a joint, crack, or opening with a sealer material. The filling of joints in bell and spigot pipe with lead and oakum.

cavity wall, hollow masonry wall, hollow wall

An exterior masonry wall in which the inner and outer wyths are separated by an air space, but tied together with wires or metal stays.

ceiling suspension assembly

A gridwork of metal rails and hangers erected for the support of a suspended ceiling and ceiling-mounted items, e.g., air diffusers, lights, fire detectors, etc.

cement

Any chemical binder that makes bodies adhere to it or to each other, such as glue, paste, or portland cement.

certificate for insurance

A document issued by an insurance company or its agent stating the dates of coverage of insurance in effect along with the types and amounts of coverage for the insured.

certificate of occupancy

A certificate issued by a government authority stating that a structure, or a portion of a structure, has been approved as complying with applicable laws, regulations, and codes, and may be occupied and put to its intended use.

chamfer

The beveled edge formed at the right-angle corner of a construction member.

change

In construction, a deviation in the design or scope of the work as defined in the plans and specifications, which were the basis for the original contract.

change order

A written order to a contractor with the necessary signatures to make it a legal document and authorizing a change from the original plans, specifications, or other contract documents, as

well as a change in the cost.

changes in the work

Changes to the original design, specifications, or scope of work requested by the owner. All changes in the work should be documented on change orders.

channel

(1) A structural steel member shaped like a U. (2) In glazing, a U-shaped member used to hold a pane or panel. (3) A watercourse, usually man-made. (4) The suspension system for a suspended ceiling.

channel beam

A construction member with a U-shaped cross section.

check valve, back-pressure valve, reflux valve

A valve designed to limit the flow of fluid through it to one direction only.

chipboard

A flat panel manufactured to various thicknesses by bonding flakes of wood with a binder. Chipboard is an economical, strong material used for sheathing, sub-flooring, and cabinetry.

chord

(1) The top or bottom members of a truss, typically horizontal, as distinguished from the web members. (2) A straight line between two points on a curve.

cinder block

A masonry block that is made of crushed cinders and portland cement. This type of block is lighter and has a higher insulating value than concrete. Because moisture causes deterioration of cinder block, they are used primarily for interior walls, rather than exterior walls.

circuit

(1) A path of conductors for an electric current. (2) A piping loop for a liquid or gas.

circuit breaker
An electrical device for discontinuing current flow during an abnormal condition. By resetting a switch, a circuit breaker becomes reusable, unlike a fuse.

civil engineer
An engineer specializing in the design and construction of roads, buildings, dams, bridges, and other structures, as well as water distribution, drainage, and sanitary sewer systems.

cladding
A covering or sheathing usually applied to provide desirable surface properties, such as durability, weathering, corrosion, or impact resistance.

clamshell
(1) A bucket used on a derrick or crane for handling loose granular material. The bucket's two halves are hinged at the top, thus resembling a clam shell. (2) A wood molding with a cross section that resembles a clam shell.

class A, B, C, D, E,
Fire-resistance ratings applied to building components such as doors or windows. The term "class" also refers to the opening into which the door or window will be fitted.

class-A
Underwriters' Laboratories classification for a component having a 3-hour fire endurance rating.

class-B
Underwriters' Laboratories classification for an interior component having a 1-hour or a 1-1/2-hour fire endurance rating.

class-C
Underwriters' Laboratories classification for an interior component having a 3/4-hour fire endurance rating.

class-D
Underwriters' Laboratories classification for an exterior component having a 1-1/2-hour fire endurance rating.

class-E
Underwriters' Laboratories classification for an exterior component having a 3/4-hour fire endurance rating.

clause
A subdivision of a paragraph or subparagraph, particularly within a legal document such as a contract document. A clause is usually numbered or lettered for easy reference.

clay pipe
Pipe that is made of earthenware and glazed to eliminate porosity. Clay pipe is used for drainage systems and sanitary sewers.

clay tile
A fired earthenware tile used on roofs. Also called "quarry tile" when used for flooring.

cleanout
(1) A pipe fitting with a removable threaded plug that permits inspection and cleaning of the run. (2) A door in the base of a chimney that permits access for cleaning. (3) A small door in a ventilation duct used to permit removal of grease, dust, and dirt blockages.

clip
(1) To cut off as with shears. (2) A short piece of brick that has been cut. (3) A small metal fastening device.

closed list of bidders
A list of contractors that have been approved by the architect and owner as the only ones from whom bid prices will be accepted.

closed specifications
Specifications stipulating the use of specific or proprietary products or processes without provision for substitution.

close nipple

A short piece of pipe threaded from both ends and leaving no smooth outside surface.

coarse aggregate

Aggregate that will not pass through a 1/4-inch sieve screen.

coaxial cable

A cable consisting of a tube of conducting material surrounding a central conductor. The tube is separated from contact with the cable by insulation. Coaxial cable is used to transmit telephone, telegraph, television, and computer signals.

code

Regulations, ordinances, or statutory requirements of a governmental agency relating to building construction and occupancy. Codes are adopted and administered for the protection of public health, safety, and welfare.

cofferdam

A watertight enclosure from which water is pumped to expose an area of formation in order to permit access for construction or repairs.

coil

A term applied to a heat exchanger using connected pipes or tubing in rows, layers, or windings as in steam heating, water heating, and refrigeration condensers and evaporators.

cold-air return

In a heating system, the return air duct that transports cool air back into the system to be heated.

collar

(1) A flashing for a metal vent or chimney where it passes through a roof. (2) A trim piece to cover the hole where a vent goes through a wall or ceiling. (3) A metal band that encircles a metal or wooden shaft.

column

A type of supporting pillar that is long and relatively slender. A column is usually loaded axially in compression.

column footing

The foundation under a column that spreads the loads out to an area large enough so that the bearing capacity of the soil is not exceeded and differential settling does not occur.

combination door

An exterior door that has interchangeable panels of glazing and screening, one for summer and the other for winter use.

common brick

Brick not selected for color or texture, and thus useful as filler or backing. Though usually not less durable or of lower quality than face brick, common brick typically costs less. Greater dimensional variations are also permitted.

compaction

(1) The compression of any material into a smaller volume; for example, waste compaction. (2) The elimination of voids in construction materials, as in concrete, plaster, or soil by vibration, tamping, rolling, or some other method or combination of methods. In specifying compaction of embankment or fill, a percent compaction at optimum moisture content is often used. Another method is to specify the equipment, height of lift, and number of passes.

completion bond, construction bond, contract bond

The guarantee by a bonding company that a job contract will be completed and will be clear of all liens and encumbrances.

completion date

The date certified by the architect when the work in a

building, or a designated portion thereof, is sufficiently complete, in accordance with the contract documents, so that the owner can occupy the work or designated portion thereof for the use for which it is intended.

composite beam

A beam combining different materials to work as a single unit such as structural steel and concrete or cast-in-place and precast concrete.

composition board

A manufactured board consisting of any of several materials usually pressed together with a binder. Compositon board is frequently used as sheathing, wall board, or as an insulation or acoustical barrier.

composition roofing

A roof consisting of several layers, thicknesses, or pieces. Also called "built-up roofing."

compound beam, built-up beam

A beam consisting of smaller components that have been assembled and fastened together to function as a single unit.

comprehensive general liability insurance

A broad form of liability insurance covering claims for bodily injury and property damage which combines under one policy coverage for all liability exposures (except those specifically excluded) on a blanket basis and automatically covers new and unknown hazards that may develop. Comprehensive general liability insurance automatically includes contractual liability coverage for certain types of contracts. Products liability, completed operations liability and broader contractual liability coverages are available on an optional basis. This policy may also be written to include automobile liability.

compression

Structurally, the force that pushes together or crushes, as opposed to the force that pulls apart, as in tension.

concrete

A composite material which consists essentially of a binding medium within which are embedded particles or fragments of aggregate; in portland cement concrete, the binder is a mixture of portland cement and water.

conduit

(1) A pipe, tube, or channel used to direct the flow of a fluid. (2) A pipe or tube used to enclose electric wires to protect them from damage.

construction documents

Drawings and specifications setting forth in detail the requirements for the construction of a project.

contingent agreement

An agreement, generally between an owner and an architect, in which some portion of the architect's compensation is contingent upon the owner's obtaining funds for the project (such as by successful referendum, sale of bonds, or securing of other financing), or upon some other specially prescribed condition.

contract documents

(1) The owner-contractor agreement. (2) The conditions of the contract (general, supplementary, and other conditions). (3) The drawings. (4) The specifications. (5) All addenda issued prior to, and all modifications issued after, execution of the contract. (6) Any items that may be specifically stipulated as being included in the contract documents.

convection

The movement of a gas or liquid upward as it is heated and downward as it is cooled. The movement is caused by the change in density. The warm, less dense material rises, and the cooler, denser material falls.

coping

The protective top member of any vertical construction, such as a wall or chimney. A coping may be masonry, metal, or wood, and is usually sloping or beveled to shed water in such a way that it does not run down the vertical face of the wall. Copings often project out from a wall with a drip groove on the underside.

cornice

(1) An ornamental molding of wood or plaster that circles a room just below the ceiling. (2) An ornamental topping that crowns the structure it is on. (3) An exterior ornamental trim at the meeting of the roof and wall. This type of cornice usually includes a bed molding, a soffit, a fascia, and a crown molding.

counterflashing

A thin strip of metal frequently inserted into masonry construction and bent down over other flashing to prevent water from running down the masonry and behind the upturned edge of the base flashing.

course

(1) A horizontal layer of bricks or blocks in a masonry wall.

(2) A row or layer of any type of building material, such as siding, shingles, etc.

critical path method, CPM

A charting of all events and operations to be encountered in completing a given process. The method is rendered in a form permitting determination of the relative significance of each event, and establishing the optimum sequence and duration of operations.

cross beam

(1) A large beam that spans between the two walls or sides of a structure. (2) A brace between opposite walings or sheeting in an excavation.

crushed stone

Stone crushed and screened so that substantially all faces result from fracturing.

culvert

A transverse drain under a roadway, canal, or embankment other than a bridge. Most culverts are fabricated with materials such as corrugated metal and precast concrete pipe.

curtain wall

The exterior closure or skin of a building. A curtain wall is non-bearing and is not supported by beams or girders.

cut and fill

An operation common to road building and other rock and earthmoving operations in which the material excavated and removed from one location is used as fill material at another location.

D

damages

Usually, per diem amounts specified in a contract and payable only when incurred loss can be proved to have resulted from a contractor's delays or breach of contract.

dampproofing

An application of a water resisting treatment or material to the surface of a concrete or masonry wall to prevent passage or absorption of water or moisture. Can also be accomplished by an admixture to the concrete mix.

date of agreement
The date shown on the face of an agreement, or the date the agreement is signed. It is usually the date of the award.

date of substantial completion
The date certified by the architect when the work, or a designated portion thereof, is sufficiently complete, in accordance with the contract documents, so that the owner may occupy the work, or designated portion thereof, for the use for which it is intended.

datum
A base elevation to which other elevations are referred.

dead load
A calculation of the weight of the structural components, the fixtures, and the permanently attached equipment used in designing a building and its foundations.

deck
(1) An uncovered wood platform usually attached to or on the roof of a structure.
(2) The flooring of a building.
(3) The structural assembly to which a roof covering is applied.

deflection
The bending of a structural member as a result of its own weight or an applied load. Also, the amount of displacement resulting from this bending.

design-build, design-construct
A term designating a contractor who provides both design and construction services to an owner.

design load
(1) In structural analysis, the total load on a structural system under the worst possible loading conditions. (2) In air conditioning, the maximum heat load a system is designed to withstand.

dewater
To remove water from a job site by pumps, wellpoints, or drainage systems.

direct expense
All items of expense directly incurred by or attributable to a specific project, assignment, or task.

direct personnel expense
Salaries and wages, including fringes, of all principals and employees attributable to a particular project or task.

distributed load
A load distributed evenly over the length of a structural member or the surface of a floor or roof, expressed in weight per length or weight per area.

distribution box
A container, located at the outlet of a septic tank, that distributes the effluent evenly to the drain tiles in the absorption field.

division
One of the standard sixteen major Uniform Construction Index classifications used in specifying, pricing, and filing construction data.

dowel-bar reinforcement
Short sections of reinforcing steel extending from one concrete pour into the next and used to increase strength in the joint.

downtime
The amount of time a piece of equipment cannot be used for reasons of repair or maintenance.

dragline
A bucket attachment for a crane that digs by drawing the bucket towards itself using a cable. The attachment is most commonly

used in soft, wet materials that must be excavated at some distance from the crane. This device is used extensively in marsh or marine work.

drain

A pipe, ditch, or trench designed to carry away waste water.

drain tile

Tile in short-length sections laid with open joints, usually surrounded with aggregate and covered with asphaltic paper or straw, and used to drain the water from an area.

drawings

Graphic and pictorial documents showing the design, location, and dimensions of the elements of a project. Drawings generally include plans, elevations, sections, details, schedules, and diagrams. When capitalized, the term refers to the graphic and pictorial portions of the contract documents.

dressed lumber

Lumber that has been processed through a planing machine for the purpose of attaining a smooth surface and uniformity of size on at least one side or edge.

drip edge

The edge of a roof which drips into a gutter or into the open. Also, the metal or wood strip that stiffens and protects this edge.

drop ceiling, dropped ceiling

A non-structural ceiling suspended below the structural system, usually in a modular grid. A drop ceiling usually contains lighting systems.

dry-pipe sprinkler system

A sprinkler system having no water in the pipes until it is activated. This type of system is particularly useful where there is danger of freezing.

drywall

The term commonly applied to interior finish construction using preformed sheets, such as gypsum wallboard, as opposed to using plaster.

dry well

A pit or well that is either filled or lined with coarse aggregate or rocks and is designed to contain drainage water until it can be absorbed into the surrounding ground.

duct

(1) In electrical systems, an enclosure for wires or cables often embedded in concrete floors or encased in concrete underground. (2) In HVAC systems, the conduit used to distribute the air. (3) In post-tensioning, the hole through which the cable is pulled.

ductwork

The ducts of an HVAC system.

dumbwaiter

A small hoisting mechanism or elevator in a building used for hoisting materials only. The dumbwaiter was originally developed by Thomas Jefferson for use in his house at Monticello.

duplex receptacle

Two electrical receptacles housed in the same outlet box.

E

early strength

Strength of concrete or mortar developed usually within 72 hours after placement.

earth berm

A small, earthen dike-like embankment usually used for diverting run-off water.

earth pressure

The horizontal pressure exerted by retained earth.

earthwork

A general term encompassing all operations relative to the movement, shaping, compacting, etc., of earth.

economy brick

A cored, modular brick with nominal dimensions of 4 inches x 4 inches x 8 inches and actual dimensions of about 3-1/2 inches x 3-1/2 inches x 7-1/2 inches.

edge form

Formwork used to limit the horizontal spread of fresh concrete on flat surfaces such as pavements or floors.

elbow

A rather sharply bent or fabricated angle fitting, usually of pipe, conduit, or sheet metal.

electric meter

A device that measures and registers the integral of an electrical quantity with respect to time.

electric outlet

A point in an electric wiring system at which current is taken through receptacles equipped with sockets for plugs, making it available to supply lights, appliances, power tools, and other electrically powered devices.

electric panelboard

A panel, or group of individual panel units, capable of being assembled as a single panel. Designed to include fuses, switches, circuit breakers, etc. Housed in a cabinet or cutout box positioned in or against a wall or partition and accessible only from the front.

electric receptacle

A contact device, usually installed in an outlet box, which provides the socket for the attachment of a plug to supply electric current to portable power equipment, appliances, and other electrically operated devices.

elevated floor

Any floor system not supported by the subgrade.

elevation

(1) A vertical distance relative to a reference point. (2) A view or drawing of the interior or exterior of a structure as if projected onto a vertical plane.

elevator

A "car" or platform that moves within a shaft or guides and is used for the vertical hoisting and/or lowering of people or material between two or more floors of a structure. An elevator is usually electrically powered, although some short-distance elevators (serving fewer than six or seven floors) are powered hydraulically.

embankment

A ridge constructed of earth, fill, rocks, or gravel. The length of an embankment exceeds both its width and its height. The usual function of an embankment is to retain water or to carry a roadway.

emergency exit

A door, hatch, or other device leading to the outside and usually kept closed and locked. The exit is used chiefly for the emergency evacuation of a building, airplane, etc., when conventional exits fail, are insufficient, or are rendered inaccessible, as by fire.

emergency lighting

Temporary illumination provided by battery or generator and essential to safety during the failure or interruption of the conventional electric power supply.

emergency power

Electricity temporarily produced and supplied by a standby power generator when the conventional electric power supply fails or is interrupted. Emergency power is essential in operations like hospitals, where even relatively short power outages would be life threatening.

eminent domain

The legal right or power of a government to take, for public use, hitherto privately owned property, usually with some degree of compensation to its owner.

employer's liability insurance

Insurance that protects an employer from his employees' claims for damages resulting from sickness or injury sustained during their course of work and based on negligence of common law rather than on liability under Workers' Compensation.

engineer

A person trained, experienced in, or licensed to practice the profession of engineering.

erection

The positioning and/or installation of structural components or preassembled structural members of a building, often with the assistance of powered equipment such as a hoist or crane.

estimate

The anticipated cost of materials, labor, services, or any combination of these for a proposed construction project.

estimated design load

The sum of: the useful heat transfer; the heat transfer to or from the connected piping; and the heat transfer that occurs in any auxiliary apparatus connected to a heating or air conditioning system.

excavation

(1) The removal of earth, usually to allow the construction of a foundation or basement. (2) The hole resulting from such removal.

exposed aggregate

The coarse aggregate in concrete work revealed when the outer skin of mortar is removed, usually before the full hardening of the concrete.

extra

An item desired or work performed in addition to that specified in the contract and usually involving additional cost.

F

face

(1) The surface of a wall, masonry unit, or sheet of material that is exposed to view or designed to be exposed in finish work. (2) To cover the surface layer of one material with another, as to "face" a wall with brick or fieldstone.

face block, faced block

A unit of concrete masonry with a plastic or ceramic face surface, often glazed or polished for special architectural uses.

factor of safety

(1) Stress factor of safety: the ratio of the ultimate strength, or yield point, of a material to the design working stress. (2) Load factor of safety: the ratio of ultimate load, moment, or shear of a structural member to the working load, moment, or shear, respectively, assumed in design.

false ceiling

A ceiling suspended a foot or more below the actual ceiling to provide space for and easy access to wiring and ducts, or to alter the dimensions of a room.

falsework

The temporary structure erected to support work in the process of construction. Falsework consists of shoring or vertical posting formwork for beams and slabs, and lateral bracing.

fan-coil unit

An air conditioning unit that houses an air filter, heating or cooling coils, and a centrifugal fan, and operates by moving air through an opening in the unit and across the coils.

fascia, facia

(1) A board used on the outside vertical face of a cornice. (2) The board connecting the top of the siding with the bottom of a soffit. (3) A board nailed across the ends of the rafters at the eaves. (4) The edge beam of a bridge. (5) A flat member or band at the surface of a building.

fatigue

The weakening of a material caused by repeated or alternating loads. Fatigue may result in cracks or complete failure.

fee

Remuneration for professional services.

fiberboard

A general term referring to any of various panel products, such as particleboard, hardboard, chipboard, or other type formed by bonding wood fibers by heat and pressure.

fiberglass, fibrous glass, glass fiber

Filaments of glass formed by pulling molten glass into random lengths that are either gathered in a wool-like mass or formed as continuous threads. The wool-like form is used as thermal and acoustical insulation. The thread-like form is used as in textiles, glass fabrics, and electrical insulation, and as reinforcing material.

fiberglass reinforced plastic (FRP)

A coating of glass fibers and resins applied as a protective layer to plywood. The resulting composite is tough and scuff resistant. It is used in construction of containers and truck bodies, and for concrete formwork.

field applied

(1) The application of a material, such as paint, at a job site, as opposed to being applied at a factory. (2) The construction or assembly of components in the field.

field order

In construction, a written order passed to the contractor from the architect to effect a minor change in work, requiring no further adjustment to the contract sum or expected date of completion.

field work

Any work performed at a job site.

fill

(1) The soil or other material used to raise the grade of a site area. (2) A sub-floor leveling material.

final acceptance

The formal acceptance of a contractor's completed construction project by the owner, upon notification from an architect that the job fulfills the contract requirements. Final acceptance is often accompanied by a final payment agreed upon in the contract.

final completion

A term denoting that the work has been completed in accordance with the terms and conditions of the contract documents.

final inspection

An architect's last review of a completed project before issuance of the final certificate for payment.

final payment

The payment an owner awards to the contractor upon receipt of the final certificate for payment from the architect. Final payment usually covers the whole unpaid balance agreed to in the contract sum, plus or minus amounts altered by change orders.

finish flooring

The material used to make the wearing surface of a floor, such as hardwood, tile, or terrazzo.

finishing

Leveling, smoothing, compacting, and otherwise treating surfaces of fresh or recently placed concrete or mortar to produce the desired appearance and service.

fir

(1) A form of softwood indigenous to temperate zones, used principally for interior trim and framing. Varieties include Douglas fir, silver fir, balsam fir, and white fir. (2) Although used most often to refer to Douglas Fir, which is also a pseudo-fir, this is a general term for any of a number of species of conifers, including the true firs.

fire alarm system

An electrical system installed within a home, industrial plant, or office building that sounds a loud blast or bell when smoke and flames are detected. Certain alarms are engineered to trigger sprinkler systems for added protection.

fire brick

A flame-resistant, refractory ceramic brick used in fireplaces, chimneys, and incinerators.

fire extinguisher

A portable device for immediate use in suppressing a fire. There are four classes of fires: A, B, C or D. A single device is designed for use on one or more classes.

fire extinguishing system

An installation of automatic sprinklers, foam distribution system, fire hoses, and/or portable fire extinguishers designed for extinguishing a fire in an area.

fire hydrant

A supply outlet from a water main, for use in fire fighting.

fireproof

(1) Descriptive of materials, devices, or structures with such high resistance to flame that they are practically unburnable. (2) To treat a material with chemicals in order to make it fire resistant.

fire-protection sprinkler system

An automatic fire-suppression system, commonly heat-activated, that sounds an alarm and deluges an area with water from overhead sprinklers when the heat of a fire melts a fusible link.

fire resistance

(1) The property of a material or assembly to withstand fire, characterized by the ability to confine a fire and/or to continue to perform a given structural function. (2) According to OSHA, the property of a material or assembly that makes it so resistant to fire that, for a specified time and under conditions of a standard heat intensity, it will not fail structurally and will not permit the side away from the fire to become hotter than a specified temperature.

fire resistant door

A door designed to confine fire to one part of a structure, keeping it from spreading through an entire building. It may be a solid-core wooden door, or one sheathed in metal, depending on the intended location. Doors are rated for the projected time they could be expected to perform their function during a fire. Most building codes require that the door between living quarters and a garage be fire resistant.

fire-resistive construction

Construction in which the floors, walls, roof, and other components are built exclusively of noncombustible materials, with fire-endurance ratings equal to or greater than those mandated by law.

fire wall

An interior or exterior wall that runs from the foundation of a building to the roof or above, constructed to stop the spread of fire.

fitting

(1) A standardized part of a piping system used for attaching sections of pipe together, such as a coupling, elbow, bend, cross, or tee. (2) The process of installing floor coverings around walks, doors, and other obstacles or projections. (3) In electrical wiring, a component, such as a bushing or locknut, that serves a mechanical purpose rather than an electrical function.

fixed fee

A fixed amount specified in a contract to be paid for all materials and services required to complete the contact.

flash

(1) To make a joint weathertight using flashing. (2) An intentional or accidental color variation on the surface of a brick. (3) A variation in paint color resulting from variable wall absorption.

flashing

A thin, impervious sheet of material placed in construction to prevent water penetration or direct the flow of water. Flashing is used especially at roof hips and valleys, roof penetrations, joints between a roof and a vertical wall, and in masonry walls to direct the flow of water and moisture.

flexible connector

(1) In ductwork, an airtight connection of nonmetallic materials installed between ducts or between a duct and fan to isolate vibration and noise. (2) A connector in a piping system that reduces vibration along the pipes and compensates for misalignment. (3) An electrical connection that permits movement from expansion, contraction, vibration, and/or rotation.

float

A tool (not a darby), usually of wood, aluminum, or magnesium, used in concrete finishing operations to impart a relatively even but still open texture to an unformed fresh concrete surface.

floor

(1) The surface within a room upon which one walks. (2) The horizontal division between two stories of a building, formed by assembled structural components or a continuous mass, such as a flat concrete slab.

floor load

The live load for which a floor has been designed, selected from a building code, or developed from an estimate of expected storage, equipment weights, and/or activity.

floor plan

A drawing showing the outline of a floor, or part of a floor, interior and exterior walls, doors, windows, and details such as floor openings and curbs. Each floor of a building has its own floor plan.

fluorescent lamp

A low-pressure mercury electric-discharge lamp in which a phosphor coating on the inside of the tube transforms some of the ultraviolet energy generated by the discharge into visible light.

foam core

The center of a plywood "sandwich" panel, consisting of plastic foam between wood veneers. The foam may be introduced in a liquid form that is forced under pressure into a space between the wood veneer skins, or the skins may be applied to a rigid plastic foam board.

foot

(1) The bottom or base on an object. (2) A unit of measurement of length in the English System. (3) A projection on a cylindrical roller used to compact a layer of earth fill.

footcandle

A unit of illumination equal to 1 lumen per sq. ft.

footing

That portion of the foundation of a structure that spreads and transmits load directly to the soil.

forced-air furnace

A warm-air furnace, outfitted with a blower, that heats an area by transmitting air through the furnace and connecting ducts.

foreclosure

The legal transfer of a property deed or title to a bank or other creditor because of the owner's failure to pay the mortgage, whereupon the owner loses the right to the property.

form

A temporary structure or mold for the support of concrete while it is setting and gaining sufficient strength to be self-supporting.

form insulation

Thermal insulation, equipped with an airtight seal, that is applied to the exterior of concrete forms to preserve the heat of hydration at required levels so that concrete can set properly in cold weather.

formwork

The total system of support for freshly placed concrete, including the mold or sheathing which contacts the concrete, as well as all supporting members, hardware, and necessary bracing.

foundation

The material or materials through which the load of a structure is transmitted to the earth.

frame

An assembly of vertical and horizontal structural members.

frame construction

A construction system in which the structural parts are wood or dependent on a wood framework for support. The balloon system consists of vertical members running from the foundation to the roof plate, and to which floor joists are attached. In platform construction, floor joists of each floor rest on the plates of the floor below.

frame house

A house of frame construction, usually with exterior walls sheathed and covered with wood siding.

framework

A network of structural

members or components joined to form a structure, such as a truss or multi-level building.

framing

(1) Structural timbers assembled into a given construction system. (2) Any construction work involving and incorporating a frame, as around a window or door opening. (3) The unfinished structure, or underlying rough timbers of a building, including walls, roofs, and floors.

French drain

A drainage ditch containing loose stone covered with earth.

front-end loader

A machine with a bucket fixed to its front end, having a lift-arm assembly that raises and lowers the bucket. A front-end loader is used in earth moving and loading operations and in rehandling stock piled materials.

furnace

(1) That part of a boiler or warm air heating plant in which the combustion takes place. (2) A complete heating unit that transfers heat from burning fuel to a heating system.

furring

(1) Strips of wood or metal fastened to a wall or other surface to even it, to form an air space, to give appearance of greater thickness, or for the application of an interior finish such as plaster. (2) Lumber one inch in thickness (nominal) and less than four inches in width, frequently the product of resawing a wider piece. The most common sizes of furring are 1 x 2 and 1 x 3.

furring strip

A wood strip used as furring.

fuse

A protective device, made of a metal strip, wire or ribbon that guards against overcurrent in an electrical system by melting if too much current is generated and breaking the circuit.

fuse box

A metal box with a hinged cover which houses fuses for electric circuits.

fusible link

A metal link made of two parts held together by a low-melting-point alloy. When exposed to fire-condition temperatures, the link separates allowing a door, damper or device to be closed.

G

gable

The portion of the end of a building that extends from the eaves upward to the peak or ridge of the roof. The gable's shape is determined by the type of building on which it is used: triangular in a building with a simple ridged roof, or semi-octagonal in a building with a gambrel roof.

galvanize

The process of protectively coating iron or steel with zinc, either by immersion or electroplating.

gambrel roof

A roof whose slope on each side is interrupted by an obtuse angle that forms two pitches on each side, the lower slope being steeper than the upper.

gate valve

A piping device consisting of a housed wedge or disc positioned perpendicular to the flow, which it regulates by being raised or lowered.

gauge, gage

(1) The numerically designated thickness of sheet metal. (2) A metal tubing or the similarly

designated diameter of a screw or wire. (3) A measuring device for pressure or liquid level. (4) The distance between rows of bolt or rivet holes in the same member. (5) A wood or metal strip used as a thickness-control guide in bituminous or concrete paving operations. (6) In plastering, a screed. (7) The act of adding or the amount of gauging plaster added to hasten the setting of common plaster. (8) In laid roofing, the exposed length of a shingle, slate, or tile.

general conditions
The portion of the contract document in which the rights, responsibilities, and relationships of the involved parties are itemized.

general contract
In a single-contract system, the documented agreement between the owner and the general contractor for all the construction for the entire job.

general contractor
For an inclusive construction project, the primary contractor who oversees and is responsible for all the work performed on the site, and to whom any subcontractors on the same job are responsible.

general drawing
A drawing that illustrates structural cross-section, main dimension, elevation plan, substructural borings, and other basic details of a construction project.

general foreman
The general contractor's on-site representative, often referred to as the "superintendent" on large construction projects. It is the responsibility of the general foreman to coordinate the work of various trades and to oversee all labor performed at the site.

general requirements
The designation or title of Division I (the first of 16) in the Construction Specifications Institute's Uniform System. General requirements usually include overhead items and equipment rentals.

generator
A mechnical or electromechanical device that converts mechanical energy into electrical power, as an alternator producing alternating current or a dynamo producing direct current.

gin pole
A cable-supported vertical pole used in conjunction with blocks and tackle for hoisting.

girder
A large principal beam of steel, reinforced concrete, wood, or combination of these, used to support other structural members at isolated points along its length.

girt, girth
(1) A horizontal member used as a stiffener between studs, columns, or posts at intermediate level. (2) A rail or intermediate beam that receives the ends of floor joists on an outside wall.

glass
A hard, brittle, inorganic product, ordinarily transparent or translucent, made by the fusion of silica, flux, and a stabilizer, and cooled without crystallizing. Glass can be rolled, blown, cast, or pressed for a variety of uses.

glass block
A hollow, translucent block of glass, often with molded patterns on either or both faces, which affords pleasantly diffused light when used in non-load bearing walls or partitions.

glaze
(1) To install glass panes in a window, door, or another part

of a structure. (2) A hard, thin, glossy ceramic coating on the surface of pottery, earthenware, ceramics, and similar goods.

glazed structural unit
A hollow or solid unit to whose surface a smooth, glassy covering, such as glazed tile, has been applied.

glazed tile
Ceramic or masonry tile having an impervious, glossy finish.

glazing
(1) Fixing glass in an opening. (2) The glass surface of an opening which has been glazed.

glue laminated, glu-lam
The result of a process in which individual pieces of lumber or veneer are bonded together with adhesives to make a single piece in which the grain of all the constituent pieces is parallel.

grade
(1) The surface or level of the ground. (2) A classification of quality as, for instance, in lumber. (3) The existing or proposed ground level or elevation on a building site or around a building. (4) The slope or rate of incline or decline of a road, expressed as a percent. (5) A designation of a subfloor, either above grade, on grade, or below grade. (6) In plumbing, the slope of installed pipe, expressed in the fall in inches per foot length of pipe. (7) The classification of the durability of brick. (8) Any surface prepared to accept paving, conduit, or rails.

grade beam
A horizontal end-supported (as opposed to ground-supported) loadbearing foundation member that supports an exterior wall of a superstructure.

grade block
A type of concrete masonry unit from which the top course of a foundation wall is constructed and above which a thicker or thinner masonry wall is constructed.

grade line
(1) A line of stakes with markings, each at an elevation relative to a common datum and from whose elevations a grade between their terminal points can be established. (2) A strong string used to establish the top of a concrete pour or masonry course.

grader
A multipurpose earthworking machine used mostly for leveling and crowning. A grader has a single blade, centrally located, that can be lifted from either end and angles so as to cast to either side.

grade stake
In earthwork, a stake that designates the specified level.

grading plan
A plan showing contours and grade elevations for existing and proposed ground surface elevations at a given site.

grate
(1) A type of screen made from sets of parallel bars placed across each other at right angles and in approximately the same plane. A grate is used to allow water to flow to drainage, but to cover an area for pedestrian or vehicular traffic. (2) A surface with openings to allow air to flow through while supporting a fuel bed, as in a coal furnace.

gravel
Coarse particles of rock that result from naturally occurring disintegration or that are produced by crushing weakly bound conglomerate. Gravel is retained on a No. 4 sieve.

gravel roofing
Roofing composed of several ("built up") layers of saturated or coated roofing felt, sealed and bonded with asphalt or coal-tar pitch which, for solar protection and insulation purposes, is then

covered with a layer of gravel or slag. Usually used on flat or nearly flat roofs.

gravel stop
A metal strip or flange around the edge of a built-up roof. The stop prevents loose gravel or other surfacing material from falling off or being blown off a roof.

grid
(1) In surveying, a system of evenly spaced perpendicular reference lines at whose intersections elevations are measured. (2) The structural layout of a given building. (3) A system of crossed reinforcing bars used in concrete footings.

grid ceiling
(1) A ceiling with apertures into which luminaries are built for lighting purposes. (2) Any ceiling hung on a grid framework.

grille
(1) Any grating or openwork barrier used to cover an opening in a wall, floor, paving, etc., for decoration, protection, or concealment. (2) A louvered or perforated panel used to cover an air duct opening in a wall, ceiling, or floor. (3) Any screen or grating that allows air into a ventilating duct.

ground
(1) The conducting connection between electrical equipment or an electrical circuit and the earth. (2) A strip of wood that is fixed in a wall of concrete or masonry to provide a place for attaching wood trim or burring strips. (3) A screed, strip of wood, or bead of metal fastened around an opening in a wall and acting as a thickness guide for plastering or as a fastener for trim. (4) Any surface that is or will be plastered or painted.

grout
(1) An hydrous mortar whose consistency allows it to be placed or pumped into small joints or cavities, as between pieces of ceramic clay, slate, and floor tile. (2) Various mortar mixes used in foundation work to fill voids in soils, usually through successive injections through drilled holes.

grouting
(1) The placing of grout so as to fill voids, as between tiles and under structural columns and machine bases. (2) The injection of grout to stabilize dams or mass fills, or to reinforce and strengthen decaying walls and foundations. (3) The injection of grout to fill faults and crevices in rock formations.

guarantee
A legally enforceable assurance of quality or performance of a product or work, or of the duration of satisfactory performance. Also called "guaranty" and/or "warranty."

guaranteed maximum cost
The maximum amount above which an owner and contractor agree that cost for work performed (as calculated on the basis of labor, materials, overhead, and profit) will not escalate.

guaranty bond
Each of the four following bonds are types of guaranty bonds: (1) bid bond, (2) labor and material payment bond, (3) performance bond, and (4) surety bond.

gunite, gunnite
Concrete mixed with water at the nozzle end of a hose through which it has been pumped under pressure. Gunite is applied or placed pneumatically, as "shot," onto a backing surface.

gutter

(1) A shallow channel of wood, metal, or PVC positioned just below and following along the eaves of a building for the purpose of collecting and diverting water from a roof. (2) In electrical wiring, the rectangular space allowed around the interior of an electrical panel for the installation of feeder and branch wiring conductors.

gypsum

A naturally occurring, soft whitish mineral (hydrous calcium sulfate) which, after processing, is used as a retarding agent in portland cement and as the primary ingredient in plaster, gypsum board, and related products.

gypsum board

A panel whose gypsum core is paper-faced on each side, which is used to cover walls and ceilings while providing a smooth surface that is easy to finish.

gypsum concrete

A mixture of calcined gypsum binder, wood chips or other aggregate, and water. The mixture is poured to form gypsum roof decks.

gypsum sheathing

A type of wallboard whose core is made from gypsum with which additives have been mixed to make it water repellent. The sheathing is surfaced with a water-repellent paper to make it an appropriate base for exterior wall coverings.

H

halon fire extinguisher

A suppressing system for use on all classes of fires. Its extinguishing agent is bromotrifluoromethane, a colorless, odorless, and electrically non-conductive gas of exceptionally low toxicity and considered to be the safest of the compressed gas fire suppressing agents. Halon systems are often used in modern computer equipment rooms.

hand

(1) Prefaced by "left" or "right" to designate how a door is hinged and the direction it opens. (2) Preceded by "left" or "right" to designate the direction of turn one encounters when descending a spiral stair, with "right-hand" being clockwise.

handrail

A bar of wood, metal, or PVC, or a length of wire, rope, or cable, supported at intervals by upright posts, balusters, or similar members or, as on a stairway, by brackets from a wall or partition, so as to provide persons with a handhold.

hanger

(1) A strip, strap, rod, or similar hardware for connecting pipe, metal gutter, or framework, such as for a hung ceiling, to its overhead support. (2) Any of a class of hardware used in supporting or connecting members of similar or different material as, for instance, a stirrup strap or beam hanger for supporting the end of a beam or joist at a masonry wall. (3) A person whose trade it is to install gypsum board products.

hardware

(1) A general term encompassing a vast array of metal and plastic fasteners and connectors used in or on a building and its inherent or extraneous parts. The term includes rough hardware, such as nuts, bolts, and nails, and

finish hardware, such as latches and hinges. (2) Computers and other machines and physical equipment that directly perform industrial or technological functions.

hatch
An opening in a floor or roof of a building, as in a deck of a vessel, having a hinged or completely removable cover. When open, a hatch permits ventilation or the passage of persons or products.

haunch
(1) A bracket built into a wall or column to support a load falling outside the wall or column, such as a hammer brace in a hammer-beam roof.
(2) Either side of an arch between the crown, or centerstone, and the springing, or impost. (3) A thickening of a concrete slab to support an additional load, as under a wall.

header
(1) A rectangular masonry unit laid across the thickness of a wall, so as to expose its end(s). (2) A lintel. (3) A member extending horizontally between two joists to support tailpieces. (4) In piping, a chamber, pipe, or conduit having several openings through which it collects or distributes material from other pipes or conduits. (5) The wood surrounding an area of asphaltic concrete paving.

heat exchanger
A device in which heat from a hot fluid is transferred to another fluid. The fluids are usually separated by the thin walls of tubing.

heating load
The number of BTUs per hour required to maintain a specified temperature within a given enclosed space.

heating system
The method and its related necessary equipment used in a given heating application, such as a forced hot air system.

heat loss
(1) The net decrease in BTUs within a given space, caused by heat transmission through spaces around windows, doors, etc. (2) The loss by conduction, convection, or radiation from a solar collector after its initial absorption.

hem-fir
A species combination used by grading agencies to designate any of various species, such as White Fir and Western Hemlock, having common characteristics. The designation is used for identification and standardization of recommended design values and because some species, in lumber form, cannot be visually distinguished.

high-density plywood
Plywood manufactured from resin-impregnated veneer and formed with heat at high pressures to render a product having at least twice the density of conventional plywood.

high-early-strength concrete
Concrete containing high-early-strength cement of admixtures causing it to attain a specified strength earlier than regular concrete.

high-intensity discharge lamp
A mercury, high pressure sodium, or other electric discharge lamp requiring a ballast for starting and for controlling the arc, and in which light is produced by passing an electric current through a contained gas or vapor.

hip
(1) The exterior inclining angle created by the junction of the sides of adjacent sloping roofs, excluding the ridge angle. (2) The rafter at this angle. (3) In a truss, the joint at which the upper chord meets an inclined end post.

hollow-core door
A flush door with plywood or hardwood faces secured over a skeletal framewwork, the interior remaining void or honeycombed.

hollow masonry unit
A masonry unit in which the net cross-sectional area is less than 75% of the gross cross-sectional area when compared in any given plane parallel to the bearing surface.

hollow metal door
A hollow-core door constructed of channel-reinforced sheet metal. The core may be filled with some type of lightweight material.

hollow metal frame
A doorframe constructed of sheet metal with reinforcing at hinges and strikes.

hot-air furnace
A heating unit in which air is warmed and from which the warmed air is drawn into ducts to be carried throughout a building or selected portion thereof.

hot water boiler
Any heating unit in a hot water heating system in which or by which water is heated before being circulated through pipes to radiators or baseboards throughout a building or portion thereof.

hot-water supply
The combination of equipment and its related plumbing supplying domestic hot water.

H-pile
A steel H-beam driven into the earth by a pile driver.

I

I-beam
A structural member of rolled steel whose cross section resembles the capital letter I.

incandescent lamp
A lamp in which electricity heats a (tungsten) filament to incandescence.

infiltration
The leakage of air into a building through the small spaces around windows, doors, etc.; caused by pressure differences between indoor and outdoor air.

inspection list
A list of items of work to be completed or corrected by the contractor.

inspector
A person authorized and/or assigned to perform a detailed examination of any or all portions of the work and/or materials.

instructions to bidders
Instructions contained in the bidding documents for preparing and submitting bids for a construction project or designated portion thereof.

insurance
A contractual obligation by which one person or entity agrees to secure another against loss or damage from specified liabilities for premiums paid.

insurance, builder's risk
A specialized form of property insurance which provides coverage for loss or damage to the work during the course of construction.

insurance, certificate of
A document, issued by an authorized representative of an insurance company, stating the types, amounts, and effective dates of insurance in force for a designated insured.

insurance, contractor's liability
Insurance purchased and maintained by the contractor to protect the contractor from specified claims which may arise out of or result from the contractor's operations under the contract, whether such operations are by the contractor or by any subcontractor or by anyone directly or indirectly employed by any of them, or by anyone for whose acts any of them may be liable.

insurance, liability
Insurance which protects the insured against liability on account of injury to the person or property of another.

insurance, professional liability
Insurance coverage for the insured professional's legal liability for claims for damages sustained by others allegedly as a result of negligent acts, errors, or omissions in the performance of professional services.

insurance, public liability
Insurance covering liability of the insured for negligent acts resulting in bodily injury, disease, or death of persons other than employees of the insured, and/or property damage.

insurance, Workers' Compensation
Insurance covering the liability of an employer to employees for compensation and other benefits required by Workers' Compensation laws with respect to injury, sickness, disease, or death arising from their employment. Also still known in some jurisdictions as "Workmen's Compensation Insurance."

interior door
A door installed inside a building, as in a partition or wall, having two interior sides.

interior finish
The interior exposed surfaces of a building, such as wood, plaster, and brick, or applied materials, such as paint and wallpaper.

invert
The lowest inside surface or floor of a pipe, drain, sewer, culvert, or manhole.

invert elevation
The elevation of an invert (lowest inside point) of pipe or sewer at a given location in reference to a bench mark.

invitation to bid
A portion of the bidding documents soliciting bids for a construction project.

irrigation
(1) The process or system, and its related equipment, by which water is transported and supplied to otherwise dry land. (2) The use of water thus supplied for its intended purpose.

J

jamb
An exposed upright member on each side of a window frame, doorframe, or door lining. In a window, these jambs outside the frame are called "reveals."

job condition
Those portions of the contract documents that define the rights and responsibilities of the contracting parties and of others involved in the work. The

conditions of the contract include general conditions, supplementary conditions, and other conditions.

job site

The area within the defined boundaries of a project.

joint

(1) The point, area, position, or condition at which two or more things are jointed. (2) The space, however small, where two surfaces meet. (3) The mortar-filled space between adjacent masonry units. (4) The place where separate but adjacent timbers are connected, as by nails or screws, or by mortises and tenons, glue, etc.

joist

A piece of lumber two or four inches thick and six or more inches wide, used horizontally as a support for a ceiling or floor. Also, such a support made from steel, aluminum, or other material.

junction box

A metal box in which splices in conductors or joints in runs of raceways or cable are protectively enclosed, and which is equipped with an easy access cover.

K

key

(1) The removable actuating device of a lock. (2) A wedge of wood or metal inserted in a joint to limit movement. (3) A keystone. (4) A wedge or pin through the protruding part of a projecting tenon to secure its hold. (5) A back piece on a board to prevent warping. (6) The tapered last board in a sequence of floorboards, which, when driven into place, serves to hold the others in place. (7) The roughened underside of veneer or other similar material intended to aid in bonding. (8) In plastering, that portion of cementitious material which is forced into the openings of the backing lath. (9) A joggle. (10) A keyway. (11) A cotter as in def. 4. (12) A small, usually squared piece which simultaneously fits into the keyways or grooves of a rotating shaft and the pulley.

keyway

(1) A recess or groove in one lift or placement of concrete which is filled with concrete of the next lift, giving shear strength to the joint. Also called a "key." (2) In a cylindrical lock, the aperture that receives and closely engages the key for its entire length, unlike a keyhole of a common lock. (3) A key-accepting groove in a shaft, pulley, sprocket, wheel, etc.

kicker

(1) A wood block or board attached to a formwork member in a building frame or formwork to make the structure more stable. In formwork, a kicker acts as a haunch to take the thrust of another member. Sometimes called a "cleat." (2) A catalyst. (3) An activator, as the hardener for a polyester resin.

kickplate

(1) A metal strip or plate attached to the bottom rail of a door for protection against marring, as by shoes. (2) A plate, usually metal, used to create a ridge or lip at the open edge of a stair platform or floor, or at the back edge or open ends of a stair tread.

kilowatt-hour

A unit of electrical energy consumption equal to 1,000 watts operating for one hour.

knocked down frame

A door frame which comes from the manufacturer in three or more parts.

knockout

A prestamped, usually circular section in an electrical junction box, panel box, etc., which can be easily removed to provide access for a fitting or raceway cable.

knot

(1) The hard, cross-grained portion of a tree where a branch meets the trunk. (2) An architectural ornament of clusters of leaves or flowers at the base of intersecting vaulting ribs. (3) Intentional or accidental compact intersection(s) of rope(s) or similar material.

L

Lally Column

A trade name for a pipe column from 3 to 6 inches in diameter, sometimes filled with concrete.

laminated beam

A straight or arched beam formed by built-up layers of wood. The method of lamination may be by gluing under pressure, by mechanical nailing or bolting, or a combination.

landscape architect

A person whose professional specialty is designing and developing gardens and landscapes, especially one who is duly licensed and qualified to perform in the landscape architectural trade.

land surveyor

A person whose occupation is to establish the lengths and directions of existing boundary lines on landed property, or to establish any new boundaries resulting from division of a land parcel.

lapping

The overlapping of reinforcing bars or welded wire fabric for continuity of stress in the reinforcing when a load is applied.

lateral support

Any bracing, temporary or permanent, that provides greater support in resisting side-to-side (lateral) forces and deflections. Floor and roof members typically provide lateral support for walls, columns, and beams. Vertical pilasters or secondary walls may also provide support.

layout

A design scheme or plan showing the proposed arrangement of objects and spaces within and outside a structure.

ledge

(1) A molding that projects from the exterior wall at a building. (2) A piece of wood nailed across a number of boards to fasten them together. (3) An unframed structural member used to stiffen a board or a number of boards or battens. (4) Bedrock.

ledger

(1) A horizontal framework member that carries joists and is supported by upright posts or by hangers. (2) A slab of stone laid flat, such as that over a grave. (3) A horizontal scaffold member, positioned between upright posts, on which the scaffold planks rest.

letter of intent

A letter signifying an intention to enter into a formal

agreement, usually setting forth
the general terms of the
agreement.

level
(1) A term used to describe any
horizontal surface that has all
points at the same elevation and
thus does not tilt or slope.
(2) In surveying, an instrument
that measures heights from an
established reference. (3) A
spirit level, consisting of small
tubes of liquid with bubbles in
each. The small tubes are
positioned in a length of wood
or metal which is hand held and,
by observing the position of the
bubbles, used to find and check
level surfaces.

liability insurance
Insurance that protects the
insured against liability on
account of injury to the person
or property of another.

licensed contractor
A person or entity certified by a
governmental authority, where
required by law, to engage in
construction contracting.

lift slab
A method of concrete
construction in which floor and
roof slabs are cast on or at
ground level and hoisted into
position by jacking. Also, a slab
that is a component of such
construction.

lightweight concrete
Concrete of substantially lower
unit weight than that made using
gravel or crushed stone
aggregate.

limit of liability
The maximum amount that an
insurance company agrees to
pay in case of loss, damage, or
injury.

line drawing
A graphic representation made
with lines and solids, as opposed
to one made with tone
gradations, such as a photograph
or rendering.

lintel
A horizontal supporting
member, installed above an
opening such as a window or a
door, that serves to carry the
weight of the wall above it.

liquidated damages
A sum established in a
construction contract, usually as
a fixed sum per day, as the
measure of damages suffered by
the owner due to failure of the
contractor to complete the work
within a stipulated time.

live load
The load superimposed on
structural components by the
use and occupancy of the
building, not including the wind
load, earthquake load, or dead
load.

load
(1) The force, or combination
of forces, that act upon a
structural system or individual
member. (2) The electrical
power delivered to any device or
piece of electrical equipment.
(3) The placing of explosives in
a hole.

loam
Soil consisting primarily of sand,
clay, silt, and organic matter.

longitudinal bracing
Bracing that extends lengthwise
or runs parallel to the center line
of a structure.

lot line
The limit or boundary of a land
parcel.

lowest responsible bidder
The bidder who submits the
lowest bona fide bid and is
considered by the owner and
architect to be fully responsible
and qualified to perform the
work for which the bid was
submitted.

lowest responsive bid
The lowest bid that is responsive
to and complies with the
requirements of the bidding
documents.

lumber

Timbers that have been split or processed into boards, beams, planks, or other stock that is to be used in construction and is generally smaller than heavy timber.

M macadam

A method of paving in which layers of uniformly graded, coarse aggregate are spread and compacted to a desired grade. Next, the voids are completely filled by a finer aggregate, sometimes assisted by water (waterbound), and sometimes assisted by liquid asphalt (asphalt bound). The top layers are usually bound and sealed by some specified asphaltic treatment.

main

(1) In electricity, the circuit that feeds all sub-circuits. (2) In plumbing, the principal supply pipe that feeds all branches. (3) In HVAC, the main duct that feeds or collects air from the branches.

main beam

A structural beam that transmits its load directly to columns, rather than to another beam.

main office expense

A contractor's main office expense consists of the expense of doing business that is not charged directly to the job. Depending on the accounting system used, and the total volume, this can vary from 2 to 20%, with the median about 7.2% of the total volume.

maintenance bond

A contractor's bond in which a surety guarantees to the owner that defects of workmanship and materials will be rectified for a given period of time. A one-year bond is commonly included in the performance bond.

manhole

A vertical access shaft from the ground surface to a sewer or underground utilities, usually at a junction, to allow cleaning, inspection, connections, and repairs.

man-hour

A unit describing the work performed by one person in one hour.

masonry

Construction composed of shaped or molded units, usually small enough to be handled by one man and composed of stone, ceramic brick, or tile, concrete, glass, adobe, or the like. The term masonry is sometimes used to designate cast-in-place concrete.

master switch

An electrical switch that controls two or more circuits.

mat foundation

A continuous, thick-slab foundation supporting an entire structure. This type of foundation may be thickened or have holes in some areas and is typically used to distribute a building's weight over as wide an area as possible, especially if soil conditions are poor.

membrane roofing

A term that most commonly refers to a roof covering, employing flexible elastomeric plastic materials from 35 to 60 mils thick, that is applied from rolls and has vulcanized joints. The initial cost of an elastomeric-membrane roof-covering system is higher than a built-up roof, but the life-cycle cost is lower.

meter

A device for measuring the flow of liquid, gas, or electrical current.

millwork

All the building products made of wood that are produced in a planing mill such as moldings, door and window frames, doors, windows, blinds, and stairs. Millwork does not include flooring, ceilings, and siding.

modification (to construction contract documents)

(1) A written amendment to the contract signed by both parties. (2) A change order. (3) A written interpretation issued by the architect. (4) A written order for a minor change in the work issued by the architect.

modular construction

(1) Construction in which similar units or subcomponents are combined repeatedly to create a total system. (2) A construction system in which large prefabricated units are combined to create a finished structure. (3) A structural design which uses dimensions consistent with those of the uncut materials supplied. Common modular measurements are 4″ to 4′.

mortar

(1) A plastic mixture used in masonry construction that can be troweled and hardens in place. The most common materials that mortar may contain are portland, hydraulic, or mortar cement; lime; fine aggregate; and water. (2) The mixture of cement paste and fine aggregate which fills the voids between the coarse aggregate in fresh concrete.

mortise

(1) A recess cut in one member, usually wood, to receive a tenon from another member. (2) A recess such as one cut into a door stile to receive a lock or hinge.

multizone system

A heating or HVAC system having individual controls in two or more zones in a building.

N **nailer**

A strip of wood or other fitting attached to or set in concrete, or attached to steel to facilitate making nailed connections.

needle

(1) In underpinning, the horizontal beam that temporarily holds up the wall or column while a new foundation is being placed. (2) In forming or shoring, a short beam passing through a wall to support shores or forms during construction. (3) In repair or alteration work, a beam that temporarily supports the structure above the area being worked on.

net fill

In excavation, the compacted fill required less the cut material available between particular stations.

net load

In heating calculations, the heating requirement, not considering heat losses, between the source and the terminal unit.

nominal dimension

(1) The size designation for most lumber, plywood, and other panel products. In lumber, the nominal size is usually greater than the actual dimension; thus, a kiln-dried 2 x 4 ordinarily is surfaced to 1-1/2 x 3-1/2. In panel products, the size is generally stated in feet for surface dimensions and increments of 1/16-inch for thickness. Product standards permit various tolerances for the latter, varying according to the type and nominal thickness of the panel. (2) In masonry, a dimension larger than the one

specified for the masonry unit by the thickness of a joint.

nominal size
The dimensions of sawn lumber before it is surfaced and dried.

nonbearing partition
A partition which is not designed to support the weight of a floor, wall, or roof.

nonmetallic sheathed cable
Two or more electrical conductors enclosed in a nonmetallic, moisture resistant, flame-retardant sheath.

normal weight concrete
Concrete having a unit weight of approximately 150 pounds per cubic foot and made with aggregates of normal weight.

O

offer
A proposal, as in a wage and benefits package, to be accepted, negotiated, or rejected.

on center
(1) a measurement of the distance between the centers of two repeating members in a structure. (2) A term used for defining the spacing of studs, joists, and rafters.

one-way slab
A slab panel, bounded on its two long sides by beams and on its two short sides by girders. In such a condition, the dead and live loads acting on the slab area may be considered as being entirely supported in the short or transverse direction by the beams; hence, the term "one-way."

one-way system
The arrangement of steel reinforcement within a slab that presumably bends in only one direction.

on-grade
A concrete floor slab resting directly on the ground.

nosing
The horizontal projection of an edge from a vertical surface, such as the nosing on a stair tread.

notice to bidders
A notice contained in the bidding documents informing prospective bidders of the opportunity to submit bids on a project and setting forth the procedures for doing so.

notice to proceed
Written communication issued by the owner to the contractor authorizing the work to proceed and establishing the date of commencement of the work.

open bidding
A bidding procedure wherein bids or tenders are submitted by and received from all interested contractors, rather than from a select list of bidders privately invited to compete.

open shop, merit shop, non-union shop
A term describing a firm whose employees are not covered by collective bargaining agreements.

operating engineer
The workman or technician who operates heavy machinery and construction equipment.

outlet
(1) The point in an electrical wiring circuit at which the current is supplied to an appliance or device. (2) A vent or opening, principally in a parapet wall, through which rainwater is released. (3) In a piping system, the point at which a circulated liquid is discharged.

outline specifications
An abbreviated listing of specification requirements

normally included with schematic or design development documents.

overburden
(1) A mantle of soil, rock, gravel, or other earth material covering a given rock layer or bearing stratum. (2) An unwanted top layer of soil that must be stripped away to gain access to useful construction materials buried beneath it.

overtime
(1) Payment for time worked over the normal number of hours. (2) Paid for at a premium, e.g., time-and-one half or double the normal rate.

owner
(1) The architect's client and party to the owner-architect agreement. (2) The owner of the project and party to the owner-contractor agreement.

owner-architect agreement
Contract between owner and architect for professional services.

owner-contractor agreement
Contract between owner and contractor for performance of the work for construction of a project or a portion thereof.

owner's liability insurance
Insurance to protect the owner against claims that arise from the operations performed for the owner by the contractor and from the owner's general supervision of such operations.

owner's representative
The person designated as the official representative of the owner in connection with a project.

P **packaged air conditioner**
A factory-assembled air conditioning unit ready for installation. The unit may be mounted in a window, an opening through a wall, or on the building roof. These units may serve an individual room, a zone, or multiple zones.

pad
(1) A plate or block used to spread a concentrated load over an area, such as a concrete block placed between a girder and a loadbearing wall. (2) A shoe of a crawler type truck.

pad foundation
A thick slab-type foundation used to support a structure or a piece of equipment.

paint
(1) A mixture of a solid pigment in a liquid vehicle which dries to a protective and decorative coating. (2) The resultant dry coating.

pan
(1) A prefabricated form unit used in concrete joist floor construction. (2) A container that receives particles passing the finest sieve during mechanical analysis of granular materials.

panel box
A box in which electric switches and fuses are mounted.

panel door
A door constructed with panels, usually shaped to a pattern, installed between the stiles and rails which form the outside frame of the door.

paneling
The material used to cover an interior wall. Paneling may be made from a 4/4 select milled to a pattern and may be either hardwood or softwood plywood, often prefinished or overlaid with a decorative finish, or hardboard, also usually prefinished.

panic hardware

A door locking assembly that can be released quickly by pressure on a horizontal bar. Panic hardware is required by building codes on certain exits.

parapet

(1) That part of a wall that extends above the roof level. (2) A low wall along the top of a dam.

parge coat

A coat of masonry cement applied to masonry for resistance to penetration of moisture.

parquet flooring

A floor covering composed of small pieces of wood, usually forming a geometric design.

partial occupancy

Occupancy by the owner of a portion of a project prior to final completion.

particle board

A generic term used to describe panel products made from discrete particles of wood or other ligno-cellulosic material rather than from fibers. The wood particles are mixed with resins and formed into a solid board under heat and pressure.

partition

A dividing wall within a building, usually non-loadbearing.

pavement base

The layer of a pavement immediately below the surfacing material and above the sub-base.

paving

The hard surface covering of areas such as walks, roadways, ramps, waterways, parking areas, and airport runways.

penalty clause

A provision in a contract for a charge against the contractor for failure to complete the work by a stipulated date.

penthouse

A structure on the roof of a building, usually less than one-half the projected area of the roof and housing equipment or residents.

percentage agreement

An agreement for professional services in which the compensation is based upon a percentage of the construction cost.

percentage fee

Compensation, based upon a percentage of construction cost, that is applicable to either construction contracts or professional service agreements.

percolation test

A test to estimate the rate at which a soil will absorb waste fluids, reported by measuring the rate at which the water level drops in a hole full of water.

performance bond

(1) A guarantee that a contractor will perform a job according to the terms of the contract, or the bond will be forfeited. (2) A bond of the contractor in which a surety guarantees to the owner that the work will be performed in accordance with the contract documents. Except where prohibited by statute, the performance bond is frequently combined with the labor and material payment bond.

permanent load

The load, including a dead load or any fixed load, that is constant through the life of a structure.

permeability

(1) The property of a material that permits passage of water vapor. (2) The property of soil which permits the flow of water.

PERT schedule

An acronym for Project

Evaluation and Review Technique. The PERT schedule charts the activities and events anticipated in a work process.

pilaster

A column built within a wall, usually projecting beyond the wall.

pile

A slender timber, concrete, or steel structural element, driven, jetted, or otherwise embedded on end in the ground for the purpose of supporting a load.

pile bearing capacity

The load on a pile or group of piles that will theoretically produce failure if exceeded.

pile driver

A machine for driving piles, usually by repeated blows from a free-falling or driven hammer. A pile driver consists of a framework for holding and guiding the pile, a hammer, and a mobile plant to provide power.

pile foundation

The system of piles, and pile caps, that transfers structural loads to bearing soils or bedrock.

pile load test

A static load test of a pile or group of piles used to establish an allowable load. The applied load is usually 150% to 200% of the allowable load.

pinch bar

A steel bar with a chisel point at one end used as a lever for lifting or moving heavy objects.

pipe

(1) A hollow cylinder or tube for conveyance of a fluid. (2) From ASTM B 251-557: Seamless tube conforming to the particular dimensions commonly known as "Standard Pipe Size."

pipe column

A column made of steel pipe and often filled with concrete.

pitch

(1) An accumulation of resin in the wood cells in a more or less irregular patch. Pitch is classified for grading purposes as light, medium, heavy, or massed. (2) The angle or inclination of a roof, which varies according to a climate and roofing materials used. (3) The set, or projection, of teeth on alternate sides of a saw to provide clearance for its body.

pitched roof

A roof having one or more surfaces with a slope greater than 10 degrees from the horizontal.

plain concrete

(1) Concrete without reinforcement. (2) Reinforced concrete that does not conform to the definition of reinforced concrete. (3) Used loosely to designate concrete containing no admixture and prepared without special treatment.

plan

A two-dimensional graphic representation of the design, location, and dimensions of the project, or parts thereof, seen in a horizontal plane viewed from above.

plaster

(1) A cementitious material or combination of cementitious material and aggregate that, when mixed with a suitable amount of water, forms a plastic mass or paste. When applied to a surface, the paste adheres to it and subsequently hardens, preserving in a rigid state the form or texture imposed during the period of plasticity. (2) The placed and hardened mixture created in definition 1 above.

plaster bead

An edging, usually metal, to strengthen applied plaster at corners.

plasterboard

Any prefabricated board of plaster with paper facings. Plasterboard may be painted or used as a base for a finish coat of applied plaster. Also called "sheetrock" or "drywall."

plaster lath

A supporting structure for plaster, such as a wood lath, metal lath, or lath board.

platform

(1) A floor or surface raised above the adjacent level. (2) A landing in a stairway. (3) (OSHA) A working space for persons, elevated above the surrounding floor or ground level such as a balcony or platform for the operation of machinery or equipment.

platform framing

A framing system in which the vertical members are only a single story high, with each finished floor acting as a platform upon which the succeeding floor is constructed. Platform framing is the common method of house construction in North America.

plenum

A closed chamber used to distribute or collect warmed or cooled air in a forced-air heating/cooling system.

plinth

(1) A block or slab supporting a column or pedestal. (2) The base course of an external masonry wall when of different shape from the masonry in the wall proper.

plot

(1) A measured and defined area of land. (2) A ground plan of a building and adjacent land.

plumb

Vertical, or to make vertical.

plumbing

(1) The work or practice of installing in buildings the pipes, fixtures, and other apparatus required to bring in the water supplies and to remove water-borne wastes. (2) The process of setting a structure or object truly vertical.

plumbing fixture

A receptacle in a plumbing system, other than a trap, in which water or wastes are collected or retained for use and ultimately discharged to drainage.

plumbing system

The water supply and distribution pipes; plumbing fixtures and traps; soil, waste, and vent pipes; building drains and sewers; and respective devices and appurtenances within a building.

plywood

A flat panel made up of a number of thin sheets, or veneers, of wood, in which the grain direction of each ply, or layer, is at right angles to the one adjacent to it. The veneer sheets are united, under pressure, by a bonding agent.

pointing

(1) The finishing of joints in a masonry wall. (2) The material with which joints in masonry are finished.

polyethylene

A thermoplastic high-molecular-weight organic compound. In

sheet form, polyethylene is used as a protective cover for concrete surfaces during the curing period, a temporary enclosure for construction operations, and as a vapor barrier.

polystyrene foam
A low-cost, foamed plastic weighing about 1 lb. per cu. ft., with good insulating properties and resistant to grease.

polyurethane
Reaction product of an isocyanate with any of a wide variety of other compounds containing an active hydrogen group. Polyurethane is used to formulate tough, abrasion-resistant coatings.

polyvinyl chloride, PVC
A synthetic resin prepared by the polymerization of vinyl chloride, used in the manufacture of nonmetallic waterstops for concrete, floor coverings, pipe and fittings.

post
(1) A member used in a vertical position to support a beam or other structural member in a building, or as part of a fence. In lumber, 4x4s are often referred to as posts. Most grading rules define a post as having dimensions of five inches by five or more inches in width, with the width not more than two inches greater than the thickness. (2) Vertical formwork member used as a brace. Also called a "shore," "prop," "jack."

post-and-beam framing
Framing in which the horizontal members are supported by a distinct column, as opposed to a wall.

posttensioning
A method of prestressing reinforced concrete in which tendons are tensioned after the concrete has hardened.

precast
(1) A concrete member that is cast and cured in other than its final position. (2) The process of placing and finishing precast concrete.

precast concrete pile
A concrete pile, either reinforced or prestressed, cast elsewhere than its final position.

precast concrete wall panel
A concrete wall panel, either reinforced or prestressed, cast elsewhere than its final position.

prefabricated joint filler
A compressible material used to fill control, expansion, and contraction joints and may be used alone or as a backing for a joint sealant.

prehung door
A packaged unit consisting of a finished door on a frame with all necessary hardware and trim.

prequalification of bidders
The process of investigating the qualifications of prospective bidders on the basis of their experience, availability, and capability for the contemplated project, and approving qualified bidders.

pressure treating
A process of impregnating lumber or other wood products with various chemicals, such as preservatives and fire retardants, by forcing the chemicals into the structure of the wood using high pressure.

prestress
(1) To place a hardened concrete member or an assembly of units in a state of compression prior to application of service loads.
(2) The stress developed by prestressing, such as by pretensioning or posttensioning.

prestressed concrete
Concrete in which internal

stresses of such magnitude and distribution are introduced, that the tensile stresses resulting from the service loads are counteracted to a desired degree. In reinforced concrete, the prestress is commonly introduced by tensioning the tendons.

prestressed concrete wire
Steel wire with a very high tensile strength, used in prestressed concrete. The wire is initially stressed close to its tensile strength. Then some of this load is transferred to the concrete, by chemical bond or mechanical anchors, to compress the concrete.

prestressing
Applying a load to a structural element to increase its effectiveness in resisting working loads. Prestressed concrete is a common example.

pretensioned concrete
Tendons stressed in a form before placing concrete and tendons released to provide load transfer where concrete has achieved strength.

pretensioning
A method of prestressing reinforced concrete in which the tendons are tensioned before the concrete has hardened.

prime contract
Contract between owner and contractor for construction of the project or portion thereof.

prime contractor
Any contractor on a project having a contract directly with the owner.

product standard
A published standard that establishes: (1) dimensional requirements for standard sizes and types of various products; (2) technical requirements for the product; and (3) methods of testing, grading, and marking the product. The objective of product standards is to define requirements for specific products in accordance with the principal demands of the trade. Product standards are published by the National Bureau of Standards of the U.S. Department of Commerce, as well as by private organizations of manufacturers, distributors, and users.

professional engineer
Designation reserved, usually by law, for a person professionally qualified and duly licensed to perform structural, mechanical, electrical, sanitary, and civil engineering services.

professional liability insurance
Insurance coverage for the insured professional's legal liability for claims for damages sustained by others, allegedly as a result of negligent acts, errors, or omissions in the performance of professional services.

professional practice
The practice of one of the environmental design professions in which services are rendered within the framework of recognized professional ethics and standards and applicable legal requirements.

progress payment
Partial payment made during progress of the work on account of work completed and/or materials suitably stored.

progress schedule
A diagram, graph, or other pictorial or written schedule showing proposed and actual starting and completion times of the various elements of the work.

project
The total construction of which the work performed under the contract documents may be the whole or a part.

project certificate for payment
A statement from the architect to the owner confirming the amounts due individual contractors, where multiple contractors have separate direct agreements with the owner.

project cost
Total cost of the project, including construction cost, professional compensation, land costs, furnishings and equipment, financing, and other charges.

project engineer
The engineer, either in the architect's office or the consultant's office, as the case may be, designated to be responsible for the design and management of specific engineering portions of a project.

property insurance
Coverage for loss or damage to the work at the site caused by the perils of fire, lightning, extended coverage perils, vandalism and malicious mischief, and additional perils (as otherwise provided or requested). Property insurance may be written on (1) the completed value form in which the policy is written at the start of a project in a predetermined amount representing the insurable value of the work (consisting of the contract sum less the cost of specified exclusions) and adjusted to the final insurable cost on completion of the work, or (2) the reporting form in which the property values fluctuate during the policy term, requiring monthly statements showing the increase in value of work in place over the previous month.

public liability insurance
Insurance covering liability of the insured for negligent acts resulting in bodily injury, disease, or death of persons other than employees of the insured, and/or property damage.

pull box
(1) A box, with a removable cover, placed in electric raceway to facilitate the pulling of conductors through the raceway. (2) A manual activator for a fire alarm system.

purchase order
A document, sent to a seller by the buyer, listing details of the order, such as stock descriptions, price, and shipping instructions.

purge
To remove unwanted air or gas from a ductline, pipeline, container, space, or furnace, often by injecting an inert gas.

purlin
In roofs, a horizontal member supporting the common rafters.

pylon
(1) A steel tower used to support electrical high-tension lines. (2) A movable tower for carrying lights. (3) A truncated pyramidal form used in gateways to Egyptian monuments.

Q

quadrant
(1) One quarter of the circumference of a circle; an arc of 90 degrees. (2) An angle measuring instrument.

quality control
A system of procedures and standards by which a constructor, product manufacturer, materials

processor, or the like, monitors the properties of the finished work.

quantity survey
Detailed listing and quantities of all items of material and equipment necessary to construct a project.

quotation
A price quoted by a contractor, subcontractor, material supplier, or vendor to furnish materials, labor, or both.

R

raceway
Any furrow or channel constructed to loosely house electrical conductors. These conduits may be flexible or rigid, metallic or non-metallic and are designed to protect the cables they enclose.

radiator
A visually exposed heat exchanger consisting of a series of pipes that allows the circulation of steam or hot water. The heat from the steam or hot water is given up to the air surrounding the pipes.

rail
(1) A horizontal member supported by vertical posts, i.e., a handrail along a stairway.
(2) A horizontal piece of wood, framed into vertical stiles, such as a panelled door.

raised flooring system
A floor constructed of removable panels supported by stringers allowing easy access to the space below.

ready-mixed concrete
Concrete manufactured for delivery to a purchaser in a plastic and unhardened state.

real estate
Property in the form of land and all improvements such as buildings and paving.

real property
Land including everything on it and beneath it with some rights to the airspace directly above.

receptacle
A contact device installed in an electric outlet box for the connection of portable equipment or appliances.

recessed fixture
A lamp fixture which has its bottom edge flush with the ceiling.

record drawings
Construction drawings revised to show significant changes made during the construction process, usually based on marked-up prints, drawings, and other data furnished by the contractor to the architect. Record drawings are preferable to as-built drawings.

reference mark
A supplementary mark close to a survey station. One or more such marks are located and recorded with sufficient accuracy so that the original station can be re-established from the references.

reinforced concrete
Concrete containing adequate reinforcement, prestressed or not prestressed, and designed on the assumption that the two materials act together in resisting forces.

reinforced concrete masonry
Concrete masonry construction in which steel reinforcement is so embedded that the materials act together in resisting tensile, compressive, and/or shear stresses.

reinforced T-beam
A concrete T-beam strengthened internally with steel rods to resist tensile and/or shear stresses.

reinforcement

Bars, wires, strands, and other slender members embedded in concrete in such a manner that the reinforcement and the concrete act together in resisting forces.

reinforcing bar

A steel bar, usually with manufactured deformations, used in concrete and masonry construction to provide additional strength.

release of lien

Instrument executed by a person or entity supplying labor, materials, or professional services on a project which releases that person's or entity's mechanic's lien against the project property.

replacement value

The estimated cost to replace an existing building based on current construction costs.

resident engineer

An engineer employed by the owner to represent the owner's interests at the project site during the construction phase. The term is frequently used on projects in which a governmental agency is involved.

resilient channel

A mounting device with flexible connectors used for fastening gypsum board to studs or joists which helps to reduce the transmission of vibrations.

resilient flooring

A durable floor covering that has the ability to resume its original shape, such as linoleum.

restoration

A series of actions to bring an object or building back to its original condition.

retainage

A sum withheld from progress payments to the contractor in accordance with the terms of the owner-contractor agreement.

retaining wall

(1) A structure used to sustain the pressure of the earth behind it. (2) Any wall subjected to lateral pressure other than wind pressure.

return system

A series of ducts, pipes, or passages that returns a substance, whether it be air or water, to the source for reuse.

rib

(1) One of a number of parallel structural members backing sheathing. (2) The portion of a T-beam which projects below the slab. (3) In deformed reinforcing bars, the deformations or the longitudinal parting ridge.

ridge beam

A horizontal timber to which the tops of rafters are fastened.

right-of-way

A strip of land, including the surface and overhead or underground space, which is granted by deed or easement for the construction and maintenance of specific linear elements such as power and telephone lines, roadways and driveways, and gas or water lines.

rigid metal conduit

A raceway constructed for the pulling in or withdrawing of wires or cables after the conduit is in place, made of standard weight metal pipe permitting the cutting of standard threads.

rise and run

The angle of inclination or slope of a member or structure, expressed as the ratio of the vertical rise to the horizontal run.

riser

A vertical member between two stair treads.

roof-deck

(1) The foundation or base upon which the entire roofing system is built. Types of decks include steel, concrete, cement, and wood. (2) A flat open portion atop a roof, such as a terrace or sundeck.

roof hatch

A weather-tight assembly with a hinged cover, used to provide access to a roof.

roofing

Any material that acts as a *roof covering* making it impervious to the weather such as shingles, tile, or slate.

roof live load

Any external loads that may be applied to a roof deck, such as rain, snow, construction equipment, and personnel.

S **saddle**

(1) A fitted device used with hangers to support a pipe. (2) A series of bends in a pipe over an obstruction. (3) A short horizontal member set on top of a post as a seat for a girder. (4) Any hollow-backed structure with a shape suggesting a saddle, as a ridge connected to two higher elevations or a saddle roof.

safe load

The maximum load on a structure that does not produce stresses greater than those allowable.

safety fuse

A cord containing black powder or other burning medium encased in flexible wrapping and used to convey fire at a predetermined and uniform rate for firing blasting caps.

safety nosing

An abrasive, nonslip stair nosing whose surface is flush with the tread against which it is placed.

roof pitch

The slope of a roof expressed as the ratio of the rise of the roof to the horizontal span. More roofing material is required to cover the roof when the slope or pitch is great.

rough flooring

Any materials used to construct an unfinished floor.

roughing-out

A preliminary shaping operation in carpentry.

"R" Value

A measure of a material's resistance to heat flow given a thickness of material. The term is the reciprocal of the "U" value. The higher the "R" value the more effective the particular insulation.

safety switch

In an interior electric wiring system, a switch enclosed within a metal box but having a handle which protrudes through the box to allow switching to be accomplished from outside the box.

safety tread

A tread on a stair which has a roughened surface or roughened inserts to prevent a foot from slipping.

safe working pressure

The maximum working pressure at which a vessel, boiler, flask, or cylinder is allowed to operate, as determined by the American Society of Mechanical Engineers Boiler Code, and usually so identified on each individual unit.

sand

(1) Granular material passing the 3/8-inch sieve and almost entirely passing the No. 4 (4.75-millimeter) sieve and predominantly retained on the

No. 200 (75-micrometer) sieve, and resulting from natural disintegration and abrasion of rock or processing of completely friable sandstone. (2) That portion of an aggregate passing the No. 4 (4.75-millimeter) sieve, and resulting from natural disintegration and abrasion or rock or processing of completely friable sandstone. *Note:* The definitions are alternatives to be applied under differing circumstances. Definition (1) is applied to an entire aggregate either in a natural condition or after processing. Definition (2) is applied to a portion of an aggregate. Requirements for properties and grading should be stated in the specifications. Fine aggregate produced by crushing rock, gravel, or slag commonly is known as manufactured sand.

sandblast

A system of cutting or abrading a surface such as concrete by a stream of sand ejected from a nozzle at high speed by compressed air. Sandblasting is often used for cleanup of horizontal construction joints or for exposure of aggregate in architectural concrete.

sand filter

A bed of sand laid over graded gravel, used as a filter for a water supply.

sand finish

(1) In plastering, a textured final coat, usually containing sand, lime putty, and Keene's cement. (2) A smooth finish derived from rubbing and sanding the final coat.

sandwich panel

(1) A panel formed by bonding two thin facings to a thick, and usually lightweight, core. Typical facing materials include plywood, single veneers, hardboard, plastics, laminates, and various metals, such as aluminum or stainless steel. Typical core materials include plastic foam sheets, rubber, and formed honeycombs of paper, metal, or cloth. (2) A prefabricated panel which is a layered composite, formed by attaching two thin facings to a thicker core, such as a precast concrete panel, consisting of two layers of concrete separated by a nonstructural insulating core.

sash, window sash

The framework of a window that holds the glass.

scaffolding

A temporary structure for the support of deck forms, cartways, and/or workmen, such as an elevated platform for supporting workmen, tools, and materials. Adjustable metal scaffolding is frequently adapted for shoring in concrete work.

scale drawing

A drawing in which all dimensions are reduced proportionately according to a predetermined scale, such as 1 inch = 40 feet.

schedule of values

A statement furnished by the contractor to the architect reflecting the portions of the contract sum allocated to the various portions of the work and used as the basis for reviewing the contractor's applications for payment.

schematic design phase, schematic drawing

The phase of the architect's services in which the architect consults with the owner to ascertain the requirements of the project and prepares schematic design studies, consisting of drawings and other documents illustrating the scale and relationship of the project components to the owner. The architect also submits to the owner a statement of probable construction cost base don current area, volume, or other unit costs.

screed
(1) To strike off concrete lying above the desired plane or shape. (2) A tool for striking off the concrete surface, sometimes referred to as a strikoff.

scupper
Any opening in a wall, parapet, bridge curb, or slab that provides an outlet through which excess water can drain.

sealed bid
A bid, based on contract documents, that is submitted sealed for opening at a designated time and place.

sealer
(1) Any liquid applied to the surface of wood, paper, or plaster to prevent it from absorbing moisture, paint, or varnish. (2) A liquid coating applied over bitumen or creosote to restrict it from bleeding through other paints. (3) A final application of asphalt or concrete to protect against moisture. (4) Any liquid coating used to seal the pores of the surface to which it is applied.

seam
A joint between two sheets of material, such as metal.

seasoned
(1) Timber that is not green, having a moisture content of 19% or less, and is air or kiln-dried. (2) Cured or hardened concrete.

section
(1) A topographical measure of land area, equal to one mile square, or 640 acres. One of the 36 divisions in a township. (2) The most desired pieces of veneer, clipped to standard widths of 54 and 27 inches, because of the ease of using

them in assembling a panel. The actual width may vary form 48-54 inches, or 24-27 inches. (3) A part of a flat log raft. (4) A drawing of a surface revealed by an imaginary plane cut through the project, or portion thereof, in such a manner as to show the composition of the surface as it would appear if the part intervening between the cut plane and the eye of the observer were removed. (5) A subdivision of a division of the specifications which covers a unit of work.

sectional overhead doors
Doors made of horizontally hinged panels that roll into an overhead position on tracks, usually spring assisted.

selected bidder
The bidder selected by the owner for discussions relative to the possible award of a construction contract.

select material
Excavated soil suitable for use as a foundation for a granular base course of a road or for bedding around pipes.

separate contract
One of several prime contracts on a job. A separate contract is not a subcontract.

septic tank
A watertight receptacle that receives the discharge from a drainage system, or part thereof, and is designed and constructed to separate solids from the liquid, digesting organic matter through a period of detention.

service box
Within a building, a metal box located at that point where the electric service conductors enter the building.

service door, service entrance
An exterior door in a building, intended primarily for deliveries,

for removal of waste, or for the use of service personnel.

service drop
The overhead conductors which connect the electric supply or communication line to the building being served.

service elevator
An elevator intended for combined passenger and freight use.

service entrance switch
The circuit breaker or switch, with fuses and accessories, located near the point of entrance of supply conductors to a building and intended to be the main control and cut-off for the supply to that building.

sewage
Any liquid-borne waste which contains animal or vegetable matter in suspension or solution. Sewage may include chemicals in solution, and ground, surface, or storm water may be added as it is admitted to, or passes through, the sewers.

sewer
(1) Generally, an underground conduit in which waste matter is carried in a liquid medium. (2) A pipeline in which sewage is conveyed.

sewerage
The entire works required to collect, treat, and dispose of sewage, including the sewer system, pumping stations, and treatment plant.

shake
(1) Roofing material produced from wood, usually cedar, with at least one surface with a grain split face. (2) A crack in lumber due to natural causes.

shear
(1) An internal force tangential to the plane on which it acts. (2) The relative displacement of adjacent planes in a single

member. (3) To cut metal with two opposing passing blades or with one blade passing a fixed edge. (4) The tool used for the operation in definition 3.

shear connector
(1) A welded stud, spiral bar, short length of channel, or any other similar connector which resists horizontal shear between components of a composite beam. (2) A timber connector.

shear wall, shearwall
A wall portion of a structural frame intended to resist lateral forces, such as earthquake, wind, and blast, acting in or parallel to the plane of the wall.

sheathed cable
Electric cable protected by non-conductive covering, such as vinyl.

sheathing
(1) The material forming the contact face of forms. Also called "lagging" or "sheeting." (2) Plywood, waferboard, oriented strand board, or lumber used to close up side walls, floors, or roofs preparatory to the installation of finish materials on the surface. The sheathing grades are also commonly used for pallets, crates, and certain industrial products.

sheave
(1) The grooved wheel of a pulley, or block. (2) The entire assembly over which a rope or cable is passed, including not only the pulley wheel but also its shaft bearings, and side plates.

shed
A small, usually roughly constructed shelter or storage building, sometimes having one or more open sides, and sometimes built as a lean-to.

shed dormer
A dormer window having

vertical framing projecting from a sloping roof, and an eave line parallel to the eave line of the principal roof. A shed dormer is designed to provide more space under a roof than a gabled dormer would provide.

sheeting

(1) Planks used to line the sides of an excavation, such as for shoring and bracing. (2) 7/8-inch tongue-and-groove board, (3) Sheet piling. (4) A form of plastic in which the thickness is very small in proportion to length and width and in which the plastic is present as a continuous phase throughout, with or without filler.

sheet metal

Metal, usually galvanized steel but also including aluminum, copper, and stainless steel, which has been rolled to any given thickness between 0.06 and 0.249 inches and cut into rectangular (usually 4 feet by 8 feet) sections which are then used such as in the fabrication of ductwork, pipe, and gutters.

sheet-metal work

The fabrication, installation, and/or final product such as the ductwork of a heating or cooling system, as performed or produced by a worker skilled in that trade.

sheet pile

A pile in the form of a plank driven in close contact or interlocking with others to provide a tight wall to resist the lateral pressure of water, adjacent earth, or other materials. A sheet pile may be tongued and grooved if made of timber or concrete, or interlocking if made of metal.

shell

(1) Structural framework. (2) In stressed-skin construction, the outer skin applied over the frame members. (3) Any hollow construction when accomplished with a very thin curved plate or slab. (4) The outer portion of a hollow masonry unit when laid.

shingle

A roof-covering unit made of asphalt, wood, slate, asbestos, cement, or other material cut into stock sizes and applied on sloping roofs in an overlapping pattern.

shoe

(1) Any piece of timber, metal, or stone receiving the lower end of virtually any member. Also called a "soleplate." (2) A metal device protecting the foot, or point, of a pile. (3) A metal plate used at the base of an arch or truss to resist horizontal thrust. (4) A ground plate forming a link of a track, or bolted to a track line. (5) A support for a bulldozer blade or other digging edge to prevent cutting down. (6) A cleanup device following the buckets of a ditching machine. (7) A short section used at the base of a downspout to direct the flow of water away from a wall.

shop drawings

Drawings, diagrams, schedules, and other data specially prepared for the work by the contractor or any subcontractor, manufacturer, supplier, or distributor to illustrate some portion of the work.

shoring

(1) Props or posts of timber or other material in compression used for the temporary support of excavations, formwork, or unsafe structures. (2) The process of erecting shores.

sill

(1) The horizontal member forming the bottom of a window or exterior doorframe. (2) As applied to general construction, the lowest member of the frame of the

structure, resting on the foundation and supporting the frame.

simple beam
A beam without restraint or continuity at its supports.

single-pole switch
An electric switch with one movable and one fixed contact.

site
The geographical location of the project, usually defined by legal boundary lines.

site built
The construction of a structure at the site where it is to remain.

site drainage
(1) An underground system of piping carrying rainwater or other wastes to a public sewer. (2) The water so drained.

site plan
A plan of the area at the proposed construction showing the building outline, parking, work areas, and/or property lines.

sized lumber
Lumber uniformly manufactured to net surfaced sizes. Sized lumber may be rough, surfaced, or partly surfaced on one or more faces.

skim coat
A thin coat of plaster, usually either the finish coat or the leveling coat.

slab
(1) A flat, horizontal or nearly so, molded layer of plain or reinforced concrete, usually of uniform but sometimes of variable thickness, either on the ground or supported by beams, columns, walls, or other framework. (2) The outside, lengthwise cut on a log.

slab on grade
A concrete slab placed on grade, sometimes having insulation board or an impervious membrane beneath it.

slab-on-grade construction
A type of construction in which the floor is a concrete slab poured after plumbing and other equipment is installed.

slump
A measure of consistency of freshly mixed concrete, mortar, or stucco equal to the subsidence measured to the nearest 1/4 in. (6 mm) of the molded specimen immediately after removal of the slump cone.

smoke and fire vent
A vent cover, installed on a roof, which opens automatically when activated by a heat-sensitive device, such as a fusible link.

snap tie
A proprietary concrete wall-form tie, the end of which can be twisted or snapped off after the forms have been removed.

snow load
The live load allowed by local code, used to design roofs in areas subjected to snowfall.

sod
The upper layer of soil containing roots of glass.

soffit block
A special concrete masonry unit used under a beam and slab concrete floor to conceal the beam soffits and provide a flat ceiling.

soffit board
A board that forms the soffit of a cornice.

soil
A generic term for unconsolidated natural surface material above bedrock.

soil pipe

A pipe that conveys the discharge from water closets or similar fixtures to the sanitary sewer system.

soldier

(1) A vertical wale used to strengthen or align formwork or excavations. (2) A masonry unit set on end so its long, narrow face is vertical on the face of the wall.

soldier beam

A rolled-steel section driven into the ground to support a horizontally sheeted earth bank.

solid-core door

A door having a core of solid wood or mineral composition, as opposed to a hollow-core door.

solid masonry wall

A wall built of solid masonry units with all joints filled with mortar and no hollow wythes.

Sonotube®

A product consisting of a preformed casing made of laminated paper used to form cylindrical piers or columns.

span

(1) The distance between supports of a member. (2) The measure of distance between two supporting members.

spandrel beam

A beam in the perimeter of a building, spanning between columns and usually supporting floor or roof loads.

special conditions

A section of the conditions of the contract, other than general conditions and supplementary conditions, which may be prepared to describe conditions unique to a particular project.

specifications

A part of the contract documents contained in the project manual consisting of written requirements for materials, equipment, construction systems, standards, and workmanship. Under the Uniform Construction Index, the specifications comprise sixteen divisions.

splice

Connection of two similar materials to another by lapping, welding, gluing, mechanical couplers, or other means, such as the connection of welded wire fabric by lapping and the connection of piles by mechanical couplers.

split-face block

Concrete masonry unit with one or more faces produced by purposeful fracturing of the unit, to provide architectural effects in masonry wall construction.

sprayed fireproofing

An insulating material sprayed directly onto steel structural members with or without wire mesh reinforcing to provide a fire-endurance rating.

spreader

(1) A piece of wood or metal used to hold the sides of a form apart until the concrete is placed. (2) A brace between two wales. (3) A device for spreading gravel or crushed stone for a pavement base course. (4) A stiffening member used to keep door or window frames in proper alignment during shipment and installation.

spread footing

A generally rectangular prism of concrete larger in lateral dimensions than the column or wall it supports, to distribute the load of a column or wall to the subgrade.

sprinklered

Said of an area of a building that is protected from fire by an automatic sprinkler system.

stack vent

(1) The extension of a soil or waste stack above the highest horizontal drain or fixture connected to the stack. (2) A device installed through a built-up roof covering to allow entrapped water vapor to escape from the insulation.

staging

(1) A temporary working platform against or within a building for construction, repairs, or demolition. Also called "scaffolding." (2) A temporary working platform supported by the temporary timbers in a trench.

stair

(1) A single step. (2) A series of steps or flights of steps connected by landings, used for passage from one level to another.

staking out

The process of driving stakes for batter boards to locate the limits of an excavation.

standpipe

(1) A pipe or tank connected to a water system and used to absorb surges that can occur. (2) A pipe or tank used to store water for emergency use, such as fire fighting.

standpipe system

A system of tanks, pumps, fire department connections, piping, hose connections, connections to an automatic sprinkler system, and an adequate supply of water used in fire protection.

static load

The weight of a single stationary body or the combined weights of all stationary bodies in a structure, such as the load of a stationary vehicle on a roadway. During construction, the static load is the combined weight of forms, stringers, joists, reinforcing bars, and the actual concrete to be placed.

steam heating system

A heating system in which heat is transferred from a boiler or other source, through pipes, to a heat exchanger. The steam can be below, at, or above atmospheric pressure.

steel

Any of a number of alloys of iron and carbon, with small amounts of other metals added to achieve special properties. The alloys are generally hard, strong, durable, and malleable.

steel-frame construction

Construction in which steel columns, girders, and beams comprise the structural supporting elements.

steel sheet piling

Interlocking rolled-steel sections driven vertically into the ground to serve as sheeting in an excavation or to cut off the flow of ground water.

steep asphalt

Roofing asphalt with a high softening point, used on surfaces with a steep slope.

stepped footing

(1) A wall footing with horizontal steps to accommodate a sloping grade or bearing stratum. (2) A column or wall footing composed of two or more steps on top of one another to distribute the load.

stock lumber

Lumber cut to standard sizes and readily available from suppliers.

stone

(1) Individual blocks of rock processed by shaping, cutting, or sizing, for use in masonry work. (2) Fragments of rock excavated, usually by blasting, from natural deposits and further processed by crushing and sizing, for use as aggregate. (3) A carborundum or other

natural or artificial hone used to sharpen cutting edges of tools.

storm drain

A drain used to convey rain water, subsurface water, condensate, or similar discharge, but not sewage or industrial waste.

story

(1) That part of a building between the upper surface of a floor and the upper surface of the floor above. Building codes differ in designations applied when a part of a "story" is below grade. (2) A major division in the height of a building even when created by architectural features, such as windows, rather than horizontal divisons. For example, an area may be "two stories high."

stranded wire

A group of fine wires used as a single electric conductor.

strapping

(1) Flexible metal bands used to bind units for ease of handling and storage. (2) Another name for "furring."

stretcher bond, running bond, stretching bond

A masonry bond with all courses laid as stretchers and with the vertical joint of one course falling midway between the joints of the courses above and below.

strike

(1) In masonry, to cut off the excess mortar at the face of a joint with a trowel stroke. (2) To remove formwork. (3) A work stoppage by a body of workers.

stringer

(1) A secondary flexural member parallel to the longitudinal axis of a bridge or other structure. (2) A horizontal timber used to support joists or other cross members.

strip

(1) Board lumber one inch in nominal thickness and less than four inches in width, frequently the product of ripping a wider piece of lumber. The most common sizes are 1x2 and 1x3. (2) To remove formwork or a mold. (3) To remove an old finish with paint removers. (4) To damage the threads on a nut or bolt.

strip foundation

A continuous foundation of which the length considerably exceeds the breadth.

structural frame

All the members of a building or other structure used to transfer imposed loads to the ground.

structural glued-laminated timber

A wooden structural member made from selected boards strongly glued together.

structural joists and planks

Lumber two, three, or four inches thick and six inches or wider, graded for its strength properties. Such planks are used primarily for joists in residential construction and graded, in descending order, select structural, #1, #2, and #3. The #1 and #2 grades are usually marketed in combination as #2 & Better.

structural light framing

A category of dimension lumber up to four inches in width which provides higher bending strength ratios for use in engineered applications, such as roof trusses. The lumber is often referred to by its fiber strength class, such as 175f for #1 & Better Douglas Fir, or as stress-rated stock.

structural lumber

Any lumber with nominal dimensions of 2 inches or more

in thickness and 4 inches or more in width and which is intended for use where working stresses are required. The working stress is based on the strength of the piece and the use for which it is intended, such as beams, stringers, joists, planks, posts, and girders.

structural steel
Steel rolled in a variety of shapes and manufactured for use as loadbearing structural members.

structural steel fastener
Any fastener used to connect structural steel members to each other, or to supporting elements, or with concrete to make a composite section.

structural timbers
Structural lumber with a nominal dimension of 5 inches or more on each side, used mainly as posts or columns.

structure
A combination of units fabricated and interconnected in accordance with a design and intended to support vertical and horizontal loads.

stud
(1) A vertical member of appropriate size (2x4 to 4x10 in.) or (50x100 to 100x250 mm) and spacing (16 to 30 in.) or (400 to 750 mm) to support sheathing or concrete forms. (2) A framing member, usually cut to a precise length at the mill, designed to be used in framing building walls with little or no trimming before it is set in place. Studs are most often 2x4's, but 2x3's, 2x6's and other sizes are also included in the stud category. Studs may be of wood, steel, or composite materials. (3) A bolt having one end firmly attached.

stud bolt
A bolt firmly anchored in, and

projecting from, a structure, such as a concrete pad, and used to secure another member, as in bolting a sill plate to concrete.

stud partition
A partition in which studs are used as the structural base. A wallboard is usually applied over the studs.

subbase
(1) A layer in a pavement system between the subgrade and base course or between the subgrade and the concrete pavement. (2) The bottom front strip or molding of a baseboard.

sub-bidder, subbidder
A person or entity who submits a bid to a bidder for materials or labor for a portion of the work.

subcontract
An agreement between a prime contractor and a subcontractor for a portion of the work at the site.

subcontractor
A person or entity who has a direct contract with the contractor to perform any of the work at the site.

subflooring
Plywood sheets or construction grade lumber used to construct a subfloor.

subgrade
(1) The soil prepared and compacted to support a structure or a pavement system. (2) The elevation of the bottom of a trench in which a sewer or pipeline is laid.

submersible pump
A type of pump with the motor and liquid handling unit in a watertight case that can be lowered directly into the liquid to be pumped.

subsidence
Settlement over a large area as opposed to settlement of a single structure.

subsoil

The bed or stratum of soil lying immediately below the surface soil and which is usually devoid of humus or organic matter.

substrate

An underlying material that supports or is bonded to another material on its surface.

substructure

The foundation of a building that supports the superstructure.

subsurface course

The top course of a pavement that acts as a wearing surface.

successful bidder

The bidder chosen by the owner for the award of a construction contract.

superintendent

The contractor's representative at the site who is responsible for continuous field supervision, coordination, completion of the work, and, unless another person is designated in writing by the contractor to the owner and the architect, for the prevention of accidents.

superstructure

(1) That part of a building or other structure above the foundation. (2) That part of a bridge above the beam seats or the spring line of an arch.

supervision

Direction of the work by the contractor's personnel. Supervision is neither a duty nor a responsibility of the architect as part of professional services.

supplemental services

The items in a schedule of designated architectural services not customarily included in the sequence from predesign through post-construction, such as renderings, value analyses, energy studies, project promotion, and expert testimony.

supplementary conditions

A part of the contract documents which supplements and may also modify, change, add to, or delete from provisions of the general conditions. Preferable to supplemental conditions.

supplier

A person or entity who supplies materials or equipment for the work, including that fabricated to a special design, but who does not perform labor at the site.

surety

A person or entity who promises in writing to make good the debt or default of another.

surety bond

A legal instrument under which one party agrees to answer to another party for the debt, default, or failure to perform of a third party.

survey

(1) To do boundary, topographic, and/or utility mapping of a site. (2) To measure an existing building. (3) To analyze a building for the use of space. (4) To determine the owner's requirements for a project. (5) To investigate and report on required data for a project.

suspended acoustical ceiling

A ceiling designed to be sound absorbent and to be hung from the structural slab or beams in an area.

switch

A device used to open, close, or change the connection of an electric circuit.

switchboard

A large panel, frame, or assembly with switches, overcurrent and other protective devices, fuses, and instruments mounted on the face and/or back. Switchboards are usually accessible from front or rear and are not intended to be mounted in cabinets.

switchgear

Any switching and interrupting devices combined with associated control, regulating, metering, and protective devices, used primarily in connection with the generation, transmission, distribution, and conversion of electric power.

T

tar-and-gravel roofing

Built-up roofing made up of gravel or sand, poured over a heavy coating of coal-tar pitch applied to an underlayer of felt.

T-bar

A light-gauge, T-shaped member used to support panels in a suspended acoustical ceiling.

temporary shoring

Shoring installed to support a structure while it is being built and removed when construction is finished.

tensile strength

Maximum unit stress which a material is capable of resisting under axial tensile loading, based on the cross-sectional area of the specimen before loading.

terminal

(1) An element attached to the end of a conductor or to a piece of electric equipment to serve as a connection for an external conductor. (2) A decorative element forming the end of an item of construction. (3) A point of departure or arrival such as a railway or airport terminal.

terminal box

A box, on a piece of electrical equipment, that contains leads from the equipment, ready for connection to a power source. The box is usually provided with a removable cover.

terneplate

Sheet steel-coated with an alloy of lead and tin, used chiefly in roofing.

test cylinder

A sample of a concrete mix, cast in a standard cylindrical shape, cured under controlled or job conditions and used to determine the compressive strength of the mix after a specified time interval.

test piling

A foundation piling that is installed on the site of a proposed construction project and used to conduct load tests to determine the size and quantity of pilings needed for the actual structures.

test pit

An excavation made to examine the subsurface conditions on a potential construction site. Also, a pit excavated to inspect the condition of existing foundations.

thermal break, thermal barrier

An element of low conductivity placed between two conductive materials to limit heat flow, for use in metal windows or curtain walls which are to be used in cold climates.

thermostat

An electric switch controlled by an element that responds to temperature, used in heating and/or cooling systems.

thin-set
Descriptive of bonding, materials for tile which are applied in a layer approximately 1/8 inch or 3 mm thick.

thin-wall conduit
Electric conduit with a wall thickness that will not support threads. Sections are joined by couplings held in place by set screws.

threshold
(1) A shaped strip on the floor between the jambs of a door, used to separate different types of flooring or to provide weather protection at an exterior door. (2) The level of lighting or volume of illumination which permits an object to be seen a specified percentage of the time with specified accuracy.

tie
A thin rectangular unit used as a finish for walls, floors or roofs, such as ceramic tile, structural clay tile, asphalt tile, cork tile, resilient tile, and roofing tile.

tie beam
(1) A concrete beam that connects individual pile caps or spread footings. (2) A horizontal timber that connects the lower end of two opposite rafters to prevent spreading.

tie wire
(1) A wire used to hold forms together so they will not spread when filled with concrete. (2) A single-strand wire used to tie reinforcing in place or metal lath to a column.

tilt-up, tilt-up-construction
A method of concrete construction in which members are cast horizontally at a location adjacent to their eventual position and tilted into place after removal of molds.

timber connector
One of a variety of metal connectors used in conjunction with bolts to form connections of timbers. Usually the bolt holds the timbers together while the connector prevents slippage.

time
Term defined in reference to a construction contract as time limits or periods stated in the contract. A provision in a construction contract that "time is the essence of the contract" signifies that the parties consider punctual performance within the time limits or periods in the contract to be a vital part of the performance. Failure to perform on time is a breach for which the injured party is entitled to damages in the amount of loss sustained.

time of completion
Date established in the contract, by calendar date or by number of days, for substantial completion of the work.

tin roofing
A roof covering of tinplate or terneplate.

title insurance
Insurance, offered by a company, that a title to property is clear or that it can be cleared by resolving certain defects.

title search
A search into the historical ownership record of a property to establish its true ownership and check the existence of liens or easements which might affect the sale of the property.

toe
(1) Any projection from the base of a construction or object to give it increased bearing and stability. (2) That part of the base of a retaining wall that projects beyond the face away from the retained material.

(3) The lower portion of the lock stile. (4) The junction between the base metal and the face of a filled weld. (5) To drive a nail at an oblique angle. (6) That portion of sheeting below the excavated material. (7) The part of a blasting hole furthest from the face.

tongue and groove
(1) Lumber machined to have a groove on one side and a protruding tongue on the other, so that pieces will fit snugly together, with the tongue of one fitting into the groove of the other. (2) A type of lumber or precast concrete pile having mated projecting and grooved edges to provide a tight fit, abbreviated "T & G."

ton of refrigeration
A measure of refrigerating effect equal to 12,000 BTU per hour.

top plate
A member on top of a stud wall on which joists rest to support an additional floor or form a ceiling.

topsoil
The surface layer of soil, usually contains organic matter.

total float
In CPM terminology, the difference between the time available to accomplish an activity and the estimated time required.

transfer bond
In pretensioning, the bond stress resulting from the transfer of stress from the tendon to the concrete.

transformer
An electric device with two or more coupled windings, with or without a magnetic core, for introducing mutual coupling between circuits, generally used to convert a power supply at one voltage to another voltage.

transit
A surveyor's instrument used to measure or lay out horizontal or vertical angles, or measure distance or difference in elevation.

transom
A glazed or solid panel over a door or window, usually hinged and used for ventilation. The transom and bar may be removable for passage of large objects.

trap
(1) A plumbing fixture so constructed that, when installed in a system, a water seal will form and prevent backflow of air or gas but permit free flow of liquids. (2) A removable section of stage floor.

trim
Millwork, primarily moldings and/or trim to finish off and cover joints around window and door openings.

trimmer
(1) A short beam that supports one or more joists or beams at an opening in the floor, a header. (2) A beam or joist inserted in a floor on the long side of a stair opening and supporting a header. (3) Shaped ceramic tile used as bases, caps, corners, moldings, and angles.

trowel finish
The smooth finish surface produced by troweling.

truss
A structural component composed of a combination of members, usually in a triangular arrangement, to form a rigid framework; often used to support a roof.

tubular scaffolding
Scaffolding manufactured from galvanized steel or aluminum tube and connected by clamps.

tubular-welded-frame scaffold
A scaffold system using prefabricated welded sections that serve as posts and horizontal bearers. The prefabricated sections are braced laterally with tubes and bars.

turn-key contract
A contract similar to design and construct except the contractor is responsible for all financing and owns the work until the project is complete and turned over to the owner.

two-way reinforcement, two-way system
A system of reinforcement. Bars, rods, or wires are placed at right angles to each other in a slab and are intended to resist stresses due to bending of the slab in two directions.

two-way slab
A reinforced concrete slab in which the main reinforcing runs in two directions, parallel to the length and width of the panel.

U

UL Label
A seal of certification attached by Underwriters' Laboratories, Inc. to building materials, electrical wiring and components, storage vessels, and other devices, attesting that the item has been rated according to performance tests on such products, is from a production lot that made use of materials and processes identical to those of comparable items that have passed fire, electrical hazard, and other safety tests, and is subject to the UL re-examination service.

ultimate load
(1) The maximum load a structure can bear before its failure due to buckling of column members or failure of some component. (2) The load at which a unit or structure fails.

unbalanced bid
A contractor's bid based on increased unit costs for tasks to be performed early and decreased unit costs for later tasks. The unbalanced bid is used in an attempt to get money early to finance later parts of a job.

undercoat
(1) A coat of paint that improves the seal of wood or of a previous coat of paint, and provides a superior adhesive base for the topcoat. (2) A paint used as a base for enamel. (3) A colored primer paint.

underdrain
A drain installed in porous fill under a slab to drain off ground water.

underpinning
To provide new substructure support beneath a column or a wall, without removing the superstructure, in order to increase the load capacity or return it to its former design limits.

uniform load
A load distributed uniformly over a structure or a portion of a structure.

union
(1) A confederation of individuals who share the same trade or similar trades and who have joined together for a common purpose. (2) A pipe fitting used to join two pipes without turning either pipe, consisting of a collar piece which is slipped on one pipe, a shoulder piece which is threaded or soldered on that pipe and

against which the collar piece bears, and a thread piece which is fixed to the other pipe. An outside thread on the thread piece and an internal thread on the collar piece are used to make the joint. A gasket is sometimes incorporated as a fluid seal.

unit price

Amount stated in the bid as a price per unit of measurement for materials or services as described in the bidding documents or in the proposed contract documents.

unit price contract

A construction contract in which payment is based on the work done and an agreed on unit price. The unit price contract is usually only used where quantities can be accurately measured.

V **value engineering**

A process of reviewing plans and specifications for the purpose of reducing the final cost without changing the intended utility or overall appearance.

vapor barrier

Material used to prevent the passage of vapor or moisture into a structure or another material thus preventing condensation within them.

variable-volume air system

An air-conditioning system that automatically regulates the quantity of air supplied to each controlled area according to the needs of the different zones, with preset minimum and maximum values based on the load in each area.

variance

A written authorization from the responsible agency permitting construction in a manner which is not allowed by a code or ordinance.

utility

(1) A grade of softwood lumber used when a combination of strength and economy is desired. It is suitable for many uses in construction but lacks the strength of Standard, the next highest grade in light framing, and is not allowed in some applications. (2) A grade of Idaho White Pine boards, equivalent to #4 Common in other species. (3) A grade of fir veneer that allows a white speck and more defects than are allowed in D grade. Utility grade veneer is not permitted in panels manufactured under Product Standard PS-1-83.

utility pole

An outdoor pole installed by a utility company for the support of telephone, electric, and other cables.

vendor

A person or entity who furnishes materials or equipment not fabricated to a special design for the work.

veneer

(1) A masonry facing which is attached to the backup but not so bonded as to act with it under load. (2) Wood peeled, sawn, or sliced into sheets of a given constant thickness and combined with glue to produce plywood. Veneers laid up with the grain direction of adjoining sheets at right angles produce plywood of great stiffness and strength, while those laid up with grains running parallel produce flexible plywood most often used in furniture and cabinetry.

vent

(1) A pipe built into a drainage system to provide air circulation, thus preventing siphonage and back pressure from affecting the function of

the trap seals. (2) A stack through which smoke, ashes, vapors, and other airborne impurities are discharged from an enclosed space to the outside atmosphere.

ventilation
A natural or mechanical process by which air is introduced to or removed from a space, with or without heating, cooling, or purification treatment.

vinyl composition tile
A floor tile similar to vinyl-asbestos floor tile except the

asbestos has been replaced by glass fiber reinforcing.

vitrified-clay pipe
Glazed earthenware pipe favored for use in sewage and drainage systems because it is impervious to water and resistant to chemical corrosion.

volume method (of estimating cost)
Method of estimating probable construction cost by multiplying the volume of the structure by an estimated current cost per unit of volume.

W

waffle slab
A reinforced concrete slab with equally spaced ribs parallel to the sides, having a waffle appearance from below.

wainscot
(1) A lower interior wall surface, usually extending three to four feet up from the floor, that contrasts with the wall surface above it. (2) The lower wall surface of an interior wall composed of two wall surfaces.

waiver of lien
An instrument by which a person or organization who has or may have a right of mechanic's lien against the property of another relinquishes such right.

wale, waler, whaler
(1) Timber placed horizontally across a structure to strengthen it. (2) Horizontal bracing used to stiffen concrete form construction and to hold studs in place.

wall
A vertical element used primarily to enclose or separate spaces.

wallboard
A manufactured sheet material used to cover large areas.

Wallboards are made from many items, including wood fibers, asbestos, and gypsum. In North America, the most common is "sheet rock," a gypsum-based panel bound by sheets of heavy paper. It is used to seal interior walls and ceilings in place of wet plaster.

warm-air furnace
A furnace that generates warm air for a heating system.

warranty
Legally enforceable assurance of quality or performance of a product or work, or of the duration of satisfactory performance. Warranty, guarantee, and guaranty are substantially identical in meaning; nevertheless, confusion frequently arises from supposed distinctions attributed to guarantee (or guaranty) being exclusively indicative of duration of satisfactory performance or of a legally enforceable assurance furnished by a manufacturer or other third party. The Uniform Commercial Code provisions on sales (effective in all states except Louisiana) use warranty but recognize the continuation of the use of guarantee and guaranty.

water-cement ratio

The ratio of the amount of water, exclusive only of that absorbed by the aggregates, to the amount of cement in a concrete or mortar mixture. The ratio is preferably stated as a decimal by weight.

waterstop

A thin sheet of metal, rubber, plastic, or other material inserted across a joint to obstruct the seeping of water through the joint.

weep hole

(1) A small hole in a wall or window member to allow accumulated water to drain. The water may be from condensation and/or surface penetration. (2) A small hole in a retaining wall located near the lower ground surface. The hole drains the soil behind the wall and prevents build-up of water pressure on the wall.

welded reinforcement

Concrete reinforcing steel joined by welding and most often used in columns to extend vertical bars.

welded-wire fabric, welded-wire mesh

A series of longitudinal and transverse wires arranged substantially at right angles to each other and welded together at all points of intersection.

well, wellhole

(1) Any enclosed space of considerable height, such as an air shaft or the space around which a stair winds. (2) A collection device for ground water. (3) A wall around a tree trunk to hold back soil. (4) A slot in a machine or device into which a part fits.

well point

A perforated pipe sunk into granular soil to permit the pumping of ground water.

well-point system

A series of well points connected to a header and used to drain an area or to control ground water seepage into an excavation.

wide-flange beam

A hot-rolled steel beam resembling an "H" on its side, and having parallel flanges.

wind load

The horizontal load used in the design of a structure to account for the effects of wind.

window

(1) An opening, usually glazed, in an external wall to admit light and, in buildings without central air conditioning, air. (2) An assembly consisting of a window frame, glazing, and necessary appurtenances. (3) A small opening in a wall, partition, or enclosure for transactions, such as a ticket window or information window.

window frame

The fixed part of a window assembly attached to the wall and receiving the sash or casement and necessary hardware.

window schedule

A tabulation, usually on a drawing, listing all windows on a project and indicating sizes, number of lights, type of sash and frame, and hardware required.

window wall

An exterior envelope using a frame containing windows that may be fixed or operable. The glazing may be clear, tinted, and/or opaque.

wing wall

(1) A short section of wall at an angle to a bridge abutment, used as a retaining wall and to stabilize the abutment.

wire gauge

(1) The diameter of a wire as

defined by several different systems. Usually, the thicker the wire is, the smaller the gauge number is. (2) A device for measuring the thickness of a wire, usually consisting of a metal sheet with standard-sized notches on one or more edges.

wiring box
A box used in interior electric wiring at each junction point, outlet, or switch, which serves as protection for electric connections and as a mounting for fixtures or switches.

withe, wythe
A partition used to separate two flues in a chimney stack.

wood block floor
A finished floor consisting of rectangular blocks of a tough wood such as oak, set in mastic with the end grain exposed, usually over concrete slab. Wood block floor is used where very heavy traffic and heavy loads are expected.

wood preservative
Any chemical preservative for wood, applied by washing on or pressure-impregnating. Products used include creosote, sodium fluoride, copper sulfate, and tar or pitch.

work
(1) All labor and materials required to complete a project in accordance with the contract documents. (2) The product of a force times the distance traveled.

wrought iron
(1) A material consisting of iron with strands of silica throughout. Once the surface iron decomposes, the silica surfacing prevents further oxidation. Wrought iron is no longer commercially available. (2) A number of easily welded or wrought irons with low impurity content used for water pipes, tank plates, or forged work.

X

XCU (insurance terminology)
Letters which refer to exclusions from coverage for property damage liability arising out of (1) explosion or blasting (designated by "X"), (2) collapse of or structural damage to any building or structure (designated by "C"), and (3) underground damage caused by and occurring during the use of mechanical equipment (designated by "U").

Y

yard
(1) A unit of length in the English System equal to three feet. (2) A term applied to that part of a plot not occupied by the building or driveway.

yard lumber
Lumber graded according to its size, length, and intended use, stockpiled in a lumber yard. Also called "general building construction lumber."

Y-fitting, wye fitting
A pipe fitting in the shape of a "Y." One arm is usually at 45 degrees to the main fitting and may be of reduced size.

yoke
(1) A tie or clamping device around column forms or over the top of wall or footing forms to keep them from spreading from the lateral pressure of fresh concrete. (2) Part of a structural assembly for slipforming which keeps the forms from spreading and transfers form loads to the jacks.

Z

Z-bar

A Z-shaped member that is used as a main runner in some types of acoustical ceiling.

zee

A tight-gauge member with a Z-like cross section. The flanges of the Z are approximately at right angles to the web.

zoning

(BOCA) The reservation of certain specified areas within a community or city for buildings and structures, or of use of land, for certain purposes with other limitations, such as height, lot coverage, and other stipulated requirements.

zoning permit

A permit issued by appropriate governmental officials authorizing land to be used for a specific purpose.

Index

D

E